The REDO Compendium

The REDO Compendium

Reverse Engineering for Software Maintenance

Edited by

H.J. van Zuylen
Delft Hydraulics, The Netherlands

JOHN WILEY & SONS
Chichester · New York · Brisbane · Toronto · Singapore

Other Wiley Editorial Offices

John Wiley & Sons, Inc., 605 Third Avenue,
New York, NY 10158-0012, USA

Jacaranda Wiley Ltd, G.P.O. Box 859, Brisbane,
Queensland 4001, Australia

John Wiley & Sons (Canada) Ltd, 22 Worcester Road,
Rexdale, Ontario M9W 1L1, Canada

John Wiley & Sons (SEA) Pte Ltd, 37 Jalan Pemimpin #05-04,
Block B, Union Industrial Building, Singapore 2057

Library of Congress Cataloging-in-Publication Data

The REDO compendium : reverse engineering for software maintenance /
edited by Henk van Zuylen.
p. cm.
Includes bibliographical references and index.
ISBN 0 471 93607 3
1. Software maintenance. I. Van Zuylen, Henk.
QA76.76.S64R43 1993
005.1'6—dc20 92-40218
CIP

British Library Cataloguing in Publication Data

A catalogue record for this book is available
from the British Library

ISBN 0 471 93607 3

Produced from camera-ready copy supplied by the editor
Printed in Great Britain by the Alden Press, Oxford

Contents

Preface

The REDO Compendium of Reverse Engineering for Software Maintenance is one of the results of the Esprit project REDO. Its purpose is to give the views of the REDO partners on the most important subject in the project: what is reverse engineering, when should it be applied, what is its role in software maintenance, how can it be done and how can it be supported by tools.

REDO has produced a toolset to support reverse engineering. The philosophy behind the toolset and its architecture are described in this compendium. The large number of references gives an overview of the present state of the art in this field.

The subject of reverse engineering is approached from many points of view, which makes the Handbook a kind of "smørgasbord" from which everybody can pick his choice.

The Compendium has been written by a rather large team of authors. The comments of the reviewers, especially from J. Foster and H. Calow have been invaluable in the process of the writing and editing of this book.

The REDO consortium acknowledges the financial support of the CEC. The continuous interest and encouragement from the CEC project officer, M. Coyle has stimulated the whole project and especially the writing of this Compendium.

List of Contributors

- A. Altes
  Centrisa
  Servicio y Desarrollo Informaticos
  Corcega 373
  08037-Barcelona
  Spain
  Tel No: 34 3 2075511
  Fax No: 34 3 4590014
  Eurokom: A Altes

- K. H. Bennett
  University of Durham
  Centre for Software Maintenance, University of Durham
  Centre for Software Maintenance
  Science Laboratory,
  South Road
  Durham DH1 3LE
  United Kingdom
  Tel No: 44 91 374 2000
  Fax No: 44 91 374 3741

- P. van den Bosch
  Delft Hydraulics
  PO Box 152
  8300 AD Emmeloord
  The Netherlands
  Tel No: 33 5274 2922
  Fax No: 33 5274 3573

- J. P. Bowen
  Oxford University Computing Laboratory
  Programming Research Group
  11 Keble Road
  Oxford OX1 3QD
  United Kingdom
  Tel No: 44 865 273838
  Fax No: 44 865 273839

Eurokom: M Harper
Email: Jonathan.Bowen@comlab.ox.ac.uk

- P. T. Breuer
  Oxford University Computing Laboratory
  Programming Research Group
  Present address: 3 Arthur Street
  Cambridge
  United Kingdom
  Tel No: 44 223 68682
  Email: ptb@eng.cam.ac.uk

- T. Cahill
  Department of Computer Science and Information Systems,
  University of Limerick
  Plassy Technology Park
  Limerick
  Ireland
  Tel No: 353 61 333644
  Fax No: 353 61 330316
  Eurokom: T Cahill

- A. G. Darlison
  Performance Technology Group, Lloyd's Register
  29 Wellesley Road Croydon,
  Surrey CR0 2AJ
  United Kingdom
  Tel No: 44 81 6814040
  Fax No: 44 81 6816814
  Eurokom: P Katsoulakos

- A. Davies
  Marconi Command and Control Systems Ltd
  Technology Group
  New Parks
  Leicester LE3 1UF
  United Kingdom
  Tel No: 44 533 871481
  Fax No: 44 533 871746
  Eurokom: M Shenton

- J. Estdale
  Performance Technology Group,Lloyd's Register
  29 Wellesley Road Croydon,
  Surrey CR0 2AJ
  United Kingdom
  Tel No: 44 81 6814725
  Fax No: 44 81 6816814
  Eurokom: P Katsoulakos

- J. Grumann
  Grumann Daten Kommunikation GmbH
  Wingertsbergweg 16
  D-6380 Bad Homberg
  Germany
  Tel No: 49 6172 44661
  Fax No: 49 6172 45011

- H. Haughton
  Performance Technology Group, Lloyd's Register
  29 Wellesley Road Croydon,
  Surrey CR0 2AJ
  United Kingdom
  Tel No: 44 81 6814040
  Fax No: 44 81 6816814
  Eurokom: P Katsoulakos

- C. Hornsby
  Performance Technology Group, Lloyd's Register
  Present address:
  Shell International Petroleum Company Ltd
  ICA/42 Shell Centre
  London SE1 7NA
  United Kingdom
  Tel No: 44 71 934 4559
  Fax No: 44 71 934 6896

- P. Jacob
  Department of Computer Science and Information Systems,
  University of Limerick
  Plassy Technology Park
  Limerick
  Ireland
  Tel No: 353 61 333644
  Fax No: 353 61 330316
  Eurokom: T Cahill, C Stanley-smith
  Email: jacobp@ul.ie

- P. Katsoulakos
  Performance Technology Group, Lloyd's Register
  29 Wellesley Road Croydon,
  Surrey CR0 2AJ
  United Kingdom
  Tel No: 44 81 6814040
  Fax No: 44 81 6816814
  Eurokom: P Katsoulakos

- I. Khabaza
  Performance Technology Group, Lloyd's Register
  29 Wellesley Road Croydon,
  Surrey CR0 2AJ
  United Kingdom
  Tel No: 44 81 6814040
  Fax No: 44 81 6816814
  Eurokom: P Katsoulakos

- K. C. Lano
  Programming Research Group, University of Oxford
  Present address:
  29 Wellesley Road Croydon,
  Surrey CR0 2AJ
  United Kingdom
  Tel No: 44 81 6814040
  Fax No: 44 81 6816814
  Eurokom: P Katsoulakos

- F. McLoughlin
  Department of Computer Science and Information Systems,
  University of Limerick
  Plassy Technology Park
  Limerick
  Ireland
  Tel No: 353 61 333644
  Fax No: 353 61 330316
  Eurokom: T Cahill, C Stanley-smith

- L. O'Brien
  Department of Computer Science and Information Systems,
  University of Limerick
  Plassy Technology Park
  Limerick
  Ireland
  Tel No: 353 61 333644
  Fax No: 353 61 330316
  Eurokom: T Cahill, C Stanley-smith
  Email: obrienl@ul.ie

- G. Ostrolenk
  Performance Technology Group, Lloyd's Register
  29 Wellesley Road Croydon,
  Surrey CR0 2AJ
  United Kingdom
  Tel No: 44 81 6814040
  Fax No: 44 81 6816814
  Eurokom: P Katsoulakos

- M. Price
  Marconi Command and Control Systems Ltd
  Technology Group
  New Parks
  Leicester LE3 1UF
  United Kingdom
  Tel No: 44 533 871481
  Fax No: 44 533 871746
  Eurokom: M Shenton

- D. J. Robson
  University of Durham
  Centre for Software Maintenance
  Science Laboratory,
  South Road
  Durham DH1 3LE
  United Kingdom
  Tel No: 44 91 374 2000
  Fax No: 44 91 374 3741

- N. Sabanis
  Performance Technology Group, Lloyd's Register
  29 Wellesley Road Croydon,
  Surrey CR0 2AJ
  United Kingdom
  Tel No: 44 81 6814040
  Fax No: 44 81 6816814
  Eurokom: P Katsoulakos

- M. Shenton
  Marconi Command and Control Systems Ltd
  Technology Group
  New Parks
  Leicester LE3 1UF
  United Kingdom
  Tel No: 44 533 871481
  Fax No: 44 533 871746
  Eurokom: M Shenton

- C. Stanley Smith
  Department of Computer Science and Information Systems,
  University of Limerick
  Plassy Technology Park
  Limerick
  Ireland
  Tel No: 353 61 333644
  Fax No: 353 61 330316

Eurokom: C Stanley-smith
Email: smith@ul.ie

- M. Tobin
Performance Technology Group, Lloyd's Register
29 Wellesley Road Croydon,
Surrey CR0 2AJ
United Kingdom
Tel No: 44 81 6814040
Fax No: 44 81 6816814
Eurokom: P Katsoulakos

- P. Welch
Grumann Daten Kommunikation GmbH
Wingertsbergweg 16
D-6380 Bad Homberg
Germany
Tel No: 49 6172 44661
Fax No: 49 6172 45011

- E. Younger
Center for Software Maintenance, University of Durham
Centre for Software Maintenance
Science Laboratory,
South Road
Durham DH1 3LE
United Kingdom
Tel No: 44 91 374 2000
Fax No: 44 91 374 3741

- H. J. van Zuylen
Delft Hydraulics
Research and Development
PO Box 177
2600 MH Delft
The Netherlands
Tel No: 31 15 569353
Fax No: 31 15 619674
Eurokom: H Van-zuylen
Email: henk.zuijlen@wldelft.nl

REDO Partners

- Centrisa
  Servicio y Desarrollo Informaticos
  Mr. A.M. Altes
  Corcega 373
  08037-Barcelona
  Spain
  Tel No: 34 3 2075511
  Fax No: 34 3 4590014

- Computer Technologies Co Ltd
  Mr. S. Psonis
  452 Mesogion Avenue
  15342 Athens
  Greece
  Tel No: 30 1 6550547
  Fax No: 30 1 6570656

- Delft Hydraulics
  Dr. H.J. van Zuylen
  Research and Development
  PO Box 177
  2600 MH Delft
  The Netherlands
  Tel No: 31 15 569353
  Fax No: 31 15 619674

- Electricité de France
  Miss A.Ferrier
  DER-IMA
  1 Avenue de Général de Gaulle
  PO Box 408
  92141 Clamart, CEDEX
  France
  Tel No: 47 654321
  Fax No: 1 47 655428

- Grumann Daten Kommunikation GmbH
  Dr J. Grumann
  Wingertsbergweg 16
  D-6380 Bad Homberg
  Germany
  Tel No: 49 6172 44661
  Fax No: 49 6172 45011

- Ingenieria y Tecnologia de Sistemas S.A.
  Mr. I.Pèrez
  Piquer 7
  28033 Madrid
  Spain
  Tel No; 34 1 3023146
  Fax No: 34 1 3021712

- Lloyd's Register
  Performance Technology Group
  Dr P.S. Katsoulakos
  29 Wellesley Road Croydon,
  Surrey CR0 2AJ
  United Kingdom
  Tel No: 44 81 6814040
  Fax No: 44 81 6816814

- Marconi Command and Control Systems Ltd
  Mr. C. Moss
  Technology Group
  New Parks
  Leicester LE3 1UF
  United Kingdom
  Tel No: 44 533 871481
  Fax No: 44 533 871746

- University of Oxford
  Programming Research Group
  Mr. J.P. Bowen
  Oxford University Computing Laboratory
  Programming Research Group
  11 Keble Road
  Oxford OX1 3QD
  United Kingdom
  Tel No: 44 865 273838
  Fax No: 44 865 273839

REDO Partners

- University of Durham
  Center for Software Maintenance
  Dr M. Munro
  Centre for Software Maintenance
  Science Laboratory,
  South Road
  Durham DH1 3LE
  United Kingdom
  Tel No: 44 91 374 2000
  Fax No: 44 91 374 3741

- University of Limerick
  Department of Computer Science and Information Systems
  Prof T. Cahill
  Plassy Technology Park
  Limerick
  Ireland
  Tel No: 353 61 333644
  Fax No: 353 61 330316

1

Introduction

H.J. van Zuylen, *Delft Hydraulics, The Netherlands*

1.1 The History of REDO

1.1.1 The Start

REDO is an Esprit project which started in 1989 and has been completed in the Spring of 1992. It was aimed at the development of methods and tools to improve software maintenance. The work has been done by a consortium consisting of 11 organizations from 7 countries. At the beginning of the project the fields of interest for the different consortium members were rather diverse. Some issues which the partners wanted to develop in the project were, for instance:

- validation of existing software
- coupling of software and its documentation
- use of formal methods in software maintenance
- the improvement of the usability of existing software by better user interfaces
- development and improvement of tools for the restructuring of source code and job control
- the development of a generic language in which the semantics of different programming languages and job control languages can be expressed.

There was also a whole range of applications areas in which the partners were interested:

- data processing applications written in COBOL and PL1, with the transaction monitoring system CICS and the database management system TOTAL,
- programs for scientific and engineering purposes written in FORTRAN, for instance for the simulation of the flow of fluids,
- real-time programs for environmental monitoring and process control.

The involvement of the partners was again quite different. Some partners felt, that they should improve their methods and/or tools, others wanted to develop new tools and methods, others did not want to develop any software themselves, but were interested in applying the results of the project in case studies or to provide the consortium with the expertise which they had in their organization.

Although there was this great diversity in the project in interests, application area, objectives and background of the partners, there was also a strong tendency for unification. The aim of REDO was to bring together all the different aspects of software maintenance, the different methods and tools, into an integrated framework, or at least, in such a way that it can be integrated afterwards: an integratable toolset.

The idea of a single language, called UNIFORM, was a cornerstone of the project. Every source code, including job control and environmental interaction (interaction with the operating system, database management system and user interface management system) should be translated into UNIFORM. All further tools had to operate on the UNIFORM representation.

Another common objective was the development of tools to extract *technical documentation* from the source code and to modify source code such that the control and data structure were improved. Both objectives could be achieved by transforming the source code into a representation in the form of a database and extracting the documentation from this database representation. Also the restructuring of the source code could be done by operations on the database representation.

Initially, the REDO objectives were rather ambitious. From the beginning it was clear, that a lot of choices had to be made in order to make the project feasible.

1.2 The Choices

In the first year, several options were investigated. First of all UNIFORM appeared to be critical in the project. All tools would have been dependent on the development of this language and the translators from the source code to UNIFORM. It further appeared that the principle of a single generic representation for the semantics of the source code, job control and environmental interaction, does not necessarily lead to the format of a language. What can be expressed in a language, can equally well be expressed in a network of objects and relations (nodes and arcs). This representation can be stored in a database on which the tools can operate directly.

Another issue was a common fine-grained repository for all tools. The original idea was to store the source code and documentation as rather course-grained objects in a database. It was clear from the beginning that interfaces were needed between the tools. The database representation which was intended originally as an internal representation for the tools which performed restructuring and generated technical documentation, appeared to be a good basis for a fine-grained common repository, which became the interface between the different tools. The original database scheme had to be redesigned and extended in order to contain all relevant data structures.

A long discussion has been devoted to the question whether the well-established technique of relational databases should be used or object management systems. The strict discipline of relational schemes has too many disadvantages when objects with different granularity have to handled. (Objects can be, for instance, representations of single variables and operators or unstructured documentation.) Also the possibilities to store the semantics in the database scheme are restricted. On the other hand, one of the partners already had tools which had been built with a relational database management system. Therefore, it was decided to use two platforms: the relational databases and the two-tier database system of the Tool Builders Kit (TBK) from IPSYS. This choice also had an impact on the way the user interface of the REDO tools was developed. TBK had its own user interface tool, which gave a certain uniformity to the look-and-feel of the different tools, but also imposed some restrictions.

In order to reduce the dependency on the development on UNIFORM, the database scheme developed was first aimed at COBOL. It can be considered to have a subset of the functions of UNIFORM. During the project more features were added: first TOTAL and CICS and later FORTRAN.

The user interaction in programs was considered to be similar to environmental interactions. Basically, there is not much difference between a call to a database management system in order to retrieve some data, and a question asked to a user on the screen and subsequently the response via the keyboard. The early investigations in the project of the state-of-the-art showed, that user interactions are less structured, have very specific problems and cannot be treated in the same way as other forms of environmental interactions. A tool was developed to extract the user interaction from (FORTRAN) source code. However, the real problem to solve was, how to (re)organize the user task and consequently to (re)develop the user interface. This work is more ergonomics and knowledge engineering than software engineering. It is reported in a separate REDO report [TN-WL-1071] and publications [359, 360]. The step to bring the user interaction in the same framework as the other environmental interaction appeared to be 'a bridge too far'. First the method for task analysis and user interface design has to be established, before a formalized representation becomes useful.

One could say that the original approach of REDO was more bottom-up than top-down. Although an integrated approach was taken, the project started from techniques and tools, more than from a well-defined maintenance task and method. During the first year the software maintenance task was studied [TN-LR-1039]. It appeared that the comprehension task is very important and takes a large portion of the resources in software maintenance. All improvements to a system to simplify this task can be seen as improvements to the maintainability.

Newly developed, well structured code is easier to understand and to maintain than old code which has lost its structure by many 'patches'. The focus of the REDO project was initially directed to restructuring [TN-LR-1027] and later to reverse engineering. The word 'restructuring' has to be understood in the sense that the existing structure of the software is analyzed, clarified and presented on a higher level of abstraction. Restructuring of the control and data and also the modularization of the code can be considered as attempts to reduce the complexity of the system and to improve the comprehensibility. The distinction which is made between reverse engineering and restructuring is explained in section 2.

1.3 The Purpose of the REDO Compendium

This compendium contains the views of the REDO partners on the maintenance problem and describes their theoretical and practical contributions to solutions of the problems. The content reflects the fact that the partners of the consortium had various interests and background. It brings together many viewpoints and approaches. It has been composed, in the first place, for readers from technical support and research/development staff. The first group (technical support staff) is actively involved in the execution of maintenance of strategic software of their company. They work in the data processing group or software development group or are part of the 'operating core' [230]. These staff members will find useful information in this compendium, which they can use to reorganize their work and to apply other methods and tools.

Research and development staff members have the task to follow the state-of-the-art and to select promising developments. They will find useful information and many references to other sources of information.

Other readers of this compendium can be found in middle management. These readers can get more an understanding of the real maintenance problems. Software maintenance in most companies is still organized on a very practical level. Compared to software development the approach in maintenance is less structured, more aimed at the ad hoc solutions of problems than a systematic approach. (This does not mean that maintenance is not well-organized.) The improvement of the maintenance practice is not only a technical problem, but has management aspects too.

The compendium is also useful for people considering the development of CASE tools to support reverse engineering. With the experience gained in REDO, the authors are able to specify what kind of tools are useful, which techniques can be applied and how tools could support the method of reverse engineering.

The compendium will be suitable as a basis for a 'cook book', tailored to a specific situation, domain and company. The method in the Compendium will not be universally applicable as it is, but should be customized to particular circumstances in an organization.

Finally, the compendium will be a good starting point for students who want to study the software maintenance domain.

1.4 The Situation of Software Maintenance

In chapters 2 to 5 the situation in software maintenance is described. One may observe that many people involved in maintenance feel uncomfortable because of the maintenance backlog and the fact that maintenance becomes more difficult the longer a system exists. The structure of programs makes them difficult to understand and to modify. Software maintainers would like to change this situation, but there is no clear way out yet. Sometimes a 'guru' or tool vendor claims that he knows how to get out of the maintenance crisis, but practice is still such, that there is no clear-cut path which can be followed with a guaranteed success. It is not even always clear which way one has to go, if one wants to improve maintenance.

The ideal situation is, of course, that one may follow a well-defined path using all kinds of tools, to move from the present status – with the maintenance backlog and programs which are difficult to maintain – to a better situation, where modifications of information systems can be made with moderate resources within an acceptable time. The reality is still far from this situation. It is not very clear to most people what are the reasons and background of the maintenance crisis. Nor is it clear what the ideal situation will look like or how one may realize the improvement of maintainability and which tools are needed.

The compendium has the following functions:

1. To show the reader the situation in software maintenance.

2. To describe a better situation, where maintenance can be seen as projects, instead of problems.

3. To discuss how one may move to a better situation.

4. To explain which problems have to be solved.

5. To show how the REDO method and tools can help to make this move to better maintainability.

It explains the readers why and how they should apply reverse engineering and which parts of their task can be supported by tools.

In order to give the readers a flavor of the content of the book, the next few pages give a summary of the topics in the compendium. These are elaborated upon in the following chapters by different authors.

1.5 The Maintenance Domain

"Software which is used in a real-world environment, must change or become less and less useful in that environment". This statement is known as the first law of Lehman [198]. The second law, in which Lehman describes one of the reasons of the maintenance crisis, is: "As an evolving program change, its structure becomes more complex, unless active efforts are made to avoid this phenomenon".

The fact that software degrades, even if it has been developed as a well-structured system, is one of the reasons that the maintenance of these systems becomes more tedious and more expensive, as the age of the systems grows. This process can be stopped and controlled if the system is 'freshened-up' at some moment when maintenance becomes too difficult. This might be done once in the life of a system, but as Lehman describes, such a 'freshen-up' action might be necessary more frequently.

The improvement of a system in order to facilitate further maintenance can be done by restructuring the source code. This means, for instance:

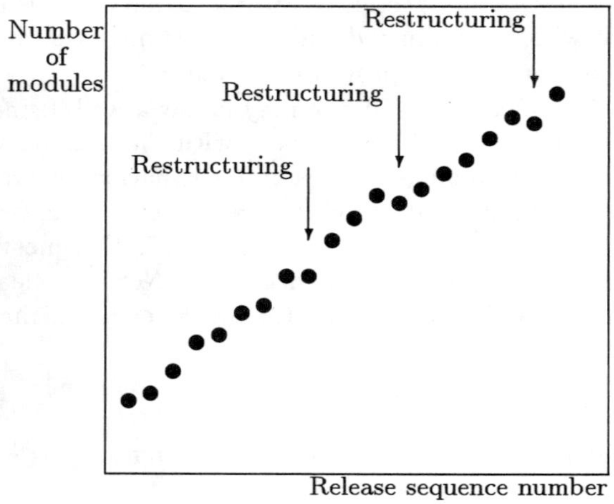

Figure 1.1: Size of a program as a function of the release number, as observed by Lehman.

- changing the data structures such that redundant variables are removed, data dependencies are made visible and variable names are used consistently over the whole application,
- simplifying the control structure, such as by the removal of unwanted GOTO instructions,
- removing redundant pieces of source code,
- cutting source code into smaller slices which have internal cohesion and are mutually independent

In fact, the software is brought to a level where it satisfies higher standards. A few of these 'freshen-up' activities can be done automatically. In most cases human interaction is necessary to make the restructuring effective. For instance the removal of GOTOs does not always improve the comprehensibility of the code and the renaming of variables is only possible if the semantics of the application is clear.

Another way to improve the maintenance of an application is to provide methods and tools to support the comprehension of the application. Often maintenance is difficult because:

- it is not clear where a modification of the code has to be made in order to implement new functions or to improve existing functions,
- it is not clear what the impact will be on the rest of the source code.

These uncertainties make the maintenance task difficult or even impossible, while the maintenance process itself is difficult to plan and control. Reverse engineering is a method to reduce these uncertainties.

1.5.1 Views and Representations

Software engineers have several views of a program in mind when they do maintenance. Examples are the control flow structure, the data structure and the interaction with the user or the environment. Each view contains the information about one or more aspects of the program. These views are used to understand the program, to verify, refine and adjust the mental representation of the maintenance problem.

Important issues for views are:

- different views should be available at the same time,
- the information should be available at different levels of detail (such as source code at statement level, or just the control structure),
- the information which is contained in the relation between different views and items in a view is also important in order to understand a program.

REDO has made a first selection of the views and representation of views which are useful for understanding and documenting an application. Tools are developed to:

- extract the data structure from the source code,
- improve the data structure and represent it as a normalized entity–relation model (chapter 19),
- extract the control flow from a representation of the source code,
- improve the control structure (by removing GOTOs) (chapter 20),
- extract the interaction with a DBMS and represent this in a comprehensible way (chapter 19),
- query the source code and present the source code at different levels of detail (an example is a tool to find the parts of the source code in which the interaction with the user is controlled),
- build documentation, establish and maintain links among documentation items and between documentation items and source code (chapter 19),
- build a formal description of the function of pieces of source code (chapters 15 and 16),
- extract metrics from the source code, both of the control and the data structure (chapter 21),
- optimize the layout of diagrams (chapter 11),
- build a representation of the dataflow,
- identify modules of code, which can be isolated as procedures, functions or subroutines,
- build call trees, cross-reference lists, etc., (chapter 22).

These tools are described in part IV and in several REDO publications. REDO integrates these views at a task and a data level. At the task level, it is possible to combine different views. When the user is studying a view, he or she may choose to browse another one, which represents another aspect of the same piece of code. The views are mutually linked, which makes it easy to select the appropriate information. The integration at data level is realized by the common repository, the System Description Database, where all data and the links between data items are stored. This ensures the unrestricted transfer of information between the REDO tools.

1.5.2 The REDO Method

Comprehension is a very important objective of reverse engineering. There are many activities which have to be done to make the comprehension process possible and meaningful. In the REDO method these activities are grouped into 6 phases which could be executed sequentially. In practice, people may wish to iterate between the phases. Some phases will be skipped over or done only very superficially. Some parts of the application may be less interesting for reverse engineering and may be omitted, while it may become clear during reverse engineering that other software modules have to be included in the process. Also the level of detail at which reverse engineering is done may be decided during the process.

A linear process for reverse engineering could be possible in those cases where the software engineer has sufficient knowledge and experience to decide in advance which information should be collected and in how much detail and in which form. In many cases an iterative process might be more suitable.

The REDO method is described in chapters 13 and 14. It consists of the following phases:

1. identify, document and recover all existing sources of information,
2. install application in the intended maintenance environment,
3. reverse engineer,
4. establish test procedure,
5. re-engineer and re-implement,
6. hand-over

The REDO method does not necessitate the use of the REDO tools. It could even be done with help of very simple tools like an editor and compiler.

1.6 The REDO Architecture.

The REDO tools are built around a repository, the SDDB, the System Description Database. The source code and documentation are stored in this repository in an analyzed form. A loader parses the source code, COBOL with calls to TOTAL CICS, or FORTRAN and stores the parse tree in the SDDB. Most of the tools use the parse tree, instead of starting from the source code itself. This makes the development of tools relatively simple. A commercial object database system is used, which provides some tools and facilities which make the development of browsers, selection tools and analyzers relatively simple. The documentation and the parse tree of the source code are all stored in the same SDDB. Therefore, the data scheme of the SDDB is rather large and complicated. In future, extensions to the database can be added, in order to cope with other programming languages, interaction with operating systems, transaction processing systems, etc.

The view of the source code, as it is stored in the SDDB can be represented either as statements in the original language, for instance, COBOL or FORTRAN, or in UNIFORM.

1.7 Conclusions

Reverse engineering is relatively new as a separate activity. This REDO Compendium provides guidance for managers to (re)organize the reverse engineering process. It provides a structure which can be used to develop a reverse engineering handbook for a company. This requires some refinement to adapt the general structure to the company requirements and local culture. Quality management can be set up, using the REDO Compendium, together with existing standards for software engineering [166] [167] (see chapter 17).

The tools developed in REDO and the environment, including the System Description Database, provide a platform for reverse engineering. Developments of new tools or improvement of existing tools is made easy by the generic character of the facilities of the environment and its open structure. The feasibility of interfaces between the REDO environment and CASE environments is also guaranteed.

1.8 Advice for Readers

The compendium contains a large amount of diverse information. Sequential reading of the whole compendium will take a long time and might be not very satisfying for readers with special interest in only certain aspects. Most chapters of the compendium have been written as independent, closed units. They can be read without reading all the preceding chapters. A few chapters have a more central role, especially chapter 2 on the Overview of Maintenance and Reverse Engineering, chapter 18 on the REDO architecture and chapter 19 on the System Description Database. Starting with these sections one may select other chapters in a rather arbitrary way.

For *managers* especially chapters 2, 3, 5, 8, 13, 14, 17, 18 contain interesting information. A good initial choice for *practitioners* would be chapters 2, 4, 6, 12, 13, 14, 19, 20, 21 and 22. *Middle management*, people responsible for the organization of maintenance and the choice of appropriate methods, will find important information in nearly all chapters. *Developers of tools* will find important information in chapters 5, 7 and 11 and in part IV of the compendium. *Researchers* will find chapters 9, 10 15, 16, 19 – 22 interesting. Finally, *students* will find a lot of interesting technical and theoretical information in parts II and IV. The reference list will be a good gateway to more information in recent literature.

Part I

OVERVIEW

2

An Overview of Maintenance and Reverse Engineering

K.Bennett, *Centre for Software Maintenance, University of Durham, Durham, UK*

2.1 Definition of Terms and Concepts

2.1.1 Software Maintenance

We shall use the ANSI-IEEE definition [168] of software maintenance as follows:

Software maintenance is the modification of a software product after delivery to correct faults, to improve performance or other attributes, or to adapt the product to a changed environment.

It is important to note that preventive maintenance is included within the scope of this definition, that is, modification to software undertaken to improve some attribute of that software, such as its maintainability, quality, etc. Also, we note that software maintenance is largely concerned with evolution of systems, and so-called bug fixing is a minor part [203].

A major problem in the software industry is coping with the software maintenance of the huge quantity of existing software that now exists. Such software represents an enormous financial investment and simply cannot be discarded due to the arrival of new technology. The largest software maintenance activity in most organizations [203] [202] is concerned with implementing modifications caused by changes in user requirements (called *perfective maintenance*). It is important to be able to carry out such modifications without degrading the quality of the system, and to complete them quickly to avoid an applications backlog. Unfortunately, much existing software has been so heavily modified that it has become extremely difficult to maintain. It is therefore useful to investigate if such software can be analyzed so that, without altering its functional specification, it can be made more maintainable. The solution of this problem is the main focus of the REDO project.

The field of software engineering has been characterized by a low level of technology. Tools have appeared and continue to appear in the market place to support code level activities, such as cross-referencers, restructurers, program analyzers, etc. Few are integrated, and there are no widely accepted commercially available maintenance methods. We may summarize by concluding that maintenance has developed in an ad-hoc way, in a bottom-up direction. A clear model of the process is urgently needed, so that methods may be defined, and integrated tools produced to support these methods.

2.1.2 History of Software Maintenance

In the 1950s and early 1960s, software maintenance comprised a very small part of the software life cycle; the major activity was the writing of new programs for new applications. In the late 1960s and the 1970s, management realized that old software does not simply die, and at that point software maintenance started to be recognized as a major activity. An anecdote about the early days of electronic data processing in banks illustrates this point. In the 1950s, a large US bank was about to take the major step of employing its very first full-time programmer. Management raised the issue what would happen to this person once all the programs had been written. The same bank now has several buildings full of data processing staff!

By the late 1970s, industry was suffering major problems with the applications backlog, and software maintenance was now taking more effort than initial development in some sectors, particularly in commercial data processing (see Lientz and Swanson [202]).

In the 1980s, it was becoming evident that old architectures were severely constraining new design. In another example from the US banking system, existing big banks had considerable difficulty modifying their software to introduce automatic teller machines, whereas new banks writing software from scratch found this rather easier. In the 1980s also, in the UK, it has been reported that at least two building society mergers were unable to go ahead, due to the problems of bringing together software from two different organizations.

In the 1990s, a large part of the business model of many organization has now been implemented, so that business change is represented by evolutionary change to the software, and not revolutionary change, and most so-called development is actually enhancement. There is, however, a major problem in understanding and recovering the underlying specification and design which are represented in many hundreds of thousands of lines of code, in order that such enhancement can take place easily, without causing errors, and without degrading the structure.

2.1.3 Software Evolution

Lehman [197, 198, 199] has argued that the evolution of a software system conforms to five laws, which he derived from the empirical observation of several large software systems. Of these five laws, the first two are relevant here.

1. **Continuing Change.** A program that is used in a real world environment must change or become less and less useful in that environment.

2. **Increasing Complexity.** As an evolving program changes, its structure becomes more complex unless active methods are made to avoid this phenomenon.

Thus, successful software will inevitably evolve, but the process of evolution will lead to degraded structure and increasing complexity unless remedial action is taken. At certain points in time the complexity becomes unacceptable, and remedial action is taken, resulting in an improvement in maintainability. Evolution continues until complexity again has degraded to such an extent that remedial action is required (for instance, the cost of software maintenance has become unacceptable, or the quality of the software has degraded).

At certain points, therefore, in the life of a software system, major preventive maintenance will take place, with the objective of making the software system more maintainable. The high-level model of this process is shown in figure 2.1. We start with our software application system which is used by the triggering activity to determine when an assessment of the software system should be undertaken.

The assessment is initiated by the trigger, and this can lead to a range of outcome, some of which are shown in the figure. The outcome may be drastic - such as discarding the system completely; or it may be considered cost effective to modify the system to improve its maintainability, giving it a further lease of life. We shall call this the *Management Decision Process.*

A further possibility, which may be undertaken as well as the other outcome, is to improve the maintenance process, so that in the future, the maintenance practice is better. This will help in avoiding the type of problems that have arisen in the past and that are indicated by the assessment. Although it is possible to improve the technology of software maintenance, it is likely that this alone is insufficient, and attention will have to be paid to the management too, in terms of project monitoring, control and quality. For example, the assessment activity may show that a programme of reviews should be introduced, and these should be supported by metrics to track error report rates.

Lehman's laws are not, however the only reason for addressing system evolution. Before introducing other aspects, we shall define important basic terminology.

2.1.4 Reverse Engineering

In this document we shall be using the terms specification, design and implementation. In an hierarchical system, these are difficult terms to define, because the implementation of one level may represent the specification of the design of the next lower level of abstraction. Generally, a requirements specification is a definition of the problem to be solved, without any reference to how it is to be solved. Typically, the specification may be non executable, and may be expressed in a notation such as first order logic, Z or VDM. It may also involve non-functional attributes such as time constraints.

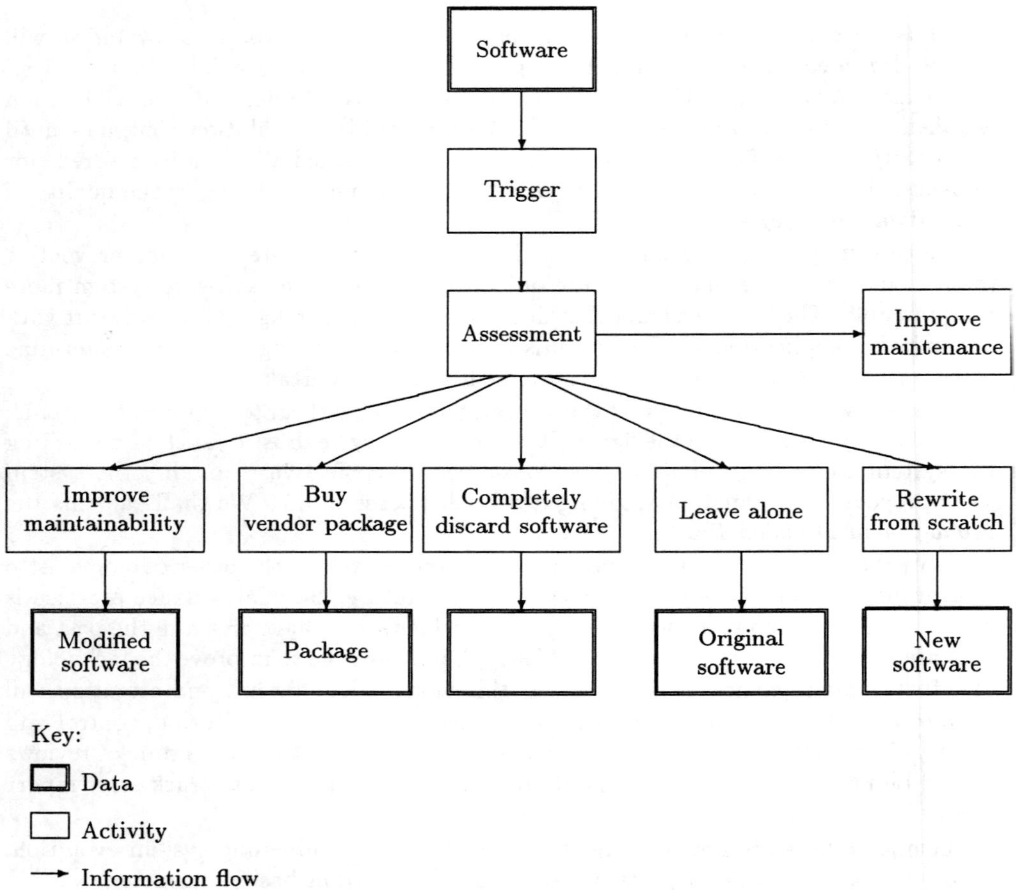

Figure 2.1: The strategic layer

The design is concerned with the description of the solution to the requirement specification. The implementation is concerned with the coding in some high-level programming language, the testing and the delivery of the operational system.

Currently, no adequate, widely accepted, quantitative definition of maintainability is available. Maintainability could be judged in terms of the effort or time required to perform given modifications arising from adaptive, perfective, corrective or preventive maintenance on the software system (e.g. mean time to repair). An alternative approach is to assess maintainability indirectly in terms of attributes of the software itself e.g. modularity, cohesion or coupling. The two approaches (process and product) should be related in some way, though the topic lacks theoretical insight and is controversial. In this report, this topic is considered in more depth in chapters 6 and 21.

No standard definition of other useful software maintenance terms exists, but Chikofsky and Cross [71] have provided a useful taxonomy. They state that:

> **Reverse engineering** *is the process of analyzing a subject system to identify the system's components and their inter-relationships, and to create representations of the system in another form or at higher levels of abstraction.*

Reverse engineering is seen as an activity which does not change the subject system, nor does it create a new system based on the reverse engineered subject system. It is seen as a process of examination and understanding (and of recording the results of that examination and understanding), not a process of change or replication. Two important examples of reverse engineering, both of which are being addressed in REDO, are redocumentation and design recovery. Chikofsky and Cross define these as:

> **Redocumentation** *is the creation or revision of a semantically equivalent representation within the same relative abstraction level.*

> **Design recovery***involves identifying meaningful higher level abstractions beyond those obtained directly by examining the system itself.*

Several equivalent representations (views) may be useful to aid human comprehension. Design recovery thus involves using domain knowledge, external information etc., to recover information about design and requirements specifications that should exist, but no longer do so. They must be deduced from existing software objects, of which the most trustworthy is the source code.

Restructuring is the transformation from one representation to another at the same relative abstraction level, while preserving the subject system's external behavior. Examples include the transformation of source code control flow structure to a structured form. Restructuring often has the objective of improving maintainability, by adopting more understandable constructs.

Finally, **re-engineering** is the examination and alteration of a subject system to reconstitute it in a new form and the subsequent implementation of the new form. In particular, we can use modern formal software engineering techniques to improve maintainability and the maintenance process.

It can thus be seen that 'reverse engineering' is a very broad term referring to many different types of activity. A checklist of typical activities is given in section 2.3. For example, we may re-engineer an existing assembly code system into its equivalent form in ADA. Rather than a simple restructuring, followed by re-implementation, we may wish to take advantage of modern approaches to concurrency by redesigning parts of the system before recoding in ADA. However, this is still likely to be a 'once only' activity.

Another example of reverse engineering is provided within the regular iterative maintenance cycle described in the next section; the maintainer must understand the system before undertaking the implementation of a change, and if this understanding is written down in some form (for instance as pictorial design) it can contribute to understanding by subsequent maintainers. This is still reverse engineering according to our definition, although the main emphasis is clearly on capturing system understanding .

The first type of example has been called a 'laundry' approach; the software is taken in its unpleasant form, and passed through a process which much improves it. A strong incentive for this type of reverse engineering is provided by the need to change technology, for instance,

- Moving from a centralized to distributed database;
- Moving from an hierarchical to a relational database system.

Thus, one of the problems inherent in reverse engineering is that the need for it can arise for many different reasons, and that there are many different ways of undertaking reverse engineering. In practice, it may also be sensible to undertake changes during reverse engineering so that the functionality changes.

It is therefore unrealistic to think of a single 'reverse engineering method'; there is likely to be a rich diversity of both objectives and techniques, in terms of management, technical and quality issues. A comprehensive understanding of reverse engineering needs to address these issues, and in REDO, they have formed an integral part of the project, as explained in later chapters in this book.

It is unlikely that reverse engineering can operate within a very rigid standard framework, because the target software system has, by its nature, to be taken as it stands, rather than as how we would like it to be. This does not mean that a set of reverse engineering principles cannot be set down, and some of these principles are now explained.

2.1.5 Cost-benefit of Reverse Engineering

Reverse engineering of any form has a cost, in terms of time and effort, software tools, training, etc. It may also have to be undertaken in parallel with evolution of the target system. At the current state of the art, it is relatively simple to estimate the cost of some forms of reverse engineering (like automated restructuring) and far more difficult to estimate, for instance, design recovery. The field lacks theory, and also good case studies are few and far between. A checklist of costs, with both qualitative and quantitative aspects, is given in section 2.6.

The benefits of reverse engineering may also be hard to quantify. Often, the rationale (as supported by Lehman) is to make an existing system 'more maintainable'. This suggests a high investment (to reverse engineer), where the returns are long term (in terms of reduced maintenance costs over many years). This is a notoriously hard type of business case to make, and at the current state-of-the-art, it may have to be based on some intuition and risk. It may also indicate an incremental approach.

As an example, an extreme case is to completely discard the current system and start from scratch to build a replacement, using current technology. This may be attractive if an up-to-date functional and non-functional specification exist. If high-level designs also exist it may be possible to reuse parts of the existing system (for instance by encapsulation using clearly defined interfaces). In many cases, however, this sort of information no longer exists; the only software in which trust can be placed is the source codes.

Typically, this type of software has been extensively modified to meet changing requirements. The source code, is the *only* form in which the organization's key procedures, data etc. are represented. We require a systems analysis activity performed, not on a manual process, but on existing software. This is a necessary precursor to a completely new system.

This systems analysis is a form of reverse engineering, with the aim of discovery (and representing) high-level designs and specifications.

To summarize, reverse engineering (particularly when undertaken as a 'laundry' activity) needs a cost-benefit justification in terms of the benefit to the business. This may be hard to estimate with great precision, but often, some attempt at quantitative analysis is better than none. To help this process, checklists for costs and benefits are given in section 2.6 and 2.7 respectively.

2.1.6 Reverse Engineering Principles

Despite the great diversity of reverse engineering activities, we can establish a set of principles to guide the planning of a particular project. The REDO interpretation of these principles is the subject of this book, and the following list provides the references to the relevant chapters.

- Supporting business needs. Any reverse engineering activity, whether of the 'laundry' model or of the continuous understanding model, needs ultimately to be justified in terms of business need. This has already been stressed in this chapter, and it is further analyzed in chapter 3.

- Reverse engineering, like any other software activity, needs careful management, including planning, monitoring and control, resourcing and motivating. It also requires quality planning and risk analysis. These topics are developed in part III (chapters 13 – 17) of the book.

- In common with other branches of software engineering, reverse engineering requires a clear method, which in turn defines the tools needed to support the method. Methods may vary according to the needs of particular application domains. Methodological issues are discussed in chapters 4, 6, 7, 13 and 5.

- System understanding is a major issue for many reverse engineering projects (i.e. those which are more than simple code restructuring). The distinguishing feature of REDO is the use of a central repository in which all data relevant to reverse engineering is stored, together with the appropriate links and relationships between such data. Furthermore, the use of such a repository allows the development of an integrated toolset which accesses and updates it. The REDO view of system understanding and documentation is central to the project, and is described in chapters 6 – 8; the REDO architecture and the design and use of the repository (or 'System Description Database') are presented in chapters 18 and 19, respectively.

- As suggested earlier, reverse engineering is of very wide scope, and key issues such as metrics, validation, static analysis are described in chapters 20 and 21.

These principles, and their exploration and evaluation within REDO, are intended to apply to many different reverse engineering scenarios, not just the 'laundry' approach.

2.1.7 Software Maintenance Processes

We have seen earlier that the reverse engineering process often extracts representations of the system at higher levels of abstraction than the source code which is usually the starting point. How do these processes relate to the iterative process of system evolution resulting from software maintenance?

Software maintenance can occur due to changing user needs, to errors which must be fixed, and to a changing environment. Although these types are different at the detailed level, at a high level they can be described by an iterative three stage process:

1. **request control**: the information about the request is collected; the change is analyzed using impact analysis to assess cost/benefit; and a priority is assigned to each request.

2. **change control**: the next request is taken from the top of the priority list; the problem is reproduced (if there is one); the code (and design and specifications if available) are analyzed; the changes are designed and documented and tests produced; the code modifications are written; and quality assurance is implemented.

3. **release control**: the new release is determined; the release is built; confidence testing is undertaken; the release is distributed and acceptance testing by the customer takes place.

Currently, these three steps are almost always undertaken in terms of source code. Design information and even adequate documentation typically do not exist. Thus software maintenance is thought of predominantly as a source code activity.

There is a growing consensus that in order to achieve major productivity gains, software maintenance must be undertaken at higher abstraction levels than code namely at the design level or specification level (for instance, Basili [17]). The implementation is then generated from the high-level designs or specifications. Ideally this would be an automatic process (as it is already in the generation of machine code from high-level languages, or code from fourth-generation languages) but currently, human assistance is usually required.

This approach to software maintenance is supported by several reasons:

1. The representation of a system at higher levels of abstraction is more compact than at lower levels, so the system is easier to understand as a whole.
2. The objects which represent the system at high levels of abstraction (for instance, modules, requirements, specifications etc.) are structures which encourage highly maintainable systems. Furthermore, they are closer to the application domain in terms of which many changes are expressed.
3. The generation of the implementation can employ reuse techniques to reuse the majority of the implementation which is not changed after a software maintenance activity (so-called 'vertical' reuse). We are thus reusing not only parts of the product, but the process too.
4. The documentation for systems maintained in this way can be clearly specified.
5. Modification can be better controlled leading to less structural degradation.
6. Modern software engineering techniques become available to the software engineer, leading to high quality in the software maintenance phase (see Collins, Nicholls and Sørensen [79]).
7. The high-level abstract level objects are appropriate vehicles in which to express the testing plan.

Thus, the three steps of software maintenance described at the start of this section are retained, but they are undertaken at a *high level* of abstraction. The second step (change control) is now more substantial because the executable code must also be generated from the specification (although this is mitigated by reuse of existing system components).

An important role for reverse engineering now becomes clear – it enables us to take an existing software system, which is being maintained in terms of its source codes, and recover an abstract representation which can be used for subsequent maintenance. The forward engineering step does not exist in the conventional sense. Instead, the executable form is generated as part of the implementation phase in the change control activity. Reverse engineering is thus primarily a systems understanding process.

To summarize, the major problems that must be addressed in software maintenance over the next decade are:

- Reducing the cost of changing software.
- Reducing the applications backlog.
- Improving the productivity of skilled personnel, particularly taking into account demographic projections.

- Allowing the software to take advantage of new technologies in implementing evolution.
- Improving the quality (e.g. reliability) of software.
- Expressing maintenance in business terms.

Experience and surveys have shown that system understanding is a major activity within software maintenance.

2.2 Management Model

2.2.1 Business Model

In this section, we amplify the decision-making model introduced in section 2.1.3. It follows from the previous section that this type of model is most relevant to reverse engineering projects which conform to the 'laundry' approach. However, REDO is not restricted to this form of reverse engineering.

There is a current trend for business units to be held financially accountable within their companies (and within universities!) (see Ward [321]). There is a growing dependence on IT, and as IT departments become larger (and more expensive), they need to provide greater accountability for their internal management and productivity. Thus IT services have to be seen as relevant to the business. This is a recent issue for software maintenance, and in many organizations, maintenance is simply seen as a consumer of large amounts of revenue. No business justification is made for investment in software maintenance.

The business may well have first sight of the problem because of the applications backlog. The software cannot change at the rate required by the business. Other circumstances include:

- takeovers and mergers
- system migration
- regulatory change
- statutory changes
- competitive pressure
- changes in the organization (e.g. expansion)
- need to reduce costs
- new markets

This suggests that a business case will be needed to justify the investment in software maintenance, in terms of the benefits and returns to be gained for money expended. As Warden [323] points out, reverse engineering of key software and subsequent re-implementation needs to be presented as a safe and well-understood process (low risk) as part of an overall strategy.

We see the first stage of reverse engineering as a decision-making process to resolve why reverse engineering may be of benefit, and to determine the requirements of it for the software under consideration. This decision-making process may be triggered by a number of activities, such as the need to be make a major upgrade to the system, the availability of third party software maintenance, unacceptable error reports, rising software maintenance costs or unacceptable application backlog. This decision process (the trigger) then prompts an assessment of the software, and three major subactivities are envisaged:

- the software to be assessed must be clearly identified and an inventory made,
- the assessment criteria must be drawn up. These can include technical issues, such as the quality of the software as measured by customer reports, and also management criteria, such as the strategic importance of the software to the organization,
- the software is then assessed based on the criteria established.

The result of the analysis can lead to one of several recommendations, including:

- carry on as now; possibly subcontract the maintenance,
- improve the maintenance process,
- replace software with an off-the-shelf package,
- re-implement from scratch,
- discard software and discontinue,
- freeze maintenance and leave well alone,
- reverse engineer and forward engineer to produce a new implementation (using some, or all of the methods listed in this document).

The main planning steps in a reverse engineering project can now be seen and summarized:

- The reverse engineering project will lead to an analysis both of the business need and the technical state of the software.
- A clear statement of the financial, business, technical and management objectives is made, not just for the reverse engineering activity, but for the longer term software maintenance of the product.
- An overall technical strategy is derived.
- A cost benefit analysis of the strategy is undertaken, leading to a business case for investment in the project.
- Assuming that the project is approved, a detailed plan is prepared, involving control and monitoring. Again, this will address both the reverse engineering and subsequent maintenance stages, and will include Quality Assurance.

- Progress is continually monitored against the plan, so that the veracity of the original business plan can be assessed.

- The final step of the reverse engineering step will be acceptance testing of the product.

2.3 Checklist for Reverse Engineering

In tables 2.1 - 2.3 a number of reasons describe why an organization may wish to undertake reverse engineering of part or all of a software system. For many reverse engineering projects, the motivation will be provided by a combination of reasons, with some having more weight than others. The list is separated into quality, management and technical issues.

Table 2.1: Checklist quality issues

1.	To simplify complex software. According to Lehman [198] successful software will inevitably evolve, but the process of the evolution will lead to degraded structure and increasing complexity (and therefore increasing software maintenance problems) unless remedial action is taken. Reverse engineering comprises part of such remedial action.
2.	To improve the quality of software which contains errors, by identifying and then removing those errors. It should be easier to remove errors from well-designed and structured systems which have been well reverse engineered, rather than the original, possibly, incomprehensible source codes.
3.	To remove side-effects from an implementation (i.e. unplanned state changes).
4.	To improve the coding quality, for example to reduce the number of control transfers, remove redundant code, adopt data naming standards, improve control structure, adopt standard layout and commenting (quality here is usually interpreted as understandability).
5.	To undertake a major design repair activity, because the original design (and therefore implementation) of the software may be erroneous.
6.	To produce up-to-date, consistent and helpful documentation, relevant to maintainers. (Often, documentation is nonexistent or out-of-date or of no help to maintainers).
7.	To establish a proper strategy and test suite for regression testing and VVT (verification, validation and testing).
8 .	To meet the need for improved performance in the software system, in terms of storage space used, speed etc. (implying design level changes).
9.	To bring the existing software into a more modern software engineering development environment consistent with other practices within the organization. This should provide higher quality of software, with lower costs for subsequent software maintenance.
10.	To allow the design to be validated as part of a financial auditing process.
11.	To allow quality and maintenance inspection to be introduced into the quality auditing of the software.

Table 2.2: Checklist management issues

1.	To enforce organizational, national or international program and programming standards (here, program standards can be interpreted in a broad sense, including the design and specification levels as relevant standards become available).
2.	To enable better software maintenance management techniques (in terms of planning, monitoring and control) to be introduced, including the acquisition of appropriate metrics. This will provide better visibility of the software maintenance to be achieved, and therefore facilitate better control.
3.	To address legal aspects. It may be necessary in the future to undertake reverse engineering because of legal arguments about copyright of software (the so-called copyright notice for the PROCOMM package explicitly forbids reverse engineering). It may be necessary to show that a competitor has reverse engineered our product illegally.
4.	To enable the organization to produce and cost more effectively impact of change reports, audit trails etc.

Table 2.3: Checklist technical issues

1.	To allow major changes to be implemented (the structure, documentation and quality of the software may be so poor that it is unfeasible to implement a major change without reverse engineering the software to a higher level of abstraction first).
2.	To discover and represent the underlying business model implicit in the software.
3.	To rediscover and record the design of the system.
4.	To rediscover and record the requirement specification of the system; in both this and the previous case, it may be appropriate and useful to provide more than one view. It is often the case that original design and specification information has been lost, or has not been kept up-to-date. By acquiring and capturing such design and specification information, we can potentially support software maintenance at higher levels of abstraction, and then generate implementations from them.
5.	To port the application to a new environment, new programming language etc., for example, to convert a system running on a single processor machine to execute on a highly parallel multiprocessor machine.
6.	To help establish and support a reuse policy for code, designs, specifications, processes etc.
7.	To redesign the exception handling in the system, including the possible introduction of fault tolerance.
8.	To reverse engineer software because software maintenance practice is itself evolving.
9.	To discover the original requirements of the software, because they were never stated or even known.

Table 2.4: Checklist technical issues (continued)

10.	To recover and record high level information about the system, including: • The system structure in terms of its components and their interrelationships expressed by interfaces. • Functionality in terms of what operations are performed on what components. • The dynamic behavior of the system in understanding how input is transformed to output. This should ideally relate closely to the static structure of the system. However, understanding the dynamic behavior involves studying the system over many modules. • Rationale. Design involves deciding between a number of alternatives at each design step. We may wish to find out and record which alternatives were chosen and why the decision was made in the way it was. • Construction. We may need to find out which modules, documentation, test suites etc., are stored in which files in the file store or database.
11.	To rediscover which tools or hardware were used to generate the system. (This is of considerable importance in long-lived host-target software)
12.	To update the source code (etc.) so that it can be compiled, linked and so on, by the tools that are currently supported, rather than those that were used when the software was built.
13.	To rediscover the contents of the software release (in terms of configuration management), possibly due to a disaster.
14.	To replace old design concepts (which at the time were well implemented) by modern techniques (for example, to replace a semaphore design of a parallel system with a design based on rendezvous).
15.	To facilitate interfacing the system to a new or modified kernel in a layered architecture.

2.4 Reverse Engineering Activities

In this section, we shall identify a number of different activities of reverse engineering. Depending on the reason why reverse engineering is being undertaken, one or more of the techniques listed below may be applicable in any given project.

Furthermore, the reverse engineering may be done incrementally or totally, again depending on the requirement. Also, the selection of the method may be application domain dependent; this is addressed in section 13.

We shall assume that the reverse engineering team starts with no prior knowledge of the system, and that the system is in a realistic, unmanaged state to start with.

1. **Loading.** We may need to bring our software system into a modern software configuration management systems (CMS), supported by a software engineering database (or so-called repository). Since configuration management is a very basic, essential tool in software maintenance, this is an important step in reverse engineering. For some applications, this may require the basic inventory of software items comprising the system to be identified (including documentation,

test suites etc.). It may be a non-trivial task, especially when there are versions and variants of software components, possibly shared between teams. For long lived software, it may be important to identify the versions of tools, hardware, systems software etc., that were used in the generation of the system releases.

2. **Structural understanding.** Having brought our software system (including all software items) into our configuration management system, it may then be appropriate to analyze the result to see if it is the best structure in terms of the configuration management system (CMS). Reorganization may be required. As a simple example, it may be helpful to reorganize the existing documentation so that links can be established in the CMS system between documents and the objects they describe. This is clearly closely linked with activities listed below.

3. **Restructuring.** We may wish to undertake restructuring at the code level (that is, we perform a code level to code level transformation without altering the functionality (the external behavior) of the code). This can include for example the untangling of complex control structures, standard data naming, chunking, aggregating or fragmenting modules, dead code removal, removal of duplicate data items, imposition of layout standards, file analysis, data normalization, and removal of side-effects. The key rationale is to help system understanding, not to execute the code.

4. **Quality Assurance.** Often, software systems do not have a properly constituted set of test suites and a regression testing procedure. An important reverse engineering task may be to prepare such test suites and link them to functional descriptions and components in terms of black and white box testing procedures. In view of the increasing importance of software quality, this may become a very significant form of reverse engineering. In terms of product, it may be necessary to institute new review procedures.

5. **Redocumentation.** Redocumentation of the system in terms of what it is, why it was produced and how it is being built may be appropriate. Redocumentation at different levels of abstraction may be required. Documentation supports system understanding (often the most expensive activity in software maintenance) in terms of: learning about the system (including incremental update); recording information during reverse engineering; reinforcing visibility for instance for Quality Assurance processes; and planning maintenance (impact analysis, cost of modification etc.).

   The output could contain documentation in a number of forms, and examples include:

   - production of a cross-reference listing (if necessary taking into account the scope of the language) and indication of variable usage,
   - call graph generator,
   - data access map,
   - dataflow analysis.
   - transaction analysis,

- cohesion and coupling analysis,
- per module functional description based on a standard form layout,
- documentation entered by maintainers in text format, as system understanding is gained.

Documentation is needed at higher levels of abstraction also. Knuth has described a very interesting approach to documentation which he terms 'literate programming'. His WEB documentation system [182] has been used to describe large software systems such as TEX. This intermixes program text and documentation, and tools (TANGLE and WEAVE) are available respectively to generate documentation for maintenance, and to produce machine executable source code. It is seen mainly as a tool for documenting new systems. Further details are given in the section on documentation.

6. **Design recovery.** The discovery of higher levels of abstraction (possibly including several views of these) for the software system. This also is taken to include discovering the business model.

7. **Porting.** As noted above, it may be necessary to port all the reverse engineered information to the customer repository (ranging from a simple filestore and paper documentation to a full software engineering repository. Hopefully, this will rarely be required.

8. **Acceptance testing.** At the end of the reverse engineering process, we suggest that an explicit acceptance test is undertaken on the system before any further maintenance is undertaken.

2.5 Checklists for Reverse Engineering: Research and Costs-benefits

In this section, we shall provide three short lists of topics in reverse engineering. The first one in table 2.5 is on open questions about this subject. The second and third one, tables 2.7 and 2.8, contain cost and benefit issues which need to be taken into account before embarking on a reverse engineering project.

In the literature (for instance Smythe, Colbrooke and Darlisson [286]) reverse engineering is often presented as a clean process with many loosely coupled component tasks; one carefully isolated operation follows another until a re-implemented system emerges from the other end. In practice, this seems not to be the approach, and it is not clear if it is a desirable objective. For example, an obvious initial reverse engineering task is to load the existing software system into the CMS. This may involve a considerable effort to understand the system, and it is only sensible to record that understanding immediately, rather than to repeat it later (or even hand the job to another team). As a second example, reverse engineering is normally presented as a very clear bottom-up activity, but practical experience suggests that it is both a top-down and bottom-up approach. The processes may depend heavily on the maintainers' existing expertise and understanding of the system, and on the state of the

Table 2.5: Checklist research issues

1.	It is not clear that manipulation of the source code control structure always is advantageous. It can replace contorted control flow by contorted use of flag variables. Not all GOTOs need to be removed. (example: those dealing with exceptions). It is not always clear that this benefits the understanding of the design and it is really attacking the symptoms rather than the solution (see Calliss [64], and Miller and Strauss [229]). However, in many cases, an improved, clearer source code control structure is more understandable, and the places where problems occur may be acceptably rare.
2.	Simple activities like standard layout, data naming, commentary etc. can be a help because programmers can readily familiarize themselves with new systems at the tactical level, and not be distracted by learning different standards. Some work was done on this area a few years ago but it is less active now. It is likely that this can be applied at higher abstraction levels for instance, for design methods, by choosing a suitable design method (Jackson etc.).
3.	The typical picture of reverse engineering shows abstraction from the code to some high-level design representation. The design representation is then manipulated to improve maintainability and/or some other attributes. The improved design is then subject to a forward engineering process, to produce new code from the design. This incorporates three fallacies: • The abstract design may be impossible to find or extremely messy. Should errors in the code lead to errors in the reverse engineered design? If not, when should they be corrected, and how does this fit into the overall process? • We may not actually forward engineer from scratch from a reverse engineered specification; often we may try to reuse heavily the existing code and design where this has changed little and is of high quality. • Subsequent maintenance should not be undertaken on code (even if reconstructed) but on high-level abstractions.
4.	It may be that a useful representation for high-level models is an object-oriented notation. At high levels it really needs to be independent of a particular method such as Yourdon, Jackson, etc.

system itself. How do we trade off a highly directed and prescriptive method for reverse engineering against efficiency of a free will cognitive process? It is certainly the case that the evolution of software can be undertaken in a highly prescriptive, visible and controlled environment. In reverse engineering it is more difficult to make generic proposals; it is highly dependent on the software, personnel etc. An interesting line is to investigate the use of process modeling languages in reverse engineering.

Table 2.6: Checklist research issues (continued)

5.	There are seen to be clear limits to the usefulness of automated design recovery. Human input is needed to give the design recovery a sense of strategy or direction. The human being constructs some hypotheses about the system as a very high-level model and then inspects the source code to test the hypotheses. Maybe the high-level model is then altered, but this gives the reverse engineering a means of identifying important abstraction using human insight, and knowledge of the application domain, and knowledge of system design. This approach is supported by the work of Foster and Munro on documentation [125], by the work of Sneed on reverse engineering COBOL systems [288], and work on the REFORM project at Durham University on inverse engineering assembly code to Z specifications [321]. As an example, reverse engineering a compiler is likely to be a relatively straightforward job for a compiler expert. Much is known about standard structures, techniques and theory for compilers, and our reverse engineer is likely to be guided strongly by this as he or she goes through the process of understanding the system. Reverse engineering involves recapturing lost information. It seems that this can only come from human experts with a knowledge of the application domain and of systems design and computer science theory. It may be that AI can provide limited automation or play an advisor role; however, we do not really understand the manual process well, so early automation seems optimistic.
6.	How does design improvement now take place? It could be that instead of reverse engineering to an abstract design, and then improving that design, we move straight to the improved design through the process of establishing tentative high-level models. We now edit the code, with heavy reuse, to match the new design (and along the way, reuse existing design information, specifications, etc). The work of Basili [17] is relevant here. He envisages the software being loaded initially into a software engineering repository. Reverse engineering is then carried out, reusing wherever possible, the old design information and its implementation (code). If reverse engineering does rediscover the requirement specification, it would not be wise to discard all design and implementation information – some of it may be useful as a 'hint', and some to reuse as is.
7.	It could be that a limited amount of automatic machine-based manipulation of code could help the initial reverse engineering step.
8.	The performance implications of using a repository containing 'fine-grained' data needs exploration and analysis.
9.	It is not clear to what extent reverse engineering is dependent upon the application domain.
10.	Inadequate case studies and 'best practice' exist.

Table 2.7: Reverse engineering costs

1.	The code may be too specific, and not generic, so that few advantages are gained when the system is re-engineered.
2.	We may have concerns about legal aspects and copyright. The legal position must be clarified before the project starts.
3.	The code may have errors and it is not clear if it is useful to reverse engineer error filled code.
4.	Reverse engineering itself may introduce errors, and revalidation will be essential in the project plan.
5.	Reverse engineering can be very expensive and the returns are not clear. A cost benefit analysis will be needed.
6.	It can be unfeasible with tight deadlines, and continuous change on the software in question. If this is the case, very careful planning and liaison with customers will be needed. A small number of releases can be made with the current system (with a deadline) while reverse engineering can proceed in parallel. Alternatively, an incremental approach might be appropriate.
7.	It reduces the programmer's task to a mundane mechanical one.
8.	Management are not sure how to cost, plan and implement reverse engineering. It is seen as a high risk option.
9.	There are no standards, or standard methods for reverse engineering. Popular commercial methods such as Jackson's do not directly address evolution.
10.	Existing commercial toolsets are inadequate, expensive, not integrated and lack a repository.
11.	It may be better to start again, using a package or fourth-generation language solution.
12.	Management are not sure how to cope with reverse engineering; it appears to have low visibility, it is difficult to control and measure etc.
13.	Little benefit for non important short-lived software is seen.
14.	No adequate measures of maintainability exist.
15.	It may be necessary to maintain the old system in parallel with the reverse engineering process, causing problems.
16.	Our model so far envisages the software being brought into a reverse eng.ineering environment (including a repository), so that reverse engineering tasks can be performed on it. However, it is not clear how the improved software returns to the user environment. The reverse engineering environment may have its own repository, configuration management system, design representation and reuse scheme. How is this ported into the user environment (which may be very different)? If we do this port, if we wish to undertake later reverse engineering, the software will have to be reloaded into the reverse engineering environment (it will almost certainly be changed by then). The sensible approach could be to have a single development, maintenance and reverse engineering environment, but this may not be commercially sensible. Perhaps the full solution will only come when appropriate standards emerge (the IBM repository could form such a standard).

Table 2.8: Reverse engineering benefits

1.	It can be foolish to discard well-tried reliable high-quality code. Therefore, it is better to modify existing code than start again. In order to start again, we may well have to understand the old system to determine the business model, and this activity is often regarded as the most expensive software maintenance activity.
2.	Existing code embodies knowledge of the application domain which may not exist elsewhere.
3.	Systems analysis is now usually done on existing software: many manual procedures are already automated.
4.	Reverse engineering supports incremental evolution, not 'big bang' development.
5.	High reuse potential of the re-engineered system may exist.
6.	Code is a mathematical object and, given the right theory, we can formally reverse engineer.
7.	The reverse engineered system is likely to be faster, smaller, more maintainable, adopt standards, use CASE, and generally be of higher quality.
8.	Reverse engineering is helped by automated tools.
9.	It is useful for important, long lived strategic software.
10.	Good studies of effective reverse engineering do exist (e.g. in CICS).
11.	Reverse engineering may allow us to move an existing system from batch to interactive, from centralized to distributed, from poor Human-Computer-Interface (HCI) to good HCI, without rewriting the whole system.
12.	Reverse engineering can be incremental (tackling hot spots first), so that it can be phased with the maintenance of the existing system.

2.6 Quality and Reverse Engineering

Reverse engineering uses both manual and automatic processes. For there to be any confidence that the reverse engineering has been undertaken successfully, we need to know that the new representations have the same meaning as the old (or, if modifications to the requirements have been undertaken, that the new behavior is correct). Even simple automated tools such as restructurers have acquired a somewhat dubious reputation for subtly changing the semantics of the target program. This undermines the confidence of the user, and it will be very difficult to provide a convincing case that reverse engineering is a sensible strategy with low risk. Also, in real-time systems, the time behavior of the system must be quality assured.

One form of reverse engineering that has already been referred to is the change from ad hoc to a proper testing strategy. This could be required without any other change to the software.

We should also prepare for validation during the reverse engineering process by the preservation, enhancement and creation of tests and regression tests linked to the code, design and specification.

This aspect of reverse engineering is addressed in further depth in chapters 12, 17 and 21.

2.7 Review

2.7.1 Maintaining at Higher Levels of Abstraction

Other than code level operations (which can be regarded as preparatory steps), the main aim of reverse engineering is to understand and represent the system at higher levels of abstraction. Now, all four types of software maintenance can be performed at this level, rather than in terms of source codes. Ideally the upper level should be the system specification, expressed in terms of application domain objects. For example, in a commercial data processing application, we would want to specify the business model at this level. Whenever change is required, we go immediately to this specification level, and change that. We then follow our design processes through to generate executable code (of course, the specification may be executable). We must not attempt to change the code directly. Of course, we would want to reuse as much as possible of the existing system, addressing our attention to those parts that have changed. Regression testing will be required to give us confidence that this is so (emergency fixes can be accommodated in this process).

Reverse engineering then provides us with the way to transform the system from source code to higher level representations. The situation is similar to that for high-level languages; once it was possible to maintain the high-level language representation, it was not sensible even to look at the generated object code.

We shall require confidence that the product as well as the process is correct, so that it will be essential to have regression testing (black box, white box) on the executable system.

2.7.2 Summary

To summarize, there is no magic, fully automated answer to reverse engineering. Like any other software engineering task, it needs a careful analysis of requirements, an investigation of the possibilities that are available, a careful choice of the techniques to be used, and an implementation based on strong quality direction. The project needs careful planning and management, and costing and metrics are needed at each stage.

The central issue in much reverse engineering is the representation of software (including that which exists, such as source codes, that which can be generated, such as cross-reference information, and that which can be formulated with human assistance such as high-level designs). The use of a central repository, together with integratable tools, which support an overall method is the focus of the remainder of this book.

3

The Business Case for Reverse Engineering

P. Welch and J. Grumann, *Grumann Daten Kommunikation GmbH, Bad Homburg, Germany*

3.1 Business Change – The Reason

To survive in the current state of national and international competition, businesses must react to a changing world, this requires change in all aspects of the business. The reasons behind this necessity to change are many, for example :

- economic growth of the company,
- pressure from competitors to improve performance,
- external influences - changes in tax regulations, new laws,
- mergers, takeovers, reorganization within the company,
- new markets, new activities, new customers.

The rate of business change required of a company for it to survive is increasing steadily. The business changes required to take account of the changing world, as mentioned above, have a direct and immediate effect on data processing needs. In order for a business to respond effectively, when something changes in the business situation, the data processing systems must change, be modified, be extended.

Nearly no company can prosper, or even survive, without large investments in data processing (or information technology if preferred). Most companies work in a way which would be impossible without the use of information technology. Data processing has improved the quality of the company for instance by decreasing reaction times or costs or increasing productivity. Further improvements are still possible, as well quantitative and qualitative improvements of the present applications of computers in a company, as with the introduction of new ones.

Economic growth leads to increased usage of existing data processing systems and thus to requirements for bigger, faster and more powerful equipment. Competitive pressures result in requirements for a higher level of productivity. At present, the same number of employees need larger, quicker and more effective data processing. A quicker response time is required in handling 'transactions' in general, needing improved speed and functional performance in data processing. Further new, more powerful, functionality in existing data processing is necessary in order to keep a company on a sufficient competitive level.

External influences can require relatively small changes to be made, but these have to be made over whole areas of the data processing systems, often at a fixed point in time. Mergers or takeovers and new markets may be the trigger for such changes.

Mergers, takeovers and other needs for reorganization of management or production leads to requirements to merge, or reorganize the data processing to reflect and support this. Frequently the data processing capacity can be spread over the entire globe.

New markets and activities, even new customers, can require changes to the data processing systems. Both modification of existing systems or totally new systems may be required, but even new systems must mesh with the existing ones at critical points.

The rate of change required of data processing is increasing in step with the increasing rate of business changes.

3.2 Data Processing Change – The Problem

3.2.1 The Situation in Business Data Processing

Systems become more complicated (knotted) and less manageable the more they are changed, modified or extended. This applies particularly to data processing systems because of the nature of most computer languages.

Most existing data processing systems were designed only to do a specific job, they were not designed with change in mind. Design strategies which accommodate future needs for change are only now becoming the subject of active research.

The original design and reasoning of the data processing system thus becomes inapplicable as functions are changed, others added or extended. The overview of the 'system as a whole' becomes progressively lost and it begins to become difficult to predict the effect on the system of even small local changes. Many older systems are in an even worse situation. They were not specifically 'designed' at all, but were developed in an ad hoc way, often without documentation. Added to the original lack of a documented concept, come the changes over the years. But many companies find themselves in the position of relying on just these old systems for their continued existence.

Even if system documentation exists, it can be mislaid, inapplicable, out-of-date. People with specialized knowledge of the system leave the company, move to other positions or retire. The knowledge about the system 'as it is' declines steadily.

Those changes which have to be made are patched onto the existing structure because there is not enough knowledge about the system to build them into it. Such patched changes can become such a significant proportion of the system, particularly at sensitive key points such as data transfer, that they themselves require changes.

The result is frequently unmanageable systems, permanently on the verge of ceasing to function, possibly with an unacceptable error rate but on whose continued existence the company relies.

3.2.2 The Consequences for Business

The resources involved to keep existing systems running requires a very large proportion of the budget for data processing. Figures of 50% are currently recognized as good – at least by data processing personnel – in some instances figures of 90% plus are more realistic. In business terms this is the cost of standing still.

The cost of adding new functionality to a system increases dramatically. It becomes more and more difficult to make minor changes and still keep the system working.

Equally serious for the business needs, is that the response time to implement such changes increases disproportionally. Business opportunities can be lost.

Data processing staff become less able to provide new systems to support the business in new directions or new markets, the meshing of new systems with the existing ones also becomes more difficult and expensive.

The ability to move existing systems to larger, quicker equipment to provide for increased usage, more users, better response times is seriously affected and the service for the individual user declines.

If data processing has difficulty in following the speed and direction of business change, if systems cannot meet new requirements, they will lag behind the business. Rather than being an 'agent of change' as was the case in the past, data processing could become a brake or even a cause for stagnation. Rather than supporting the business aims of the company, the lack of an effective data processing strategy can begin to positively restrict business opportunities.

3.3 System Change – The Solution

It is obvious that the situation painted above has not gone unnoticed either by senior management, or by data processing management and staff. Two alternative solutions which are often proposed are :

- new development of the system from scratch, including modern design methods so that the situation does not arise again,
- buying in standardized, finished software from outside.

Both these options have many disadvantages. They are generally very expensive. It takes a considerable time to show any benefits as it is difficult to implement either solution in a stepwise manner. Its introduction involves reschooling of employees to use the new system, both data processing and other staff. Both decisions have a high risk, as one cannot be sure of benefits until a substantial amount of the work involved has been carried out.

The 'cleverness' invested in the system when it was written will be lost, at least when software from outside is bought. Also the 'built-in experience' is lost, which is represented by the current system. The systems have evolved to 'fit' the user and this evolutionary knowledge is lost along with the 'feel' of the old system for the user.

Finally, one has to face the prospect of repetition of the problem in 5-10 years time for the same reasons.

The alternative of overhauling the old system, keeping the same functionality, but rearranging and cleaning it up internally so that it is once more maintainable, usually falls down not because of the difficulty of physically making the changes but the difficulties involved in finding out what to do and where to do it while still retaining the same functionality: "we don't understand it, no-one understands it, and no-one ever will understand it" is a complaint often heard from software engineers doing maintenance.

A critical factor in this equation is time. Presented with a huge pile of program code, thirty programmers will take longer to understand the system fully than one programmer. This amount of time is simply too long in business terms to be practical. Understanding an existing program is difficult and takes a long time. The software engineers know in principle what questions have to be asked in order to be able to understand the system and to make the changes, but they have no way of answering them, unless they can use tools which help them to get the answers to their questions: reverse engineering tools.

3.4 Reverse Engineering Tools – A Helping Hand

Reverse engineering and re-engineering of old systems may be a solution to maintenance problems, if there are sufficient tools available to support this task. These tools should offer a solution to the maintenance problem, the tedious tasks of debugging, simplify program modification and change. They should give the programmer once again time to concentrate on his real work, new developments.

Using such tools, the distribution of effort between day to day business – with which one earns money now, and development – with which one will earn ones money in future can come once again in the correct balance.

The first line of attack is represented by tools with which complete applications can be documented in a manner so precise that it would be impossible, or at least completely uneconomic, to do it manually.

Corresponding to the exact wishes of the software engineer, not only single program modules can be documented, but also the data structures for libraries, files and databases, system control routines, call sequences for subroutines – simply everything which is, or could be, important for the software engineer.

It is worthwhile for a data processing department to have a set of standard documentation for an application in its files. The scope and format of the documentation can be made to satisfy the software quality standards of the company. When, however, a particularly large, complex or wide reaching change is envisaged, it is often necessary to prepare special documentation. This can be to estimate the amount of change necessary, and also to assist in carrying out the change. Such documentation can be produced to the wishes of the client and customized to various purposes such as those below.

- **Migration:** from one computer installation or operating system to another.
- **Cross-compilation:** transferring an application, or module, from an 'out-of-date' language to a new one.
- **Restructuring:** changing the control structure of the source to comply with structured programming rules.
- **Implementing a DBMS:** or changing from one DBMS to a new one.
- **Generation of interfaces:** to other programs, or to modularize a particular source to enable reuse.

Although, in principle, practically anyone in the business of software engineering and data processing can benefit from reverse and re-engineering tools, we see the maximum potential economic benefit from these tools principally in the area of individualized software. This kind of software is made specific for a particular company or for a specific situation.

However, reverse engineering can also be applied by companies who make generic software for sale. A whole range of possible candidates for reverse engineering can be seen:

- operating systems and system software and compilers,
- basis software, such as the classical access methods up to complete database systems, online monitors, macro libraries for driving terminal applications up to transaction monitors such as CICS,
- Service programs, all the useful software, without which the computer cannot work for instance, editors, generators etc.

Special cases are 'quick and dirty programs': programs which are thrown together to meet an immediate need or to see quickly if something works.

In theory, such programs should not be economically viable candidates for the tools, but it is surprising how long lived, and how essential such programs can become.

Once something 'works' within a stressed environment, the driving force to clean it up, document it and catalog it is often strongly negative. There are always more important things to do. Later, various 'variants' are derived by copying and editing. Since they work too, there is no reason to document them. It would be difficult anyway since there is no documentation for the original.

After a few years, the situation can easily arise that one or other of these variants is situated at the heart of an entire application, still undocumented.

3.4.1 Individualized Software

This represents the main area of benefit, in our view. Whenever an idea, a method, a technique is turned into software for a specific company and purpose there will come a time when reverse engineering and re-engineering will be needed to document, migrate, optimize or integrate it.

PC-programs. In general the user of PC software has either no access to the source code, or the scope of the problem is not large enough to be a financially viable proposition. The boundary between PCs and workstations, however, is constantly becoming less clear and many companies have installed large PC networks to deal with day-to-day business of its employees. Where customized solutions are installed within these networks, rather than standardized software, the same problems with maintenance arise as on larger installations and such individualized software can become a realistic candidate for the tools.

Individualized workstation programs. Normally here, software houses will be the people who realize such applications. As the boundary to PCs melt, in hardware terms, the tendency will increase towards the installation of standardized software for the normal functions such as text processing. As is the case with PCs, however, there is a growing tendency to connect workstations over network software between themselves and to servers, mainframes etc. Where individualized software is installed, it falls into the maintenance trap. In particular, if a system on a mainframe computer needs maintenance which has interfaces with applications running on workstations, it is necessary either to investigate the interface at both ends or keep it constant, which may not be in the best interests of either application.

Large company DP systems. From a certain size upwards, the necessity will always arise that a company requires individualized software. This need can be real, or in some circumstances imagined. Such systems represent the largest volume of software applications and classically fall into the maintenance trap. Most applications are still developed especially for each company, although sometimes by software houses, so the source code is normally available. Even though increasingly so-called 'standard applications' will be used, they are normally, often very extensively, modified to accommodate local needs and conditions. Additional functionalities are often included to cope with the specific needs or market of individual customers.

External DP computer centers. Here we refer to computer centers operating external to the company but often running software which is individualized especially for the company. The situation is similar to that of company owned computer centers except that the responsibility, risk and work involved in maintenance is moved from the 'internal' DP department to an external firm. Some companies already have separate accounting for their data processing departments and the boundary is rather fluid.

In 'external' computer centers, though, the team is often trimmed to the bone and under continuous pressure. If only 50% of their resources are used for maintenance then it would be an unusual case, normally over 70% of the team is occupied with the maintenance of existing systems. Managers are normally under pressure to the question why so many programmers produce so few new applications. Here, the need for effective help from tools is perhaps the greatest.

3.4.2 The Decision to Apply Reverse and Re-engineering Tools

The major factor, as in all such business decisions, is economic. The languages to be developed, possible new diagramming standards implemented, and other customer requested customization must be balanced against the volume of software, its current status, and the potential rewards of 'rescuing and revitalizing' it.

Immediate user/business related benefits can be :

- improved level of service of current requirements,
- improved user response times,
- substantial cost savings compared to new software,
- no investment in user retraining,
- same 'look and feel' of system.

There are, however, longer term gains to be made in the data processing department direct, which are more difficult to assess but which can be potentially greater than the direct savings and must also be taken into account. The improved level of knowledge about the system and improved maintainability of the system will lead to an increased productivity on future changes, extensions or migrations of the system. This will free data processing staff to concentrate on new applications.

4

Reverse Engineering in Practice

J. Estdale, *Lloyd's Register, Croydon, U.K.*

4.1 Introduction

As we saw in section 2.1.4, 'reverse engineering' is a relatively new term for a whole range of overlapping activities. It covers the complete process by which the maintainability of an existing application is improved, including:

- identification and assessment of its components,
- selection, construction and initialization of an appropriate environment for future maintenance, including tools, techniques, standards etc.,
- imposition of reliable configuration management procedures,
- creation of an appropriate set of documentation of all types, for instance functional requirements and design,
- provision of regression testing facilities,
- improving the application's source code and design,
- re-implementation of the worst parts,
- replacement of the currently used version.

The complete process requires considerable time and money, which are generally in short supply during the maintenance phase of the software life cycle. It is therefore common to perform only a small fraction of it at a time. However, we are careful to distinguish this case, which is one instalment of the complete reverse engineering process, useful in itself, from something done in the course of completing some normal maintenance request. Although many of the techniques are shared, the objectives are different. Maintenance is often done under stringent constraints on time or cost, so quality and future maintainability suffer accordingly (see section 3.2). The objectives of reverse engineering are to repair the accumulating consequences, and to reduce the resources needed in future while keeping quality high. Taking short cuts in producing a baseline that all future maintainers are expected to rely on, has a much higher probability of affecting future costs and quality than something similar perpetrated while handling a single request. We suggest that perfection must be the target for reverse engineering, so that the solution to mounting costs during the exercise must be acceptance or a carefully specified reduction in scope.

4.2 Historical Background

Fragments of what we now call the reverse engineering process have been in use for many years. They include:

- documenting the application after it goes into production,
- disassembly of object code when the source has been lost,
- display of object code in assembler form by debuggers, patch utilities etc.,
- recreation of source listings from internal (semi-compiled) forms, such as the LIST command with the simpler BASIC interpreters [55]. This can usually be recognized by the standardization of layout which it imposes. It can also result in the loss of comments, 'noise' words (optional items in the language syntax which do not affect the meaning as in COBOL [295]), unnecessary brackets in expressions etc.,
- interfacing to an unpublished interface, as permitted by the European Directive [116],
- creating a 'me-too' product. The most famous example is probably the Phoenix BIOS which is highly compatible with the IBM PC ROM BIOS [175].

The earliest reverse engineering service in the UK appears to have been Sysalog's 'Product Decomposition and Structuring' in 1981 about which they said: "The idea of applying software engineering methods in reverse doesn't seem to have crossed anybody's mind" [81]. Their service was adopted from its French developers, Tesci-Software.

4.3 Maintainability

The 'maintainability' of an application is clearly a complex multi-faceted measure of the ease with which it can be maintained, which should enable us to predict maintenance costs given a profile of the kind of maintenance to be done.

The factors which affect maintenance costs can be grouped as in table 4.1. 'Requirements for change' is clearly the independent variable which will be used to predict maintenance costs. It is however moderated and in some cases, motivated by current user satisfaction and the political relationsip and comparative strengths of the users versus those who are responsible for maintenance. The 'development process' and 'history' are already determined and are represented by the current 'user satisfaction' and 'implementation' of the application. The other areas are, to a varying extent, under the control of management.

Some areas are virtually independent of the application concerned. These are the 'staff', the 'working environment' and 'management'. All the other areas are part of the application or part of its relationship to its specific technical environment. They therefore cover the issues that determine the maintainability of individual applications. Clearly, this is far broader than current attempts to measure the 'complexity' of source code.

4.4 The Communication of Understanding

The reverse engineer (or the subsequent maintainer) has a number of channels available for gaining understanding about an application:

- looking at existing documentation, source code, analysis reports, records etc.,
- listening to, watching and prompting, those with knowledge of the application or the domain,
- observing the application's output devices and triggering its input devices,
- interacting with tools which observe the application in real-time,
- thinking about the results of the above.

Information about the technical aspects of the implementation of the application can be divided up on the basis of the usual waterfall life cycle model [28]: the clients' requirements, external specification (this is the complete interface between the application and its external world including a functional specification and all externally significant non-functional attributes), architecture, design, source code, unit, integration and system test procedures, validation and afterwards: delivery, installation, acceptance, operation and maintenance. Of course, the precise terminology, divisions and content are determined by the organizations involved.

While their boundaries may be 'fuzzy' or overlap, there are widely accepted distinctions between them and these are just as valuable during maintenance as they are during the development process. For example, the external specification specifies the

Table 4.1: Maintenance cost factors

Area	**Factors**
User satisfaction	Importance, extent to which the application meets and exceeds current requirements, current level of satisfaction, user expectations, number of users, frequency of use, variety of usage, number and remoteness of sites.
Requirements for change	Urgency, importance, mix, outstanding wish-list, rate of change, compatibility with current implementation.
Operating environment implementation	Facilities, rate of change, spare capacity size, complexity, flexibility, programming languages used, understandability, structure, reliability, documentation, quality.
Bought-in components	Quality, supplier relationship and support level, charges.
Development process	User involvement, quality control, use of an appropriate development method, standards.
History	Number, extent and quality of changes made to date.
Management	Resource budgets, determination of value and priority, grouping and paralleling of changes, delay, release timetable.
Staff	Relevant experience and capability, availability, motivation, turnover, training, salary, overtime rules.
Working environment	Office environment, standards, machine access, availability of software tools and testing environment.
Application-specific environment	Remote diagnosis and control, self-testing and instrumentation, support for component testing and system testing, availability of test material.

commitments made by the developers to their clients, so it acts as a kind of 'contract' between them and should be agreed by both. It is therefore appropriate to continue these distinctions in maintenance documentation. Dividing it up into sections accordingly has the advantage of being similar to existing good practice during development and is therefore likely to be acceptable. The major problem is the lack of clear relationships between the details in the different sections. Support for traceability from a requirement to a function, to a component design, to a source component and to test cases has been much discussed, but is rarely provided. This is because:

- Such relationships can be many-to-many, n-ary or distributed in some non-uniform way.
- It is expensive to document them using normal text editing tools.
- Suitable machine support is rare, for instance hypertext-like links between sections of formatted documents.
- It is common for the various different perspectives to be structured in different ways: requirements are according to interested party, external specification in groups of related functions, design by software component, system test by testing environment used. This can make the mapping between them too complex for its maintenance to be feasible.

It should be recognized that each document produced by a structured development process is generally developed to be a 'solution' to the 'requirements' placed on it, given as statements in preceding documents. The resulting solution may be in the form of a specification, setting requirements for further documents or in the form of a notation to be interpreted by a computer. Both are specifications of intent at this point. Neither is a description derived from observing the application in operation. The point of testing is to display any differences between what the application was intended to do, and what it actually does. It may also reveal areas where the development team interpreted the client's wishes incorrectly. The resolution of these defects normally results in revised documentation, which together with a list of known defects, is intended to describe the application as it is. Maintaining a list of known defects in the application, including those in its documentation, is a pragmatic solution to bridge the gap between intention and observation, giving the documentation a currency beyond the next bug fix. Maintenance documentation should also include some results of observation, particularly performance and resource usage, which are 'holistic' properties of the system as a whole, and which may differ widely from both their intended and any predicted values.

Maintenance documents sometimes include copies of original items such as linkage editor command files, and derived items such as linkage editor address maps. Maintenance of the documentation is generally easier if these are held as individual configuration management items and referenced, rather than being physically included.

A major problem is that the technology currently in common use does not support the means to provide a detailed commentary on an item, side-by-side with the original.

Support personnel often have requirements not included in the original requirements specification, covering installation, upgrades, compatibility, migration, import/

export, environment dependence and recovery. Failure of the developers to recognize these will result in unofficial 'enhancement' by support staff, such that the application as seen by its users may differ considerably from the view intended by the developers. Commonly this includes the setting of local defaults for options, the disabling of user control over options, and embedding the application in a restrictive environment.

4.4.1 Structuring the Information

The average maintainer is not blessed with omniscience and is therefore unable to simultaneously apprehend all the attributes of even the most trivial application. He or she must therefore rely on a series of partial views from different perspectives. For such views to be simple but complete the relationships shown between their 'components' must be limited. Furthermore, it must be possible to inspect such views and decide which is the appropriate component for further work, so the views must be easily intelligible and the import of each component must be clear. Thus in a diagrammatic view, a symbol is commonly used to denote a component; its shape indicates the type; a label is used to name the component for future reference, but more importantly, to imply all aspects of the component it represents; and links, positioning and enclosure [31] are used to show all the relationships relevant in this view. The use of the word 'all' here is deliberate. Whereas development methods such as SSADM encourage the use of design diagrams as sketches, omitting minor details which might obscure the main points, the maintenance engineer requires all relationships to be shown explicitly, so that searching the appropriate view for affected components is guaranteed to find all those relevant.

4.4.2 Modularity

It is widely acknowledged that a major risk in managing maintenance stems from the unexpected implications of proposed changes and the resultant tendency of changes to propagate throughout a system. These reduce the areas that are unchanged and which can be assumed to be unaffected at least until second-order or 'knock-on' effects become apparent. Thus it is crucial that components should be created which are as independent as possible. Myer's scale for measuring interface coupling [238] is useful here:

Once components are relatively independent, they should be independently maintainable, so each should have an independent specification, design documentation, source files, build procedure, test suite, etc. This will, incidentally, help to support concurrent work by several maintainers, component replacement and reusability.

Inevitably the components will have a network of runtime dependencies. If we define interfaces so that they are always provided by exactly one component (beware such things as FORTRAN COMMON areas) and avoid designs using recursion and coroutines, most dependency networks will degenerate to trees, whose root is the main program and whose leaves are completely independent components.

Some of the subtrees will normally have been designed as intermediate level components in their own right with all the attributes of independent components previously discussed. This will complicate the choice of which component requires maintenance

Table 4.2: Scale for interface coupling

Content coupling	.95	direct reference from one module to the contents of another.
Common coupling	.7	reference to a shared global data structure (named after FORTRAN COMMON).
External coupling	.6	reference to named external data items.
Control coupling	.5	use of parameters which dictate the control flow in the called module.
Stamp coupling	.35	reference to a shared data structure passed as a parameter.
Data coupling	.2	all references are to local data or individual data values passed as parameters.

but makes it more likely that a maintenance task can be restricted to something smaller than the whole application.

The documentation should allow speedy identification of the relevant components for any change.

Independent, 'standalone' compilation is not a requirement of independent maintenance since although it provides some confidence that components are truly independent, the idea generally assumes that the provider and its consumers are given equivalent definitions of the interface provided. The term 'separate compilation' [195] is used for the compilation of components in their appropriate context, so that effectively, there is a global block surrounding each defining the available interfaces.

5

Domain-Specific Issues in Reverse Engineering

M. Price, M. Shenton, A. Davies,
Marconi Command and Control Systems Ltd, Leicester, UK
I. Khabaza, *Lloyd's Register, Croydon, UK*
H.J. van Zuylen, P. van den Bosch,
Delft Hydraulics, The Netherlands

5.1 Introduction

The need for reverse engineering occurs in all domains in which computers are applied. For programs in 'third-generation' languages like COBOL and FORTRAN, reverse engineering is a means to get the design structure from the source code, to find cross-correlations, data usage, data structures and similar aspects which are hidden in the code. There are several similarities between the different domains. However, there are also large differences. This is partly due to the differences in the kind of programs. The complexity of data processing programs comes from the complexity of the data, the volumes of the data, the constraints on it and the many different ways in which it is used. In scientific programs the complexity is often in the algorithm which is applied to the data, while in real-time programs hardware interfaces and timing are important aspects. Furthermore, the organizations in which the different kind of programs are used have different 'cultures'. This means that aspects that are strategic in the data processing domain, may be irrelevant for real-time programs and vice versa.

If people apply reverse engineering in one of these domains, they will try to solve their short and long-term problems. Due to the differences in these problems and the emphasis on certain aspects of the programs, differences can be observed between the way reverse engineering is done in each domain. There are also large similarities, especially when one considers reverse engineering on a higher, abstract level. One can consider reverse engineering as comprehension of all important aspects of the system and (re)documentation. Even the aspects are more or less the same: reverse engineering is aimed at data, functions of the program, functions of modules, data usage, performance etc. The differences come in the level of detail in which one wants to understand these aspects and their complexity.

The first sections of this chapter discuss reverse engineering for real-time applications and data processing. These sections consider reverse engineering quite generally and give a description of important aspects in these domains. The other three sections are focused on reverse engineering for specific purposes: for reuse, the improvement of the user interface and the porting to high-performance computers. In these cases reverse engineering has a well-defined purpose, although all aspects might play a role. The level of detail with which each aspect is investigated cannot always be chosen in advance. The information required to understand the relevant aspects only becomes visible when one has already investigated a part of the program. Therefore, reverse engineering for such a specific purpose has a more or less ad hoc character.

5.2 The Real-Time Domain

The real-time domain is discussed in two parts within this book. This section explores the characteristics of the real-time domain that sets it apart from other application domains and therefore introduce particular problems for the reverse engineer. In section 14.1 the methods and techniques suited to the reverse engineering of the real-time domain are discussed.

First of all we shall use the following definitions to recognize the nature of real-time systems [188], [220]:

If, given an arbitrary input or event and an arbitrary state of the system, the system always produces a response by the time it is needed, then the system is said to be real-time.

One which controls an environment by receiving data, processing them, and returning the results sufficiently quickly to affect the environment at that time.

The responsive nature of real-time systems and their ability to influence the surrounding environment are usually a central requirement, and often dominate the whole system design and testing to meet an acceptable performance criteria.

The following list describes the characteristics of the real-time domain that are unique, or are particularly important within the domain. The reverse engineering process needs to take account of these points in the development of tools and methods to address the particular needs of the real-time domain.

1. *Functional Requirements*
   Functional requirements for real-time systems are often formulated by an end

user in terms of isolated statements or concerns about desirable function and invariant constraints. For example:

"Power must be applied to the four sub-systems in sequence allowing a 5 second interval between each one"

"In the event of power failure critical parameters must be preserved"

"The moving parts must not get within 1 meter of each other"

Deriving such real-world measures from the code requires a considerable knowledge base about the machine, operating system and the natural interrelationships between external actuations and events.

Where more direct static functions, numerical, logical or transfer processes are concerned the reverse engineering aims for real-time systems are very similar to the other software domains.

2. *Performance*
   The most prominent non-functional requirement for any real time system is the performance criteria. Although accuracy can be an important issue, the most usual requirement relates to the speed of execution of the software. Some of these requirements are purely dictated by the need for the application to produce the results within an acceptable time interval. Although other domains have time constraints (for example, it would be unacceptable for a payroll job to take many days), there is fundamentally a distinct nature to many of the timing constraints or requirements on performance for real-time systems.

   The system performance may be defined in terms of guaranteed recognition of external events. In such cases it is usual to refer to some minimal time for which the event must occur to be valid, say 1 millisecond and a maximum repetition rate, perhaps 10 times per second. This sort of criteria is then translated into a worst-case demand on the system both to recognize the event and also to process it before the next one can occur.

   If trying to reverse engineer such information the constraints applied by the environment cannot be discovered from the code but constraints on events might in principle be discovered.

   It may be counter-intuitive but consistency may have priority over performance because a real-time application must guarantee to function in a worst-case condition of inputs. This factor often means that an algorithm which is more constant in its execution time is preferred over an algorithm that has a better performance in typical operating conditions but has a longer worse case execution time.

   Recognizing such performance considerations requires knowledge about the application and the domain, a method to help extract this information from the application code is for a representation of feasible input conditions to be generated and used to evaluate the worst-case behavior.

3. *Internal and external state*
   State is defined as representing an externally observable mode of behavior [322]. Associated with state is the event that causes a transition from one state to

the next, and action which is the response to the event when in a particular state. State can exist within the application (internal), and where the application interfaces with the external world, the external objects may also exhibit state. This can lead to complex relationships between the application and the external objects due to the inter-dependencies between internal and external states.

As an application changes from one state into another, it does so in response to some form of event. If events occur during the wrong internal program state it may fail to recognize the event or respond with the appropriate behavior.

An analysis of the internal and external state can provide essential information to the understanding of an application for discovering what are invalid state/event/action relationships as well as those that are valid.

To construct a model of the possible internal and external states, a reverse engineering tool would need to incrementally build the state transition model. The need for human involvement in the process is likely to remain an essential role in the creation and refinement of a useful application state model. Using their knowledge they can then study 'what if' scenarios and declare known invariants of the environment or constraints on the system outputs.

Further to the above it is important to consider that there is often a close relationship between the hardware interfaces to the external world and the software which controls that hardware. This is because the hardware can be used to control, recognize and store short status level changes with the external world which the software system would otherwise have great difficulty in achieving. Taking due account of the hardware operation can be important to build a complete state transition model.

4. *Languages*
A number of more specialized languages have been developed for real-time systems while others have been adapted. All must have a range of input/output facilities to support the interactions required by such systems. Assembler language programming has always been of great importance but other languages include CORAL , PLM , Babbage, adaptions of Pascal and ADA. FORTRAN is also used, especially where numeric higher level functions are concerned. In each case efficiency is often important with the use of code optimizers generally for memory or speed.

5. *Concurrency*
Many processes within real-time systems are data driven in nature. Often there are many separate inputs into a system, this can easily lead to sub-systems or modules which are in different processors with some form of control coupling. This could take many forms such as polling, interrupt, handshaking, semaphores or rendezvous. A precise terminology has developed to distinguish between processors and processes, these being: active, blocked, scheduled, pending etc. In each case these concepts help create a tight coupling within the architecture of the software product to support the tight external coupling with the environment.

Other aspects of task control are commonly designed to suit the application, these include: activation, suspension, priority control, resource ownership and memory management.

6. *Execution and development environments*
Real-time systems have a strong relationship with the execution environment in which they operate. This environment includes a number of external sources that interface with the real-time application and operate independently of the software design. The physical and performance constraints applied to real-time systems often means that the execution environment is significantly different to the development environment.

   The development environment provides facilities for the developer which use terminal networking, operating system, man-machine interface and other services. Typical tool support required includes: software engineering, simulation, configuration control, documentation, editing, compilation, cross-referencing, static and dynamic debugging, emulation, source formatting, linking and help.

   In contrast with the development environment the execution environment can be a different hardware platform with a much reduced set of features. The need to optimize the physical space demands and system performance will mean that facilities are restricted to those required to maintain operational performance. Those provided would typically handle serial interfaces, memory management, timer and interrupt handling and perhaps some file handling although even this is not common.

   A whole range of constraints and influences follow from the isolation of these two environments which add to the more common features of all software development. The reverse engineering process must encapsulate or allow the user to apply knowledge of the execution environment in order to interpret the behavior of the application at any of its interfaces.

7. *External sensors*
Non real-time systems generally have inputs that occur at discrete points in time and are highly structured, for example keyboard entries, command control lines. The real-time system however deals with inputs that are unstructured representations of real-world characteristics, for example sensors for temperature, light and movement, these combine with internal processes and system outputs to produce control loop relationships, in much the same way as the human hand to eye coordination takes place.

   These types of relationships make particular demands on processing time and accuracies that have to be addressed in the reverse engineering process.

8. *Diversity*
Real-time software applications are rarely portable in their entirety because of the close coupling associated with their interface drivers. The diversity of applications is also quite broad which often represents a problem for a reverse engineer. Initially they want to gain a broad view. This would involve points of interface with the environment and any hints as to what they represent. Next,

they might try to determine an overall function and attempt to discover the subdivisions used in the design. There is however a trend to use low-level real-time kernels in some equipment which may develop the scope for portability in some real-time applications.

Section 14.1 develops the task definitions in more detail as a step towards a prescriptive guide for reverse engineering.

5.3 Data Processing Application Domain

5.3.1 Introduction

This section describes aspects of the data processing application domain relevant to reverse engineering, emphasizing the following aspects:

- database management systems,
- transaction processing systems,
- environmental interaction.

Chapter 2 on the reverse engineering process and chapter 13 on the REDO method describe aspects applicable to all domains. This section is intended to supplement them by providing descriptions of background problems and techniques relevant to the data processing application domain.

5.3.2 General Issues

1. Data processing applications are characterized by the relative importance of data in comparison to processing. Processing tends to be relatively simple : updating quantity by adding or subtracting, accumulating totals, etc. In contrast data tends to be a problem because of its size (large number of records), structure (fields, sub-fields, etc.) and complex overlapping interrelations (for instance suppliers, invoices, inventories, orders, customers and accounts) of the kind where a normal form design to maintain consistency and integrity is not straightforward.

2. A major and common type of modification is due to the changeover from the well tried and understood batch transaction processing, dominated by sort-merge and sequential access technology, to the hazards of online database processing with the need to lock/unlock fields/records/files due to simultaneous access from a large number of online terminals.

3. In comparison with other application domains, data processing applications are relatively well documented initially, with established and distinct analysis, design and implementation stages. Unfortunately the need to maintain initially good and correct documentation is often overlooked, and the need to modify applications in the face of changing business rules and requirements is very frequent. Often the problem in the modification of a data processing application is not so much the absence of documentation as its invalidity due to minor but subtle and numerous changes over long periods of time.

4. COBOL dominates data processing applications and, as explained later, COBOL presents several difficulties when applying otherwise well-established reverse engineering tools.

5. Record definitions occupy a large space in the file section. A quick inspection reveals that this is partly due to the absence of the facilities to define a record type and declare a record to be of a particular type. Thus the language does not help the reverse engineer to keep track of the type structure.

6. COBOL has a 'COPY' facility which is sometimes used to help in the above and similar problems involving repetitions of complex structures. 'COPY' is an 'include' facility with a 'REPLACE' option providing some form of macro processing. Thus, before applying a CASE tool (cross-referencer, call diagrams, etc.), the 'COPY' files have to be inserted and expanded as necessary.

7. Many tools have to keep track of references and usage for each 'variable' to detect such things as unassigned variables, variables used in read mode only, etc. These tools often have to be adapted for COBOL usage as illustrated in the next three examples.

8. Consider the following COBOL definition:

```
        WORKING-STORAGE SECTION.
        01  CUST-RECD1.
                02  FLD11     PIC X(10).
                02  FLD12     PIC X(10).
                02  FLD13     PIC X(10).
```

   It is not easy to decide whether the variable FLD13 has been initialized, even if the tool were to recognize an assignment to CUST-RECD1 as possibly affecting FLD13.

9. Next consider the following possible definition:

```
FILE SECTION.
FD CUST-FILE LABEL RECORDS ARE STANDARD.
        01  CUST-RECD1.
                02  FLD11     PIC X(10).
                02  FLD12     PIC X(10).
                02  FLD13     PIC X(10).
        01  CUST-RECD2.
                02  FLD21     PIC X(15).
                02  FLD22     PIC X(15).
```

   Here we have different mappings of the same record, and a cross-referencer tool needs to be aware of the problems involved; similar or worse problems are involved in the COBOL 'REDEFINE' and *level 66* 'RENAME' facilities.

10. The procedure division (code) of a program presents many problems peculiar to COBOL which need to be taken into account by control-flow tools, call diagrams, etc.. The 'PERFORM' verb with its many formats is at the heart of COBOL control flow. The ANSI COBOL 74 form is:

```
PERFORM para1 UNTIL ..
```

whereas COBOL 85 has in addition the *inline* form:

```
PERFORM UNTIL ..
        statement1
        statement2
        ..
END-PERFORM
```

Thus, COBOL 74 encourages a proliferation of paragraphs or sections. This has its advantages in that it supports top-down development, but it makes comprehension difficult because the body of the loop must be physically separated and may be several pages away from the loop statement.

11. Many basic reverse engineering tools are concerned with following the flow of control through various paragraphs. COBOL presents many problems because a paragraph may be invoked from many places in different ways. A call graph or a simple table listing paragraph calls can be a great help. In addition to interaction with the database indicated by the use of fields and records, the usage of the working storage section through a suitable cross-referencer can reveal where a paragraph or group of paragraphs are in effect a procedure or a subroutine. The working storage acts as an all engulfing common area, making it very difficult to limit side-effects. Impact analysis may indicate a disciplined naming convention and working storage usage which will make it possible to factor out independent areas of code; this is often the first step in any attempt at an object-oriented structure (see below).

12. Impact analysis is the study of how changes to a variable in one location can invalidate code in another, possibly remote location. This is one of the most common and most difficult problems in maintenance work.

13. If a major reconstruction is envisaged then reformulation in terms of reusable components is an important goal. As the term indicates, a reusable component is a generalization of the conventional concept of subroutine. The method of communication with a reusable component is more general, the use of subroutine parameter type is extended, sometime using *generic* parameter types, and generally a reusable component is equivalent to a collection of related, possibly *generic*, subroutines. The notion of a reusable component is closely related to that of an abstract data type and of an object in object-oriented methods.

14. Some programming languages are designed to make it much easier to use these methods, but the concepts are general and amount to a programming style or policy which can be introduced into COBOL or any third-generation programming language (although the reverse engineers need to help themselves by introducing their own conventions and discipline).

15. For an existing application, a reusable component is disentangled from the rest of the surrounding application with a view to minimizing and isolating side-effects. This is similar to the principles of maximizing cohesion and minimizing coupling in the design of modules. The introduction of reusable components during reverse engineering is fruitful and somewhat easier than when developing a new application. The reverse engineer has the benefit of hindsight; it is easier after the event to see much commonality there is among apparently distinct data processing operations.

16. Such major reconstruction is often rejected as it is difficult to quantify the benefits. Generally, the benefits are greater when dealing with a complex application with a long life and subject to regular and frequent modification. A payroll application, the most common data processing application, is one such example. A firm will always need a payroll application; but the rules for tax, pension, overtime etc., change frequently.

5.3.3 Database Management Systems

1. A data processing application often consists of a number of related programs and related files. The following is an example of interrelated files:

   - suppliers
   - customers
   - stock
   - purchase orders
   - accounts payable
   - sale orders
   - invoices
   - accounts receivable

   In traditional data processing applications, data was frequently duplicated, files were program-dependent with little, if any, sharing of common data. With the introduction of database management systems (DBMSs), the situation is reversed. Data independence is sought and database administrators aim at independence from the programs using the data. Different programs have access to different, and only limited subsets or *views* of the full set of fields stored.

   The reverse engineer is often faced with an application which predates the introduction of DBMS. Much of the work needed to understand an application is the same as that required to convert to a DBMS and this may very well be the outcome of reverse engineering, although the original aim may have been less ambitious.

2. The reverse engineering process of data comprehension involves a number of overlapping and successively ambitious activities (or tools):

   (a) The simplest activity is to find out all occurrences of a particular variable, preferably distinguishing usage, for instance:

   - Find all occurrences of CUST-TOT.
   - Find all updates of CUST-TOT.
   - Find where CUST-TOT is initialized.
   - Find all usage of CUST-TOT in read mode.

   In this and similar discussions, attention has to be paid to COBOL's propensities for aliases. Examples of this problem were given above. Other examples involve the COBOL facilities to 'REDEFINE' and 'RENAME' (*level 66*).

   (b) The next more ambitious tool is a cross-referencer. This is a tool which produces a list answering the above requests for *all* variables in a program. Many compilers produce a cross-reference list as a by-product of compilation but in a rather illegible form. A cross-referencer reverse engineering tool should be more user-friendly and more comprehensive, distinguishing different usage modes, i.e. read, update or initialize.

   (c) The next more ambitious tool is a *data dictionary.* There is no strict definition of the facilities to be provided by a data dictionary. Data dictionaries provided by various software suppliers differ in the degree of generality and amount of information. The kind of information provided includes a definition for each file, record, field and variable. The definition may include type, range and other more involved rules.

   The attempt to construct a data dictionary often reveals various anomalies:

   - synonyms (i.e. different names for the same thing),
   - homonyms (the same name for different things),
   - different structure, attributes, etc. to describe the same entity, for instance a slight difference in the definition of customer record in different programs of the same application.

   (d) Other terms and products which overlap with data dictionaries, and which depend upon the degree of generality, include:

   - directory,
   - catalog,
   - encyclopedia.

   A catalog tends to be associated with a DBMS and is usually defined using a Data Definition Language (DDL). Usually the catalog is held in the database and can be interrogated like other parts of the database, (although strictly this file contains *meta-data*, (data about data), rather than data, and some additional control is needed for instance, only the database administrator can modify it).

   (e) The degree of generality determines whether the product is concerned with:

- a particular program,
- all programs of an application,
- all applications of the organization.

The type and amount of information (range, rules, etc.) also differ. In their more comprehensive and ambitious form, an encyclopedia constitutes a corporate data model encapsulating the business rules of the organization.

3. Reverse engineering often leads to the introduction of a DBMS or to the conversion from one DBMS to a more up-to-date one. There are several tools and software products available to help in this common process.

   Another important related activity in reverse engineering is the construction of an Entity-Relationship-Attribute (ERA) diagram. This is a useful and illuminating step prior to the introduction of any DBMS but is also useful in its own right. There are a number of graphics tools which help with the drawing of an ERA diagrams.

   Such tools are indispensable, as the derivation and construction of an ERA diagram is an evolving process with several false starts and restarts (for example, what is an entity in one design may be a relationship in another), with various trade-offs between alternative designs.

   The construction of an ERA diagram is usually carried out before proceeding to the design of a database which satisfies the various *normal forms.* The main objective of normal forms is to avoid update anomalies and to ensure consistency and integrity. Integrity is not quite the same as consistency, it is more general; but at this level they are used interchangeably for brevity.

   Normalization of the database is often achieved by considering the simple rule:

   one fact in one place

   This means that, for instance, part numbers may be stored in several places, but the price of the product should be stored in one place only. There are many pathological situations where normalization is difficult, but fortunately these seem to be infrequent in data processing applications.

   The file section of the data division of a COBOL program contains a large amount of detail on the possible structure of the database, file organization, access methods, keys, etc. It may be possible to detect normalization problems and possible file restructuring improvements even before considering conversion to a DBMS or studying the code, which forms procedure division.

4. Database integrity and consistency are an important reverse engineering issue. Many obscure errors result in the loss of integrity. This is an issue which arises independently of the use of a DBMS. But DBMSs usually help a lot in this respect. Normalization is very much concerned with database consistency: the price of the same product should not be different in different places.

   Some integrity rules are simple, they are concerned with range or format. Others involve more or less simple rules, including more involved business rules. An example of a rule is:

```
TOT = COST1 + COST2 + COST3
```

It is envisaged that the 4 attributes COST1, COST2, COST3 and TOT are separately stored but should satisfy the above rule. (This is of course contrary to the basic rules of normalization, but is considered for illustration).

Many DBMSs include various facilities for checking ranges and some for enforcing rules. It is not always obvious whether this kind of data validation should be carried out by the DBMS or in the application program. The first is generally preferred where the validation rules are not likely to change and are not too involved. There are many overheads and performance penalties if the DBMS is given too much to do. In particular, some changes to the validation rules, and certainly any changes in the database design, for instance adding a field, may involve reconstructing or reloading the database. For the larger databases this can be very disruptive. It is often mentioned that for most DBMSs, a change in the design of the database does not usually require a change in the application program; this is due to the use of *views* or *subschemas*. But the cost of reconstructing the database is often overlooked.

5.3.4 Transaction Processing Systems

1. Transaction processing (TP) systems (or monitors) are concerned with data processing applications which require simultaneous use from several data terminals. An example of such a system is concerned with airline seat reservation, involving hundreds of operators over a wide (geographical) area. On a smaller scale, a stock control/sales invoicing system involving half a dozen operators might justify the use of a TP system.

2. Traditionally, the use of such system involved entering a large number of transactions, which were then batched, say once a day, sorted and processed against a master file. The need for quick response has made such systems non-viable although they were very efficient in the use of the then scarce and expensive computing resources.

3. Prior to the introduction of TP systems, the computer industry has had to develop data transmission technology, the associated complex communication software, and the design of online multiuser (timesharing) operating systems.

4. TP systems require much more than the above. They raise problems concerned with simultaneous access to the same file, record or even field, with the possibility of lost updates due to concurrent interleaved access by two or more users to the same record or field. To solve these problems, TP systems have to use locking mechanisms at various levels: file, record or field.

5. When locks are applied to more than one resource, the possibility of deadlock arises: a situation where two or more users lock each other out, each one waiting for a resource locked by the other. Efficient methods had to be developed to avoid or resolve such deadlocks which occur frequently in peak periods.

6. Finally, 'commit'/'rollback' facilities have been developed to deal with situations when a transaction is unsuccessful for various reasons when the failure occurs halfway through its various update actions risking loss of database integrity or consistency.

7. The reverse engineer contemplating conversion to a TP system does not need to be fully conversant with the above complications but some knowledge of the background is needed, and explicit 'commit'/'rollback' statements have to be used in the correct place.

8. Mainly because of the various possible problems outlined above, the previously large scale batch processing program has to be converted to short *atomic* steps. Each such step constitutes in effect a transaction which is terminated by a 'commit' if successful or a 'rollback' if unsuccessful.

9. In addition to the major restructuring explained above, another difficult aspect of the use of TP monitors is concerned with the use of a number of predeclared variables to communicate with the TP system. An example of this in the case of CICS is the EBI (EXEC Block Interface) group of variables such as EBICALEN (EBI Communication Area LENgth). These variables often have to be interrogated by the application and sometimes updated. They are introduced by the TP monitor through copy or include files and make impact analysis very difficult because they are non-transparent.

5.3.5 Environmental Interaction

1. Most COBOL implementations allow the inclusion of *foreign* components (subprograms, modules or segments). These components may be written in COBOL, but more often they are written in assembler or some other programming language such as C, Pascal or BLISS. In addition the source is usually not available for analysis, let alone modification.

2. The following is a list of the main types of foreign components which occur in data processing:

   - TP monitor,
   - DBMS,
   - user interface (window/menu/mouse systems),
   - operating system services not directly available from COBOL.

3. In addition to the problem of source inaccessibility for analysis, foreign components are a major obstacle when an application has to be ported to a different hardware platform. Reverse engineering is often carried out prior to the transfer (porting) of the application to different hardware or software environments. Sometime even transfer to a different version of the same hardware or operating system may cause the application to fail, the reverse engineer is then called to adapt the application to the new environment. Portability is a major reverse engineering issue. It is easy to be wise after the event and realize that one should

avoid foreign components. Where this is not possible, we consider below various aspects of the problem and methods of minimizing it.

4. Calls to TP monitors and DBMS are carried out from within COBOL programs. These calls have specified user-friendly formats which are not part of the COBOL syntax. In the case of DBMSs , the calls conform to SQL or DML (Data Manipulation Language). These calls are converted to legal COBOL CALL statements by appropriate preprocessors. The parameters used to pass are usually defined by the system and inserted by the preprocessor as copy/include files. For example, the EBI group of variables is inserted by the preprocessor as a COBOL linkage section of the data division. The reverse engineer may need to analyze the output of the preprocessor, which is often more difficult to follow than the original source.

5. Calls to user interface facilities should conform to the latest widely agreed graphics user interface (GUI) protocols such as X Window, OSF/ motif, etc. In general, these protocols form successive layers:

Application Program
Application Program Interface(API)
Windowing level
Graphics level (i.e. pixels and icons)
Device drivers (screen, mouse, etc.)
Operating system
Hardware/firmware

In this layered hierarchy, hardware is the lowest layer and the application program is the highest layer. Each layer should call on services only from the layer immediately below it. This ensures that any changes in lower layers or the hardware need not involve any changes in the application program. At most only recompilation is needed, but sometimes not even that.

Many operating system services tempt the application programmer to skip the hierarchy and enable the application program to communicate directly with lower layers. This is very undesirable for the maintainability and portability. In general, the lower the level the more frequent are the changes which invalidate the program. Sticking to the highest level, API, is the optimum policy to achieve portability.

5.3.6 Concluding Remarks

The introductory section referred to the desirability of restructuring to reusable components and emphasized that reusable components involve a form of data abstraction and object-oriented programming. Reusable components establish a narrow channel of communication with the application program, minimize coupling, maximize cohesion and hide much of the details, especially local variables (*information hiding*), as misuse of shared variables is the most common cause of obscure errors and makes impact analysis very difficult.

The use of *layered products* such as TP monitors, DBMS and API was discussed in detail above. It is instructive to reflect that they are another form of reusable components. They involve the same principle, although they do not completely succeed in information hiding (as we saw in the case of the EBI group of variables in CICS). The introduction of a layered product into an existing (old) application usually results in making programs much more compact, consisting mainly of TP or DBMS calls. Most of the intricate details are hidden by the layered products.

Various report generators, including the report section of COBOL, are other examples of *generic* reusable components. Producing reports is a very common data processing activity; despite their extensive varieties, reports have much in common (such as control totals, control breaks, headers, footers, etc). Report generators illustrate the power of *generic* reusable components.

The reverse engineer is encouraged to reorganize code in terms of *do-it-yourself* reusable components. Although COBOL does not have explicit facilities for abstract data types or object-oriented programming, it is possible to use the concepts and easy to enforce them: reorganize code and data in chunks or objects or modules which maximize cohesion and minimize coupling.

5.4 Reuse

5.4.1 Introduction

Software engineers often reuse components which they have developed in the past. The components can be source code, data structures or design concepts. Also methods and processes for software development are often reused. In this compendium we will restrict ourselves to reuse of source code in its original or re-engineered form. The usual way is, that old components are tailored to fit a new application.

The process of reuse is often informal. Often, it gives a direction to the development process, since the software engineer tries to guide the design to known and available components. This results in a top–down approach in the worst case and a mixed top–down / bottom–up strategy in the case of a more structured project [158]. The value of experienced software engineers can be found for a great deal in the large amount of reusable knowledge and source components they have from previous projects.

Reuse among different software developers is much more complicated. The problem here is not just to find a suitable component and tailor it to a new application. The identification of reusable components, the storage in a repository and the subsequent retrieval from the repository also have to be done in a more formal, controlled way than on the individual level. Furthermore, the commitment of the managers and the developers to the reuse system is essential, since the effort to select an existing component from the library of reusable components, to comprehend the range of its applicability and to adapt the component to the new application is, in the beginning, a large threshold to reuse.

A system for reuse should increase the productivity of developers, but it should not decrease the quality of the new applications, because they had to be fixed with existing components. Optimization of the choice of reusable components has to be a feature of the reuse system. This can be promoted, for instance by multiple implementations of the same function [78].

5.4.2 Reuse of Source Code

Although development concepts, such as high-level design, are often more reusable than the actual source code [82], we will restrict this section to the reuse of source code. The first step to make reuse on a larger scale possible, is to realize a system to support reuse. Coomer *et al.* [82] and Caldiera and Basili [61] distinguish the following phases:

- Identify a suitable component
    1. state criteria for reusable components,
    2. search for source code which meets this criteria,
    3. extract the component and make it suitable for reuse.
- Prepare the component and store
    1. make a functional description of the component,
    2. verify the functional description,
    3. classify the component.

The next phase is the actual reuse. This should be supported by facilities to select components from the repository with components, to check the interfaces, to adapt it, etc. Caldiera and Basili [61] describe the *Care* system, which supports the identification and qualification process. Schuurman and Loeve [277] describe a system which supports the storage of components in a repository and the retrieve them afterwards.

Reverse engineering methods and tools, such as the ones described in this compendium, can provide support in the following activities:

- evaluate source code for reusability,
- assess the interface of the component,

- extract the description from the source code,
- verify and test the component.

For the evaluation of source code for reusability metric tools can be used, as described in [61]. The identification of the function and the assessment of the interface are products of the REDO method as described in chapter 13 and is supported by static analysis tools. Verification of the components can be seen as an application of the REDO method as described in chapter 21.

5.5 Reverse Engineering for User Interaction

5.5.1 The Need for Better User Interfaces

The user interface of an application can be considered as a separate part, with a special function. It may be modified, without the need to modify the application itself. This separation is present in modern windowing systems [352], but to a lesser extent in older applications, where the coupling between user interface and application is often strong. Maintenance of user interfaces is basically similar to the maintenance of the rest of the application, as long as it concerns only small modifications. Differences are still present, since all maintenance of user interfaces has not only software engineering, but also ergonomic aspects.

Reverse engineering for user interaction will normally only be necessary if a major modification of the user interface is required. At present such requests are rather common. The evolution of computer hardware and software has opened new ways of communication between computers and users. Types of interaction which were unthinkable in the past, are now standard for cheap PC programs. The modes of operation in the past, such as batch operation and editing of fixed format input files, are now often unacceptable for users. Since programs have a long life, especially if they have a good functionality, there are many programs with user interfaces which need to be upgraded.

There may be several reasons and triggers for the request to upgrade a user interface, for instance:

- the introduction of applications on personal computers with good user interfaces may invoke the wish to have the same kind of user interface for all existing applications,
- the downsizing of mainframe programs to workstations of personal computers,
- the change from batch processing to interactive processing,
- the integration of two or more programs with different styles of user interaction,
- the wish to simplify the effort of the user in preparing input, running programs and analyzing output, in order to have the same work done by less skilled staff members, or to increase the productivity or to make the work more pleasant,
- the need to reduce errors due to complicated interaction between the application and the user,

- the need to have a single user interface as a front-end for a system which is distributed over several processes (either on one computer or distributed over a network),

- the wish to improve the distribution of tasks between the user, the user interface and the application, i.e. work that had to be done by the user is taken over by the program and, if needed, the user can take over control over the execution of the program, which was originally done by the application itself.

Many of these reasons have a link with the *modality* of the system [139]. This is the distribution of tasks between the user interface, the application and the user and the way in which the user executes the task. An example is the way a user selects data about a geographical location, which is stored in a file. The simple approach is, that the user has to know in which file the information about a location is stored, in which directory this file can be found and with which program the information can be inspected. Another modality is, that the system contains a description of the information. The user selects the information he wants from a list of descriptions. The system makes the link to the directory and the file name and automatically chooses the appropriate program to view the data. A step further could be, that the selection from a list is replaced by a selection from the map, where the conversion of cursor coordinates to the location and the appropriate file is made by the system. Such a change in modality moves the memory load and the need of making all kinds of transformations from the user to the program.

In most cases, the replacement of a user interface will be a major effort. A balance has to be made between the effort to improve the user interface and the profit one can get from an improved program. The upgrading of the user interface can be done on different levels. For instance, the upgrading can be that the user still has the same task and executes it in the same way, but is supported by the system. The utility remains the same but the usability increases. This may increase the productivity for instance, by reducing the error rate .

It is likely, that a new user interface will affect the user task in a more fundamental way [359]. The ease of use for certain functions makes it possible to execute a task in a different way. For instance, in a batch system a linear approach is most appropriate:

- input preparation (preprocessing),

- processing,

- output analysis (postprocessing).

However, if quick feedback can be given for the input preparation, an iterative approach may be more efficient. Such a change in the task execution is only sensible if:

- information from the output is important for the decisions taken in the preparation of the input,

- the appropriate output can be generated in a time which is short compared to the time needed to prepare the input.

In transaction processing, as alternative to batch processing, the effect of a single transaction can be analyzed, the transaction can be undone and modified if it contains errors or unwanted effects. The execution of a transaction may have influence on later transactions, such as in reservation systems. The feedback mechanism which is provided, makes not only the task more efficient, but imposes also new requirements for the function of the program. In a first upgrading step, transaction processing may be seen as a 'quick batch': one transaction is executed and the results are shown. The introduction of the undo and modify function as an easy way to correct a transaction might be a next step. Also a function to see the effect of a transaction without executing it, could be a useful new function. The situation that a new user interface gives a new kind of task execution, which leads to requirements of new or modified functions, is observed quite frequently [67].

5.5.2 Characteristics of the User Interface

In her "Method for User Interface Analysis and Redesign" [TN-WL-1071], Smit lists the general characteristics of good usability as:

1. visual clarity,
2. consistency,
3. compatibility,
4. informative feedback,
5. explicitness,
6. appropriate functionality,
7. flexibility and control,
8. error prevention and correction,
9. user guidance and support.

The development of a good user interface has to take all these characteristics into account. It is an interdisciplinary task, in which information analysis, user profile analysis, task analysis, dialogue design, graphical design, software specification and design are involved. In the report [TN-WL-1071] a method is described to define and analyze the task and requirements and to redesign the user interface for existing programs. The report assumes that the user interface is logically and physically separated from the application.

There is, in many cases, a rather close link between the user interface and the application. This may lead to functional links. A new dialogue style gives the user an other view on the system. Direct manipulation in a graphical user interface gives the user new possibilities to select an action or information. This new style requires new functions, at least functions in the user interface to transform user input to a form which is accepted by the application.

In order to improve flexibility and give the user control over the application, the control of the execution of the functions can be moved from the application to the user interface. If in the original program input verification and input processing is done automatically in a sequential order, the new user interface may require that the control of these functions is done by the user: he decides whether the input is processed, how far the processing is done. and which information he will get to monitor the process.

So several characteristics of good usability, such as 'appropriate functionality', 'flexibility and control' and 'error prevention and correction', imply a logical and possibly physical link between the user interface and the original application. The boundaries between the original user interface and the rest of the application may move, so that part of the processing control, input verification and output presentation are moved over the boundary to the user interface.

This restructuring of parts of the original application is a form of re-engineering combined with the development of a new user interface. Reverse engineering is a necessary part of the development process. It provides the information about the technical possibilities to perform the re-engineering, gives an estimate of the effort needed. Reverse engineering can provide the information about the functions which should be modified and about the new control structure in those cases that this information cannot be found in the existing documentation.

5.5.3 Separation Versus Integration

In a user interface three layers are distinguished [141]:

1. presentation,
2. dialogue,
3. application program interface.

This logical separation is not always present in the physical structure of the implementation. However, if the physical design of the user interface has the same separation, the maintainability and portability of the user interface is much better [352].

On the *presentation* level the elements of the user interface are described. For instance, the menus, forms, help windows, scroll bars, drawing canvasses, graphical elements like characters, boxes, arrows and circles are output elements, keystrokes, mouse movements, mouse clicks are the input elements which are used most frequently. The presentation layer can be separated in a lexical and a syntactical aspect. The lexical aspect just concerns the description of the elements, the syntactical aspect concerns the valid combinations of the lexical elements. For instance, a scroll bar may be considered to be a lexical element, which can be combined with a window to a valid element of the user interface. The function of these elements and their mutual relations are described at the dialogue level. Here the semantics of the function keys, mouse clicks etc., is defined in terms of what happens in the user interface.

On the *dialogue* level the sequential and causal structure of the user interface is described: what happens under which circumstances and what is the consequence of a certain action. Representations which are frequently used for the dialogue level are:

- state transition networks,
- event specifications.

User interfaces can be considered as a kind of real-time system, where the user interface interacts with two processes: the user and the application. Many aspects of the control structure representation can therefore be borrowed from real-time systems.

The *application program interface* consists of all calls from the application to user interface functions or, when the application is called by the user interface, by all returns. Parameters passed, global parameters shared by application and user interface and returned data are part of the interface. It contains as well the exchange of data as control.

On the application interface level, the semantics of the user interface in terms of the application is described. When control or information is passed from the user interface to the application or vice versa, this is described in this layer. Many of the lexical elements in a user interface are default keys, mouse movements and clicks. The function of these elements is not specified in the user interface or the application code, but in the device drivers and other parts of the environment. The description of the lexical elements and their syntax is a list of data structures or objects. These objects can often be arranged in an inheritance tree.

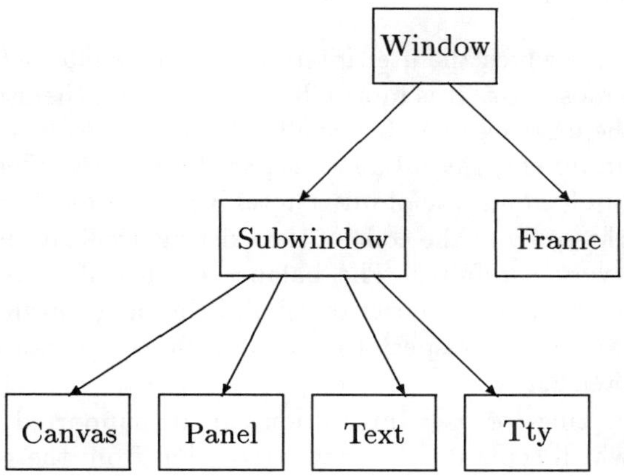

Figure 5.1: Inheritance tree for SunView objects

If an existing program is provided with an enhanced user interface, the application program interface relates as well to the existing program as to the new data processing functions which are necessary for the user interface. The word 'application' does not only mean the existing application, but also new functions, either appended to the existing application or to the user interface.

The enhancement of the user interface will consist of all design activities for new user interfaces for new programs, extended with:

- an analysis of the user interaction in the existing application,
- an analysis of the control structure and functions of the existing application,
- an analysis of the present user task,

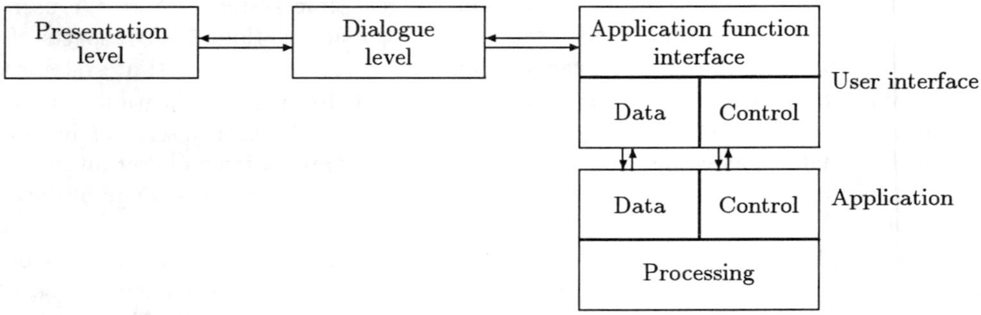

Figure 5.2: Layers of the user interface

- a redesign of the existing application, if one decides to modify the control structure or functionality.

Many systems for which the user interface is to be enhanced, have a very low-level user interface. In most cases it is more efficient to rebuild the user interface completely than to modify the existing one. Especially if one chooses to bring the user interface in a window environment, the interaction paradigm is so different from the old one, that reuse of components of the old user interface is, in most cases, not worthwhile.

The same might apply to the code of the existing application, but here the decision has to be taken very carefully. The balance of the effort to reverse engineer the application compared with the costs to rebuild the program in a more suitable form, has to be analyzed. In this respect the decision process is not different from the one described in chapter 2.

Reverse engineering for user interaction can be supported by tools. First of all, tools are useful which separate the user interaction from the rest of the application. This does not only mean that the statements are marked which contain calls to the user interface functions, but also that the control structure around these statements and the parameters involved are made visible. Such a tool can be built as a special case of a control-flow and dataflow analyzer.

Attempts to obtain the specification of the present user interface from reverse engineering will be successful only for very simple user interfaces. Most user interfaces have been built with library functions. The dialogue can be derived only from the code, when information about the library functions is used. For instance, the function of help keys is often invisible in the source code, since this is handled completely by the user interface functions. Just the help text may be traced from the source code or data files.

Other views on the application which are useful for the redesign of the user interface, are the control structure, the interaction with the environment (operating system, files, database management system, transaction processing system etc.). If one wants to study the possibility to move the control over certain functions to the user interface, an analysis of the cohesion of functions and coupling between functions is useful to determine how difficult it will be to modify the control structure.

A further view can be obtained by a dynamic analysis of the program. The computing time for certain functions of the application can be measured by performance analyzers. This information is necessary to decide whether it is worthwhile to give the user control over such function.

For the decision to restructure a part of the control structure and the data interface of an application, the situation is not much different from other maintenance tasks, where the same kind of modifications are made. Therefore the same kind of tools can be used. In the redesign of the user interface decisions have to be made about which functions should be separated from the user interface and which ones might be integrated. These decisions often have large implications for the usability of the application as well as for the effort needed to implement the new system, consisting of the re-engineered application and user interface.

Re-engineering with the objective to rebuild the user interface requires also a more specific analysis of the application. If the user wants more control over the application, the feasibility of such a requirement depends on details about execution performance of certain functions weighted agains the effort needed to give the user control over these function, the need of the user to use this function under his own control etc. Information about data interfaces has to be analyzed from the point of view of the user as well as the software engineer. From the user's point of view the data which he/she has to provide or has to interpret, should be analyzed for complexity, the possibility to derive it from other data, to verify it, or to present it in a different form. From the point of view of the software engineer, the technical feasibility of alternative user interfaces, the costs of the restructuring and further implementation have to be assessed. Generic software engineering methods and tools should be used together with more specific techniques coming from psychology, such as task and complexity analysis.

5.6 Reverse Engineering for High-Performance Computers

5.6.1 Introduction

In high-performance computers parallel processors are applied to improve the speed of computation. Parallel processors are defined as: A collection of processing elements that can communicate and cooperate to solve large problems fast [6].

The computers with the von Neumann architecture operate with single instructions and single data. Vector processors apply the same instruction on multiple data. Especially in the execution of loops, this feature can improve performance. The more general parallel computers have different processors which each operate on their own data.

Porting software from a sequential computer to a high-performance computer in order to obtain a better performance, generally does not give the expected success straightaway. The compilers for high-performance computers try to generate executable code, which uses the hardware as well as possible. They try to distribute the process over different independent subprocesses and coordinate the execution of these subprocesses. The objective is, to get the subprocesses as large as possible with as little coordination as possible. Small subprocesses give a large overhead due to the control, i.e. the loading and starting, of each process and much coordination may imply that the subprocesses are often waiting for each other.

In order to distribute the computing task over several independent subprocesses, the compiler analyzes the data and control dependencies of possible parallel subprocesses. Since the compilers only have the information from the source code, they are not always able to take the optimal decision. Semantic information is needed, for instance, in a loop with a variable number of iterations, on the maximum number of iterations, for nested IF statements whether certain combinations of conditions ever occur. The programmer can help the compiler to create optimal executable code, by inserting compiler directives into the code.

Further, the possibilities to parallize or vectorize code can be improved considerably by restructuring the algorithms or replacing them completely. For instance, the Quicksort sorting algorithm is very efficient on sequential scalar computers. It is not suited for parallelization or vectorization. The Diamond Sort algorithm, which performs less on scalar machines, appears to be much better on vector computers than Quicksort [262].

To get the best value for money from a high-performance computer, the source code has to be restructured and compiler directives have to be inserted. This task requires knowledge about the hardware, the compiler, optimization techniques and about the program. The program knowledge refers to the basic constructions like the loops, the algorithms applied to solve some problem and alternative algorithms, data models etc. This kind of knowledge can be obtained partially by reverse engineering. Reverse engineering is therefore a technique which is applied in the optimization of existing programs after porting to a high-performance computer.

The profit gained by a tailoring of a program to its new environment can be large. In a case study a improvement of a factor 17 has even been achieved [TN-WL-1051]

5.6.2 Vector and Parallel Processors

High-performance computers are, in this section, defined as those architectures which have vector or parallel processor facilities or both of them. These computers belong to the *Single Instruction, Multiple Data* or *Multiple Instruction Multiple Data* class [TN-WL-1004].

Vector processors are functional units which can perform a number of successive steps. For instance, when two floating point numbers have to be added, the following steps have to be performed:

1. compare the exponents,
2. shift the coefficient with the smaller component,
3. add the coefficients,
4. normalize the resulting coefficients,
5. adjust the exponent.

By splitting the functional add unit into five segments which can perform *simultaneous* operations on different operands, the add process for large quantities of data (for instance adding two arrays) is accelerated considerably. The data to be processed starts in the first segment; after the operation it moves to the second segment, while the next pair of data enters the first segment. In the next clock cycle operations are performed on both pairs simultaneously. After four cycles all segments are active, which means that the speed of the operation is five times higher than with a single processor.

Vectorizing is only efficient, when the same operations are applied to large amounts data.

Parallel computers have several central processors, which can operate independently and concurrently. From the users point of view four levels of parallelism can be distinguished:

- job level,
- program level,
- instruction level,
- arithmetic and bit level.

Parallelism at the program level and above is called 'coarse-grain' parallelism, at the instruction level and lower 'small-grain' parallelism. Vector processing, as described above, is a form of small-grain parallelism.

When an existing program is ported to a high-performance computer, the code is recompiled by a compiler which optimizes the object code. The optimization is such that the characteristic features of the hardware are used to minimize the execution time. This means that pieces of code which are applied to several data sets consecutively are vectorized. If the hardware has several processors, pieces of code that can run independently are assigned to different processors (parallelization). The newer compilers are very sophisticated in the sense that they apply all kinds of transformation to the code, such that parallelization and/or vectorization is maximized. Even some re-engineering is applied: existing software constructions are replaced by equivalent code, which can be vectorized properly.

Reverse engineering can help to improve this process. Report [TN-WL-1004] describes some modifications in the design and implementation, which are advantageous for vectorization and parallelization. Some constructions in the existing code, which have to be replaced in order to improve the efficiency of the code, are:

- *GOTOs*

  Such constructions have to be replaced by IF-THEN-ELSE or loop constructions.

- *subroutine calls in loops*

  Substitute the subroutine code inside the loop.

- *I/O instructions inside loops*

  Perform all input before the loop, output afterwards.

- *IF-constructions inside loops*

  Modify loop and place IF construction outside the loop.

- *inefficient matrix operations*

  Inefficient matrix operations can be replaced with other implementations, where the operations can be executed independently; this applies to searching, sorting, matrix inversion and multiplication. The more efficient procedures are available in libraries (for instance the BLAS routines [101]).

- *data structures*

  Data structures can sometimes be redesigned so that the operations on them can be vectorized/parallelized more efficiently.

- *functional blocks*

  Code can sometimes be rearranged in functional blocks which can be executed independently (on parallel processors).

- *vectorize code*

  Sometimes compilers cannot vectorize pieces of code, because the decision that the operations are vectorizable can only be taken at a semantic level; this problem can be solved by forcing the compiler to vectorize these pieces of code by use of a compiler directive (an instruction in the code which controls the compilation process).

For the reconstruction actions described above, tools can be invented to support the optimization of code:

1. A re-engineering tool which replaces GOTOs by IF-THEN-ELSE or loop construction. Such tools are already on the market and also some compilers do this kind of re-engineering.

2. A tool which recognizes the construction

```
        DO <label>
              ...
        CALL <subroutine>
          ...
<label> CONTINUE
```

   and replaces the CALL with the complete code of the subroutine. This is also a re-engineering tool.

3. A tool which recognizes the construction

```
        DO <label>
          ...
        READ or WRITE
          ...
<label> CONTINUE
```

A general recipe for replacement is not possible. A replacement has to be done by the software engineer. It is sufficient that the code is marked.

4. A tool which recognizes the IF construction inside a loop. If the IF clause is invariant in the loop (directly and indirectly independent of loop counters), the loop can be vectorized, otherwise the IF construction has to be modified by the software engineer.

5. If a library of efficient algorithms exists, a pattern matcher could be made, to search the code for units with the same input/output behavior as the library algorithm. Tools as described in section 15 could derive a specification from pieces of code, while another tool could match that specification with the specification of the more efficient algorithms. The tool should cooperate with the software engineer. He should identify the pieces of code, which are fed into the recognizer, which derives the specification and performs the match.

6. More efficient data structures are sometimes easy to identify. Many dimensional arrays can be treated more efficiently when the indices are in a particular sequence (the first index has to run faster than the second one etc.). Situations which might be improved, can be detected automatically. The pattern to look for is: nested loops with a many dimensional array with indices depending on the loop variables, while the first index goes slower than the second one. Much more complicated situations arise, when sparse arrays are packed. There are several packing techniques. The possibility of vectorizing code may depend on the technique applied. It is possible to make a tool which supports data restructuring. The tool should monitor the length of loops to be vectorized. This cannot be detected from the code alone. A runtime analysis is necessary. The detection of all pieces of code which can be vectorized can be done by a compiler for a high-performance computer, the length of the loops could be determined by an adapted runtime analyzer. The evaluation of the vectorizable code could be done with help of some rule-based system. An alternative could be a system where a rule base with heuristics gives an estimation of the efficiency of the vectorization.

7. 'Object-oriented restructuring' as it is called, brings together coherent chunks of code. The different chunks are mutually independent or weakly dependent. If the number of such chunks is increased, parallellization of the code can become much better. The chunking of code could be done (semi-)automatically by a tool, which can also show, whether two chunks are independent. If chunks are independent, they can be executed simultaneously on parallel processors. In section 22.2 this issue is discussed further.

8. A tool which recognizes all pieces of code that could be vectorized and which also shows why vectorization cannot be done automatically, can be derived from existing compilers. The software engineer could decide whether vectorization can be enforced by a compiler directive, if he has semantic knowledge about that piece of code.

5.6.3 Suggestions for Tools.

Reverse engineering for high-performance computers is aimed at the recognition of implementation constructions which should be redesigned in order to improve the performance of the compiler. The process of searching, recognition and redesign can be supported by the following tools:

1. A tool which recognizes all constructions which can be vectorized and which determines whether the vectorization can be done automatically. The tool evaluates the efficiency of vectorization and gives suggestions how a better performance could be realized. In fact this is already done by a compiler. The compiler output has to be picked up by a tool and presented to the software engineer.

2. A tool which recognizes constructions which can be vectorized after modification.

3. A tool which restructures code into chunks and shows whether these chunks are independent.

4. A runtime analyzer which shows which parts of the code take most of the processor time and gives statistics on the vector length of vectorizable pieces of code. Also the occurrence of 'memory conflicts', multiple references to the same variable within a vectorizable section of code, should be reported. A source code browser is necessary to find the relevant pieces of code [45].

5. A tool which derives specifications of sections of code and stores the specification. Another tool should match the derived specification with specifications of algorithms stored in a library.

Part II

ANALYSIS

6

Understanding in Reverse Engineering

H.J. van Zuylen, *Delft Hydraulics, The Netherlands* [1]

"Einstein argued that there must be simplified explanations of nature, because God is not capricious or arbitrary. No such faith comforts the software engineer." Fred Brooks [6]

6.1 Understanding and Documentation

Understanding is one of the main objectives of reverse engineering. In order to take the right decision and to know its impact completely, the software engineer has to study the source code. Tools are very useful to support this task by giving the information for the comprehension process in the form which is most suited. The kind of information which tools should provide depends on the objectives of the software engineers and the questions on which they want an answer.

Written documentation or documentation as text or hypertext files can be very useful information sources. If good documentation existed, it would make reverse engineering unnecessary. On the other hand, new documentation is generated during reverse engineering. This records the understanding which has been acquired. Documentation methods and standards help to structure the comprehension process. If documentation has to be made according to some standard, the software engineer has

[1] This and the following chapter will appear in a modified form in the Proceedings of the NATO ARW on User-Centred Requirements for Software Engineering Environments.

to investigate all relevant aspects of the system. The prescribed structure of the documentation will guide the software engineer along the path to be followed. Such a situation is especially helpful for the comprehension process if the software engineer participates actively in the generation of the documentation. If tools exist which generate documentation fully automatically, the software engineer is not helped in his understanding by using these tools until the moment he studies the generated documentation. Documentation tools which require some level of user interaction can be useful not only to generate documentation, but also because the software engineer has to think about the system when he uses the tool. In that way he gradually gains more understanding.

Using documentation which is already available may give rise to some problems. Documentation is often no longer consistent with the actual state of the program. The source code itself is often the only reliable documentation. The problem with the source code as documentation is that the comprehensibility is often low. Restructuring of the source code can be a means to make the source code satisfy certain standards and at the same time clarify the contents.

Another problem is that most documentation is written during the development of the system. Therefore, it is not sufficiently tailored to the needs of the software engineer. Development documentation is made for special purposes, for instance to record design decisions, to review a part of the development process, to freeze the state of a part of the development process, to verify the completeness and consistency of the design or to validate the design. The purpose of this documentation is not to serve the software maintainers. They will often need different documentation than the development documentation, such as call graphs, cross-reference tables, coverage information, performance data, data dependencies.

Documentation especially suited to software maintenance can be generated by reverse engineering. This can be added to the existing documentation. The amount of information which can be obtained in this way, and the number of ways to present it becomes very large. Therefore it is necessary to have ways to select information and to choose the presentation format.

The subject of this chapter is the process of understanding and creation and maintenance of documentation, including the source code.

6.2 Tasks and Skills for Reverse Engineering

Many activities have to be done, before the process of studying and (re)documenting can start: collecting documentation, verifying the completeness, identifying the right version of the source code and documentation, etc. The skills and knowledge needed for these activities are not very specific for reverse engineering. In this section we will focus on activities which are more specific to reverse engineering.

When the documentation has been collected, the most recent version of the source code has been loaded on the computer, then the documentation has to be completed, updated and, in some cases, rewritten.

Documentation can be considered a collection of different views of the system. Some of these views, can be generated automatically from the source code. This is the case for low-level technical documentation such as flow charts and cross-reference tables. The higher level documentation, representing the design and specification of the program, cannot be derived completely automatically. Human intervention is necessary.

All kinds of knowledge about programming, the application domain, the function of the program and the program itself, are necessary to understand what the design and the specification of the program are.

Reverse engineering does not exist as an activity in isolation. It is often applied in a partial way as a technique for debugging and program modification. The skills, knowledge and information structures used in these activities are the same as the ones needed for reverse engineering. Therefore, the research on human factors for programming and debugging (see for instance Hoc *et al.* [158]) can be used to find the role of human factors in reverse engineering.

In the next sections the human factors in the comprehension process are discussed. Conclusions are formulated which can be used as recommendations and guidelines for tools to support this process. First the process of human comprehension is described. This is applied to reverse engineering. The difference between expert and novice programmers is explained. Afterwards, the factors which influence the comprehension of the program code are discussed. This leads to some conclusions and recommendations for supporting tools.

6.3 Comprehension and Memory.

In order to understand a source code, the software engineers have to find the internal structures of the code, to establish the links between the code and knowledge which one already has and to store the facts and structures in their memory (Shneiderman and Mayer [284]). After the comprehension process they know what the code does in terms of known operations, the conditions under which the operations are performed and the final states. The knowledge about the program can be very precise, certain and complete, but in most cases the knowledge obtained is incomplete, only sufficient to answer certain questions, and fuzzy, which means that most knowledge has a vague character: some figure is in a certain range, an operation will give a result which is somewhere in a set of possible outcomes. A part of the knowledge might also be uncertain: "probably this array is sorted because it has to be used by some other procedure...".

Our memory is an essential component in the comprehension process. It can be seen as subdivided in three different parts: the sensory register, a short-term store and a long-term memory. The **sensory registers** are just a very short-term memory of visual, auditory or touch sensations. They are out of our control. The visual sensory register or iconic memory makes it possible to see the separate pictures of a film as smooth motions. The auditory or echoic memory makes it possible to perceive whole words instead of a sequence of sounds.

Our **short-term memory** can contain about 7 separate items. It is fed from our sensory registers and our long-term memory. Information in this part of our memory decays rather rapidly, unless actions are taken to keep it. People are able to control their short-term memory, for instance by repeating the word corresponding to the memory items silently or aloud.

Long-term memory is fed by the short-term memory. It contains facts and structures. Factual knowledge is unstructured for instance, knowledge about the spelling of words or the decimal numbers of pi. This knowledge is specific: it cannot be transferred to some other concept or domain. If this knowledge is not used frequently, it may become 'lost', this means that the access path becomes too weak to be retrieved.

Another kind of knowledge is called *semantic knowledge*. This kind of knowledge is structured and the structure is a part of the knowledge. It is knowledge which has been integrated in a network of links. Our cognitive process uses the links to retrieve knowledge directly or indirectly. For example, the question whether Pythagoras had feet cannot be retrieved directly from our memory. We have never seen Pythagoras, but we know that he was a man, that a man normally has feet and it is so exceptional if a man has no feet, that it is normally mentioned. Since we never heard that Pythagoras had no feet, ..., etc. Our semantic memory seems to be very similar to an object-oriented system with multiple inheritance [227].

A part of our semantic knowledge is *meta knowledge*, i.e. knowledge about our knowledge, how and when we can apply our knowledge.

There is no evidence that knowledge, which has once been stored in our long-term memory, disappears or fades away. The knowledge may become hidden or the access path become unused. The knowledge is still there, but it becomes very difficult to retrieve it. Unused memory becomes difficult to access. Memorizing is making good access paths [348]. Knowledge which is accessed frequently makes access paths in our brain which become 'wide'. Such knowledge is retrieved easily. In most cases this knowledge becomes linked to other knowledge, such that several access paths are possible. For instance, the equivalence construction in FORTRAN might be just a fact in our memory after a beginners course. When we have used the construction, get experience with it, read about the risk of the use of this construction, all kinds of relations grow. After some time we may access the equivalence concept in different ways for instance, as a way to give an alias to a variable, as a trick to save computer memory, as a way to do something which is not allowed in standard FORTRAN, etc.

When knowledge is used frequently, many links to new and existing knowledge grow. If we try to retrieve the information from our memory, we sometimes get other knowledge, which might be sufficient for our present problem. Experts have much practical knowledge, often heuristic rules, which has been derived from basic knowledge and practical facts. The expert knowledge replaces and hides the basic knowledge, which becomes subconscious.

The logical structures in our semantic memory can be very general. The same structure may be applicable to different domains. This makes it possible to transfer and generalize semantic knowledge. This process is called **analogical transfer**. Transfer of knowledge structures make it easy for someone who has learned a programming language to learn another language in a short time, if the new language is similar in character to the first one, as for instance, when both languages are procedural [158].

Semantic knowledge is structured in many layers. Networks of interrelated knowledge on a lower level might be a single item on a higher level. For instance the body of knowledge about electrical currents, mechanics, acoustics can be considered as a single item 'physics' when considered in the framework of science. The layering of semantic knowledge is not unique: there are different ways to form 'chunks' out of pieces of interrelated knowledge.

Semantic knowledge contains different **views** of the subject. For instance, a computer program can be seen as a set of source files, a collection of modules, as a tool which executes certain actions, as a product of some group of developers etc. Each view can be high-level or very detailed, structured in a top-down or bottom-up fashion, as a network or unstructured. The amount of semantic knowledge about a program, which a software engineer wants to acquire depends on his task and the strategy he applies.

Semantic knowledge is not standardized between people. Each individual builds his or her own structure of knowledge. The resulting structure depends on skills, knowledge, experience, intelligence and other personal characteristics. The difference between experts and novices is especially in the structure of their knowledge. Novices may begin with little or much knowledge, but most of their knowledge has still a factual character. Experts have a rich semantic network, containing relations between the different facts. As an example, McKeithen *et al.* [224] show that novice programmers have little or no structure in the language elements of a programming language. When they become more experienced, they organize the elements which are related to each other into chunks. Further, there is evidence that experts rely on their semantic knowledge. They appear to spend more time building a complete, coherent semantic model of the problem than novices do [158].

The pattern of relations are called schemas or plans. The existence of a schema in which knowledge fits makes it easier to interpret the information and to memorize it. Meaningful information is easier to memorize and to remember. De Groot [94] observed that expert chess players are able to memorize game situations very accurately because they were able to interpret the situation in terms of strategy or plan. Adelson [2] mentions that expert programmers understand a program at a more abstract level than novices do. That means that experts remember the function and structure of the program and are able to reproduce a program with the same functionality and structure, while novices remember more details from the program, instead of its functionality. So, at statement level novice surpass experts. Technical details which are remembered by novices escape the attention of experts. However, experts are able to recognize structures and plans, where novices still do not have as many plans in their memory as experts do.

6.4 Comprehension in Software Engineering

Shneiderman and Mayer [284] distinguish three knowledge categories which are relevant for software engineering: **syntactic knowledge, semantic knowledge of software engineering** and **semantic knowledge of the application domain.**

- **Syntactical knowledge**: Facts and rules about the computer language, the operating system, the hardware. This knowledge contains the lexicon of the language (the elements which can be used in a valid program, such as the word 'program', 'integer' and the symbols like '=' and '+'), the meaning of the lexical elements and the grammatical rules, the program syntax. Syntactic knowledge is specific for a language. When the knowledge is not used frequently, it becomes inaccessible, difficult to remember. One of the reasons is that the syntactical knowledge has a nearly flat structure: there is no internal logic which connects facts. Memorizing simple facts adds syntactical knowledge. This process can be better supported when the facts are given some meaning and internal structure [348].

- **Semantic knowledge of software engineering**: This is the software engineer's knowledge of programming structures, data structures, algorithms, implementation schemas. It takes a long time to acquire this knowledge and there is no limit to it: one may always develop more semantic knowledge. Semantic knowledge is independent of the application domain and, although it is language dependent, it may be transferred rather easily to other computer languages. It remains relatively stable in long-term memory. It is level-structured. Low-level items are, for instance, the meaning of an assignment statement or a conditional statement. These items are clustered into knowledge about patterns of use (such as: three assignment statements to form a swap operation, or nested conditionals, or arithmetic expressions). These mid-level patterns are grouped together into higher order programming schemas, for instance there is a schema for the implementation of a database search, for a matrix multiplication or a numerical integration. There is no limit to still higher levels: the schema for the solution of a numerical differential equation can be a single high-level memory item, composed out of several other (high-level) items. Apart from knowledge of schemas, the semantic knowledge also contains strategic knowledge of how and when these schemas have to be applied [136].

  The accessibility and stability of semantic knowledge is supported by the logical structure of the knowledge. When one item is retrieved from memory, the logically related items are remembered afterwards. Adding to the semantic knowledge implies understanding and structure.

- **Semantic knowledge about the domain**: knowledge which a software engineer has about payroll practice, fluid dynamics, traffic control or whatever is the domain of the application. This knowledge is independent of a programming language, but may include knowledge about the usage of programs in the domain. Semantic domain knowledge contains facts (for instance the rules of the chess game, the elementary facts of physics) and higher level patterns, such as game strategies. Novices start to learn the facts, the low-level details. Afterwards they spend the rest of their lifetime to acquire more and more high-level knowledge about strategies, plans, experience. Domain knowledge is level-structured and hierarchically organized.

Software engineers should have sufficient knowledge from these three categories in order to work efficiently. Programmers starting in a new domain, have to invest a lot of time and effort before they become productive. An expert in one domain has to learn a lot of low-level details and high-level goals when he switches to a new domain.

In software maintenance there is a tendency to keep the same person on the maintenance of a program because it is very impractical, if not impossible, to transfer all relevant knowledge from one person to his successor. The role of documentation in the process of knowledge transfer is restricted [158, 218]. Documentation is never complete in the sense that all relevant aspects are included. Common sense, basic knowledge about the domain and software engineering are not documented separately for every program. Often, authors of documentation assume that they share a lot of knowledge about the domain and software engineering with their readers. Furthermore, most documentation has been written with another purpose than the transfer of knowledge about a system. The semantics of the documentation depends on its purpose and on the context in which it has been written (see for instance Winograd and Flores [343] on the hermeneutics of design documentation.) These facts make it very difficult or even impossible to transfer all necessary knowledge to understand a system by documentation only [255].

Experience and knowledge play an important role in the comprehension of a program. So novice software engineers will perform differently when compared to experts. Several studies have shown that the skill of experts to recognize, remember and structure the program code is superior to novices, unless very detailed information on statement level is involved (for instance, Adelson [2]) or when the program code conflicts with their experience. For instance, a swapping operation is characteristic of sorting procedures and experts recognize sorting procedures by the few statements which perform the swapping. If they study a program code where swapping is done, but no sorting, the experts need more time to understand what is going on than novice programmers.

Another important fact is that, in practice, there is a difference between software engineers who do maintenance and those who develop new programs. Often, the people involved in maintenance have a less academic, more professional education or have got their training mainly in practice. Furthermore, it seems to be common practice that junior software engineers get their first experience in a company by doing maintenance work. New systems are developed by people with a higher education, which means that they have developed more skills for abstraction, know more about theories and methods. Maybe this is not generally true, but in companies where the author had the chance to investigate this situation, this phenomenon had been consistently observed.

6.4.1 The Mental Representation of Software

Comprehension of a program means the construction of a multi-leveled, multi-view internal semantic structure to represent the program. There are many features, or aspects of a program, and even if someone knows the source code by heart, that does not mean that he understands the program. The software engineer performing reverse engineering has to understand the internal structure and the semantics of the program. Most of the semantics can be derived directly from the source code. Most programs contain a mixture of source code in a certain computer language, interaction with the environment, for example a database management system, a transaction processing system, an operating system, and calls to procedures which are external to the program such as user interface libraries. The semantics have to be found by combining the information from the language semantics with information from documentation of the software environment and the specification of libraries. We shall call all these aspects *software engineering knowledge* which is partly stored in the mind of the software engineer and partly stored in the documentation. The source code has to be interpreted, which means that the semantics must be determined by transforming the information from the source code and the software engineering knowledge into a representation of the semantics of the program.

Some research has been done about the question of how software engineers study program code. Two different mental processes have been identified for studying programs. One is top-down, the other bottom-up. The bottom-up process has been described by Shneiderman [283] and Basili and Mills [18]. It starts from the program statements and builds up higher level concepts by grouping together statements which perform a certain function. A hierarchical model of the operation of the system is developed, up to the level that all code has been assigned to a function. Similar models may be built for data.

The other approach is characterized by hypothesis selection, verification, refinement and adjustment. It is introduced by Brooks [49] and verified by Gilmore [135]. The process is illustrated in figure 6.1.

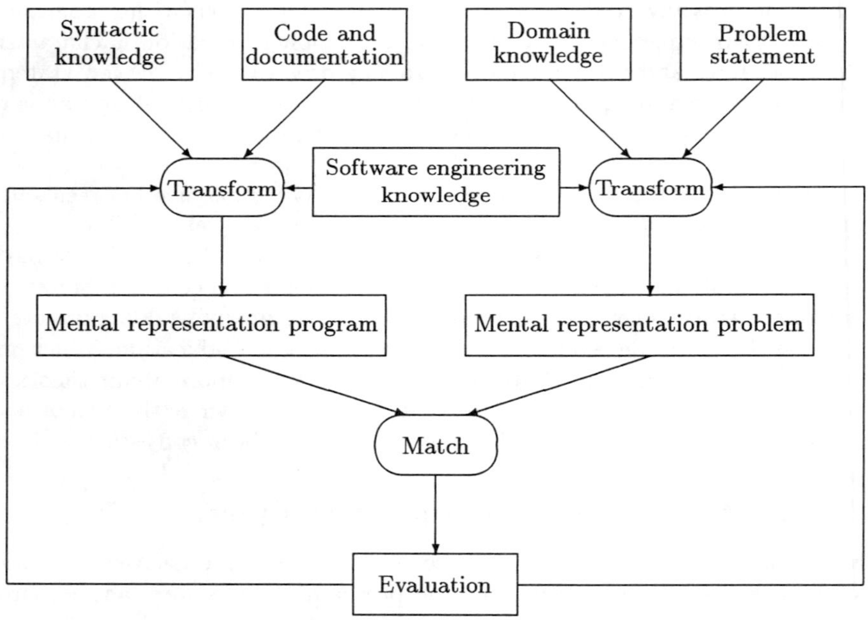

Figure 6.1: Inference structure for program comprehension

The software engineer studying a program, develops a mental representation of what the program *should be*. In figure 6.1 this is represented by the box with the name *mental representation of the problem*. This mental representation is easier to develop, when the software engineer has more knowledge about the specification and design of the program. He tries to match his ideas about the program with the code. If there are inconsistencies between his representation of what the program should do and the representation he gets of the actual behavior of the program, (*the mental representation of the program*), the software engineer may decide to change his representation of what the program should be, or he may decide that there is a bug in the program.

It is likely that novice software engineers have not enough semantic knowledge to work in this way. They probably have to study the code 'bottom-up': deriving the semantics from the statements and building the macro structures from them.

Pennington [256] shows, that the best programmers use a mixture of domain and software engineering knowledge, which has been linked together ('cross-referenced'), to understand a program. She further shows that novice programmers rely more on either domain knowledge or software engineering knowledge alone, than on the combination.

In studies of programming activities it is shown, that programmers use an opportunistic strategy, as well for programming as for debugging [255]: They switch from one strategy to another and choose the most appropriate views of the program.

An example of the changing strategies is the way in which software engineers read program code. Robertson *et al.* [267] showed that when a software engineer studies a program, the reading process is not linear, but that the direction in which the program statements are read is often reversed. Especially at the end of an episode (a set of coherent statements, for instance an iteration, a conditional construct or a function), the direction of reading changes often from forward to backwards, while at the beginning of an episode the direction often changes from backward to forward. (These changes of direction occur also at other locations in the code, but the end and beginning of episodes are especially turning points.) Robertson found that questions about the function of the code are often asked when the reading changes from backward to forward, while in the opposite case the question were more related to the strategy of searching. From this result a recommendation can be derived for the kind of comment to be inserted. Comment about the function of the episode is useful at the beginning of an episode. At the end of the episode comment about the structure of the program could be given, for instance how far the algorithm is at that point and what has to be done next.

6.5 Improving the Comprehensibility

From the considerations described above we can now derive some conclusions about possible ways in which the comprehensibility of computer program code can be improved.

1. *Provide program specification*

   When the software engineer knows what the functions of the program are, it is easier for him to build a representation of what the program has to do and to recognize the functions of chunks of code. Recognizing is much easier than analyzing or remembering. Remembering is made much easier when the appropriate cues are presented. This means that if some information has been given about the function of the program and its requirements, it is easier to recognize the program constructions and to retrieve the appropriate knowledge. When design documentation is used, one should be aware of the fact that the specification at the requirement and functional level are more reliable that at design and code level.

2. *Provide design information*

   Design information gives (experienced) programmers cues to find program plans or schemas. Therefore tools which abstract design information and support the identification of plans are essential for reverse engineering [275]. These plans are, according to Soloway and Ehrlich [293], necessary to understand the program. Experts try to find such schemas, but can be seriously hampered if they try to understand a program with the wrong schema in mind. If a program seems to fit a schema, but is in some aspects inconsistent with the schema, the expert often wastes a lot of effort in solving this inconsistency [2].

   Some research has been done on the presentation of design information and the comprehensibility of different presentations. Context diagrams and other coarse-grain representations which show few details, are easily understood. Medium level flow charts are not always helpful understanding the code. Brooke and Duncan [47] showed that they help to find bugs, but do not support general understanding. Low-level flow charts have little or no value and are to be avoided as a means to clarify the function of a program. A description of the design in a Program Design Language (PDL) program design language is more helpful, while Data Structure Documentation is a quite effective information source [330].

3. *Use meaningful names*

   Programmers almost unanimously agree that variables should have meaningful, consistent names. Often variable names are a reliable link between a program and the application domain. There has been some research by, for instance, Mynatt [239] which shows that only novice programmers comprehend a program more quickly when meaningful names are used. Expert programmers appear to do their work equally efficiently when the variables have random names or even confusing names. An observation which can be made of this research is that it has been done for very small Pascal programs. It is unlikely that the result is also true for programs of, say, 100 000 lines of COBOL.

4. *Use comments*

   Comments are useful, if written at the right level of abstraction and inserted in the right places. Weiser and Shneiderman [330] state that too many comments the code. The work of Robertson *et al.* [267] shows that comments could be useful at the beginning and end of chunks or episodes of code. The comment should primarily give information at the design or specification level.

5. *Structure the code in 'chunks'*

   A chunk is a section of code which can be understood as a unit. An instance is a function, an IF-THEN-ELSE construction, a loop or a sequence of statements in which a single dataset is processed. The control structure of a chunk is closed (one single entry, one or a few exits). GOTOs which jump into a chunk, make it difficult to understand. However, GOTOs used as an imitation of a WHILE construction may be easily understood - sometimes even better than the WHILE [330]. Another property of a good chunk is that it is a complete function in itself. That means that operations on a dataset are concentrated in single chunks. The comprehension process can be improved when the program is presented in a structured way and additional information is provided to identify the chunks.

6. *Use pretty printing.*

   Pretty printing (indentation) gives some visual cues to identify chunks. The literature [330, 158, 142] gives no consistent opinion whether the comprehension task is improved by pretty printing. Pretty printing can be enhanced on screens by using colors for certain groups of statements or for certain variables. On paper, cues can be emphasized in the code by using different fonts and bold printing.

6.6 Conclusions

1. The task of (re)documentation requires human intervention. The software engineer doing this work has to comprehend the program.

2. All available information for instance, old documentation and experience from users, is useful for the comprehension process as long as the information is not misleading. The value of this information is so that it can give guidance towards a representation of the domain, the function and requirements of the program.

3. Experts comprehend a program on a higher level of abstraction. They can discover the design and specification more efficiently than novices.

4. It is recommended that training be given to the software engineer who has to do the redocumentation.

5. Tools which support the identification of 'chunks' will be very useful.

6. Renaming of variables, such that the names are meaningful and consistent, could be a useful technique.

7. Tools which extract the data structure from the code and generate data structure documentation are very helpful.

8. The design specifications derived from the code should be flexible. It should be possible to 'zoom' in and out, to change the granularity of the view and the level of visible detail.

9. Graphical representations of the design structure could be helpful (for example control-flow graphs). They should not be too detailed. A representation of the design in a Program Design Language is more useful for program comprehension than diagrams.

   Generally, the user should have the option to select the representation which is most appropriate for him and for his task.

10. Comments should be inserted in a disciplined way. The locations which are recommended are the beginning and the end of chunks. At the beginning, functional information is useful, while at the end of chunks declarative information and information about the structure of the program is appropriate.

11. GOTOs should be removed, except if they are an implementation of well structured constructions, like DO WHILE.

12. Tools should provide a representation of the code at different levels of abstraction and in different views. The user interface for reverse engineering tools should provide the possibility of switching between different views and levels, combining them and changing the level of detail.

13. The process of cross referencing information from the source code with domain knowledge should be supported.

14. The tools should especially provide help for expert users (otherwise they will not be used by novices when they become experts). They should provide support for a representation of the code functionality (like normal forward engineering CASE tools), and match this with the actual code.

15. Tools which abstract the functionalities from the code are especially suited to expert users. While novices concentrate on the code and try to infer the functionalities from it, experts neglect this approach. Therefore they may overlook details. A tool which supports the interpretation of lines of code will therefore be very helpful.

7

Views, Representations and Development Methods

H.J. van Zuylen, *Delft Hydraulics, The Netherlands*
J. Estdale, *Lloyd's Register, Croydon, UK*

7.1 Views

A computer program has many aspects. For example it can be seen as:

- an artifact formed by certain files,
- an architecture of program modules, data structure files and other hardware and software components,
- an artifact which executes certain activities, shows certain behavior etc.

A mutually coherent and more or less closed set of aspects is called a *view*. The aspects within a view have a mutual relationship and can be understood without referring too much to aspects outside the view. Within a view a certain internal logic exists. Different views have mutual relations for instance, a view may be deduced from another view by abstraction or specification. Some views distinguished in software development are as follows:

The **physical view** concern the files and file content as well as the physical properties. The first step of the reverse engineering process focuses on the collection of the appropriate physical items. Another view in this category is the physical system on which the program runs, the different pieces of hardware, the network and the assignment of processes to the different pieces of hardware.

The **architecture** describes how the program is built up from components and how these components interact.

The **control-flow view** considers the flow of activities in the job, the transaction and in the program itself.

The **data view** aims at all information about data, variables, external input and output files, databases.

The **behavior view** contains the information about what the system does. Timing aspects and state transitions are parts of this view. Also, the interactions between the system and the environment and users are part of this view. Furthermore, a declarative description of the system for instance, in terms of pre- and post-conditions and invariants may give a contribution to the behavior view.

A program can be also considered as the product of a process. This view is called the **project process view**. This view contains information about the history of the system, the project in which the system has been developed, the management decisions and the resources used.

Another view is the **domain view**. It contains all knowledge about the domain for which the program is used. Also the link between the program and the problems which it is supposed to solve, is a part of this view for example, the high-level semantics of the program. Two aspects of this view which can be derived from a program are the user task and the business model.

Finally, one may distinguish a **management view**. The information in this view concerns the project aspects of the development, introduction and maintenance of the system, the resources used and those necessary for the future, people involved etc.

A software engineer has many views of a program. Some of these views have been discussed in literature, for instance by Olle *et al.* [246]. In terms of human understanding, views play an important role. Knowledge about a subject consists of mutually linked views. The way people communicate and reason about these views depends on the character of these views as well as the kind of information that is contained in them. The fact that software engineering uses diagrams to represent many views shows that a spatial representation can be very useful to determine views, to reason about them, to recognize properties etc. Some views – for instance the specification of the functions of the system – may be less suited for a graphical representation. A mathematical representation may be more appropriate because of its accuracy, precision and the possibility to formally verify certain properties.

The choice of an appropriate representation for the views depends on the purpose of the views. In forward engineering the identification of inconsistencies, conflicting requirements, conformance with other views and the requirements are important issues. The representations are used to breakdown the objects (functions, states or data) into smaller units.

The objectives in reverse engineering differ from forward engineering. Abstraction of higher order design views is an important objective, as well as the documentation and verification of assumptions about the system. The aggregation may be important too. For instance, if one starts with a call graph of a program, generated from the code, this may be transformed to a dataflow diagram and a state transition diagram (not a simple task to do!). The dataflow diagram may be transformed by 'chunking' the processes and hiding of internal data stores. The result may be a high-level dataflow diagram or context diagram [355].

This process as described is 'bottom-up', which, at best should be done by reverse engineering tools. However, in reality this process is not possible in an automatic way. If the process is executed with human intervention, the strict bottom-up approach

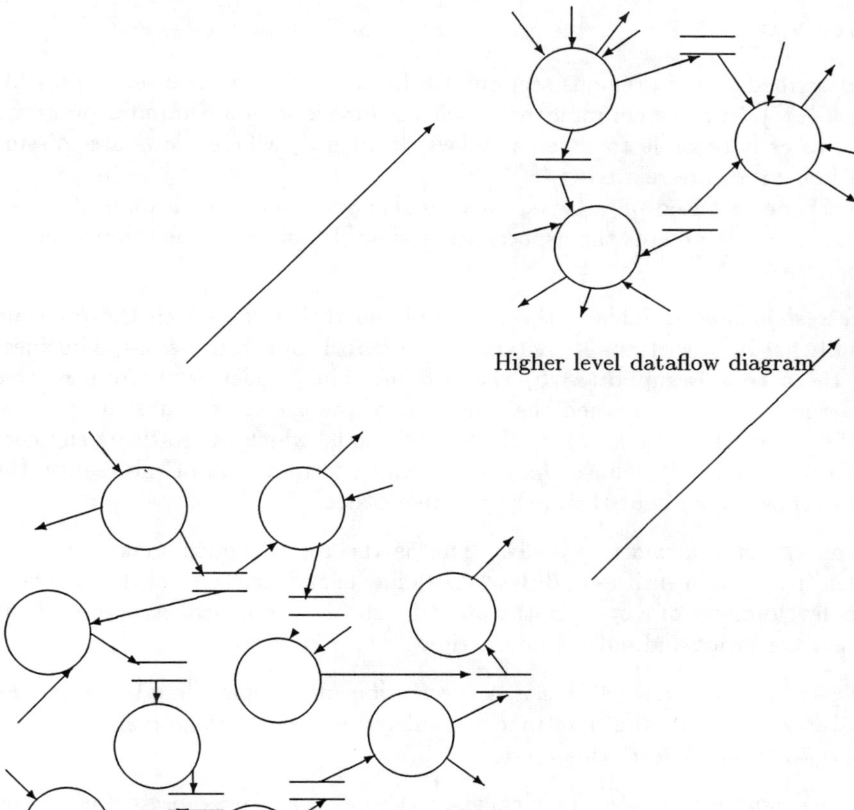

Figure 7.1: Bottom-up generation of diagrams

is less suitable for experienced software engineers. They tend to start from some hypothesized high-level view which they try to verify, as explained in the previous section with the code of the program, the system documentation, the user manual, the actual behavior of the program etc. Drawing up new documentation may be an appropriate intermediate step to verify or adapt the hypothesized view.

7.2 A Comprehensive Classification Scheme for Views

The views described in the previous section still form a rather ad hoc set of possible views. Essink [115] defines a comprehensive scheme for views of a computer program. His scheme makes it possible to organize views, to identify where views are missing and how various views are related.

Essink's scheme is based on a two-dimensional space. One dimension is the level of abstraction, the other one is the aspect of the view. He distinguished four *levels of abstraction*:

1. *Object system model.* This is the model of the reality for which the program originally has been written. It contains the organizational processes, the business rules, the activities supported by the system. This model arises from reverse engineering of the code, when the functions of the system are abstracted. On the other hand, it is also a part of the mental model which the software engineer has of the domain. It defines the entities which form a part of the reality, the relevant knowledge about them, the possible states.

2. *The conceptual information model.* This is the model which makes the link between the domain entities and the data elements and functions of the program. In the development of a system, this model contains the logical structure of the data and the input and output interactions.

3. *The logical system model.* This is a description of an operational system. So the database content, the man-machine subsystem and the algorithms applied to the data together form this model.

4. *The implementation model.* This contains the physical data representation and the physical structure of the program.

The object system model is close to the domain problem for which the program is used. The implementation model is logically far away from the domain problem, but closely related to the actual, operational system. The mental process to understand a program (the *problem model* as it was called) will often start on the object system level and go down to the implementation level. The mental model of the program (the *program model*) starts from the implementation level and moves up to the logical and possibly the conceptual level. The comprehension process may be characterized as *specification* (from object to conceptual level etc.), *abstraction* (deriving logical meaning from implementation aspects) and *matching*.

The second dimension of the classification scheme concerns the *aspects*. Essink [115] derives them from systems theory:

1. The *goal structure*, the organization of elements to realize a goal.
2. The *environmental interaction*, the interface between a system and its environment.
3. The *functional structure* is the subdivision of the system into atomic functional units, which cannot be divided any more into smaller meaningful subunits.
4. The *entity structure*, the relations between entities and their properties. The entities are viewed as passive elements whose status can be seen as the result of active elements of the functional structure.
5. The *process structure* describes the transformation process.
6. The *system dynamics* is the adaption of the system in time to the changing situation in the environment.
7. The *allocational aspects* contain the equipment used to perform the process.
8. The *realization considerations* are the organizational and social constraints that play a role in the decisions made in the design process.

As one may observe from this scheme, it has been developed originally for the classification of views in forward engineering, views which are used to clarify design decisions, to reveal inconsistencies in requirements etc. The scheme is useful for a classification of reverse engineering views too, if one accepts that many categories will remain empty.

Table 7.1: A framework for views and representations

	Levels of abstraction			
Aspect	Object system model	Conceptual information system model	Logical system	Implementation model
Goal structure	1.1	2.1	3.1	4.1
Environmental interaction	1.2	2.2	3.2	4.2
Functional structure	1.3	2.3	3.3	4.3
Entity structure	1.4	2.4	3.4	4.4
Process structure	1.5	2.5	3.5	4.5
System dynamics	1.6	2.6	3.6	4.6
Allocation aspects	1.7	2.7	3.7	4.7
Realization considerations	1.8	2.8	3.8	4.8

Realization considerations, for instance, can give useful information about a lot of technical decisions which are discovered in the code. If, for instance, a certain programmer was involved in the development of a system, traces may be found in the code of his style and preferences. In reverse engineering this background information, which fits in category 4.8 might be important. Generally speaking, one may say that categories 4.1 up to 4.7 have to be discovered in reverse engineering and that 4.8 may give useful background information.

Compilers and static analysis tools are able to derive views in category 4.2, 4.4 and 4.5 from the source code. The system dynamics of the implementation model could be studied from the source code, but there are several reasons to use at least debugging tools or just a study of the actual behavior of the system as a source of information.

The analysis of the functional structure of the implemented system can be done by the derivation of formal specifications from the code or by applying 'slicing' techniques (chapter 22.2). Units with certain functions can be identified and their behavior can be expressed in a formal specification.

The goal structure for example, how the functions and data work together to realize a certain external behavior, is not easily derived directly from the source code using tools. Here human experience and intuition are a useful source of information.

In the REDO project, tools have been developed to fill the categories 4.2 – 4.6 to a certain extent. Views on a higher level of abstraction are difficult to generate with tools. Logical data models can be derived from physical datamodels, with some human interference. All other categories remain rather empty up to now. A dataflow diagram could be generated from the code, which would fit in 3.5, but at this moment there is no tool which can do that completely automatically.

If we move further to the left, it becomes clear that the views of the *mental model of the program* become scarce. Here, we find more views belonging to the *mental model of the problem.*

7.2.1 An Example: User Interfaces

As an example to illustrate the different views the user interaction in a program is considered. If one starts from the source code, first of all there is a view of all input and output statements which provide the communication with the user (screen, keyboard, mouse etc.). This view fits in 4.2. If we make a list of variables which are involved in user interactions, with the text linked to them (field names in forms and names of topics in a menu), we get an entity structure (4.4). The control process in which the user interface is embedded, for instance the call-back functions or the decision tree in a more conventional user interface, is a view of the process structure (4.5).

The assignment of the output devices for the user interaction (mouse, keyboard, screen, files etc.) can be allocated to category 4.7. If the user interface is adaptable to hardware, for example the quality of the screen resolution or colors, the keyboard, the existence and type of the mouse, the code corresponding to this part of the system represents the dynamics aspect (4.6).

Often the user interaction is implemented using library functions. These libraries are a part of the environment and the calls and parameters involved in these calls form category 4.2: environmental interaction.

On the logical level we can distinguish the same aspects, but here the meaning is considered more than merely the data, source code or other physical components. In category 3.2 the behavior of the external functions are considered, for instance, the behavior of windows of a certain kind, menus etc. In category 3.3 belong the description of the appearance of the screen, the windows, the menus, the keys. Category 3.4 contains the list of lexical dialogue elements, while the syntactical structure of the dialogue (the valid sequence of lexical elements) is a part of category 3.3. The system dynamics, for example in the form of state-transition diagrams, belong to group 3.5.

As an exercise the reader can try to fill in the other categories. A few other relevant examples of views will be given below. On the conceptual level, category 2.1 contains the *user task* as far as it concerns the operation and control of the program. Category 1.1 is again the user task, but here the task is on domain level, for instance the task to solve a problem where the program can be used for. In category 1.1 the task to write a thesis could be considered and in category 2.1 the task to use a particular word processor.

In this way it is possible to find, in each category, views on the program or parts of the program. Not all categories are equally important. Sometimes a category can only be filled using much imagination. Still the scheme is useful to organize views and to verify whether one really covers all relevant aspects and levels of abstraction.

As a last example, category 1.8 is considered: If a request exists to enhance a user interface or to replace it, one should verify whether this request solves the real problem. Often such requests hide a deeper problem. Then the problem with the user interface are only symptoms of the real problem such as the lack of functionality of the program or insufficient training for the users. Improving the user interface does not solve the real problem. Such an analysis fits in category 1.8.

7.3 Representations and Development Methods

The representation of a view is in fact the language in which the view can be documented, which can be used to reason about a view of the system or to communicate with other people about the system. In some cases natural language is an appropriate representation, for example for the project process view. However, due to the ambiguity it is less suited to describe aspects like the behavior of a system or the control flow.

Many representations have been developed in the last 30 years to be used in the development process of software. A few have been developed especially for existing programs, such as cross-reference tables and other tables produced by compilers. Most representations have been developed, however, for the forward engineering process. They are a part of a design philosophy, method and process. In order to appreciate the differences between the different representations, it is important to know in which development method they are used and for what purpose. Some development methods are especially suited for real-time software, other for data processing software. This can be derived from the properties of the representations (see for instance [363, 115]). In table 7.2 the suitability of different development methods are given.

The fact that some methods do not have an X for a category does not mean that it cannot be used for this kind of programs. It just indicates that only a part of the development process for this kind of programs is supported and that a mixture of methods has to be used.

The different methods are not independent. For instance, many methods relate to the Yourdon method and have adopted representation techniques from the dataflow diagram technique (for example Pirbhai, Ward and Mellor and SSADM). Sometimes the diagrams used slightly differ in form and semantics. Martin and McClure [218] describe the relation between different representations. In most cases, it is possible to select such a representation, that it fits in one of the development methods. In

Table 7.2: The applicability of a development method to certain domains

Method	Data processing	Scientific	Real-time
SSADM [209], LSDM [194], Merise [269]	X		
ISAC [213]	X		
Yourdon [355]	X		
Hatley and Pirbhai [150]		X	
Ward and Mellor [322]			X
Jackson [174]	X	X	X
Information Engineering [219]	X		
Formal Methods [171]		X	X

table 7.3 some representations are given and their relation with development methods. The representations have been grouped together in categories which have similar views which can be expressed in them, but it is not possible to simply connect a view with one category of representations or vice versa.

Design representations have been developed to be used in forward engineering. This means that they support a stepwise definition of a goal and the identification of conflicting constraints in the requirements and the solution of these conflicts [318]. The suitability of these representation to express properties of an existing system and to support the process of extracting it from the code, is still unknown. The operations of the representation will differ in forward and reverse engineering. Forward engineering means specialization (filling in the details), conflict identification and solution and taking design decisions by choosing from the many possible ways to implement a function or requirement. Reverse engineering means reorganizing the representation, aggregating to another granularity, abstraction, standardizing, finding inconsistencies etc.

The representations of views were originally static: the views were printed or plotted on paper. With the case and reverse engineering tools the representations have become more dynamic. This means that views may be represented for example by the original source code, with some line marked in color, dependent on the request of the user. For instance, the user may ask for all statements which refer to a certain variable. Another example of a dynamic view is the representation of a part of the source code as a control flow diagram. The user can get the content of a node of the diagram by clicking on that node.

7.4 Granularity and Presentation Format

The information in a view should be presented on the right level of granularity and in the appropriate format. This concept is determined by the size of the smallest entity which is distinguished in the view. On source code level the lowest level is the complete source code. A more coarse level of granularity only shows the control structure, by hiding the sequential statements. One step further gives only the module structure etc.

Table 7.3: Some connections between design representations and development method

Representation	Development method								
	SSADM LSDM Merise [209, 269, 194]	ISAC [213]	Yourdon [355]	Hatley Pirbhai [150]	Ward Mellor [322]	Jackson [174]	Inform-ation Engng [219]	Formal Methods [171]	Other methods
Decomposition diagram				X					
Context diagram	X		X						
ISAC A-scheme		X							
English text	O	O	O	O	O	O	O	O	O
Formatted text	O	O	O	O	O	O	O	O	O
Data definition language									X
Program Design Language			O						X
Programming language									X
Formal language (e.g. Z)								X	
Dataflow diagram	X		X				X		
Entity relationship diagram	X		X			X	X		
Data action diagram							X		
Warnier-Orr chart									X
ISAC D-schema		X							
Information diagram Niam [242]									X
ISAC-I scheme		X							
Entity life history	X	X							
ISAC-M (Hardware allocation)		X							
HIPO									X
Yourdon structure chart	X		X						
Nassi Shneiderman diagram									X
Jackson structure chart	X					X	X		
Action diagram				X					
Warnier-Orr function chart									X
ISAC-D scheme		X							
State transition diagrams	X		X						
Petri nets								X	X
Decision table									X
Memory table/map									X
Cross-reference table									X
Make file									X
Configuration									X
Data dictionary	O	O	O	O	O	O	X		X
Directory tree									X
Numerical metrics									X
Informal diagram									X

X means that the representation is used in the development method
O means that the representation is optional.

In some cases the change in granularity implies already a change towards a new view. For instance, when dataflow diagrams are brought to a higher level of abstraction by combining different processes and hiding internal data stores, one may finally arrive at a context diagram [355].

Changes in the granularity are often useful in order to combine an overview (top-down) with low-level details. An example is the Turing Tool [84], which can display the source code as modules, without showing the internal structure, while the user may ask for the details of the module if he wants, such as the control structure or the complete source. Another example is the static analyzer REPROBATE for FORTRAN, one of the reverse engineering tools developed in REDO. The control structure of the modules is displayed as a graph. By clicking on a node, the user gets the content of the node (the source code of the module) displayed.

In the enumeration of the different representations of the views one may distinguish the following categories:

- text (make files, verbal description of the system, source code),
- numbers (quality and quantity measures, such as lines-of-code, budget, McCabe metrics),
- diagrams (entity-relationship diagram, context diagram, Petri net),
- links between views and view elements.

Tables can be considered as text and/or numbers in a specific format and with specific semantics. In fact diagrams also have properties that are similar to a language. The objects in a diagram can be compared with the words in a language. The constraints on the connection between objects are a kind of lexical rules, while the layout can be used for both text and diagrams to structure the presented information and emphasize important elements. Much information is represented by the layout of the text (pretty printing), numbers (tables) and diagrams. The *semantics* of the representation is the interpretation of the elements, but also the links they have with other objects and the operations which are allowed.

A support system for reverse engineering should have facilities to store, edit and retrieve these kind of views and to present them in a natural way to the end users. There are not many problems on an implementation level. Graphical objects can be stored like text and manipulated in various ways. Hypertext techniques can be used to represent links between text, nodes or arcs of a diagram and/or statements or data definitions in the source code. The problem to solve is how these representations should be accessed by the users, so that the diagrams are aesthetically and well-structured, that the text is well formatted and the logic of the links is visible. For this problem several methods have been developed (see chapter 11). The problem which remains is how a software engineer involved in reverse engineering wants to use these views, for instance how a satisfactory task support can be realized. The first problem to be solved here, is how the task of reverse engineering can be described (or better prescribed).

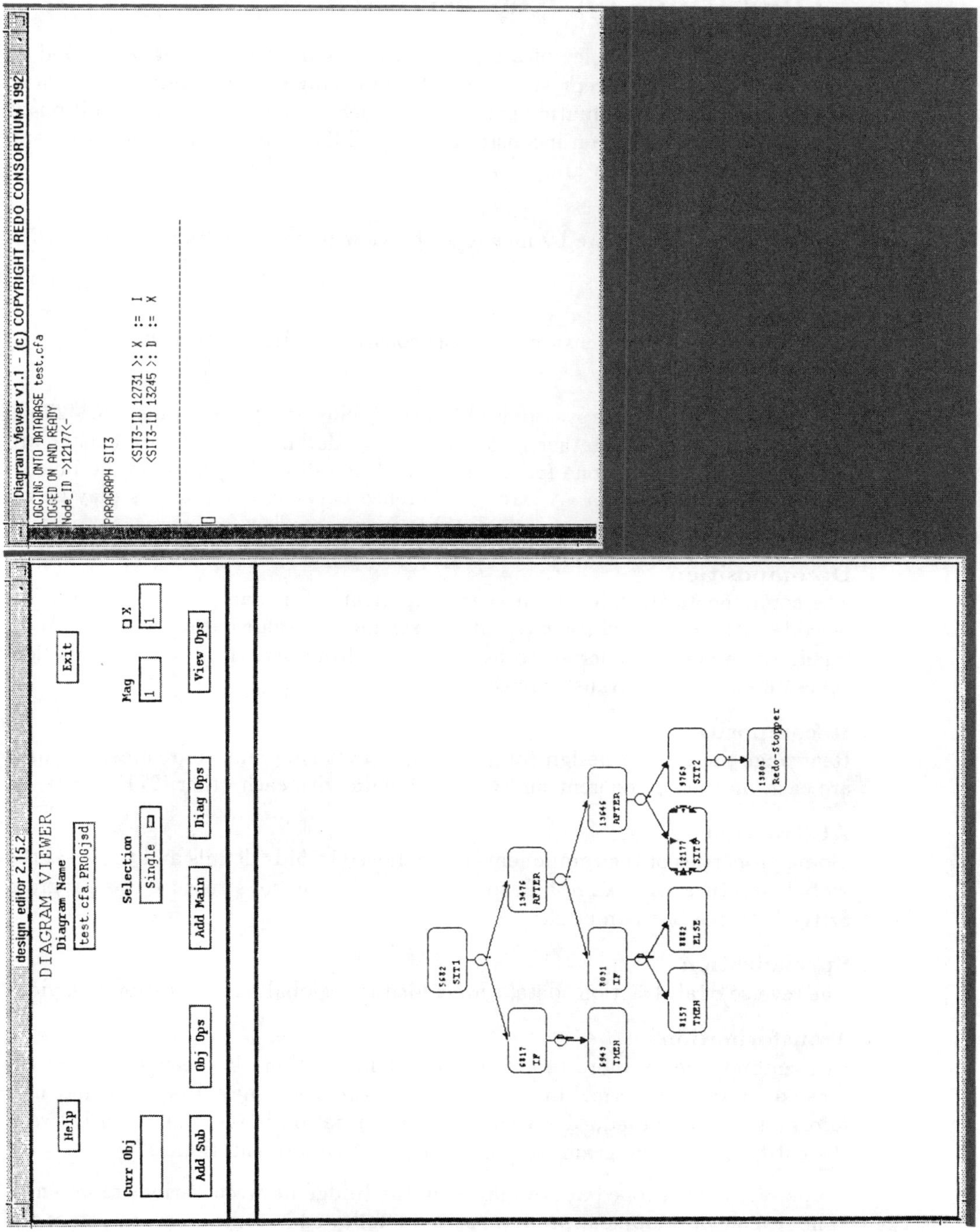

Figure 7.2: The diagram viewer of the REDO toolkit

7.5 Operations on Representations

An important issue in the choice of a representation is the question of what kind of operations are possible on a representation. Natural language is a very general way to represent a view, but automatic operations of such a representation, definition of consistency rules and a check on inconsistencies are difficult to realize. Some relevant operations on a representation are:

- **Validation**
  Evaluation of the software by means of the view to ensure that it complies with the requirements.

- **Verification**
  Evaluation of a view to ensure that it is consistent with another view.

- **Aggregation**
  A larger scale view of the system is obtained by clustering (see for instance [278]). Objects are grouped together into clusters and details internal to a cluster are removed. This can be done for instance, with dataflow diagrams, as the inverse process of decomposition. A strong coherence between components may be an indication that these components could be aggregated.

- **Decomposition**
  The components are split up into subcomponents. An example is the separation of code into chunks which have little exchange of information and a definite function (sometimes referred to as 'objects'). Rotenstriech [271] calls this 'low cohesion elimination transformation'.

- **Recomposition**
  Rearrange the code or design components, so that new chunks are created which are each internally coherent and exchange data with each other [271].

- **Abstraction**
  Some properties of the components are removed to hide details and to reveal the global structure. An example is to show only the control structure of a program or the call tree of the modules.

- **Specialization**
  The reverse of abstraction: details are added to a global representation of a view.

- **Transformation**
  Elements of one or more representations and relations between them are expressed in another form. In this process information may disappear and new information may be added. A simple transformation is the transition between the entity-relation diagram and the Warnier-Orr representation [218].

The operations mentioned above may form the bridge between various representations. The reverse development process has to be followed in some cases, but since the development process is only well understood on paper and less in practice [158], the derivation of a new representation from existing ones is in most cases not a straight forward process.

7.6 Tools to Generate Views

Before a sensible abstraction of a view is possible, the source code has to be interpreted. Parsers are the basis of most reverse engineering tools. Most reverse engineering tools can do their work on the parse tree. Chapter 19 describes how the parse tree is stored in a permanent database, a repository, on which different tools can operate.

Chapter 19 also describes a browser on the source code that displays the source code in the granularity required by the user and displays the parse tree down to a certain depth. A search for a certain construction in the program for example, all nested loops, can be implemented as a query on the repository. The user interface of the browser has to help the user to specify this query and translate the query into a form which can be executed by the database manager of the repository.

Browsers on the parse tree may display the results of a query in the format of the original programming language but, depending on the abstraction level and the operations involved, a graphical representation (call graphs, control flow, data structures) or tables may be preferable.

Restructuring of the source code is done by manipulation of the tree subject to certain rules. Complexity measures can be defined as statistical properties of the parse tree and can be calculated by counting certain types of links and nodes.

The tools which parse the program and build up the parse tree, can be extended to interpret also job control language and interactions with the environment such as transaction processing systems, embedded SQL or user interface management systems.

Another approach in reverse engineering is, to interpret the semantics of the source code. Here, one has to surpass the representation from the parse tree. One has to identify what certain pieces of code do with parameters. The resulting view can be expressed as invariants (parameters and relations between parameters which remain unchanged in a certain module, pre-conditions and post-conditions (conditions which exist before and after the execution of a module respectively). This approach may lead to a formal, mathematical description of the specification of the source code. In chapter 15 it is explained how this view can be extracted from source code.

Links between certain components are very important. Almost every programmer has the experience that he is browsing through a pile of compiler listings and has to use all his fingers to point to all lines of code he wants to compare. In chapter 19 the environment is described which makes it possible to produce these links, store them in the repository and to display all pieces of information which are linked together.

Another activity, which is often carried out in software maintenance and which is supported by the REDO environment, is the making of notes. Notes are important aspects of the views and often represent the beginning of new views. Tools to collect the notes and get an overview are important in the creation of new views.

The character of notes may be:

- clarification: this may be stored afterwards as comment in the source code,
- questions,
- activities that still have to be done.

The REDO tools described in part IV aim at reverse engineering from the source code in a bottom-up way. Additionally to REDO, standard CASE environments can be used to build the views top-down. These views are, of course, the same as for forward engineering. Currently CASE tools do not have much support to build these views from existing code or to verify these views with the actual program.

Other very useful tools to support the building of views are debuggers, dynamic analyzers and test environments. But there the main problem is that no links exist between these different tools. One single environment with one shared repository on which CASE tools, reverse engineering tools, debuggers, test environments and dynamic analyzers work and where each tool can use the result from the other tools would considerably improve the possibilities for maintenance.

7.7 Language Semantics

The most important representation of an application is the source code of the programs. In most cases it is written in programming languages like COBOL and FORTRAN. These languages have been designed to serve as a means to specify the intention of the software engineer in such a way, that a compiler can generate executable machine instructions. The source code has other functions too. In reverse engineering, it is one of the most important sources of information. Software engineers doing reverse engineering study an application for a great deal by reading and interpreting the source code. Most reverse engineering tools start from the source code and perform transformations, decomposition, abstraction, aggregation etc., on the source code. Therefore, the source code gives a very important view of the application and is a basis for many other views.

The meaning of a fragment of source code is defined by the semantic definition of the language used. In the mid 1960s, the practice began of providing a formal definition of language semantics. For languages with earlier roots, such as COBOL and FORTRAN, their 'official' or intended meaning is specified informally, in natural language. The usual problems of such specifications apply, including lack of precision, ambiguity, unclear scope of general rules. Indeed some features of FORTRAN 77 are specified the way they are to maintain a chain of compatibility which reaches back to unplanned features of implementations of the early 1960s.

Where programs affect their environment for example, operating system state, file contents and devices, the standard of specification tends to be much worse.

Generally, maintainers assume that source code means what they think it means, but they need to be open to the possibility, when inexplicable effects are observed, that they are mistaken or that the language implementation is faulty.

The constructs of algorithmic programming languages can be split into a number of categories:

- data definition: the description of the data values to be processed,
- evaluation of expressions,
- assignment to variables,
- control flow,

- communication with the environment.

It is important that tools should recognize and 'understand' these, supporting the reverse engineer in his activities. However, it is not necessary to capture a complete semantic definition of the language implementation being used when communication between tool and user is in terms of the source language (the only language one can guarantee they have in common). So, the fact that neither precisely knows the result of say, a floating-point divide, generally passes unnoticed.

7.8 Presentation of Source Code and Diagrams

The ideal view for a particular purpose will be the one that makes the required information most obvious. This means, it:

- includes all required information,
- minimizes extraneous information,
- uses a compact, but simple and adequate representation,
- is part of a complete, integrated set of views, e.g. uses one consistent notation for each view of the same type, and identifies a component structure with a defined relationship to that shown in other views.

For a few classes of views one may give the following recommendations.

Requirements

They belong to the groups 1.1 – 4.1 and 1.2 – 1.8 in table 7.1. These are generally written by clients, from their point of view and in their own terms. Rewriting them in a form which is more compatible with the developers' outputs risks losing the clients' commitment to them, so is not appropriate. True requirements are rarely very detailed. If a single sentence is really sufficient, the developers should not feel the need to bully their clients into writing more and needlessly constraining the end result.

External specification

External specification is in the groups 2.1 – 2.8. This is the developers' response to the requirements – what they propose to build in the belief that it will satisfy all or most of the clients' requirements. The developers normally attempt to persuade the clients to sign this off, hoping that if this specification is met, the clients will automatically accept the software, worse still if the current, or even the original requirements have not been met.

The structure of this document is the responsibility of the developers. It is helpful to adopt a structure compatible with that of the top-level architectural design, for instance common operations and functions such as error handling and field editing during user input, other functions in task-related groups within user classes and finally system administration or support.

Writing it as an early draft user manual should reduce costs and make it easier for the clients to understand, although a complete specification of an interactive interface will need careful handling.

Architecture

The architecture is mainly in the groups 3.2, 3.3, 3.4 and 3.7. During the development of a system it is the responsibility of the chief architect. It should define any standards, procedures, techniques etc., to be applied to all relevant components, then specify the breakdown of the application into components and the requirements on them, including their interfaces. This may be a multi-stage, multi-level activity. Ideally the components should have a simple relationship to the structure of the external specification. If not, then the reasons for this and the future maintenance implications must be evaluated.

Design

This covers the low-level design of individual components, particularly the algorithms and data structures to be used. It is in groups 3.3 – 3.6 and 3.8.

Source code

The usual way to display source code (in group 4.1 – 4.8) is in its original language. However there are other possibilities in which the design of the source code becomes better visible, such as:

- a lower level language used in the translation process for instance, assembler, object code, binary,
- a more powerful language, for example a later variant, ADA, C++, UNIFORM
- a very high-level language or fourth-generation language (4GL) which abstracts away from implementation details towards a solution or preferably problem, description. Formal notations and pseudo code come in the former category,
- English. This has been found to be less ideal than one might think, because of the lack of precision in common terms, the wordiness compared to the abbreviated notation provided by most programming language and our inability to automatically convert a changed description to machine interpretable text. In any case, acceptable free text is still hard to generate,
- diagrammatic. Traditionally these have been 'extractions', rather than abstractions, for instance control flow and module call trees,
- composite. CASE tools with an automatic prototype system generation capability can produce enormous quantities of code. One claims 1300 lines of CICS COBOL from 5 lines of pseudo-code. Note that this is not the same as saying that the 5 lines contain the meaning of the 1300. It only means that, in the context of the CASE tool and its repository, assuming that there are no standard

proformas which are always generated and that the generated code is reasonably compact, the 5 lines imply the 1300.

Of course different representations suit different people and some are not interpretable without appropriate training and experience.

Given the known difficulties in porting programs between unrelated languages, today's major contenders are the original programming language, an improved variant or a formal notation. One can effectively invent one's own variant language by the disciplined use of specially-marked comments, although automatic checking of the enhanced language is unlikely to be cost-justifiable.

Formal notations are useful for algorithmic languages once the following conditions have been met:

- a formal algebraic specification of the language is available,
- the code is WHILE structured: there are no GOTOs or exception-handling,
- loop invariants can be acquired from an application expert,
- runtime exceptions/errors never occur.

Once the necessary simplifications have been done, formal notation can offer a summary of the effect of the program in the form of a formula for each output value in terms of input values.

8

Documentation

E. Younger, *Centre for Software Maintenance, University of Durham, Durham, UK*

In a broad sense, documentation is anything which provides information about the software system. Thus it includes the source code, JCL, test suites, as well as development documents, user documentation and code analysis results. In the following however we restrict the use of the term to mean information generated specifically for the purpose of describing the system; thus we exclude the application code and its data from our classification. The contents of documents may include natural language text, diagrams, mathematical expressions, and may be in the form of flowing text, tables, structured diagrams etc.

8.1 Problems with Existing Documentation

Many applications in daily use were developed 15 or 20 years ago, before the advent of well-defined development methods, and certainly before there was much concern about the problem of maintenance. Such systems are likely then to have little or no documentation of use to a maintainer.

Major software development projects are frequently behind schedule and over budget. Towards the end of such a project, the pressure is on the development team to meet deadlines for the release of the software. The result is that anything considered non-essential to the release is postponed, often indefinitely. Generally, documentation (other than that which accompanies the released system) is considered to fall into this category. Development documentation therefore becomes out of date as refinements and amendments are made to the system and never documented — this also applies to the post-release maintenance phase of the product's life. In the worst case some documents are never written at all.

The advent of IPSEs and software engineering databases allows documentation to be stored in a common repository with the rest of the application. This in itself goes some way towards overcoming the above problems: the status of the documentation is implicitly elevated to that of an integral part of the application, rather than a optional extra. It is also possible to include the documentation in the same quality assurance procedure which is, or ought to be, applied to the application as a whole. Similarly, where a configuration management system is used to manage different versions of a system, the documentation can also be brought under its control.

This technology is however very recent. Existing applications were, with very few exceptions, developed without the aid of such project management systems, and so the documentation is typically stored separately from the rest of the application, either online in a dedicated document preparation system, or more probably on paper only.

There are a wide range of document preparation systems, often even within a single organization, and these evolve rapidly. The original documentation may have been written using a system which is not available to the maintainer, and so it becomes impossible to maintain the documentation other than by rewriting it completely using a new system. This is typically considered uneconomical as part of a single maintenance task, and so changes to an application are documented, if at all, by amendment documents. Thus a maintainer who wishes to discover the present state of the application is forced to follow through a series of amendment documents, perhaps written in different styles by different programmers, which can prove confusing and difficult to understand.

The system under consideration may have been developed using ad hoc methods, or a development method unfamiliar to the maintainer. This may mean that any development documentation which does exist is difficult in itself for the maintainer to understand.

Thus the maintainer approaching an unfamiliar system is often faced with documentation which is incomplete, out of date, inconsistent, difficult to access, difficult to understand, or in the worst cases inaccurate. Even good quality documentation may not be useful to the maintainer if it does not convey the information required to carry out the task at hand. In many cases the documentation is so poor that it is not used at all, and the maintainer relies solely on the source code to understand the system. It is this situation which redocumentation seeks to rectify.

8.2 Types of Documentation

1. **Development documentation**

   This term is used to mean documentation of the type produced during a modern systematic software development process, though the actual documentation in question may actually be generated during a post-delivery redocumentation effort.

   Modern system development methods follow a well-defined path of stepwise refinement from requirements capture and specification through descending levels of design abstraction to the implementation of the system. Documentation is generated at each stage of the process and includes complete, consistent specifications, records of design decisions with rationale and descriptions of the design. In systems in practice, any or all of the above may be missing or unreliable. Older systems, or even modern ones, may have been developed in an ad hoc manner following no well-defined development process. Such a process is unlikely to have been documented in a fashion useful to maintainers, if it was documented at all.

Development documentation, which is reliable and of good quality, is valuable to the maintainer. Given reliable documentation, its utility is determined by *traceability*. Maintenance requests are generally expressed at a high level of abstraction: a particular system requirement needs to be changed, or a function is performed incorrectly. It is important that the documentation includes cross-references which allow the maintainer to trace through from the specification documents to the relevant design information and from here to the affected sections of code. The sheer volume of text which accompanies a well-documented application of even moderate size makes this essential.

2. **User documentation**

This includes all documentation delivered to the user as part of the system package. It comprises information needed to install and use the system, ideally without intervention from its developers [TN-ITS-1003]. It is almost certain that some form of user documentation will exist, though its contents and scope may depend on the relationship between the developer and user.

The minimal form of user documentation contains the information required to operate the system. This should include:

- pre- and post-conditions for execution,
- descriptions of input and output data,
- descriptions of user interaction procedures,
- external file formats,
- details of any execution options and how these are selected,
- error conditions, error messages and recovery procedures.

These may be in the form of examples, informal descriptions, formal functional or syntactic specifications, or combinations of these.

When an application is developed internally by an organization for in-house use this may be sufficient documentation for the end user; installation and support will probably be carried out by the developers. However systems delivered to client organizations must be accompanied by more extensive documentation which ought to include:

- Installation instructions, unless installation is carried out by the supplier. This will give instructions to load the system from the distribution media, install the component files on the user's disk store, and build the application from these files if appropriate. In the simplest case, installation of a PC application may involve inserting a diskette and typing 'install'. In such cases the useful information will be contained in the installation script, or *makefile* for a Unix application. There may also be an inventory of the files which make up the application and their location in the disk store. This information may also be contained in the installation script.

- An overview of the system, the problem it is intended to solve, and its constraints. This may be interpreted as a requirements specification.
- The hardware and software operating environment. This will specify the computer system on which the application will run, its requirements for main memory and disk storage, also any peripheral devices required and configuration instructions when alternatives are possible.

User documentation is a potentially rich source of information about the application. As noted above, it may provide information about the requirements specification for the system. It may also describe the input/output behavior, and will almost certainly give detailed information about user interaction and/or data file formats. However the information may well be in a descriptive form which is insufficient to provide a complete specification of any part of the system. Even so it is useful to the maintainer. At a high level, installation instructions or script files will provide an inventory of the files which make up the application and perhaps also relations between them. At a lower level, the user interaction and input/output format descriptions aid the maintainer in identifying the roles of various variables in the programs. Although functional and other requirements may be described, user documentation is unlikely to give any information about how these are refined at design and implementation stages. However the fact that these are stated will give clues about the functional constructs that a maintainer might look for when studying the system.

3. **Technical documentation**

Technical documentation is the term we use to denote low-level documentation generated purely from analysis of the application code by automatic tools. Technical documentation is useful in maintaining at the code level, and in reverse engineering. Almost all commercial tools sold as redocumentation or reverse engineering tools are of this type.

Technical documentation tools typically generate low-level documentation such as identifier cross-reference listings, call graphs, control-flow diagrams, and also more abstract information such as dataflow diagrams and structure charts. The former is useful to maintainers trying to understand the details of the code, the latter in reverse engineering: in understanding the application at a more abstract level.

Technical documentation of this type is generally cheap to produce, as it is generated automatically, hence it can be readily produced and kept up to date. Again, a requirement for it to be useful is traceability. This is much less of a problem than with development documentation – technical documentation is generated from code and so the tools which produce it can be constructed to insert appropriate references back to the code (in the case of a cross-referencer, this is the object of the exercise). A greater problem is traceability between development and technical documentation – each is generated in isolation from the other, and so tracing logical connections between them may typically have to be done indirectly, via the code for example.

8.3 Redocumentation

Redocumentation is the process in which new documentation is generated for an existing system either to replace or augment any documentation which already exists. The process of redocumentation will record the outputs from any reverse engineering which is performed – it is concerned with making available to the maintainer the information required to understand the system. This is an essential part of any maintenance task; system understanding has been identified as the single most expensive part of the maintenance process [297]. A survey of maintenance programmers has shown that they perceive poor documentation to be the greatest problem facing them in their work [69].

8.3.1 Approaches to Redocumentation

The approach to redocumentation adopted will vary depending on the aim of the activity. Redocumentation may take place in response to a variety of triggers, for example:

- In response to a maintenance request, parts of the system may be (wholly, or more probably, partially) redocumented as a side-effect of the maintainer's efforts to understand the system.
- As part of a full-scale reconstruction of the application to improve its maintainability, complete redocumentation of the application may be carried out. The reconstruction process may itself be triggered by various stimuli (see chapter 2).

These two scenarios correspond conceptually to the two system comprehension strategies identified by Littman *et al.* [206], namely the *as needed* strategy (wherein the maintainer studies and understands only as much of the application as is necessary to carry out the maintenance task) and the *systematic* approach (in which the entire system is studied to gain a complete understanding). In studies involving small programs, the latter was found to give superior results, however in large systems it is impractical for a maintainer to fully understand the entire system.

We now consider two approaches to redocumentation. These are mutually complementary, and may overlap.

1. **Recreate the development documentation**

   This may involve rewriting any existing documentation to make it consistent with the current state of the system, to conform to standards, to import it into a repository, etc.

   Where documentation does not exist, it will be necessary to recreate it by examination of the application itself. This is reverse and inverse engineering in its strict sense. We attempt to reverse the process of stepwise refinement by which systems are (ideally) developed. This is not to say that we assume the system was in fact developed in this way; in fact systems which are many years old were very probably developed by ad hoc methods and subsequently modified repeatedly. Reverse engineering will recover a description of the current state of the system, but its design may be so bad that the resulting documentation may not be very helpful to the maintainer. Also, the reverse engineering method may attempt to describe designs in a different fashion entirely from those used by the original developers. Even a well-designed application may then give rise to unhelpful documentation. For example, using the language of Object-Oriented Design to describe the design of a system developed in a top-down procedure-oriented manner is obviously inappropriate and will probably give rise to an unhelpful and confusing design description document. An experienced software engineer may be able to recognize probable design methods from the type of code produced.

Recovery of specifications directly from application programs by formal methods is another approach which is under investigation in REDO. While it may be possible to recover a high-level functional specification the problem of abstraction from this to recover the requirements specification for the system is non-trivial. It is quite possible that the original requirements were never properly recorded or correctly translated into the system design. The best we can do in the absence of additional information is to hypothesize that the requirements are accurately refined to the functional specification recovered from the code. If a requirements specification does exist, or requirements can be identified from other sources such as user documentation, it will be possible to verify that the system in its current state satisfies these.

Using formal methods it is in principle possible to generate documentation corresponding to part of the development process directly from the application. However, it is not possible to discover some information which is important to the maintainer. It is possible for example to discover *how* the system is designed but not *why* it is designed that way. Unless the various design decisions were documented with their rationale by the original developers, it is possible to rediscover these only by talking to the developers or by inferences based on the maintainer's experience.

Another type of information required by maintainers is the mapping between objects and processes in the problem domain and their representation in the application. Use of meaningful identifiers can help the maintainer to infer these relationships if they are not documented. An experiment has shown that programmers whose mental models of systems incorporate concepts both from the problem domain and the system itself develop a better understanding of the system [256].

Recovery of development documentation using current methods is expensive [287]. It generally ties up large numbers of maintenance personnel in studying the system and is not well supported by software tools. Those redocumentation tools which do exist are mainly confined to the COBOL/data-processing sector, and support reverse engineering to specific design representations only (e.g. [8]).

2. **Incremental redocumentation**

   This second approach is generally the result of the 'as needed' strategy noted above. Maintainers engaged in satisfying particular maintenance requests must gain an understanding of parts of the application in order to modify it. The understanding required is quite wide-ranging and at various levels of abstraction. A general understanding of the high-level design may be needed to identify those modules which need to be modified. Partial knowledge of the control- and dataflows may be required to identify potential side-effects elsewhere in the application. A detailed knowledge of the implementation details in the vicinity of the change(s) is of course essential (assuming, that is, that the application is maintained at the implementation level, rather than (partially) re-implemented from a modified design).

   This knowledge may be gained using a variety of methods, for instance code-reading and analysis of code using software tools. The knowledge gained is very often not recorded for the benefit of future maintainers, resulting in duplication of effort (research has shown that large parts of a typical application remain stable over time while particular 'hot spots' are modified repeatedly). Failure to record the understanding gained represents a waste of resources that must be addressed. Incremental redocumentation is the recording of knowledge about the application as it is acquired. It is generally a side-effect of some other maintenance activity rather than a task in its own right. We are not aware of much research in this area. Tools have also been described which allow the user to enter informal text and link this to program code [123, 125] (see section 19.7.5). If this approach is adopted, then a information base of knowledge about the application will be built up as a natural part of the maintenance process, concentrated on exactly those parts of the of the application which are most likely to be the subject of future maintenance activities.

   The process of system understanding has been studied from the point of view of the cognitive processes involved and the mental models constructed during the process (chapter 6). The recording of programmers, conceptual knowledge in a useful form has many potential problems, not least the fact that different programmers may express what is substantially the same knowledge in completely different ways, or may form subtly different models of the same system. Thus programmers may be unable to understand one anothers' representations of their knowledge, particularly if they record it in an unrestricted or unguided way. Nevertheless, given that the processes (such as hypothesize, validate, refine) and concepts (such as plans and beacons) used in building mental models are now well researched, the possibility of providing support for the processes and of documenting systems in terms of the concepts used is worthy of investigation. This area has been touched upon by systems such as PROUST [178], which uses KBS techniques to identify plans in programs. However, such automated systems are very limited in their range of applicability (PROUST is limited to analysis of programs which attempt to implement a given requirements specification). Human maintainers in contrast can examine and understand a wide range of applications, but at present there is no accepted framework for representing the mental models which are constructed.

8.4 Documentation Systems for Maintenance

In this section we consider how documentation fits into the maintainer's conceptual model of a system, and how it may be stored and accessed to reflect this model. The objective of a documentation system for maintenance should be to support the process of system understanding and redocumentation. As such it should be based on a conceptual model of the task and the data. Each of the three categories (development, technical, user) of documentation are potentially useful to maintainers.

Conceptually, complex relationships exist between an application and the documentation which describes it. These vary in granularity; at the highest level, a document *describes* an application. At a lower level, particular parts of a document *refer* to specific parts of the application. These references may be *explicit*, for example they may represent the development path from an initial statement of a requirement through to the code which implements the required functionality. Others may be *implicit*, in the sense that they may be inferred by the maintainer during the comprehension process. Some of these implicit references may be specific to a particular maintainer's mental model: a second maintainer may make different logical connections. References from documentation to the application are generally represented in conventional linear documentation by explicitly naming part of the application in the text. These references are unidirectional, from the documentation to the application. References back from the application to the documentation may occur in module header commentary, but are otherwise rare.

Some systems exist which allow and encourage more extensive documentation to be embedded in the application itself. A good example is Knuth's WEB system [182]. WEB supports a programming/documentation concept known as 'literate programming'. Documentation and application code are intermixed in a WEB source file. Compilers then run on this source to generate source for a Pascal compiler and for the TeX document formatter. WEB has been used in major software projects, for example the TeX document typesetting system is written in WEB. Maintenance of the WEB source rather than the program source encourages and facilitates keeping the documentation up-to-date and consistent with the application. However, WEB has several shortcomings. The WEB source is linear, as it is stored in a conventional file, thus there is no possibility to set up links between related information. It is also very large, comprising intermixed documentation text and program code. This gives rise to similar problems encountered with more conventional systems, in locating relevant information in the WEB source file. The great advantage is however, that WEB encourages a *style* of programming which results in high-quality documentation for systems developed using it.

The literate programming concept is valuable, both for development and maintenance. It can be readily supported in a more modern IPSE-type environment, to take advantage of the additional facilities which are available. Rather than mixing code and documentation in a single file, it is possible to store the two separately but to take advantage of those linking and windowing facilities which are available to maintain the intimate relationship between them. Brown and Childs [53] describe an experiment investigating the use of a hypertext tool for literate programming. Users familiar with the WEB system preferred to work with this tool rather than the typeset output from WEB or the raw WEB source in an editor. In maintenance, the practice of 'literate maintenance', of documenting changes visibly and clearly at the time they are made could go some way towards reducing the degradation over time of an evolving application.

Where the application and documentation are stored in a repository/database, the possibility is given to represent references by links in the database. Explicit links can be set up permanently when the database is loaded; implicit or conceptual links may be built up as part of the incremental comprehension and redocumentation process. It may also be appropriate to annotate the links themselves to explain the relationships which they represent.

This data model, in which the application and its documentation are interrelated by a set of links at various levels of granularity, corresponds closely to a maintainer's conceptual model. A documentation tool, which uses this data, will allow both text and links added to be modified, and will also allow links to be traversed to retrieve related information. Such tools form part of the REDO toolkit and may be used to examine the information in the REDO repository, to edit documents and links, and to annotate parts of the application.

The features we have described, namely a system of inter-linked information and a tool which retrieves related information by following these links, are typical of a hypertext system. However the partitioning of data into small frames which is a feature of many hypertext systems is perhaps not entirely suitable for a documentation system. A user may typically wish to follow a link to a section of a document (a hypertext-style navigation), but then to browse forward or backward through this document in a linear fashion.

Documentation, which is subject to maintenance, is likely to show the same tendency to degrade with time as is exhibited by applications. Good practice in the maintenance of both can combat this trend, but is unlikely to eliminate it completely. A tool for documentation which supports the casual incremental addition of information is likely to speed up the degradation of quality unless steps are taken to prevent this. Factors which could contribute to deterioration of quality include:

- maintainers entering incorrect, inconsistent, duplicate or conflicting information,
- modification of the application without corresponding changes to the documentation,
- proliferation of information, resulting in duplicate or redundant information, and a poorly structured database with 'spaghetti' links.

Consistency checking between the application and its documentation may be performed automatically if appropriate links are set up in the database. Correctness and consistency of the documentation itself can be maintained by a quality control process for the application as a whole, and by version and configuration management procedures. There is a clear need to mark documentation so that information, which has been quality-checked and found to be reliable, can be identified as such. Proliferation of information is perhaps the flip-side of ease-of-use in this case. Restricting the update facilities offered by the tools according to the identity of the user can go some way to alleviating this, but a periodic restructuring/reconstruction of the database might still prove necessary.

The desirable features of a (re)documentation system for software maintenance can now be summarized (see also [123]):

1. **Integrated source code**
   Traceability from documentation to the related source code is essential in maintenance. The direct embedding of documentation in the code itself is possible, using either the commenting facilities of the language or systems such as WEB, but is not desirable for the reasons discussed above. The system should therefore use some form of linkage between separately stored code and documentation, preferably with stronger semantics than merely 'a relationship exists'.

2. **Integrated technical documentation**
   Technical documentation should be linked both to the code and to other documentation in the system, to allow it to be used efficiently. Links should be created by the tools which extract the documentation from the application.

3. **Integration of existing documentation**
   It should be possible to incorporate any existing documentation for the application, whether online or on paper, into the system. This should not require the re-typing of all existing documentation, as this will prove very expensive, but it should be possible to incorporate references to external material unavailable online.

4. **Incremental documentation**
   It should be possible to build up the documentation for the application gradually over time, as described above, and the system must be usable despite the documentation being incomplete.

5. **Informal update**
   It must be easy for the maintainer to add information to the documentation base while engaged in studying the application. The intention is to provide a system which encourages maintainers to record their understanding of the application as it emerges. A system which is cumbersome to use or which causes the user's train of thought to be broken is not likely to be used in the manner intended.

6. **Quality assurance**
   In order to prevent degradation of the documentation over time, quality assurance procedures are essential. These can be aided by stamping new information with the identity of its author and the date and time its entry. Existing information can be consolidated and summarized periodically to prevent the documentation base from growing in an uncontrolled way.

7. **Configuration management**
   Where an application is evolving, configuration management must allow the documentation appropriate to a particular version to be recovered.

8. **Information hiding**
   The documentation base for a well-documented application of even moderate size will be very large. It must be possible to view this information at various levels of abstraction, and to screen out unrequired parts of the documentation.

9. **Team use**
   The team involved in maintaining or reverse engineering a typical application will have many members. Therefore the documentation system must support concurrent access and update by multiple users.

8.5 Conclusions

Documentation is crucially important in maintenance as an aid to understanding the system. The documentation which accompanies typical systems in use today is very often of poor quality and not oriented towards the needs of maintainers, who frequently do not use it at all. Thus the need for redocumentation is clear.

Types of documentation which are useful sources of information for maintainers have been identified. Some possible strategies for the redocumentation of an application have been discussed. Documentation systems for software are in the main aimed at the development phase of the software life cycle. We have identified some desirable features of a documentation system for software maintenance to support some of the processes involved in redocumentation and use of documentation, together with some potential problem areas.

9

UNIFORM

T. Cahill.
Department of Computer Science and Information Systems, University of Limerick, Ireland

9.1 Introduction

From the outset of the REDO project, it was realized that it was highly desirable to carry out maintenance at the specification level or the design level, rather than at the programming level, where the programmer has to maintain the source code of the implementation languages used. However it was also realized that obtaining appropriate specification or design-level descriptions depended on in-depth analyses of the source code of the implementation languages. Any large system is going to consist of components written in *several* implementation languages. Therefore it seemed desirable to devise a 'language' or notational system which would describe in a uniform manner, the actions specified in several different implementation languages.

To obtain specification or design-level descriptions of an application meant that reverse engineering of data-processing systems had to be done at the level of the entire application system, not just at the individual module level. Application systems consist of many programs, whose *joint effects* determine their overall functionality, and understanding of an individual program frequently requires that it be seen in context. That is, understanding a program consists of determining the contribution that the program is making to the overall functionality of the system.

It was also realized that most third-generation languages had substantially common constructs, even if this similarity was disguised by widely varying syntactical forms. If this semantic commonality can be exploited then there could be substantial reuse of tools which by their very nature were not dependent on the syntax, or irrelevant semantic details of individual languages. For example, diagramming tools do not generally depend on the detailed semantics of assignment statements, and many diagramming conventions do not distinguish between FOR and WHILE loops.

Subsequent sections will argue that Language Independent Representations are *necessary* for meaningful reverse engineering of large applications, and that they are *desirable* in many other situations.

UNIFORM is a language which was designed in an attempt to find an implementation language independent representation of application systems. About one and a half man years of effort was put into the design of this language in the first year of the project, and many useful insights resulted from this effort. However it became clear that the majority of tool-producers in the consortium were interested in two languages, FORTRAN and COBOL, and there was not a large overlap of functionality in the tools handling the different languages. Most importantly, once the consortium agreed on the platform and on the initial structure of the System Description Database (SDDB), they wished to implement tools without further delay. Consequently, the need for a fully language-independent representation scheme became less urgent, and the work was discontinued. The University of Limerick has now resumed work on language-independent representations of applications, mainly because several organizations have requested that the REDO tools (especially the metrication tools) be adapted to other languages.

9.2 Language Independent Representation is Necessary for Large Systems

Most large commercial systems involve a wide variety of 'languages' which are used to specify different components of the system. For example, an application running in a VAX installation can involve:

- COBOL as the base compiled language;
- Digital Command Language (DCL) as the language for binding actual resources to formal resources, and for scheduling the execution of programs;
- Forms Management System (FMS) to describe the layout of forms, and to trigger the display of help screens and the invocation of data-validation routines;
- DBMS-11 for specifying database schemata;
- Datatrieve for specifying retrievals from databases or conventional files;

Therefore, to get a full understanding of what happens during the operation of a system, it is necessary to understand the contributions that individual 'programs' written in these languages make to overall functionality of the system, in terms of their actions on shared objects. Since these actions may be described in several different 'programming languages' it is necessary to describe these actions in ways that are independent of the languages used in implementing the system. This requires a common notation for specifying such actions.

9.3 Language Independence is Desirable in Many Cases

Even if reverse engineering is to be carried out on systems implemented in a single language, there is scope for substantial reuse of reverse engineering tools if they do not have to be rewritten from scratch for each new language. This is especially true for tools that are not dependent on the full semantics of specific programming languages. Such tools would include:

- Control Flow Restructuring tools;
- Data Flow Analysis tools, especially those which only required knowledge of whether a variable was assigned a value, without having to know what value was being assigned to the variable;
- A large number of diagramming tools;
- A large number of metrication tools;

However it should be noted that the greater the variety of tools to be provided, the more detailed the semantic analysis will have to be if a single representation scheme is to be used.

9.4 Approaches to Achieving Language Independent Representations

There are a number of approaches to achieving language-independent representations of applications, including:

1. Formalize the semantics of each language, using a single notational scheme, such as VDM or Z. This provides a single notational scheme for expressing the effects of many languages. There are three main problems with this approach:

    (a) It is a highly skilled task, requiring substantial mathematical maturity, and a deep knowledge of the semantics of the languages concerned. There are very few organizations with the required mix of skills. The REDO project was fortunate in having partners such as Durham and Oxford, who have both been involved in formalizing CICS.

    (b) When the individual programs have been translated into this notation, sophisticated tools are required to reason with this notation. In particular, if specification level descriptions are required, it will be necessary to develop expression simplification and theorem proving tools, which can handle extremely complex expressions (possibly several megabytes in length). Work has been reported by the Programming Research Group of Oxford University which deals with this problem.

(c) Since Z and VDM are unlikely to become the preferred specification language for the majority of data-processing software practitioners, and since they are not executable languages, they cannot be the implementation language. Therefore, it is necessaryto:-

- devise front-ends which hide the mathematics from the maintainers to enable them to maintain the specification;
- devise tools to repartition the functionality into modules;
- devise tools to regenerate executable code in appropriate implementation languages for each module.

All of these problems are still areas of active research and it is unlikely that solutions would have emerged that could have been adopted within the timescale required by the project.

The problems associated with using Z or VDM specification languages are unavoidable when one wishes to maintain at a much higher level than the source code of the implementation languages. That is, it is not specific to VDM or Z.

2. Design a 'narrow-spectrum' textual intermediate language. That is, a language at roughly the same level as the set of languages being reverse engineered, and translate all the languages into this language. Formalize the semantics of this language, and develop the tools around representations based on this language.

   This approach is intuitively appealing because many languages do have constructs which vary considerably in syntax, but whose semantics are very similar, including:

   - named constants,
   - variables with declared initial values,
   - programmer-defined types (or type construction mechanisms),
   - arrays,
   - slices of arrays,
   - files,
   - records,
   - pointers,
   - conditional execution of statements,
   - WHILE loops and FOR loops (i.e. loops over the elements of a set),
   - functions,
   - procedures,
   - processes or tasks,
   - parameter passing mechanisms.

   Therefore it seems worthwhile abstracting from the terminology and syntax of the individual languages. There are three main problems:

(a) Within each construct, there are considerable semantic variations between the different languages. Tools which carry out restructuring on the intermediate form may yield 'programs' which are not directly representable in the ultimate implementation language, because certain 'statements' are transformed by the restructuring operations into a semantic variation not allowed in the implementation language. For example, FORTRAN may only allow functions to return a REAL or INTEGER values, while the tools operating on the intermediate language might create a function which returns BOOLEAN or CHARACTER values. If FORTRAN code was required as output, then this function may have to be retransformed into an allowable function.

(b) When reverse engineering operational software, one is not reverse engineering a standard language. Generally, a piece of operational software has been compiled using a vendor-specific compiler which may not apply the 'standard' meaning to a construct. This means that the meaning of the operational software is dependent on the compilers, linkers, and environments in which that software runs. Therefore, to translate an operational notation into a common intermediate format, requires detailed knowledge of the specific compilers and hardware. This is especially true of languages such as COBOL, where data is described in terms of its storage attributes, and where there are verbs such as the unedited MOVE statement which are highly dependent on the storage attributes, and the characteristics of the target machine. The effort involved in devising such a notation, and in articulating the translation into that notation will only be repaid if tools are being developed for a very wide range of languages, or if a sufficiently wide variety of tools are being developed to justify the effort.

(c) The introduction to this chapter mentioned a variety of languages used in the implementation of large commercial applications. These languages are not at the same level, and consequently the intermediate language will, in some sense, be 'larger' than any of the languages. For example, most third-generation languages do not have facilities for instantiating processes or tasks, but every shell or command language has this feature. Therefore it must be included as a construct of the intermediate language. In fact, a cursory inspection of many large applications will show that while a language such as COBOL does not have facilities for process instantiation, many COBOL programs will contain calls to operating system services to spawn sub-processes. Therefore it is impossible to avoid introducing the concept of process into the intermediate form.

3. Develop a 'wide-spectrum' language. A wide-spectrum language is a language which can be used throughout the life cycle. That is, it is suitable for specification, design, and implementation of a system. Such languages must have a firm mathematical basis, and effectively the task of developing such a language would be equivalent to designing modularization and procedural extensions to Z or VDM. Such languages include the COLD and Munich CIP languages. This option was proposed, but not acted on by the REDO consortium.

4. Develop a 'broad-spectrum' language, which would somehow incorporate the types of objects encountered in command languages, database definition and manipulation languages, and screen description languages. By 'broad-spectrum' we mean a language that can express concepts appropriate to 'programming in the large' as well as 'programming in the small'. This is even more difficult than devising a narrow-spectrum language, but it was felt that the difficulties were not insuperable, especially if the language was mainly going to be used as a representational mechanism, and that transformations carried out on representations could be devised and verified as the need arose.

   While the design of a broad spectrum language may be more difficult than the design of several specialized narrow spectrum-languages, careful design should ensure that the number of new concepts to be introduced can be kept under control.

   A language like ADA provides many features of a broad spectrum language, and has been a major influence on the design of UNIFORM. It can describe many features of command languages through its TASK specification mechanisms, and it can describe screen-based forms and commercial database management systems as abstract data types.

   Extensions to ADA, such as ANNA, can be used to widen the spectrum of ADA. However, we lacked the courage to go this route, as the consortium was not sure if it could implement tools which could successfully bring COBOL programs up to this level of abstraction.

   However, one of the main problems was that ADA did not provide the right kind of BASE TYPEs for COBOL. COBOL does not have a TYPE system *per se*. Instead it allows the programmer to specify the storage attributes, and the formatting characteristics of variables. If we wished to represent these in ADA, we would have had to implement complex PACKAGEs to do so.

   In retrospect it may have been wiser to go this route.

9.5 Considerations in Designing an Intermediate Form

In designing an intermediate form of representation for applications, one must first decide on the objectives of an intermediate form, and what are the benefits to be gained from such a form. That is, one must decide what kind of tools will need this form, and what kind of tools can use this form. From previous sections it will be obvious that design and specification levels will need the form, while conventional program analysis tools can use the form. In the case of REDO, it was hoped that UNIFORM would be capable of representing all the semantically relevant aspects of an application using a single 'notation' or 'language'. In retrospect this can be seen as too ambitious, given the resources assigned to the task, the resources available within the time-frame of the project for tools which needed such a form, and the requirement for tools which are language specific and which therefore could not exploit this form.

However there are a number of criteria that UNIFORM attempted to satisfy:

1. It is a truism to say that the nature of a system is defined by the relationships between its components. These relationships are effectively sharing relationships, and since the structure of a system is determined by the structure of the objects it shares, then understanding a large system can be decomposed into steps, where the first step consists of understanding the most shared objects, and subsequent steps deal with understanding the objects in decreasing order of their shareability or globality. The more shared an object is, the more influence it will have on the overall design of the system.

   Therefore, any notation used to describe systems, should contain features which can describe shared objects in the simplest possible terms. In large data-processing systems, data and meta-data are the two most shared 'substances'. While full-object orientation encourages sharing of code as well as data, simply improving the articulation of how data and meta-data are shared in commercial systems, leads to considerable improvement in the description of the system.

2. As very few people consciously wish to damage the quality of their software, the language should be such as to promote the use of good software quality standards, even if these are not directly representable in the implementation language.

   For example, enumerated types are not directly representable in COBOL or FORTRAN, but it may be useful to note the fact that a particular variable can assume a small set of values either through comments, or through associated external documentation.

   Indeed COBOL describes individual variable instances and does not have the ability to declare types independently of instances. The use of COPY libraries can be regarded as an attempt to factor out common type information. Therefore the language should have an expressive type system, in order to ensure that type declarations can be put into their correct scope, thus ensuring that the sharing of meta-data implied by type declarations is visible to the reader.

3. The constructs in the intermediate language should be reachable by either conventional parsing techniques, or after a reasonable amount of abstraction recovery work has been done by automated tools. Thus one can test that a variable is an instance of an enumerated type, by checking that that variable is only assigned literals, or that it is only assigned values from variables that have been established to be instances of enumerated types. However it may be very difficult to determine whether two procedures could be equivalent to two distinct instantiations of a generic procedure.

   Not all abstractions may be reachable by fully-automated reverse engineering tools, in which case there is a need for training of users, and sophisticated front-ends to facilitate abstraction by hand.

4. As the structure of most commercial systems is dominated by the design decisions concerning the most shared objects, generally data stored in files or databases, it is very important that the effect of alternative designs for such files or databases can be established. Therefore the language should facilitate a wide variety of correctness-preserving transformations, which can model such alternatives.

5. There is a great deal of over-specification in most third-generation languages. This is particularly true as regards the sequence in which operations can be carried out. A modern high-level language should include facilities for specifying concurrent systems, and the use of conventional dataflow analysis techniques should be used to reverse engineer a sequential program into a number of concurrent tasks. This is important given the availability of multiprocessor configurations, and the advent of distributed computing environments.

6. The characteristics of the source languages must be taken into account. This is particularly true of languages such as COBOL, which contains many constructs which make abstraction recovery extremely difficult. COBOL makes extensive use of VARIANT structures, which forces the programmer to reason about the effects of an operation in terms of the effect on the storage which is allocated to the operands. This means that it is frequently necessary to reason about the bit-patterns in such storage. This makes dataflow analyses very machine-dependent. In effect, such analyses must descend to the machine level before ascending to higher levels. Consequently an intermediate representation must concern itself with all the storage attributes of data.

   Arithmetic is also a problem in most commercial programming languages. Each language has its own type-conversion rules. COBOL generally uses decimal arithmetic with truncation as a default, that is, it uses modular arithmetic. Consequently, it is very difficult to establish whether the specification of the PICTURE of a variable reflects what the programmer intended, or simply reflects a decision which happens to work. If a programmer uses PIC 999 for a variable, does this mean that the values assumed by the variable are constrained to the subrange 0...999 and that no attempt will ever be made to assign any other value, or does it mean that no error has ever been detected with this PICTURE? In fact COBOL compilers generally have options to detect and highlight situations where a variable can be assigned different values. However most programmers disable this option, simply because it causes too many warnings to be issued.

It must be confessed that the difficulties caused by lower-level reverse engineering problems, such as those outlined in (5), have forced us to defer much of the higher level abstraction recovery activities. However we have now developed a range of tools to cope with these problems, and once we have consolidated our findings we can go on to improve the design of the higher-level features of UNIFORM.

10

Decompilation

J.P. Bowen, P.T. Breuer
Programming Research Group, University of Oxford, UK

10.1 Introduction

The *Dictionary of Computing* [170] gives the following (abridged) definitions for a *compiler* and *decompiler* (or reverse compiler):

> **compiler** A program that translates high-level language into absolute code ...
>
> **decompiler** A program that attempts to ... translate back from machine code to something resembling the source language. The task is difficult and not often attempted.

The following sections are intended to show how a decompiler may be constructed given only a knowledge of or access to the specification for a forward compiler, and some facility with Prolog [35, 75] or other high-level languages. It is easy to do and should be attempted more often.

Decompilation is only useful, of course, if the object code is available and it is required to reproduce the higher level 'original' as an intermediate stage to aid understanding or restructuring. The decompiled code can then be abstracted to a specification by other techniques developed by the REDO project [42, 190].

10.2 Decompilation

A compiler may be specified by a description of how each construct of the source language is translated into a sequence of object code instructions [157]. It is possible to produce a compiler prototype almost directly from such a specification, and this is quite a usual route for the construction of a compiler nowadays – first the specification is written, and then a *compiler-compiler* such as the UNIX **yacc** tool [3] reads the specification and writes the code for the compiler. But the specification can be read in the other direction too, allowing one to construct a decompiler from it, either using a *decompiler-compiler* [TR-PRG-1047] or working more directly. [TN-PRG-1044]

A quicker route to a working compiler prototype than applying a full-blown compiler-compiler to the compiler specification is to simply write down a version of the compiler specification in a declarative language such as Prolog [326]. This should be executable immediately, if reasonable care is taken. Writing the compiler in Prolog is a key idea in producing a decompiler here: in theory a Prolog program can be run backwards if certain provisos are met, because the source code has no procedural directionality [207]. Each Prolog program declares a relationship between input and output variables, but 'input' and 'output' can be switched round if the user calls the program in a slightly different way. The rest of this section is devoted to explaining the idea.

The trick to making a compiler in the form of a logic program [34, 156], is to read the compiler specification as defining a relation between valid high-level and low-level program constructs. Normally a high-level program is supplied as input to a compiler and object code is returned, but what is wanted here is to supply object code and return the equivalent high-level program(s), resulting in a decompiler, and the switch-round will be entirely external to the Prolog code. In practice, however, some alterations to the program will have to be made: the clauses of the forward compiler logic program will have to be *reordered* to ensure termination when it is run 'backwards', and in particular, all the arithmetic clauses will need to be reversed from '$\mathtt{x} = \mathtt{y} + \mathtt{z}$' to '$\mathtt{z} = \mathtt{y} - \mathtt{x}$', (or be written as reversible relations '$\mathtt{plus}(\mathtt{x}, \mathtt{y}, \mathtt{z})$'). The reordering is necessary because of Prolog's very simple depth-first and left-to-right search strategy. In actual use, it will probably be necessary to make judicious use of the cut pseudo-clause ('`!`') as well for efficiency reasons.

Compiler specifications may be presented in Prolog as a three-way relation $\mathcal{C}$ between high-level code p, the matching object code $m[s : f\rangle$ (lying between a start address s up to but not including a finish address f), and a symbol table of addresses Ψ which lists the memory locations (used in the object code) against each name (used in the source code) [34, 157, 156]:

$$\mathcal{C}(p, m[s : f\rangle, \Psi)$$

For example, the clause of $\mathcal{C}$ which says that 'the compilation of the sequential composition of two programs p and q depends on compiling the two subprograms contiguously in memory' derives from the following specification statement:

Specification {sequential composition}
    If $s \leq j \leq f$
    and $\mathcal{C}(p, m[s : j\rangle, \Psi)$

and $\mathcal{C}(q, m[j : f\rangle, \Psi)$
then $\mathcal{C}(\ p\,;q\ , m[s : f\rangle, \Psi)$

Note that this specification introduces an intermediate address j between start address s and finish address f. During forward compilation, the code p will be compiled first and since the start address s is known, its finish address j can be calculated (it is just $s + n$ where n is the length of the compiled code segment produced from p). Then, compiling q, knowing the start address j results in the final finish address f being calculated in the same way. This can be coded in *standard* Prolog [75, 260] as follows:

```
c(P;Q,M/S:F,Psi) :-
  c(P,M/S:J,Psi),
  c(Q,M/J:F,Psi),
  ensure(S=<J=<F).
```

Here the **ensure** clause checks that $s \leq j$ and $j \leq f$. (Actually this is superfluous in the forward direction because negative length sections of the address table m will never be generated.)

For decompilation, the object code $m[s : f\rangle$ will be known, but the high-level program $p\,;q$ will be unknown. The logic program must ensure that the unknown intermediate address j ranges between s and f, and some reordering of clauses is necessary because of Prolog's naive left-to-right depth-first search of clauses during execution. The '**ensure**' term must come first in order to generate plausible values for j:

```
cr(P;Q,M/S:F,Psi) :-
  ensure(S=<J=<F),
  cr(P,M/S:J,Psi),
  cr(Q,M/J:F,Psi).
```

So some clever encoding of the **ensure** clause (and other arithmetic clauses) is necessary when using standard Prolog. However, the newly emerging field of *constraint logic programming* [76, 80] – which allows a variety of constraints (including numerical constraints) to be added to a logic program – allows the clause `ensure(S=<J=<F)` to be encoded as a simple constraint `{S=<J, J=<F}`, and then the same program may be used for both forward and reverse compilation without alteration. So if a reversible language is used to encode a compiler, then it can be used as a decompiler too!

A complete forward and reverse compiler for a simple imperative language, including recursion, has been produced as a prototype in Prolog using this technique [TN-PRG-1044], and the use of constraint logic programming languages looks promising for the future.

10.3 Decompiler-Compilers

Another approach to constructing a decompiler from the compiler specification is to arrange for a *decompiler-compiler* tool [TR-PRG-1047] to read the specification and write the code for the decompiler. Again, it is advantageous to use a high-level language (such as Prolog or ML [336]), but not completely necessary. It is only required that the language allow the use of subroutines as parameters, and even 'C' [181] does that.

The concept behind a decompiler-compiler is that the clauses of the specification for the compiler can be read as instructions on how to explicitly *enumerate* all the source codes which could give rise to a given object code. The following is the appropriate version of the specification to work from:

Reverse Specification {sequential composition}
$\mathcal{C}(\_, m[s:f\rangle, \Psi)$ contains $p\,;q$
where j is from $[s \ldots f]$
and p is from $\mathcal{C}(\_, m[s:j\rangle, \Psi)$
and q is from $\mathcal{C}(\_, m[j:f\rangle, \Psi)$

and what it describes is a *set* (unary relation) $\mathcal{C}(\_, m[s;f\rangle, \Psi)$ which contains the source code construct $p\,;q$ under certain conditions. The conditions are that p and q are to be found in the sets $\mathcal{C}(\_, m[s:j\rangle, \Psi)$ and $\mathcal{C}(\_, m[j:f\rangle, \Psi)$ respectively. Imagine that we want to write a procedure which enumerates all the elements of these sets in a list structure. It could look like:

```
list function rce(m,s,f,Psi){
local j,p,q,r
  r := EmptyList
  for j from list ListFromTo(s,f) do
    for p from list rce(m,s,j,Psi) do
      for q from list rce(m,j,f,Psi) do
        r := AppendToList(r,Seq(p,q))
  return(r)
}
```

and all a decompiler-compiler has to do is construct this code *automatically* from the specification given.

The only difficulty arises from multiple clauses in the specification. The full compiler specification from which this example is taken also contained the clause

Reverse Specification {abort}
$\mathcal{C}(\_, m[s:f\rangle, \Psi)$ contains $ABORT$

and the proper approach is to:

1. write an enumeration function for each alternate clause of the specification ('sequential composition' and 'abort' above), and,
2. define the enumeration function for the whole specification as the *concatenation* of the enumerations of the clauses, thus:

```
list function rce(m,s,f,Psi){
  return(ConcatenateLists(rce0(m,s,f,Psi),rce1(m,s,f,Psi))
}
```

Here `rce0` is the enumeration function associated with the 'sequential composition' clause, and `rce1` is that associated with the 'abort' clause:

```
list function rce1(m,s,f,Psi){
local r
  r := EmptyList
  r := AppendToList(r,Abort())
  return(r)
}
```

In fact this method of constructing a decompiler only 'works' if there are only a finite number of source code constructs which could have given rise to a particular object code. If there is an infinite number, the program may find itself attempting to append one more element to the end of an already infinite list, which will bring a long pause to the procedure!

The way out of the difficulty is to replace the **ConcatenateLists** function with an 'interleave' function, which does not place the elements of the second list after all the elements of the first list, but instead interleaves them together as fairly as possible. But one also has to 'interleave' the **for x from list y** operations too, and it is simple to do this by using an explicit list-valued function instead of the two-deep **for**...**list**... loop, thus:

```
list function rce0(m,s,f,Psi){
local j,p,q,r
  r := EmptyList
  for j from list ListFromTo(s,f) do
    for (p,q) from list XLists(rce(m,s,j,Psi),rce(m,j,f,Psi)) do
      r := AppendToList(r,Seq(p,q))
  return(r)
}
```

and here **XLists** does the complicated interleaving of the product of the two lists in a fair way. For a discussion of the general computational problem and the complete decompilation algorithm (see [TR-PRG-1047]).

The method given here is expensive on *space* if the substrate language does not use some form of 'garbage-collection' to reclaim abandoned list structures (as Lisp [1] and ML [336] do). Even with garbage collection the method is expensive on *time* because the structures are at least made before being abandoned, and the problem then is that the substrate language is *eager* to evaluate them even though they will not ultimately be needed. In a *lazy* language like Haskell or Orwell [26], however, these structures will never be completed and the time-behavior will be better. We can simulate the action of a lazy language by using a slightly different concept as the basis of the decompiler technique, and the remainder of the section will deal with that.

Laziness can be simulated by using *objects* instead of lists. The objects are procedures which when given the **NEXT** command, respond with the next item in the corresponding list, and when given the **FIRST** command give the first element in the corresponding list, and reset their internal counter, and we use an object to stand in for the set $\mathcal{C}(\_, m[s,f\rangle, \Psi)$. The decompiler can construct the object for the 'abort' clause of the specification as follows:

```
class com(s,f)->rce1(m,Psi){
  case com in
  NEXT)  return(0)
  FIRST) return(Abort())
  esac
}
```

meaning that the response to a '**FIRST** element of list' request is always the **ABORT** code construct, and to a '**NEXT**' command the response is always 'sorry, already finished' (here signalled by a zero). The class takes the variables **m** and **Psi** as parameters because these do not vary significantly. Since a class is a generic object, one will create an object **o** with these parameters already set when one calls '**o** := **rce1**(**m**, **Psi**)', and one has to send it its remaining parameters with the message:

```
NEXT(s,f)->o
```

The distinction between classes (generic pattern for an object) and objects is not particularly important in this case, because there is no *internal state*. But the object constructed from the 'sequential composition' clause of the specification does give rise to an object with internal state (represented by the **persistent** local variables ***j**, ***p**, ***q**) however, and because of the possibility of inadvertently sharing internal states, the object must set up distinct private copies **rce1** and **rce2** of the **rce** enumerators at initialization, because these are required to count through their enumerations independently of each other. This is handled by the declaration of **rce1** and **rce2** as being instances of the class **rce(m, Psi)** at the top of the file, along with the other local variables. Which ***j**, ***p**, ***q** one gets is intended to be dependent on the message parameters **s** and **f**, and this is handled by shifting the variables address to the correct place in an array.

The final object (see figure 10.1) looks complicated, but is easy to construct automatically. Further alterations are required to make it count in an interleaved way, and some extra objects are still manufactured and discarded, but the overall semantics is closer to call-by-need (lazy evaluation) than in an imperative language with lists.

10.4 Conclusions

In practice, the object code from an optimising compiler will be considerably more complicated than any of the examples which have so far been attempted. However, the Prolog approach does have the advantage that extra clauses of the compiler specification will be accommodated without affecting the existing clauses.

The efficiency of the Prolog decompilers generated so far is not great, but decompilers produced by the decompiler-compiler are more efficient. And when multiple answers are possible, the first answer returned will normally be of greatest interest (and the program can be structured with this in mind), so it is not necessary to search through them all (for instance, all the possible combinations of sequential composition).

Additionally, the layers of the source code language can be treated separately. For example, individual subroutines can be recognized and isolated early on in the decompilation process, so that smaller blocks of code may then be decompiled separately.

```
class com(s,f)->rce0(m,Psi){
persistent array j[*,*],p[*,*],q[*,*]
persistent object rce1,rce2 of class rce(m,Psi)
  j:=&j[s,f]; p:=&p[s,f]; q:=&q[s,f]   -- instantiate j,p,q
  case com in
  NEXT) if  (*q := NEXT(*j,f)->rce2)    -- stepped q
         then return(Seq(*p,*q))         -- return p;q
        if !(*q := FIRST(*j,f)->rce2)   -- reset q
         then return(0)                  -- q empty, give up!
        if  (*p := NEXT(s,*j)->rce1)    -- finished q, stepped p
         then return(Seq(*p,*q))         -- return p;q
        if !(*p := FIRST(s,*j)->rce1)   -- reset p
         then return(0)                  -- p empty, give up!
        if  (s≤++*j≤f)                  -- finished p, stepped j
         then return(Seq(*p,*q))         -- return p;q
        return(0)                        -- finished j, give up!
  FIRST) *j := s
        if !(*p := FIRST(s,*j)->rce1)
         then return(0)                  -- p empty, give up!
        if !(*q := FIRST(*j,f)->rce2)
         then return(0)                  -- q empty, give up!
        return(Seq(*p,*q))
  esac
}
```

Figure 10.1: Code for the final object class

Assuming that subroutines are all approximately of the same order of magnitude in size, the computational complexity is then linear in the number of subroutines. Indeed, if parallel computation is available, separate subroutines could be decompiled in parallel, thus reducing the computation time still further – essentially to a (large) constant time.

The decompiler-compiler approach is based on functional rather than relational concepts. Because of the irreversible nature of functions when there are implemented on a machine, compilation and decompilation must be handled separately. A different set of concerns arise with this approach, particularly with regard to the enumeration of sets of possible high-level programs or object codes to ensure that the required programs are enumerated fairly.

10.4.1 Future problems

The problems of parsing has so far been ignored by using the abstract syntax directly. Fortunately, this can be made fairly readable using modern declarative programming languages since infix, prefix and postfix operators with specified associativity and precedence are normally allowed. However, in practice a real compiler would need a parser (and a static semantics checker). A decompiler would require a concrete syntax to be generated from the abstract syntax produced be the decompiler presented here.

Luckily, this is far easier that the reverse procedure since only correct abstract syntax is generated and thus error checking is not necessary. All these extra phases are possible in Prolog, or some other high-level declarative language, although perhaps not as efficiently as other approaches [251].

The development of techniques of *inductive logic programming* [235], which aim at the derivation of Prolog programs from examples and background knowledge, could provide the possibility of automatically synthesizing the compiling specification program from examples of triples (p, Ψ, m) of an input source program p, symbol table Ψ, and the compiled object code m. This then obviates the need for (perhaps unfounded) assumptions on the part of the decompiler writer about the semantics of the source code.

11

Diagramming Techniques

F. McLoughlin,
Department of Computer Science and Information Systems, University of Limerick, Ireland
J. Estdale, M. Tobin, *Lloyd's Register, Croydon UK*

11.1 Introduction

Many different types of model exist to represent real-world processes and activities; one of the most expressive is the diagram, which may be used to represent many different things in many differing areas of human endeavor. This chapter concentrates on automatic drawing algorithms used to generate design diagrams for use within the field of software engineering. It also describes the Control-Flow Diagrammer tool, developed in REDO.

11.2 Design Diagrams

Traditional informal and structured development methods generally rely on a process of decomposition based on one or more kinds of diagram and diagrammatic notation. Diagrams may also be used for program documentation [183] or even for 'visual programming' [237]. In recent years, there has been an explosion of new design methodologies which rely heavily on diagrams to express relationships and concepts within the domain. Traditionally, the systems analyst manually extracted the information required to model the real-world problem for each diagram-type used, rather than utilizing information which may have already been derived via some other technique.

Considerable time is spent drawing diagrams (and revising them until they look 'nice'). According to Charles Martin [217], "the most important second-generation CASE improvement will be automated production of systems-analysis diagrams".

The meaning of a diagram is contained in its nodes, their relationships and what they each represent. Relationships are usually indicated by links, sometimes by physical enclosure and sometimes by the availability of navigation operations. In some diagrams, the spatial layout is significant; for instance direction indicators are sometimes omitted when control flow is from top-left to bottom-right or a hierarchy runs from top to bottom.

With the advent of Integrated Project Support Environments (IPSEs), it is possible to store project information in one central repository and manipulate the data residing within it as required. With all project data stored in a central database, it is possible to interrogate automatically the model of the system stored within and derive any diagrams, dependencies etc., from it. As a result, the derived information may be used, with the aid of an automatic graph-drawing tool, to produce diagrammatic models of the system in question. This approach has been taken in REDO and is described in chapter 19. IPSEs can also support the correlation of design diagrams with the applications they depict. As well as linking complete diagrams to document sections, source files etc., it would be useful to link diagram elements to corresponding fragments of source code. Examples include call graphs, flow charts and state-transition diagrams. The precise correlation can be reviewed and updated when required. This is helpful when studying source code, as one's emerging understanding of the underlying design can be recorded, checked and improved. The notion of correlating designs with code is further described in chapter 18.

11.3 What Constitutes A Nice Diagram?

The reason that diagrams are used as models is because they can represent real-world activities effectively. This implies that they must be readable and understandable by the human reader. Automatic graph-drawing algorithms must therefore draw diagrams in such a way as to communicate their meanings effectively and clearly.

11.3.1 Classification Of Automatic Diagramming Algorithms

Tamassia *et al.* [304] suggest that graph layout algorithms can be classed using the following criteria:

class of graph: each algorithm is usually directed at a certain class of graph, for instance trees, directed graphs, planar graphs;

graph standard: in general, diagrams tend to be drawn to one of two standards:

- **straight line:** all connections joining nodes on a graph are straight lines;
- **grid standard:** all connections run along the lines of a rectangular grid in which the diagram is embedded.

aesthetics: the criteria which aid in graph readability;

constraints imposed by the model: certain diagramming techniques impose constraints on the possible layout of models of that technique. For instance, in dataflow diagrams it is usually desirable to position sources and sinks on the outside of the diagram and process bubbles towards the center;

computational complexity: due to the complexity of the algorithms involved, it may be impossible, or at least very difficult, to produce 'good' diagrams within a small space of time. Many graph layout algorithms make extensive use of heuristic layout techniques, to minimize the time involved while maintaining a 'good' diagrammatic standard.

As an example, Batini[20] suggests the following criteria for the layout of dataflow diagrams using a grid standard approach:

- minimization of crossing lines;
- minimization of the total number of bends in connection lines;
- minimization of the global length of connections;
- minimization of the area of the smallest rectangle covering the graph;
- placement on the external boundary of symbols representing interfaces.

11.3.2 Aesthetic Criteria

Aesthetic criteria are the 'human' elements in diagram drawing which give the diagram a more 'pleasing' appearance to the human eye. Like most human perceptions of real-world objects, individuals tend to be very subjective in their ideas of what a pleasing diagram should look like and in many cases where people do agree on a set of pleasing aesthetic criteria they do not necessarily agree on what criteria should have the highest priority. In any case, certain criteria may conflict with each other, for instance it could be possible to minimize the area of a diagram at the expense of, say, increasing the number of crossing lines.

Tamassia *et al.* [304] has suggested that the following criteria allow a diagram to be at its most effective:

area: the minimization of the area occupied by a drawing;

balance: the drawing should look 'balanced';

bends: minimization of the number of bends in the drawing;

crossings: minimization of the number of crossing arcs;

degree: vertices of highest degree should occupy the center of the diagram;

length: minimization of the global length of edges;

symmetry: sons in a hierarchy should be symmetrical;

density: uniform density of vertices throughout the drawing.

This is not an exhaustive list but the more important criteria do appear in it.

11.3.3 Data Structure Representations

Two methods are used to represent graphs within a computer, an *adjacency matrix* and an *adjacency list*; they may be used interchangeably.

Adjacency Matrix

An *adjacency matrix* for the graph $G = (V, E)$ is an $n \times n$ matrix A ($n = \mid V \mid$) such that:

- $A(i,j) = 1$, if $(i,j) \in E$;
- $A(i,j) = 0$, otherwise.

Note that if G is an *undirected* graph then $A(i,j) = A(j,i) = 1$.

Adjacency List

In an *adjacency list* representation of a graph structure, each vertex is associated with the vertices adjacent to it. For example, if vertex a is adjacent to vertices b, c and d then a's adjacency list will contain the vertices b, c and d. If the graph is *undirected* then each of the vertices b, c and d will also contain entries for a.

A *sparse* diagram is one where the $\mid E \mid /n$ ratio is low. Bearing in mind that many diagrams (especially in the field of software engineering) may be defined as *sparse* diagrams, it is clear that time and space advantages are to be gained, by using an adjacency list representation of graphs.

Figure 11.1 shows an example of a graph and how it is represented by both methods.

11.4 Directed Graph-Drawing Algorithms

Many different graph-drawing algorithms exist. Generally, each particular algorithm is aimed at a particular class of graph. For example, algorithms exist for drawing trees, hierarchical structures and planar/nonplanar graphs. Each one is specialized for drawing its own class of graphs and algorithms may not be readily interchanged.

Control-flow graphs are *hierarchical* by nature; the hierarchy implies that certain nodes in the graph occur before certain others, as would happen in program control flow. Unfortunately, program control flows are not strictly hierarchical, e.g. a loop resulting from structures such as `REPEAT`s and `WHILE`s would be *cyclic* (the problem being that as a cycle has no beginning or end, no node in a cycle may be thought of as being before another node).

Sugiyama *et al.* [301] published an algorithm based on Warfield's paper [325]. This algorithm shows how a strictly hierarchical graph may be drawn in a small time-bound using certain heuristics. It has become the *de facto* standard and the basis for many other hierarchical algorithms [228, 93, 272, 127] which allow for the modeling of graphs which contain cycles.

Initially, a set of aesthetics were formalized for hierarchical drawings:

- a hierarchical layout of vertices as an ordering between 'levels';

A simple graph

A->C->B->A

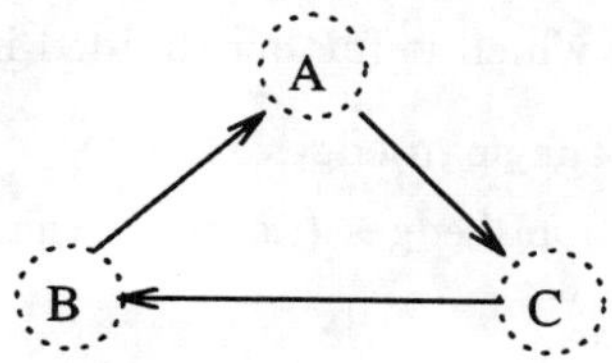

Adjacency matrix representation

	A	B	C
A	0	0	1
B	1	0	0
C	0	1	0

Adjacency list structure (doubly linked)

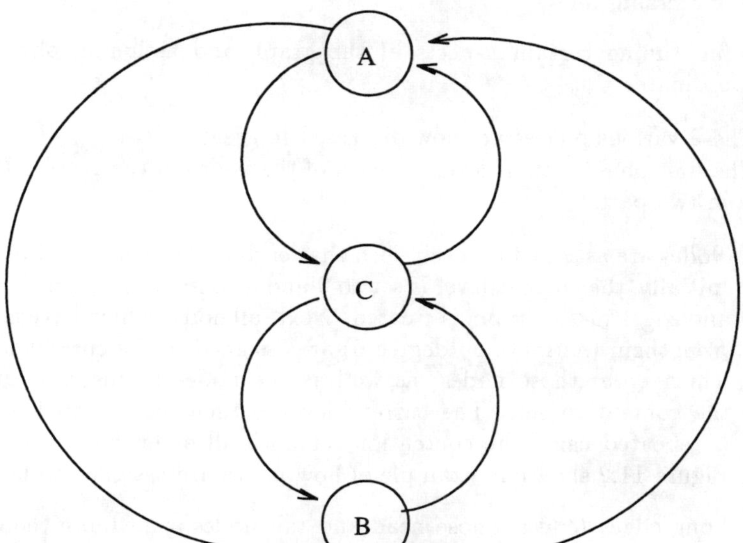

Figure 11.1: Examples of a graph with its adjacency matrix and list representations

- a minimum of crossing edges;
- straightness of lines, which is further divided into:
  - straightness of one-span edges;
  - straightness of 'long' edges (i.e. more than one).
- close layout of vertices;
- a 'balanced' layout;

and a set of drawing rules:

- vertices are placed on horizontal lines in each level of the hierarchy without overlapping;
- all edges to be drawn in straight lines.

The algorithm proceeds in three phases:

- assigning nodes to levels;
- sorting the nodes within each level in order to produce an 'acceptable' number of crossing lines;
- fine-tuning certain aspects of the graph and assigning physical x and y co-ordinates.

These various phases are now discussed in greater detail.

The first phase assigns levels to each of the nodes in the graph. This process takes place in two parts.

1. Nodes are assigned to levels such that each node is on a level below its ancestors. Initially, the current level is set to 0 and a contention set, consisting of all nodes and edges in the graph, is created. Next, all nodes which have no edges extending *from* them (nodes of outdegree 0) are assigned to the current level and all edges which *enter* those nodes, as well as the nodes themselves, are removed from the contention set. The current level is then incremented and the procedure is repeated using the contention set until all nodes have been assigned a level. Figure 11.2 shows an example of how nodes are assigned to levels.

2. Long edges (edges whose head and tail nodes span more than one level of the hierarchy) are broken into segments, each of which goes between adjacent levels and 'dummy' nodes are inserted in the intervening levels. By prioritizing the layout of dummy nodes later in the algorithm, it is possible to keep long edges as straight as possible. Figure 11.3 shows an example of dummy node insertion.

The second phase minimizes the number of edge crossings in the diagram. Since the minimization of crossing lines is combinatorial in nature, Sugiyama *et al.* [301] made use of a heuristic to aid them in their positioning of vertices within each level. The heuristic employed is the *barycentric method.*

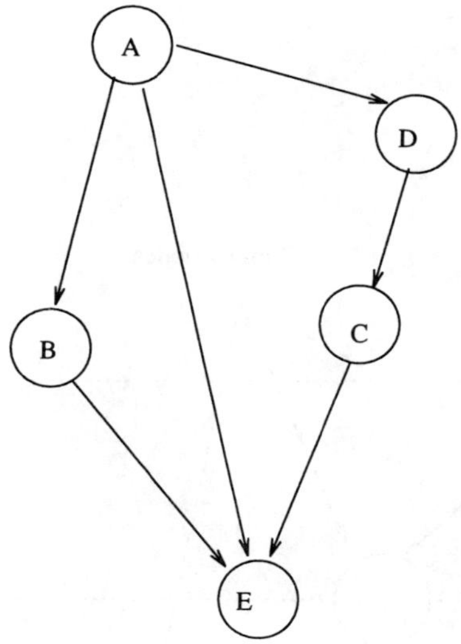

(a) Initial graph

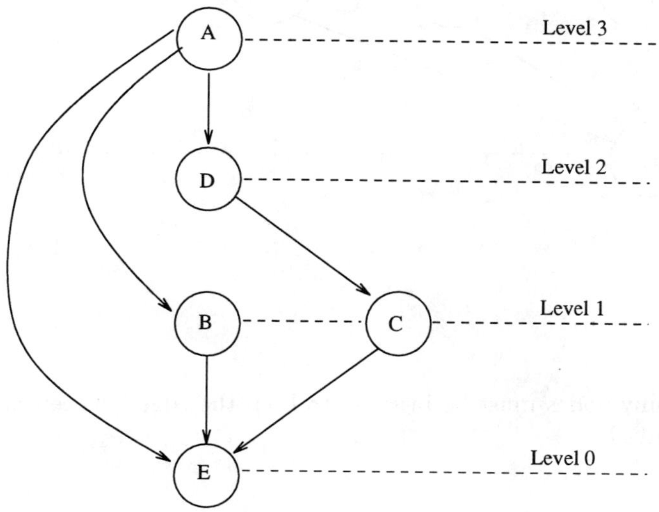

(b) After assigning levels

Figure 11.2: Assigning levels to nodes

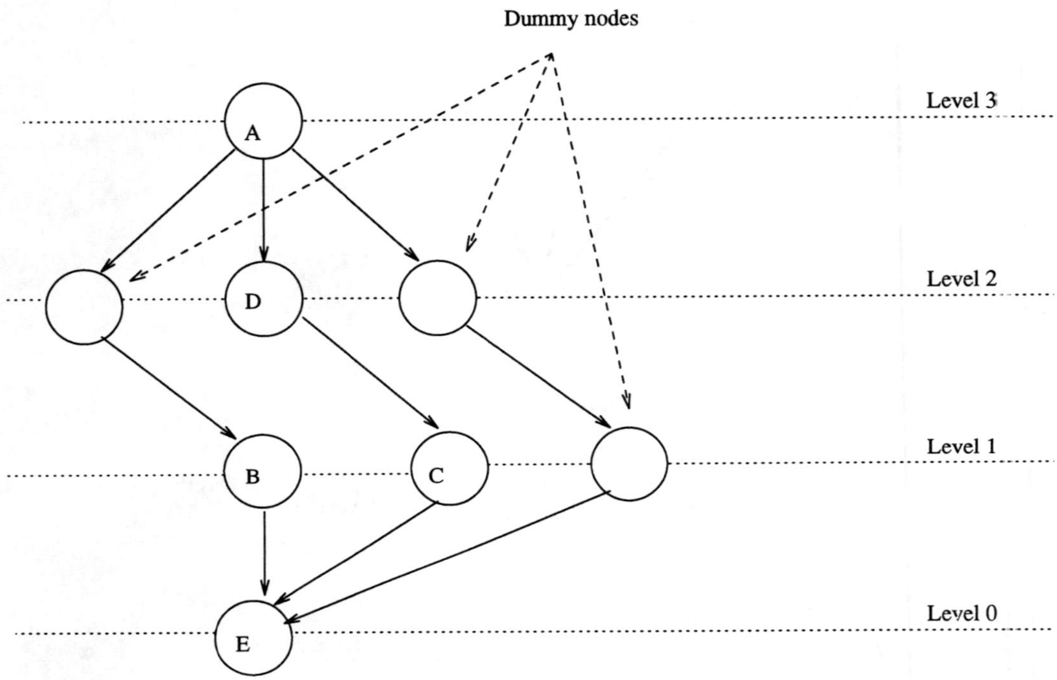

Figure 11.3: Dummy nodes must be inserted to keep the edge between nodes A and E and nodes A and B.

This method helps to achieve a reduction in the number of crossing lines, because it is heuristic in nature (it does not guarantee a minimum number of crossings but reduces them to an acceptable level). In all cases, except when a node is on level 1 or level n, a node will have two barycenters: an *up-barycenter* and a *down-barycenter*. The up-barycenter of a node is the average position of its *predecessors*, while the down-barycenter of a node is the average position of its *successors*. To 'balance' the diagram, all nodes on each level are assigned an initial value. The Sugiyama algorithm then makes alternate passes up and down the levels in the hierarchy, sorting nodes by their up-barycenters on the downward passes and by their down-barycenters on the upward passes. The passes continue until either a predetermined number of passes take place or the number of crossings falls below a specified limit.

The third phase fine-tunes the horizontal positioning of nodes within levels; it may be approached as follows:

- assign x coordinates to all nodes on a level before going to another level;
- keep track of the next available position within each level;
- if the desired barycenter of a node is less than the next available position, then assign the node to the next available position;
- if two or nodes have the same up/down barycenter then let the node of higher priority be positioned at the desired barycenter and position the other node(s) as near as possible to their barycenter (a 'dummy' node has a higher priority than an ordinary node).

Full details of the algorithm are described in Sugiyama *et al* [302]. Davis [93] improved the algorithm so that allowance could be made for cycles within hierarchies. In his adaptation, whenever a cycle is detected, the edge which completes the cycle is *temporarily* reversed. This then allows a 'proper' hierarchy to be created and nodes may be assigned to levels. When drawing the edge, in phase three, the edge is drawn in its original direction. Figure 11.4 demonstrates why it may happen that this heuristic may lead to increased edge-span.

While a graph with cycles may now be drawn using the hierarchical layout algorithm, this technique tends to lengthen some edges. Davis also improved the Sugiyama algorithm in the way in which y coordinates are assigned to the nodes on each level. It is suggested by Davis that the spacing between two levels should be such that the slope of any edge between the levels is 2/3. This heuristic may enlarge the diameter of the graph but it eliminates tightly packed edges with nearly horizontal edges.

11.5 The REDO Control Flow Diagrammer

The aim of the tool is to draw control-flow diagrams using an application's code syntax stored in the REDO repository. The repository is also used to store information about the diagram: a diagram is composed of objects, which are regarded as nodes and edges.

The tool may be thought of as consisting of two parts: the *display engine* and the underlying system-provided facilities. The display engine is based on the Sugiyama

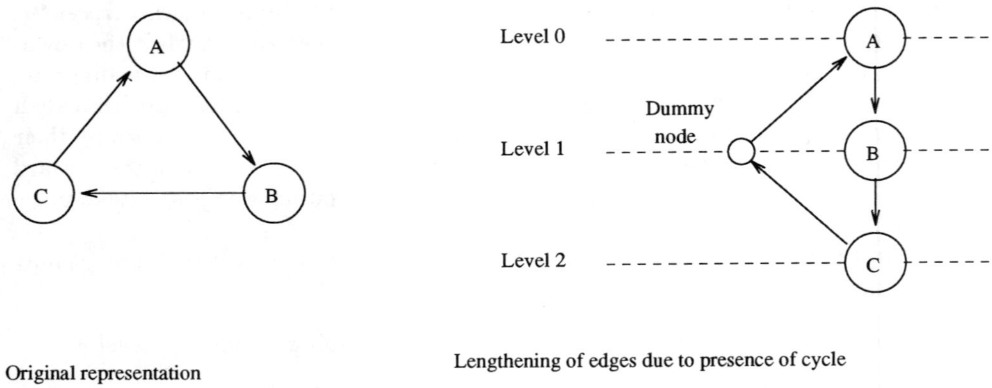

Figure 11.4: Lengthening of edges due to the Davis heuristic

algorithm [301] and incorporates the enhancements to the algorithm as defined by Meyer [228], Davis [93], Rowe [272] and Gansner [127].

In brief, all required data is loaded from the repository into a set of C linked lists and then manipulated in the following sequence:

1. levels are assigned to each node in the graph (a partial ordering is assigned, which is based on the closure of each node), cycles are broken if necessary;

2. using alternate passes of up/down barycenter calculations and sorts, *relative positions* (relative to each other) are assigned to the nodes in each level. This has the effect of creating a full ordering on all the nodes in the graph;

3. the nodes are then loaded into the repository and their physical coordinates are calculated;

4. the diagram is then fine-tuned. Any nodes which are unconnected to any other parts of the diagram tend to be placed on the bottom-left of the graph and this phase will place them on the top level, just after the last node on that level. (There should not be any unconnected nodes, as all code must be reachable within the program in order to be executed.)

The resulting diagram is presented to the user via a diagram editor, where enhancements and revisions can be made. The shapes available and their associated semantics are constrained to conform to those used in constructing the original diagram.

One of the novel aspects of this approach to diagramming has been the use of an *adjacency list* representation of the nodes and arcs of the graph. The implementation uses the adjacency list approach throughout the coding, from the calculation of the number of crossing edges (this was adapted from the Warfield [325] definition using adjacency matrices as the appropriate data structure) to the level assignment phase.

12

Regression Testing

D.J. Robson, *Centre for Software Maintenance, University of Durham, Durham, UK*

Software maintenance requires changing programs as a result of errors, or alterations in the user requirements. However, during such modifications, new errors may be introduced, causing unintended, adverse side-effects in the software. To combat such occurrences, regression testing is utilized in order to revalidate the modified programs. Ideally, the existing baseline set of test cases should be executed to ensure conformance with the specifications. As a result, this testing phase can prove to be expensive in terms of both human and computational resources. Thus, this section discusses some of the problems involved with regression testing and examines current selective retesting strategies which attempt to reduce the retesting effort and describes their advantages and limitations.

12.1 Introduction

In general, the issue of selective revalidation during the software maintenance phase appears to have been neglected for many years. The degree of disinterest becomes apparent when considering the literature concerned with revalidation methodologies and regression testing tools [149]. In order to accurately retest both the existing functionalities and enhancements, and to re-establish confidence in the software's ability to perform according to the specification, it is essential to employ some form of regression testing. However, the execution of an entire baseline set of test cases to validate small numbers of modifications may consume a large amount of time and computational resources, while intuitively or randomly selecting test cases to exercise the main system facilities is simply insufficient. Thus, it would be highly desirable to establish a systematic and sensible approach to rectify this situation.

Two types of regression testing have been identified, namely progressive and corrective regression testing [201]. The former involves testing major changes to the specification, so whenever enhancements, or new data requirements are incorporated into a system, the specification will be altered to reflect the modifications. In general, such alterations are expressed in terms of new modules or routines being added, and perhaps old ones being eliminated. On the other hand, corrective regression testing is performed on a specification that essentially remains unchanged, so that only minor alterations that do not affect the overall program structure require revalidation.

Typically, progressive regression testing is performed after adaptive or perfective maintenance [203]. Therefore, it is usually employed at regular, fixed intervals, while the corrective retesting strategy is undertaken after corrective maintenance activities, that can occur at any time and may be invoked at irregular intervals, as after every correction.

A further problem associated with testing in the maintenance phase is the maintenance of the testing suite itself. In most organizations, the test suite grows, but never decreases in size. Obsolete test cases are defined as those test cases for which the reason that they were included initially is no longer valid. Redundant test cases are test cases whose removal does not affect the testing coverage. Other test cases are now covering those attributes. The test suite will almost certainly contain obsolete and redundant test cases, but there are few methods of systematically identifying such test cases. Identifying the minimum sized test suite is an NP-complete problem [129], so obtaining the optimal solution is often unfeasible. One possible solution has been described by Harrold and Soufa [148]. This is a heuristic method. The method identifies a set known as the hitting set which identifies a set of test cases. Any test cases which are not in the hitting set can be eliminated from the test suite. The technique is independent of any testing strategy. The heuristic is as follows:

Suppose that there is a test set TS, a list of testing requirements r_1, r_2, ..., r_n and a list of subsets of TS, T_1, T_2, ..., T_n such that for each r_i, T_i contains test cases which satisfy the requirement r_i. Thus the hitting set, as the representative set is known, must consist of at least one test case from each T_i.

First, all elements in single (that is cardinality of one) T_is are included in the hitting set. All T_is containing these test cases are then marked as covered. Next, all unmarked T_is of cardinality 2 are considered. The test case which occurs in the maximum number of T_is is then chosen to be included in the hitting set. Again, all T_is containing this test case are marked. The process is repeated for unmarked T_is of cardinality 3,4,..., max where max is the maximum cardinality of the T_is. The algorithm stops when all test sets are marked. If there is a clash, then the T_is of cardinality n+1 are considered for those test cases and the maximum one is chosen. If this also leaves it unresolved, the algorithm continues with T_is of higher cardinality. If none of these resolves the problem, a random choice is made.

Consider the following:

Requirements	1	2	3	4	5	6	7	8
Test Cases	{2,5}	{5}	{1,2,3}	{3,6}	{1,4}	{1,6}	{3,4,7}	{2,3,4,7}

In this case, the hitting set is 1,3,5.

The authors also describe how the algorithm is implemented. They then analyse the runtime complexity which they estimate as O(m*Max(n,m)), where m is the number of test cases. They also briefly describe that they have compared the hitting set generated by their algorithm with the hitting set generated by the optimal algorithm and found the hitting set generated by their algorithm is at most log n times the size of the optimal hitting set.

The authors have presented a technique for reducing the size of a testing suite. It eliminates obsolete and redundant test cases from the test suite. The technique is independent of any testing method and only requires links between testing requirements and test cases. However, the method has not been evaluated in a non-academic environment.

12.2 An Overview of the Retesting Strategies

In the past, few publications have appeared which exclusively address the issues of revalidation strategies. In 1977 and 1981, Fischer [122, 121] developed a selective retest model and test criteria that were based upon adaptions of mathematical optimization algorithms [91]. His 0-1 integer programming model for retesting expressed the degree of connectivity, reachability and test coverage of program statements, and considered the data dependencies between them. In 1987, Yau *et al.* [350] presented a revalidation methodology utilizing concepts such as input partitioning and cause-effect graphing of the program specification, symbolic execution trees and test information tables for selective determination of test data, and data-driven symbolic execution for final test execution and debugging. Leung *et al.* [201] have discussed retesting using the concept of a retestable unit, that captures the program portion which may be affected by the maintenance modifications, and utilizes it to establish new test cases or delete obsolete ones from the existing test library. Furthermore, an algorithm for computing such a retestable unit is presented, involving program slicing [329].

This section will attempt to examine current selective retesting strategies, comparing and contrasting their respective advantages and limitations.

The following discussion will present two existing revalidation strategies, together with their individual advantages and limitations. The work of Yau *et al.*[350] is presented as an overview, while the methodology of Fischer is discussed in more detail. Retesting criteria attempt to ensure that all modified program statements have been exercised, as well as those program sections that are directly, or indirectly addressed by the modified code and which share any data dependencies with it.

12.2.1 The First Revalidation Methodology

The revalidation technique developed by Yau *et al.* [350] can be illustrated in the form of a flow chart. The process is based on a derivation of the input partitions for the modified program, in which the input domain of the program is divided into a number of classes [333, 265]. The test criterion then requires at least one test case to satisfy each class. The method derives the partitions by identifying different types of paths through the program code, and various combinations of input conditions taken from the program specification.

In order to minimize the number of existing test cases which need to be re-executed after modifications, the retesting algorithm makes use of symbolic execution trees and test information tables obtained in the form of the reaching set for each node in the program graph. After determining a subset of original test cases, which may cover several of the input partitions, those classes that remain must still be satisfied. If it is found that none of the test cases in the original baseline set can be reused, then an entirely new set of test data may have to be generated in addition to those required to cover any 'open' classes.

After the test criterion has been satisfied, these newly generated test cases, together with the subset of original test data are executed using data-driven symbolic execution, producing both symbolic and real outputs, and domain information. These results are then utilized for the validation and debugging of the target software.

The revalidation methodology was demonstrated using sample FORTRAN programs and executed with versions of the dataflow analysis tool, DAVE [249], and the symbolic evaluation package, ATTEST [74]. The advantages of this retest strategy in comparison with other techniques are twofold. First, the technique is capable of validating the initial set of test cases, and second it can handle modifications including changes to the program control structure. In practice, it appeared that the technique worked satisfactorily for simple programs that performed input classifications, such as the classification of a triangle with given three sides, but did not impress when executing more algorithmic processes such as sorting routines.

Furthermore, the retest strategy is based on the evaluation of a cause-effect graph [112] [236], representing the program specification, and the use of symbolic execution in selecting and executing test cases. These two techniques are ill-suited for use in large-scale revalidation procedures. For example, the article suggests that symbolic execution should be applied only to numerical programs and process control applications, as it proves to be both costly and can produce unmanageable large quantities of output.

12.2.2 The Second Revalidation Methodology

In his two publications, Fischer [122, 121] discusses a retesting methodology based on the concept of 0-1 integer programming models [91], in which the connectivity, reachability and test coverage of program statements, and their usage of both local and global variables are identified. Furthermore, Fischer describes program segments with reference to FORTRAN, defining them as "a contiguous sequence of executable statements with one entry point at the beginning and one exit point at the end". To monitor the ripple effect [349], the overall retest strategy includes two algorithms that distinguish those segments, that are affected by the data conditions used or set in a modified segment, and which reach to and from that segment, respectively.

The Zero-One Integer Programming Model

Fischer's retesting model is based on an objective function Z, and a series of inequalities as shown below by Equation 12.1. The minimizing function Z is given by:

$$Z = c_1x_1 + c_2x_2 + ... + c_nx_n$$

which is subject to the following constraints:

$$\begin{aligned} a_{11}x_1 + a_{12}x_2 + \cdots + a_{1n}x_n &\geq b_1 \\ a_{21}x_1 + a_{22}x_2 + \cdots + a_{2n}x_n &\geq b_2 \\ &\vdots \\ a_{m1}x_1 + a_{m2}x_2 + \cdots + a_{mn}x_n &\geq b_m \end{aligned} \tag{12.1}$$

These equations can also be represented in a matrix notation as illustrated in Equation 12.2

$$\begin{vmatrix} a_{11} & a_{12} & \cdots & a_{1n} \\ a_{21} & a_{22} & \cdots & a_{2n} \\ & & \vdots & \\ a_{m1} & a_{m2} & \cdots & a_{mn} \end{vmatrix} \begin{vmatrix} x_1 \\ x_2 \\ \vdots \\ x_n \end{vmatrix} \geq \begin{vmatrix} b_1 \\ b_2 \\ \vdots \\ b_m \end{vmatrix} \tag{12.2}$$

(a) The objective function Z, represents the optimal, or minimal number of test cases required to be rerun after a modification is made to a particular program segment.

(b) The coefficient c_j represents a cost element of the objective function Z. In this model, the cost elements are set to 1, as it is assumed that all test cases have an equal cost to set up and run. In future, one hopes to vary this factor in order to further investigate the influences of test case costs on the revalidation process.

(c) The variable a_{ij} is given as an element of the constraint coefficient matrix, and is set to 1.

(d) All values indicated by the b_i elements represent the lower bound of the constraint row/column i.

(e) The variable x_j represents the test case existence variable, which depending on whether its value is 0 or 1, determines whether or not a particular test case exercises a specific program segment. For example, where $x_j = 1$, the corresponding jth test case needs to be rerun, otherwise $x_j = 0$ in which case, the particular test does not require repeated execution.

Considering Four Different Types of Matrices

Initially, Fischer's algorithm relies on a general flow analysis of the target program, in order to accumulate information concerning the connectivity, reachability and test coverage of segments and their usage of both local and global variables, and parameters. This data is represented by four matrices including the connectivity, reachability, test case dependency or cross-reference matrix, and the variable set/use matrix, respectively.

The connectivity matrix reflects the program's control flow by indicating any direct interconnections between the different segments. It is represented in the form of a square matrix, containing m^2 elements, in which a 1 entry shows that the control flow of the program directly transfers between two particular segments, while a 0 entry shows otherwise.

The reachability matrix describes both the direct and indirect interconnections between the various program segments. It can be automatically generated from a connectivity matrix by applying Warshall's Algorithm [327]. Fischer also suggests a slight alteration to this algorithm, resulting in all diagonal elements of the reachability matrix being set to 1, to ensure that whenever a particular segment is modified, it is actually included in the retest procedure. The reachability matrix is of the same dimensions as the connectivity matrix, with a 1 entry indicating whether a particular segment can be reached either directly or indirectly from another, a 0 suggesting otherwise.

The test case dependency matrix reflects the test case coverage of the individual program segments, by placing a 1 entry against segments that have been exercised by a given test case, a 0 stating otherwise.

Furthermore, the variable set/use matrix is used by the retest algorithm to monitor the ripple effect [349] during maintenance modifications. It records the usage of both global and local variables, and parameters in the different program segments, by placing an 'S', 'U', or 'X' in the matrix to represent a variable being either set, used or set and used, respectively.

Outlining the Fischer Retest Algorithm

After determining which particular program segments have been modified, a number of constraint expressions are derived from Equation 12.1, in which each expression corresponds to a row of the test case dependency matrix. These expressions are incorporated into the 0-1 integer programming model on the left hand side of Equation 12.1, whilst those values (b_i) on the right hand side are established as a result of logical *OR*ing operations performed between the respective rows and columns of the reachability matrix associated with each modified program segment. The model can be further simplified by several reduction methods [122, 91] and any redundant constraints removed, resulting in an optimal value for the objective function Z.

In order to analyze the data dependencies between the various program segments and to further reduce the number of selected, reusable test cases, Fischer developed two additional algorithms which should be regarded as part of the overall retesting methodology.

The first algorithm, simply known as Algorithm A, identifies those program segments, which could affect the data conditions used in the modified segment, and which reach to this particular segment; the emphasis being on the usage of variables in the modified segment. In contrast, the second algorithm, called Algorithm B, determines those program segments, which could be affected by the data conditions set in the modified segment, and which are reached from the particular segment; the emphasis in this case being on the setting, and setting and usage of variables in the modified segment. The results of both Algorithm A and B are then logically *AND*ed with the column and row of each modified program segment, producing a set of values, which are utilized on the right hand side of Equation 12.1, instead of the previously determined set of b_i values.

To identify whether a particular variable in a program segment is set ('S'), set and used ('X'), or used ('U'), a set of rules was defined by Fischer. These suggest that:

- a variable is set, if its value has been changed, and thus an 'S' may be entered in the set/use matrix,
- a variable is used, if its value has been accessed and used, and thus a 'U' may be entered in the set/use matrix, and
- a variable is set and used, if its value has been set and used in a statement and thus an 'X' may be entered into the set/use matrix.

The Fischer methodology has been defined only for the FORTRAN language. Its major limitations are its incapability of dealing with modifications to a program's control structure, and the assumption that the initial baseline set of test cases correctly reflects the user specifications. Furthermore, Fischer's publications only discuss and demonstrate the algorithm for segments within a program routine, in which the modifications are constrained to changes within a particular segment and only very tentative approaches are made in the application of his technique outside the scope of the example routine.

However, the advantages that accrue from the Fischer strategy appear favorable when comparing the complexity and cost factors involved in the two retesting processes. The retest strategy described earlier [350], required the use of cause-effect graphing and symbolic execution in order to revalidate the modifications, whereas the Fischer methodology, although currently less sophisticated, relies on the establishment of four, relatively simple data structures and a few logical operations. Thus, it appears that the Fischer strategy would be more suitable for large scale revalidation procedures.

12.3 Summary

This section has given an overview of some of the problems associated with regression testing. It has also described two techniques which have been proposed to tackle the selective revalidation problem. Neither of these techniques have been fully evaluated and thus it is not possible to comment on their utility. Strategies for regression testing are not yet fully developed and more research is required in order to develop such strategies.

Part III

METHOD

13

The REDO Method

J. Estdale, *Lloyd's Register, Croydon UK*

13.1 Introduction

The preceding chapters have described a variety of scenarios in which application analysis techniques are used. The REDO project has combined these techniques and others, into a prescriptive 'REDO method', which can be applied to any existing application whatever its state and which will then produce a 're-engineered', 'renovated', 'reconstructed' or 'reverse engineered' application, with the same (or similar) functionality, but improved maintainability. The REDO method is very generic and must be customized to specific circumstances

The REDO method is based on a variety of earlier techniques described in the rest of this compendium and benefits from previous ideas, including post-hoc documentation [226], K3's method [324], Holloway's stages [159], Retrofit Procedure [276], LBMS's REVENG 4 level model [193] – taking over a system [52] and the software engineering maintenance cycle [108] – and most extensively, Rock-Evans [270]. Precursors of the REDO method have been used for over a decade.

13.2 Principles

Section 13.2.1 specifies the features that are desirable for a re-engineering method, 13.2.2 gives the central concepts that underlie the current method, and 13.2.3 summarizes the lessons learnt so far.

13.2.1 Objectives

The REDO method is intended to be:

- practical: it can be followed today,
- simple to follow: many of the activities can be done by junior programmers,

- comprehensive: includes all the necessary tasks, covers quality and project management,
- systematic: schedules tasks in an optimal order,
- reliable: always produces a reasonable result,
- based on established techniques where these exist,
- up-to-date: incorporates the latest research results,
- independent of any maintenance environment: is effective and efficient without REDO tools (although obviously easier with !),
- efficient: only include activities that are actually needed,
- incremental: can be done in parts, as needs require and resources permit, each increment bringing benefits,
- totally configurable (see section 13.6),
- supportable by automatic tools.

13.2.2 Central Concepts

The desirable features noted in section 13.2.1 led to a number of design decisions:

1. Although there are many 'methods' in existence today, few are sufficiently well-codified to make it clear what needs to be done at each step. The REDO method must be simple to follow, and is therefore expressed as a sequence of activities described in natural language.
2. The REDO method must be incremental and efficient, so one must be able to reference the individual activities. It is divided into a series of numbered stages, which are themselves subdivided into numbered steps and sub-steps in the sequence to be followed. Letters are used to label unsequenced and concurrent activities.
3. Redocumentation should be done, as far as possible, 'top-down' so that the more significant decisions, such as replacement, porting, addition of new sub-systems etc., are supported as the first priority. High-level documentation is useful for most maintenance activities whereas documentation of details, such as a particular fragment of code, may only be relevant when that fragment itself is to be changed. Rather than attempting to reverse the sequence and processes of forward engineering as most reverse engineering approaches do, the REDO method recovers information in the most efficient order for supporting ongoing maintenance activities.
4. There is a generic REDO method which is independent of any maintenance environment, but the baseline refinement (see section 13.5) is described as though everything is done by humans who record their results on paper. Use of computer support is discussed in section 13.7.

5. The use of a repository is not specified, because currently available repository products center on data dictionary-like facilities, which do not support the majority of maintenance activities. In addition, the take-up of CASE technology is by no means as universal as their suppliers would like us to believe. When repositories commonly include the full range of design information and the textual and diagrammatic tools to manipulate them, then they will have become maintenance environments in their own right.

6. After re-engineering each component must have a single, simply expressed, but precisely defined purpose (not necessarily in the target language). This is an important design principle for all kinds of design activity, generalized from Constantine's work [353].

7. Any change to the implementation must be retested: even changes to comments can and do go wrong.

8. Information is available from many sources: the most appropriate should be chosen each time.

9. The method is structured around 'products', tangible outputs from each step, rather than around techniques. This makes the method more maintainable as new techniques are invented and more easily configurable, based on available inputs and desired outputs.

10. Modern applications incorporate a mixture of approaches besides the traditional compiled source code. These may include library modules, communication with an independently executing DBMS, use of interpreted languages such as JCL and SQL, event handling of graphical user interfaces, specification languages for database schemas, and even user interface definition tools [306, 357] which avoid explicit source code altogether.

13.2.3 History of the REDO Method

Version 1 of the REDO method was created to bring together existing manual techniques into as complete and concrete a prescriptive method as possible and thus provide a common background and framework for the REDO tool designers. It also provided a place to record our growing knowledge of practical re-engineering including techniques, tips and hints.

The Version 1 method rapidly grew to over 150 sequential steps with associated checklists, standards etc. At the same time, we had problems in providing a clear economic justification for complete re-engineering. Commercial practice indicated that this is rarely attempted and that incremental redocumentation (see chapter 8.3) is the norm. We had therefore recognized the need to support an incremental approach, which could be continued when resources were available. Originally we felt that this could be dealt with by the sort of adjustments or interpretations commonly applied when following the original waterfall life cycle model [28] such as:

- staged release of functionality, now called incremental development by Gilb [134],

- doing independent activities in parallel, for example coding different modules,
- backtracking to remove defects resulting from earlier work.

However, we soon realized that these mechanisms were inadequate since the choice of increments is central to the economic justification for re-engineering them, so a commercially viable method could not reasonably treat them as trivia to be handled by the reader, but should examine the issues fully and incorporate suitable mechanisms explicitly in the method.

Meanwhile, the REDO tool designers and domain experts had been developing their understanding of the maintainer's problem. This led to the agreement to move to Version 2 of the REDO method, which would be a 'logical method' with a number of different 'physical' options using different tools.

13.3 The REDO Methodology

REDO now provides more a methodology than simply a method. It comes in four parts:

- the generic REDO method for re-engineering, described in 13.4, which needs refinement before it can be applied to practical situations,
- a baseline refinement of the generic REDO method for manual re-engineering (see 13.5),
- alternative refinements of the generic REDO method for different application domains, maintenance environments (see chapters 14 and 16),
- ideas for justifying and planning a re-engineering project, based on the above items (see section 13.6.4).

It has proved difficult to explain such a complex system in a clear, easy-to-follow way. The methodology separates the generic REDO method containing the technician's view of what needs to be done, from the manager's view which includes the choice of what exactly is to be reverse engineered, how far the reverse engineering will go, controlling the process and the key decision points, estimates etc.

13.4 The Generic REDO Method

The generic REDO method is intended to specify the overall way to tackle any particular re-engineering project. The approach is shown in the information flow diagram 13.1, which is then explained and justified.

Notation

This convention shows each 'process' as a labeled rectangle or 'box', each datastore as a pair of vertically aligned, horizontal line segments, the system, i.e. method, boundary as a rectangle drawn using a dashed line and external entities as ovals outside it. Information flows are shown as line links with arrowheads indicating direction.

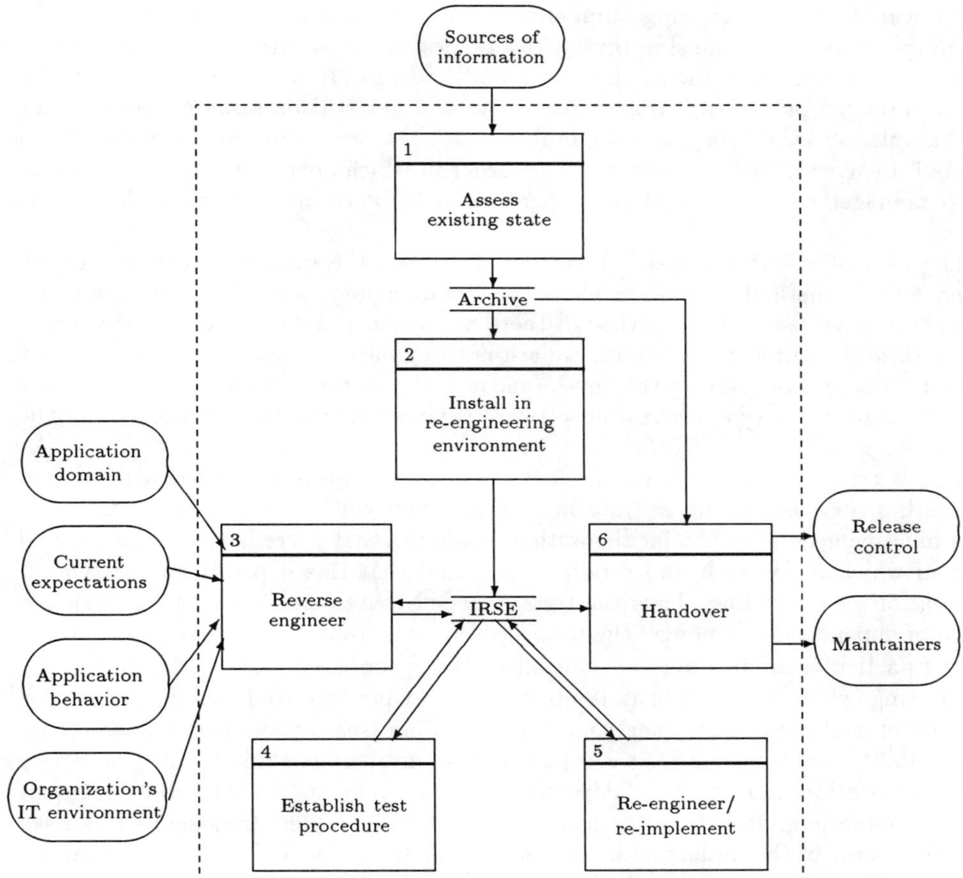

Figure 13.1: The generic REDO method: information flow

The use of a process box does not imply anything further about its behavior, for instance, that outputs are triggered by inputs, or that there is only a single processing server in each process box. Additional incidental information flows may occur where a process requires some small piece of information to complete its task.

Ordering

The processes in the method fall into a single logical sequential order as we shall see, indicated by the increasing number at the top-left of each process box. We take advantage of this significant simplifying feature, describing the processes as a numbered sequence of 'stages' that the application could undergo. However, a process may be entirely omitted or may apparently terminate and yet still be resumed later. Thus for example, SSADM [209], is not simply a 'task list' to be allocated one-by-one to the staff involved. Nor is it necessarily the order in which operations must be started, unless management decide that each operation is to be completed before the next is started.

The idea of a single sequential task list has been the most controversial aspect of the REDO method since it is clear that gaining understanding is generally an iterative process (see 6.4.1). Although there are sound practical reasons for wishing to minimize the number of options, we are not dogmatic on this issue and have not made it an objective. During the development of the method to date, the author has never encountered a case where the software engineer should make a decision about what to do next!

This is crucial. It depends on the fact that the method is concerned with reverse engineering, i.e. producing an information package which is comprehensive, so all parts must be generated. So far the author has found that there is always an optimal order in which to research and produce these and that this depends on the type of information each requires. Thus the recommended process takes a path through the lattice of dependencies amongst the proposed outputs from the process.

The particular application does not affect the optimal sequence except indirectly, by affecting what information it is appropriate to produce and hence causing the omission of irrelevant steps when generating the plan (see section 13.6.4). We ignore the possibility that someone has a complete and accurate understanding of some aspect of the application and wants to skip that step, i.e. refuses to verify and document that understanding. In the end he has to produce the complete package and he risks forgetting some of the details he knows today if he delays, so it is clearly efficient for him to continue with the prescribed step.

The method is not designed to improve our understanding of specific aspects of an application during the maintenance change. It does not attempt to indicate the most efficient way to produce any desired selection of information, given what we already know about the application. Instead the REDO methodology supports managers in planning the next logical increment in a complete reverse and re-engineering project, which would include an efficient way to produce the desired information.

The existence of this optimum ordering with no alternative sequences depends on considerations of efficiency:

- preparatory activities are delayed until required,

- almost all operations benefit from information derived earlier in the method,
- each view can be built up in a logical order,
- related activities should be clustered to reduce the overheads of switching between areas,
- if the above do not indicate a preferred ordering, an arbitrary choice has been made.

The extent to which this applies will become clearer at the lower levels of the REDO method, where the method is refined and instantiated to give concrete details.

Where a conflict occurs, such as when there are advantages in one particular operation following another, and also in its preceding it, this has been taken as a signal that the operations concerned require further decomposition, so that their dependent fragments can be given a single optimum sequence. This is one reason why the granularity of the documented operations varies widely.

Effectively we have adopted simplifications common in planning, namely:

- once a task has started, it continues until completion, i.e. is not suspended,
- all dependencies are from the end of one task to the start of the dependent task, i.e. not start-to-start, end-to-end, lagged etc.

This approach makes it easier to follow the method and to configure it.

13.4.1 Stage 1: Assess Existing State

This covers the gathering, recording, classification and assessment of existing sources of information, for instance, design documents, source files, configuration management records. The major tangible output is an archive of all the relevant items identified and an analysis of the current state of the application.

The assessment needs to be sufficiently detailed to plan the rest of the re-engineering project and to establish the best available baseline set of items on which to base future work, thus reducing the volume of material to be processed. The assessment should not go further as this would require the level of understanding generated in Stage 3 and beyond, so is more efficiently left until then.

The search for information should in principle be open: look for anything and everything about the application. This sounds expensive. However, one will generally be able to get a good picture of what exists and be able to find say 95% of this, at a reasonable cost. Once one has found something significant, such as a draft User Manual, the search can be directed towards more recent and more definitive versions. There is normally a fairly obvious distinction between high payoff activities which may produce complete items, for instance source files, specifications and test reports, and low payoff activities, which will tend to produce small 'snippets' of information, such as searching departmental progress reports.

Snippet-hunting is rarely cost-effective, but is useful when:

- the obvious high payoff possibilities have been exhausted, and snippets may provide clues to, or even unexpectedly copies of, important material,

- the search is for something specific and it can be localized to a small area, for instance, which variant was released on such and such a date? Did it contain any outstanding problems?

13.4.2 Stage 2: Install Application in Re-engineering Environment

A suitable re-engineering environment must be designed, acquired and set-up. This will include a variety of facilities, including at least:

- editing facilities for the implementation and for documents,
- configuration management (can be implemented by clerical procedure but automation is preferred).

The baseline chosen in Stage 1 must be imported and upgraded to be maintainable during the re-engineering project in the new environment. The environment and its contents constitute the IRSE: the *Integrated Re-engineering Support Environment.* Stage 2 is separated from Stage 1 because assessment of the application's current state and future requirements should precede the design of the re-engineering environment. This in turn means that when information is first identified, there is normally no suitable re-engineering environment in which to record it: hence the *archive.* The archive should be a low-cost solution: a record of what exists and where to find it, in case we need to repeat or extend the search for information later. Improving on this is strictly the business of Stage 2 and beyond.

13.4.3 Stage 3: Reverse Engineer

Stage 3 takes the existing information recorded in the IRSE in Stage 2, analyses it and merges in a range of other information, in order to create a complete 'documentation package'. This may include not only traditional paper documents, but also online query and hypertext facilities, animated or simulated specifications and other modelling and analysis tools.

The external entities used in Stage 3 provide additional information about the application's relation to the external world now, rather than historically. This could be in a variety of forms: word processor document files, commented source files, screen-dumps, sample reports, handwritten notes, a CASE repository etc., or most likely some mixture of these.

The externally-supplied information includes:

Application Domain: knowledge of the aspects of the external world relevant to this type of application and knowledge of a range of other attempts to build similar or overlapping applications

Current Expectations: the current requirements, wishes, assumptions and preferences of those with responsibilities dependant on the application. This includes the circumstances in which the application is used, the 'business rules' it should embody, and the expectations of systems which encompass or interface to it, whether automated or human. More precisely it includes knowledge of the information to be processed, the operations required and the results expected. The original requirements can be useful as a basis for this and in explaining the intended and thus the actual behavior.

Application Behavior: behavioral knowledge, i.e. observations of, and beliefs about, what the application does when in operation. Particularly important are observations of its interactions with its external world and mental models of the processes it is carrying out, particularly if derived from the original designers of the application. (Some interactions may be obscure, for instance, the use of machine resources affects other applications sharing them).

Organization's IT environment: knowledge of the organization's current and historical development, maintenance and operating environments: standards, procedures, methods, techniques, tools, training, project management, quality assurance, IT strategy etc.

One should not forget the reverse engineer's own resources: knowledge of the semantics of any source languages, the ability to reason about, dry-run, trace and instrument the implementation, to conduct experiments with carefully chosen data values, to intercept communications, to observe the changing program state etc.

Stage 3 produces whatever documentation package is required, within the constraints of the available data, knowledge, and resources. This is returned to the IRSE for possible further refinement in later stages and to facilitate transfer to subsequent maintainers. It may therefore, sometimes be sensible to restart the search for information. This is not done within Stage 3, but by resuming Stage 1 and bringing any useful new material through Stage 2 into the IRSE.

13.4.4 Stage 4: Establish Test Procedure

Stage 4 establishes an appropriate test procedure for the application, incorporating any suitable existing material. It follows Stage 3, since most forms of testing presuppose a specification of what behavior is expected, for instance, functional testing assumes that functionality has been specified, which is produced in Stage 3. It precedes Stage 5 because of the need to have adequate regression testing facilities before making changes to the implementation. Clearly, one should not make a significant investment in implementation-specific testing of components to be re-engineered (for instance structural or 'white box') unless this is needed to unravel the existing implementation.

If we exclude the 'black box' testing of components, implementation-specific testing is uncommon, due to the effort needed and the lack of commercially available tools to support it. Like code walkthroughs and the addition of pre- and post-conditions and loop invariants, it requires or at least generates a very high level of understanding of the existing implementation, which may exceed that of the original developers if they did not do the same originally. The cost will certainly exceed that which would have been incurred had this work been done initially, unless better tools are now available. However, it is rare for this level of understanding to be needed for more than a short section here and there. Indeed, if the reliability requirements indicate this level of testing is needed, one must ask why this was not specified originally and whether the application generally is upgradable to this level.

We therefore, recommend that if re-engineering or re-implementation is to be attempted, the creation of any required implementation-specific tests should be included as part of those activities.

13.4.5 Stage 5: Re-engineer/Re-implement

Stage 5 is concerned with improving the implementation, in contrast to Stage 3 which is concerned only with establishing an appropriate documentation package. Thus any change to an application's source code will be done in Stage 5, even if the intention is merely to improve its intelligibility. Source files generally include varying levels of documentation (section 8.4). Re-engineering and re-implementation are treated as one, because they are the extremes of a continuum with no precise distinction in practice. Re-engineering, at one extreme, would be the restructuring of source with no access to any design information, while at the other, re-implementation would be the recoding of the design with no access to the existing source. In the former case, it is not sensible to remove design information from the source before operating on it: even automatic analyzers will normally look for patterns corresponding to design abstractions, and are therefore extracting design information, if only 'on-the-fly'. In the latter case, since the purpose of re-implementation must be to make some improvement, access to the existing version is useful to check that any proposed new approach will in fact deliver an improvement.

This stage includes the preparation of any required implementation-specific tests. Previous implementation specific tests may well be helpful. Ideally these would be upgraded automatically as the implementation is changed/replaced.

Similarly if the re-engineering project is being combined with other changes, one can usually leave the testing of areas planned to undergo substantial modification to those responsible for those modifications, pointing out the relevance of any existing test material.

Stage 5 follows Stage 4, which establishes a test procedure, because of the need to check that the Stage 5 changes have not adversely affected the application. It follows Stage 3 because of the need to understand the application before making changes. However, the intention to proceed to Stage 5 would affect the objectives of Stage 3, since one would wish to minimize the documentation of aspects which are to change. Stage 5 includes steps to update the documentation package as necessary.

13.4.6 Stage 6: Handover

This is the final stage of the REDO method, which installs the definitive version of the application in operational use through whatever release control mechanisms are applied by the organization and transfers responsibility for it back to the maintainers, along with the documentation package, appropriate tools etc.

Clearly, Stage 6 must always be the last stage of any re-engineering project, whatever other stages are omitted. It may, however, occur several times, as significantly improved 'increments' become available, particularly if the re-engineering project is lengthy, and significant maintenance is frequently required.

13.5 The REDO Method for Manual Re-engineering

The generic REDO method has been refined to produce a detailed re-engineering method capable of being implemented with a minimal set of tools, ie tools to change sections of the existing implementation, a reliable file store and means to cause the execution of the revised application, such as a compiler, a linker and appropriate libraries and invocation facilities.

The result is similar in scope and detail to Version 1 of the REDO method (see section 13.2.3) and will be published in a future manual for re-engineering.

13.6 Customizing the REDO Method

Customization can take place in various ways:

- the development of a new refinement of the generic REDO method,
- modification of an existing refinement to suit a particular group of applications,
- configuration to suit a particular environment or organization,
- the planning of a particular re-engineering project involving the creation of a suitable work breakdown structure from an existing refinement.

Each will be examined in turn.

13.6.1 Developing a New Refinement

The generic REDO method specified in section 13.4 lacks detail about precisely what activities could be required, their inputs, outputs, quality criteria etc, etc. The REDO method for manual re-engineering in section 13.5 serves as a useful pattern to show the sort of detail needed. It also acts as a reservoir of good practice which other refinements should draw on and make use of wherever possible.

Section 13.2 gives the major design principles behind the REDO method and these should be maintained in future refinements. Section 13.4 defines a diagrammatic notation and the ordering principles to be used.

13.6.2 Modification of an Existing Refinement

Again, the principles of the REDO method should be preserved (see sections 13.2 and 13.4). The creation of a modified refinement is a significant investment and should only be undertaken if a reasonable number of re-engineering projects are expected to use it. If not, a project-specific plan may be more suitable, which can then be reused and modified for any further similar projects.

13.6.3 Configuration for a Specific Environment

This is undertaken when an organization wishes to make the REDO method specific to its environment, mentioning particular tools, machines, people, standards etc, that are to be involved in their re-engineering projects.

13.6.4 Planning a Re-engineering Project

One must first identify, adapt or create an appropriate refinement of the REDO method. One should then select the 'increment', the tasks and areas which will produce the best cost-benefit mix in the circumstances. This requires appropriate experience, which will be codified as it emerges and a consensus is reached.

One can then estimate and schedule the activities based on staff skills, availability of tools etc. We hope to provide further guidance as to reasonable 'norms' when more experience is available. However, it should be remembered that these are still very rough in the software development field. There is no equivalent of the building trade's manual of standard costs.

Quality criteria are included in the task descriptions, so can be used as the basis for reviews. These issues are discussed further in chapter 17.

13.7 Computer Support For The REDO Method

This section examines the generic REDO method to find opportunities where automated support would be helpful. REDO has developed tools which tackle the majority of these. We look at each stage in turn.

13.7.1 Stage 1: Assess Existing State

The collection of existing material is largely done by interviewing parties involved and searching records on existing systems. The only significant opportunity for computer support is in recording the results of the search. This seems to be a very straightforward application.

The assessment of material is limited to choosing the best baseline from which to start further work. It requires access to the material, analytical skills and experience. At the current state of knowledge, opportunities for automated support are limited to comparing components and displaying their differences.

13.7.2 Stage 2: Install Application in Re-engineering Environment

The creation of a suitable Integrated Re-engineering Support Environment requires the ability to install, and possibly to build, new tools, so normal development facilities should be appropriate. The loading of the baseline material into the IRSE is clearly essential, but largely determined by the proposed content and structure of that database.

13.7.3 Stage 3: Reverse Engineer

Reverse engineering is a complex activity and can be supported in many ways, for instance:

Mechanization:

- interrelating loaded components for complete multi-language, multi-component applications and allowing them to be viewed and updated,
- support for ad hoc queries and analyzers, producing simple, structured and diagrammatic views of the implementation and its behavior, in a variety of notations including highlighted source code, object-oriented Z, data models, user-defined metrics, control flow, dataflow and static analyses, slices and traces,
- capturing external information and relating this to existing material,
- writing new or improved documentation.

Procedurization:

- assessing existing user interfaces,
- a hypertext version of this compendium.

All of these avenues have been pursued within REDO. Interestingly, none of these tasks have yet been entirely automated – all benefit from some user input to supply external data or direction.

13.7.4 Stage 4: Establish Test Procedure

If a test procedure has to be created from scratch during maintenance this is often done by recording a selection of real data and results for later repetition and comparison. The automatic generation of test procedures from functional specifications and from source code has been much researched in the past [146]. Being concerned with maintenance, REDO's interest is primarily in regression testing.

13.7.5 Stage 5: Re-engineer/ Re-implement

REDO chose to pursue a number of topics under re-engineering:

- control flow simplification,
- remodularization to a JSD-based design, ie data-based restructuring,
- data remodelling,
- 'inverse engineering', deriving a formal specification and then automatically generating a new system from that,
- user interface improvement,

- conversion to vector and parallel architectures.

As was discussed in section 13.4.5, there is no clear division between re-engineering and re-implementation. We have used the latter term for the replacement of an existing area using a normal development process, given initial specifications derived during Stage 3 and additional requirements chosen to improve on the existing version based on the assessment of it done at the start of Stage 5. Since REDO is about maintenance rather than development, we decided against pursuing further research in the re-implementation area.

13.7.6 Stage 6: Handover

The delivery of improved material back to the operating environment and to the maintainers is an essential step. However, the problems are mainly practical issues: what maintenance tools are available, what import facilities do they have, how can REDO's data be mapped onto them? Standardization is coming, through IRDS, CDIF, AD/Cycle etc, so we expect the problems to reduce over the next few years. We do not see any maintenance-specific problems which require our attention.

13.7.7 General

Reverse engineers will also find it useful to have access to a range of other general-purpose facilities, such as word processing and planning and progress monitoring.

14

Domain-Specific Issues in the REDO Method

M. Shenton, A. Davies, M. Price,
Marconi Command and Control Systems Ltd, UK

14.1 The Real-Time Domain

The characteristics of real-time systems were discussed in section 5.2. Here we will develop task definitions in more detail as a step towards a prescriptive guide for the reverse engineering of real-time systems.

Section 14.1.1 gives an overall strategy to the reverse engineering process in the context of the REDO method.

Section 14.1.2 analyzes further particular stages within the overall strategy and provides some detail on how an understanding of some of the characteristics of real-time systems might be achieved.

14.1.1 Steps In The Reverse Engineering Of Real-Time Systems

This section identifies the most significant activities associated with the reverse engineering of real-time systems. The emphasis is on Stage 3 of the REDO method, where the particular characteristics of real-time systems need to be addressed. The overall process of reverse engineering real-time systems is however performed in the wider context of Stages 1 through to 6, and these stages are referenced in the text where applicable. The rigorous list of activities in the REDO method permits an assessment to be made on the level of analysis and detail to be applied at each stage. The level of analysis and detail cannot be defined precisely, this will be dependent on the overall business objective of the reverse engineering process and the amount of time and money available. This may vary from a short time duration examination of a precisely defined section of the source code, to a full and exhaustive analysis of a system, e.g. for re-engineering purposes.

The terms used in this section are those normally used in the real-time domain. There are areas where this notation differs to that used in the REDO method, if the underlying purpose is not identifiable then a description of the term is provided.

The main steps in the reverse engineering process for real-time systems are shown in figure 14.1. The starting information shown in the top row of blocks is used with the processes shown to generate the information representations at the bottom. These forms of representation are typical of those which can be used to describe real-time systems, but are neither unique nor exhaustive, and other representations may be appropriate in particular situations.

When the reverse engineering process is started the information listed below should be available. The collation of this information is performed in Stage 1 of the REDO method and forms a part of the archive of all the relevant items:

1. Supporting documentation. This covers a variety of different information that may be available, all of which may provide corroborative evidence as to the function and performance of the program. For example: feasibility report; technical proposal; requirements specifications; functional specifications; test procedures, test rigs and records; bug reports; or other engineers' notes.

2. The source code. This may only be available as a result of the disassembly of the runtime program image. In which case it will be at assembly level, contain no comments, and have no meaningful labels, names, etc. If it is available in the original source form, then it may be at a higher level, and may have meaningful comments and labels (these, if present, should be treated with due caution, as often when modifications are made to code during its lifetime, the comments are not always meticulously updated).

3. Information about the environment in which the system is intended to run, the operating system, library functions, computer architecture, compiler. Features like interrupt handling, process scheduling and direct-memory-access capabilities will be of particular significance in real-time applications.

4. Information on how to build (compile, link and locate) the software. This is particularly important in many real-time applications. There may be multiple tasks separately compiled and linked for concurrent (or pseudo-concurrent) processes running in one or more processors, where for example the sequence in which modules are compiled can affect the runtime performance of the system.

Stage 3 of the reverse engineering process can be divided, very broadly, into three areas, characterized by the views which are generated. It is these areas where analysis tools, which take into account the needs of real-time systems, would aid the reverse engineer:

1. Data analysis and functional analysis

   This corresponds to the aspects of the *entity* and *functional structure* as described in chapter 7.2. Syntactic analysis of the source code will lead us initially

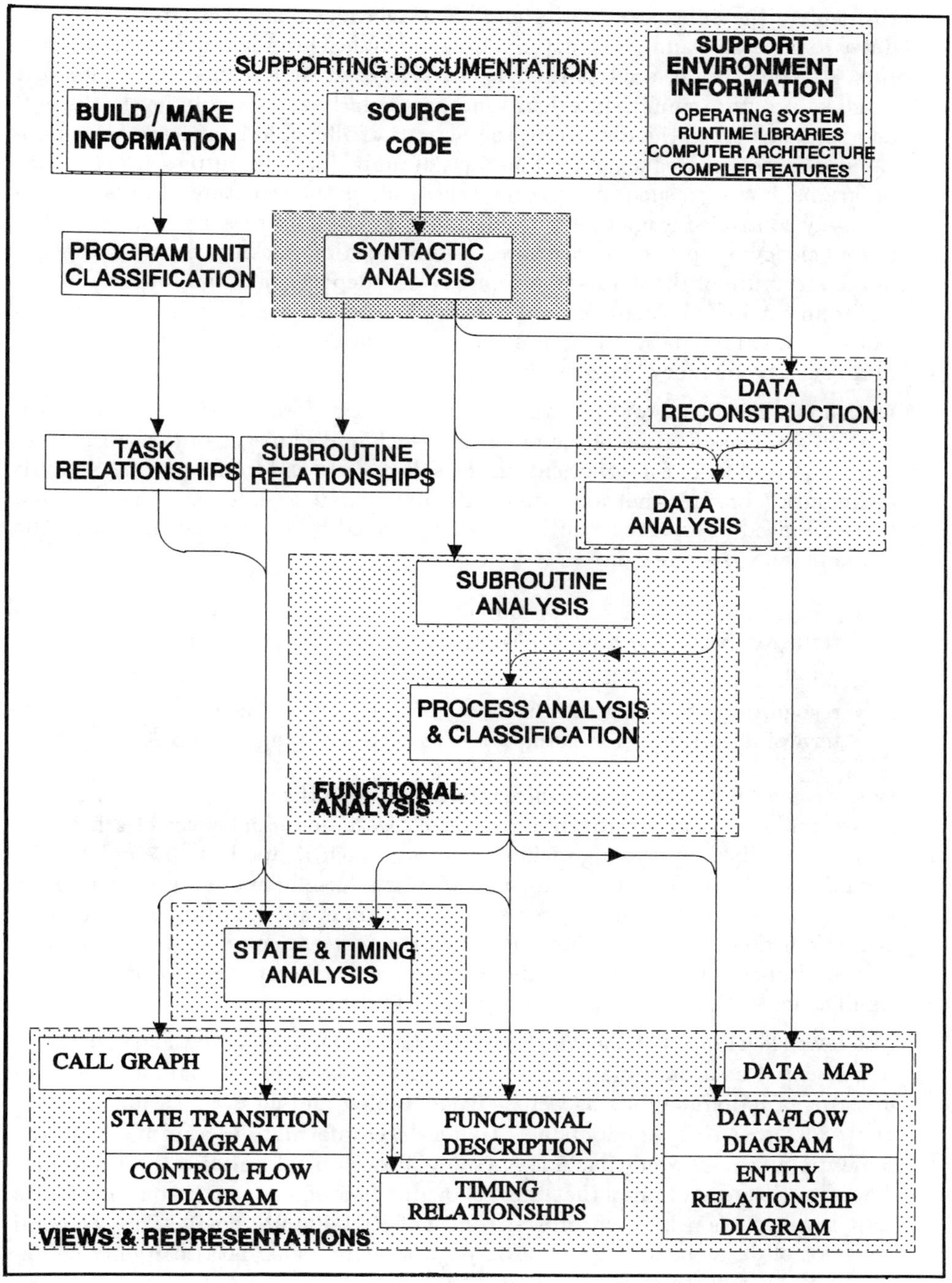

Figure 14.1: The main steps in reverse engineering real-time systems

to identify the subroutine units and their relationships. Also to identify the data, its location, and its structure. In some higher-level languages, data structure is explicitly declared (although not always in well-defined places like the heads of program units). In others, and particularly at assembly-level, it is not, and reconstructing the data from the actions of the code is at least as complicated a process as deducing the functions of individual subroutines. In real-time programs, however, such information is critical, as the structure of data is often precisely controlled, sometimes at individual bit level, for reasons of speed, memory efficiency, mapping to hardware, communication packing, etc. An analysis of the structure of the data will also, therefore, depend on details of the support environment information; computer word/byte sizes; compiler memory allocations for different data types; possible permutations of the computer memory map (such as memory bank switching).

Data analysis and subroutine analysis must proceed closely together. The identification and classification of the processes which make up each of the subroutines can be derived from the comments in the source code and from semantic analysis techniques (consider that any comments may be out of date with the code and therefore need to have their authenticity confirmed by a semantic analysis). The semantic analysis relies on:

- recognition of the effects of individual instructions, and of instruction patterns, on particular data types (for instance: "This is adding a data slot to a linked list"),
- recognition of the algorithmic effect of a sequence of instructions on a pattern of data types (for example: "This is performing a bubble-sort").

Both of these processes may require interaction with the user (perhaps to decide, for example, whether or not in a given context the nominal effect of a function is best described by the algorithmic process which it appears to emulate). It should also be noted that in real-time systems a technique often used is look-up tables, where a functional requirement in the form of an algorithm or calculation is implemented in data rather than code to increase speed. This technique may be impossible to deduce without some knowledge or speculation as to the significance of the preset values in such a data array.

The lower-level information which results from an analysis of data structure can be presented as a data map. This will need to be capable of mapping the data in terms of individual bits as well as fields, tables, and files (which may be adequate for other software domains). Higher-level information, resulting from the semantic analysis, would include entity relationship information, and dataflow diagrams (bearing in mind that these show the functional transformation of data as it is acted upon by each process, and not its temporal flow). The temporal behavior of data (including input/output, or source/sink data) can only be determined by a state analysis. This is because of the possibility of concurrent processing, pre-emptive process interruption and synchronization effects.

2. State and timing analysis

   State and timing analysis give the views of the *process structure* and *system dynamics* on the levels of the *implementation model* and *logical system* (chapter 7.2). From the build information we can establish the general relationship between tasks in the system. Tasks in separately linked, concurrently running, units will not have a direct call graph relationship with one another. Although the running of a process in one unit may be influenced or enabled (or even interrupted) by circumstances in another.

   Combining information about the subroutine relationships within each task, and the inter-task relationships, a call graph can be derived to show the relationships between the executing functions. Combining this information with the subroutine functionality, expressed in terms of its impact on data which is critical to or characteristic of system state, will yield a state analysis. This can be expressed, for example, as a state transition diagram, control matrix, and/or a control flow diagram.

   What is critical in a real-time system is the time-relationship between states, or between controls (stimuli) and states. The time to change between any two states or events may have a maximum and/or a minimum value. Additional effort to the standard state analysis would be required to derive this information, and an appropriate form of presentation also needs to be devised. The techniques that can be used to derive the state information are explored in the following section.

3. Information views and representations

   Each of the bottom group of rectangles in figure 14.1 is not simply a representational entity, but is itself a process, or rather two processes. The information produced by one or more of the analytical processes above it must be selectively extracted, combined and interpreted in a way suitable for the context of the particular representation. For example, the dataflow diagram needs the data's identity and its various relationships, but not its structure. Then the information must be formatted as necessary for presentation. Different back-ends might be applied here to generate, for example, textual, tabular, or graphical output.

   Ultimately we will arrive at some form of functional description. This can be presented textually or graphically, the level of detail or abstraction will depend upon the needs of the reverse engineer and on the nature of the real-time system. For example, the textual information at the top level will describe the nature of the application, such as being an aircraft control system or a computerized manufacturing plant. In graphical form this could be represented as a context diagram (the highest level dataflow representation) showing the major external interfaces. This can be extended to the lower levels of code by adding globally descriptive labels on segments of the program, or individual processes, by user interaction with the outputs of the analyses (perhaps by using some form of template).

   The descriptions obtained are on the level of the *conceptual information system* as described in chapter 7.2.

14.1.2 Analysis Techniques

This section provides analysis techniques that can be used to reverse engineer the characteristics of real-time systems (that were described in section 5.2, and the steps involved in reverse engineering real-time systems (described in section 14.1.1). The techniques described are in places adaptions of techniques described elsewhere in this compendium, here the focus is on the needs of the real-time domain.

1. Reverse engineering tools

   The techniques described below can be formulated as a reverse engineering tool. The level of automation of such a tool will be dependant on the complexity of the particular process. This can vary from a simple text search facility, through to a fully automated tool operating on scoping type instructions. There will be areas where current technology does not permit a fully automated process to be achieved, here syntactic and semantic analysis combined with reverse engineer interaction would provide an effective iterative analysis tool. For example, the Views & Representation section of figure 14.1 can be split into two levels as shown in figure 14.2.

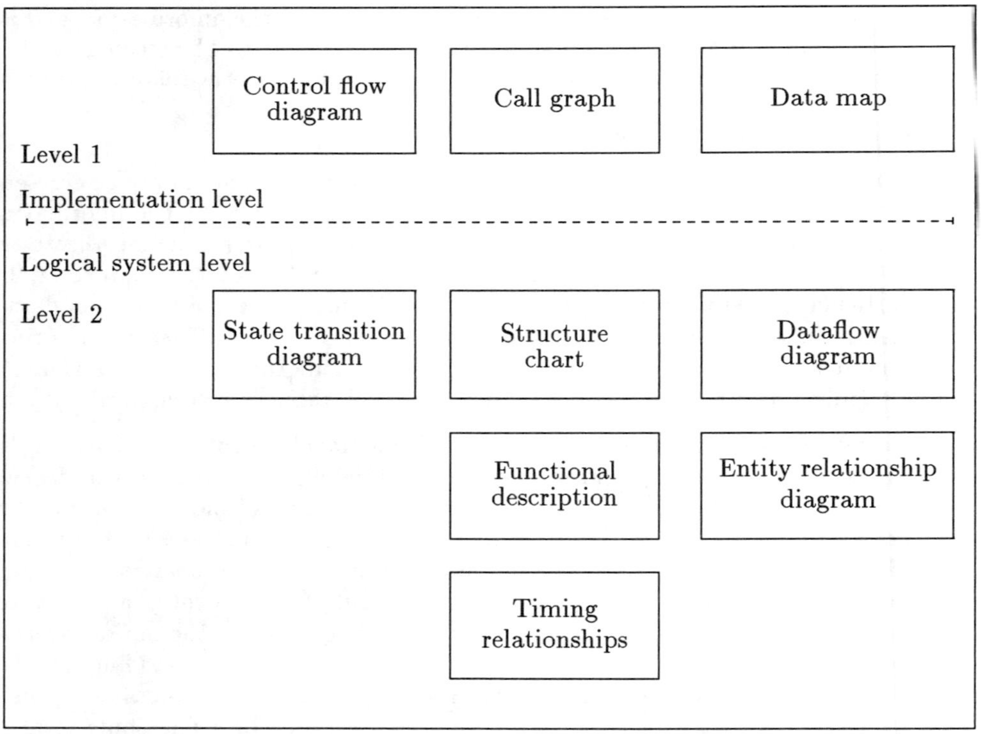

Figure 14.2: Views representation levels

Level 1 is the *implementation model level.* It represents the information that could be largely derived from the static analysis (information is derived from the textual content) of the source code. For example, the subroutine calling relationship required to develop a call graph.

Level 2 is the *logical system level.* It represents that which will require interaction with the reverse engineer. For example, to develop the call graph into a structure chart (this provides information on dataflows, sequential and conditional operations) the reverse engineer may need to provide the sequential and conditional information. Also dynamic analysis (simulation of part or all of a system) can be used to verify a particular hypothesis. The level of simulation may vary from the answering of a 'what-if' scenario to the full animation of a set of events and associated processes for state transition models.

This may be considered a simplification of the problem but it recognizes that tools can primarily perform the mechanical process of identifying relationships. The basis for, and the reasoning behind, those relationships requires the reverse engineer.

2. Management of the design analysis process.

   The amount of reverse engineering performed on a system will depend on a number of business related factors. An important consideration is that software maintenance exercises are often targeted at particular problems or areas of a system. This requires that piecemeal reverse engineering should be permitted to allow an overall view of the system to be developed over a period of time.

   During the analysis of source code and supporting documentation the reverse engineer will develop a number of ideas as to the operation of the system. During the pursuit of these ideas, some will provide good operational information, others will come to a dead end, others will divert from the main path but be considered worth following. In addition, the method of analysis used may need to change to cope with type of information available. For example, having identified a particular data structure the reverse engineer may wish to confirm the functionality of that structure by applying state transition analysis. These different analysis techniques may also be at different levels of completion at times. In order to coordinate these ideas and the information extracted from the use of specific techniques a management system is required.

   Some requirements for such a management system are:

   - A number of views of a system are required to cover: the information source (source code or system documentation), different system representations (dataflow, state analysis, etc.), textual entries from the reverse engineer explaining a particular part of a system.
   - The applying of schemas and sub-schemas against the different views permits the scope of operations to be restricted. This provides the potential for optimizing the execution time of an analysis process by reducing the amount of data analyzed, this in turn optimizes the data returned for the reverse engineer to assess. Such a schema may be applied to a number of

source code modules to separate operating system code from the different tasks and processes performed.

- Control of the attributes for the different views. For example, text fonts to be tailored to suit the application, (a common occurrence here is the use of 132 column mode for source listings).
- Editing facilities:
  - Text string searches within selected schemas, with options for different language naming syntaxes (e.g. case sensitivity, space sensitivity). String match information such as: number of occurrences, files, modules, line numbers. Operations against the match list such as: saving, editing, jumping to the position identified.
  - Adding of explanatory text to source code without modifying the source file. With printing options to show the additional text or not. This represents the traditional way that explanatory notes are added to source listings while the understanding is developing.
  - To transfer areas of text between the views.
- A version control capability, to identify design information that is affected by changes to the source code.

3. Structured analysis examination

Depending on the prime objective of the reverse engineering exercise there are different optimum methods for representing the structure of the real-time system.

There are three principle views to be understood during the analysis:

- processes: the actions to be performed against the data input to the system,
- control: the events that trigger the processes to start and control their order of execution,
- data: the data that is input into, manipulated and output from, the system.

Shlaer and Mellor [281] identified three basic strategies to software analysis (note this reference refers to the forward engineering context, the following applies the same strategies to reverse engineering):

(a) Functional decomposition [95].

The order of assessment is: Process, Control, Data. The system is presented as a single large primary process, which is sub-divided into a number of sub-processes that describe the data connections between each other, this is repeated until a number of primitive processes exist, see figure 14.3. The controls that trigger the events and the state model analysis of the primary process and primitive processes are then developed. Finally the data identified in the process and control phases is organized. Advantages: It is the oldest strategy and therefore probably the most widely used method, having intuitive appeal and therefore easy to use and understand. Disadvantages: In a forward engineering context it is non-reproducible, that is two engineers working on the same problem will probably produce different implementations. This may impact on the future reuse policy of the system knowledge extracted.

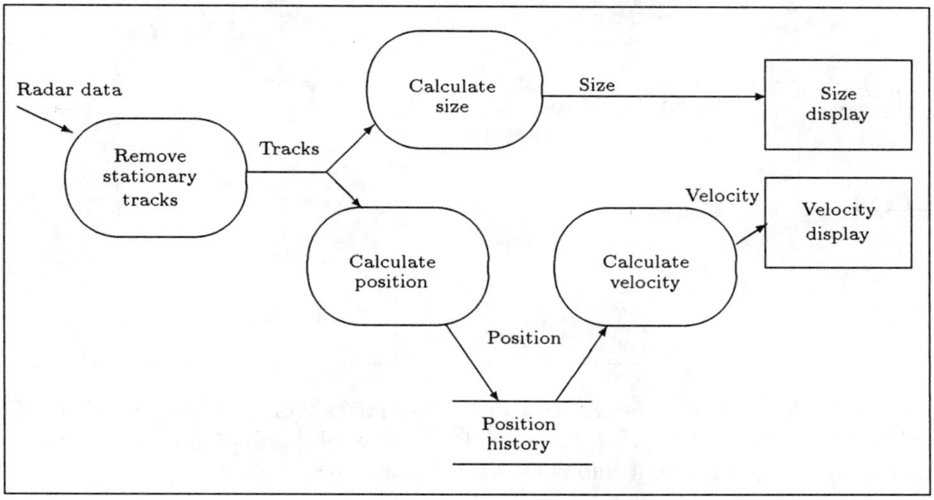

Figure 14.3: Process identification in a dataflow diagram

(b) Event response [322].

The order of assessment is: Control, Process, Data. The system is viewed as a black box that receives a number of external stimuli and makes a number of defined responses, see figure 14.4. The response required for each external event defines the control transformations and the process(es) to be performed in each case. The data requirements then evolve from the need to interconnect the different processes. Advantages: identifies the system interface readily. Disadvantages: in a forward engineering context this technique is sensitive to system interface changes.

(c) Object-oriented [282].

The order of assessment is: Data, Control, Process. Data is the driving force of this approach. The objects and their attributes are identified, see figure 14.5, the life cycles or states of the objects are then assessed to define the control aspect. The processes are then created to perform the implementation of the objects and their life cycles. Advantages: provides very tight control of the data aspect of a system. The techniques were developed for real-time systems. Disadvantages: can be difficult to recognize the system interface. It is a new technique and does not have the same intuitive feel of acceptability as the previous two methods.

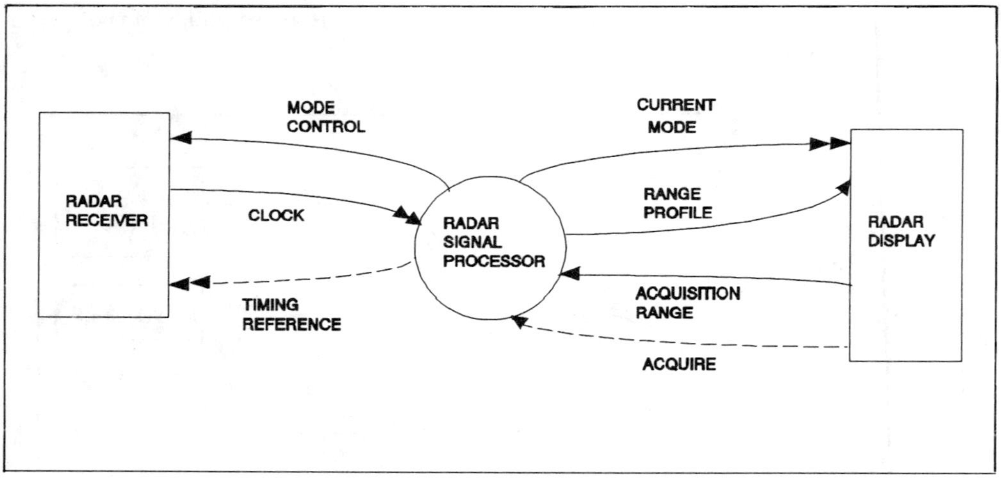

Figure 14.4: A Context schema identifies external events. Notations are used to differentiate between events: data (solid line), control (dashed line), time discrete (single arrowhead), time continuous (double arrowhead)

The order of assessments are as stated in reference [281], it is worth noting however that the methodology references [95, 322, 282] offer some flexibility on the two lower order aspects, depending on the nature of the application.

The different techniques emphasize particular system characteristics that can be used to make the reverse engineering task easier. For example, if the reverse engineering objective is to allow performance optimization then the functional decomposition may be the most suitable. If it is to satisfy that all customer interfaces are correctly dealt with, then the event response techniques may be the most suitable. If it is with the aim to maximizing reuse, then an object-orientated approach may be the most suitable.

An overriding factor may be to adopt an approach that most closely resembles the original approach taken. This is most likely to give the simplest representation with the highest level of automation (and therefore the lowest level of reverse engineer interaction). There are though certain approaches that can be taken to reduce the size of such problems to an acceptable level. Such techniques for the object-oriented strategy are discussed by Duntemann and Marinacci [104].

A tool to cover the above strategies needs to provide analysis facilities for data, control and processes. To permit a particular strategy to be adopted the tool must allow flexibility in how the dependencies are specified, and provide different notations to suit the different methodologies available.

4. State, control and timing analysis

Within real-time systems the study of one of the state, control or timing characteristics invariably develops an understanding of the other two areas. For

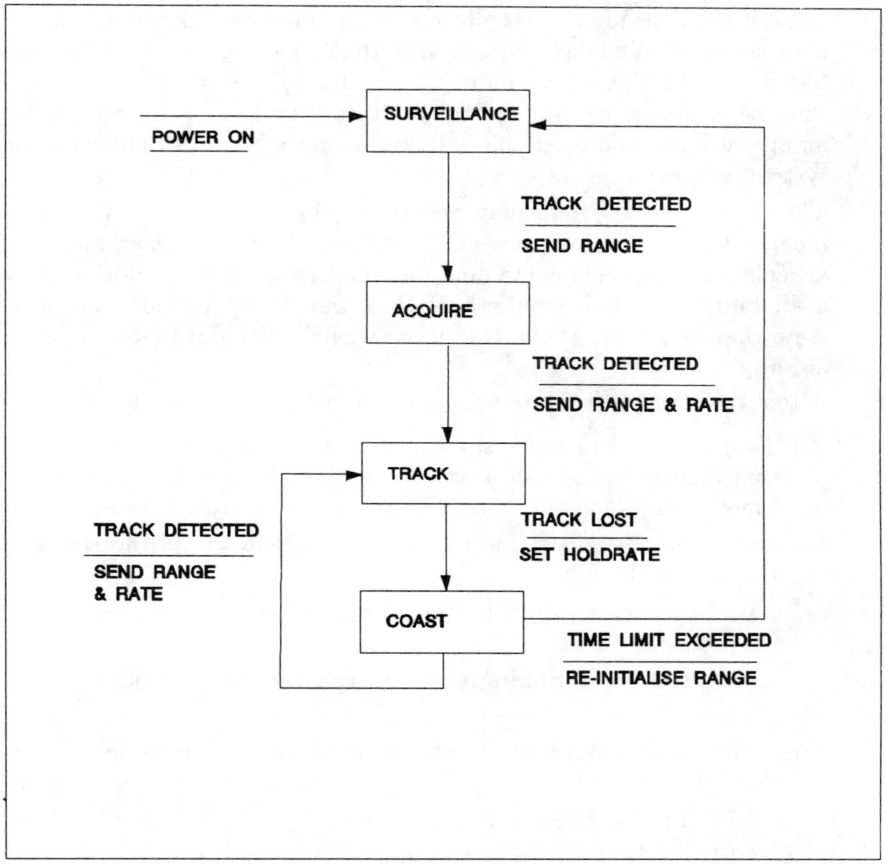

Figure 14.5: An information structure diagram

each control parameter there is a state relationship, both analyze triggers that cause changes within the real-time system. Derived from these changes is an understanding of the time relationships between states and events.

(a) State analysis

The concept of state recognizes that the interactions with people or machinery will depend on what has happened in the past. For example, a cash dispenser will only release money after the correct password and an amount has been entered, the two numbers may have the same value but because the system has gone into a different state they have a different meaning; an operation invalid when in the power up state becomes valid when in the system configuration state.

The analysis of a system may well reveal that the concept of state exists independently in many places and at different levels. For example, an operating system typically containing mechanisms to control priority, resource availability, time slicing and others, these though will be independent of the state that may exist at the task level, where human or machine interfaces are implemented.

A tool to assist in the state analysis of a system needs to identify:

(i) The characteristics of a state model. These are, the number of states that may exist, the title associated with each state, the conditions that cause changes in state, and the actions performed on the state change.

(ii) Areas where engineer interaction can be used to aid the efficiency of the tool, such as:

- The identification of an area of code where the state transitions are assessed.
- Title of the variables that represent the states, conditions and/or the actions.

(iii) Coding techniques that are used to implement state models. Common techniques are:

- IF, THEN, ELSE statements.
- SWITCH or CASE statements.

(iv) Rules that can be applied to analyze the level of completeness:

- Can all states be reached.
- Can all states (except possibly the final state) be exited.
- Are all condition and action relationships covered.

(v) Suitable view formats: State transition diagram, tabular matrix, see figure 14.6.

(vi) Performance assessment of the state model against system functionality. This simulates the state model developed, logging conditions and actions to engineer-controlled stimuli and 'what-if' type analysis. Such simulators exist in forward engineering tools [309], the ability to interface into such a tool would offer the scope for reduced purchasing and training costs.

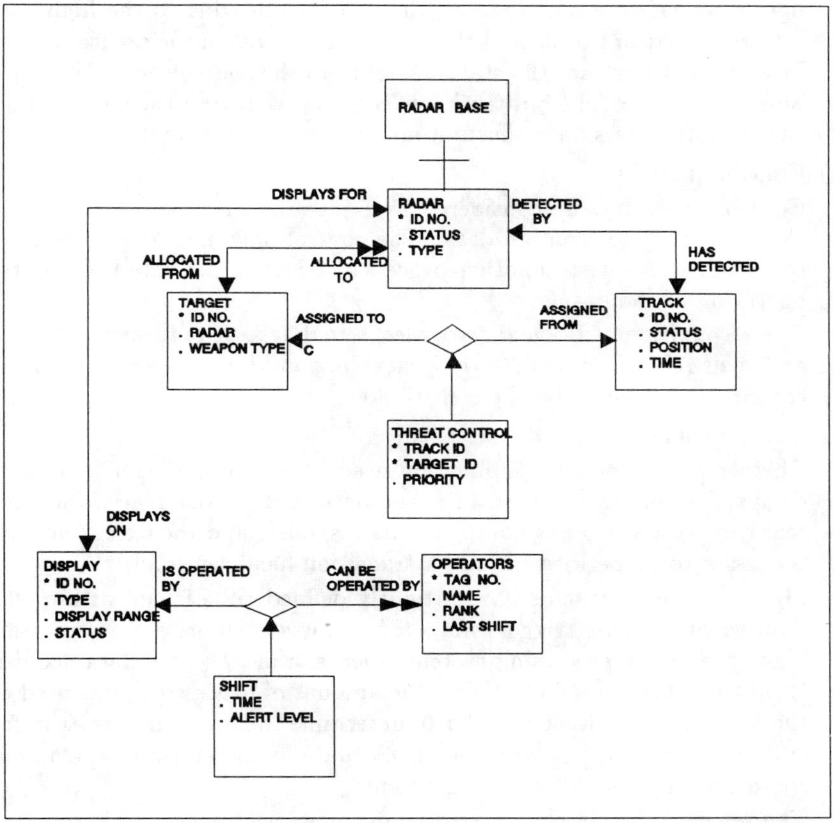

Figure 14.6: A state transition diagram identifying the states, events causing a change in the state and the actions to be performed for each event

Real-time systems have a further level of state embedded in the hardware interface devices used, e.g. interrupt controllers, interval timers, interface controllers (serial, parallel, asynchronous, synchronous). Modern integrated circuits provide a variety of operating modes within a single device. The identification of the mode used and the different states within that mode provides valuable knowledge on the interface characteristics between the real world and the software system. Although the device control and configuration information is within the source code, due to the high usage of bit-orientated protocols and the functionality within the device, it may not be possible to extract the state model from the source code. The ability to build a state model from the knowledge derived from the source code and the manufacturers data sheets would assist interface analysis.

(b) Control analysis

Control flows may be considered as a pipeline that can carry a go/no-go signal, but do not contain data. The control flow is sent from one process (or external event) to another process in order to activate it or control its operation in some way.

The recognition of Boolean variables, semaphore or rendezvous operations, and their relationships with the generating and receiving tasks or processes can be used to describe the control flow.

(c) Timing analysis

There are two aspects of timing that need to be considered. The transitional delays that occur between an event occurring in the real world and the real-time system having completed its response, and the execution times of processes to be performed once a transition has been made.

Many real-time systems have a tightly defined time frame within which a number of external triggers may occur. Such systems are associated with high-speed data processing systems such as radar, sonar, data acquisition. It may be important to establish the amount of processing time used out of the total time available in order to determine the operating margins for the current system, or for re-engineering situations to determine the amount of spare capacity for future enhancements.

The relevant system characteristics include:

- Determination of the principal timing constraint, for instance for a radar system this would be the transmitter trigger timing. It would also be necessary to take into account any variations or jitter in that signal, and changes due to a change in system state.
- Identification of the combinations of additional external events that could occur within the time frame.
- Consideration of the data buffering techniques used. This may affect the software system processing cycle times, for example a cyclic buffer store can be used to allow an instantaneous peak load to be absorbed over a number of time cycles.
- Consideration of the times taken by different processing paths through the software. This needs to identify the variation in execution times

as well as the average execution times, since worse case times may be important to the system operation. The efficiency of instruction types may need to be considered, for example floating point instructions normally have longer execution times than integer instructions.

- Identification of processes and time intervals where an external event(s) is disabled. This is important when making a system change since extending these periods unduly can cause external events to be missed. The technique is used during times of important numeric processing or during the exchange of control flags (such as semaphores). It can be analyzed by the recognition of certain instructions (for instance enable and disable interrupts) in relation to the overall system timing.
- Suitable graphical or tabular representation methods.

The linking of the reverse engineering analysis with forward engineering tools generally termed 'performance analyzers' provides a possible timing analysis technique. These give histogram comparisons of time against identified blocks of code, see figure 14.7.

5. Hardware interface analysis

Real-time systems have a high dependence on their hardware interfaces. The special-to-type interface circuits used are often responsible for manipulating the external interfaces to provide the software system with a more concise and manageable set of events. Typical operations are: combining a number of external interfaces into a single trigger with a status word that can be interrogated; using a single external trigger to generate a number of additional time-controlled triggers; use of external interfaces to control other signals. Such techniques are used for both human and machine interfaces.

Two areas of tool assistance are envisaged:

- Graphical representation of the hardware interfaces. Representations for logical operations, time delays, switches, knobs, keyboards, etc., can be used to describe the individual interfaces.
- Cross-checking that all software interfaces are covered in the hardware representation.

6. Data analysis

(a) Data types

Aspects of data analysis are required for all types of software systems. Points important to the real-time domain are:

- Bit operations. These can be identified from variable declarations at the head of or within the program structure, or by the recognition of bit-type logical operations such as AND, OR, XOR.
- The tracing of changes in bit significance through FIXED type data manipulations.

Event	Duration	No. of occurences	% of time
read data	4.00	2	5.7
show data	6.00	2	8.6
set mode	8.00	6	34.3
sort data	6.00	12	51.4
calc. rate	0.00	0	0
o/p rate	0.00	0	0
store data	0.00	0	0

Duration	No. of occurences	Accumulated time	% of time
100 μs – 200 μs	4	605 μs	4.7
200 μs – 400 μs	6	2.15 ms	16.8
400 μs - 800 μs	10	6.00 ms	46.9
800 μs – 2.0 μs	4	4.05 ms	31.6

Figure 14.7: Possible representations of the performance of a system or particular components of a system

- The ability to analyze the data content to determine if there is any redundant information. A method is by the analysis of data lexical listings where similar data names would be checked to ensure there is no unnecessary duplication.

(b) Databases

The use of significant database systems within real-time systems is increasing with the improvements in hardware and system engineering technologies. The different database techniques possible include: piles, sequential, index, hashed, ring [335]. The identification of the database type and key performance characteristics enables the reverse engineer to determine the current performance criteria and the capacity for further additions/changes without producing unacceptable hit rates and overflow buffer management techniques. This area is also typical of data processing applications.

(c) Look-up tables

Look-up tables are a special type of database used in real-time systems. They are used to replace algorithms that would take an unacceptable amount of processing time if executed at the time of use, or, are simply too difficult to express mathematically. They invariably require more memory than the algorithm they replace, but have the advantage of uniform execution times, independent of the seed data value. Types of algorithms implemented as look-up tables are:

- scientific formulae, for instance trigonometric functions, logarithmic.
- mathematically undefinable characteristics, such as linearizing a thermocouple characteristic, cursor speed control.
- pseudo random number sequences,

They are often characterized by the need to perform off-line processing in order to determine their data content. This is then combined with the source code during the system build. This can form a set of fixed data for use during system operation. Or it may form the basis for a data set that is modified during operation by calibration operations (if the characteristics of some real world sensors change with time, temperature or other environmental property).

Reverse engineering of a look-up table directly from the source code would be difficult in many cases. There is a need to access off-line programs that are used to develop the data from the algorithms. This can present additional difficulties where the off-line program is in a different language to the main system program, due to:

- greater range of scientific functions required,
- better text and file manipulations required,
- developed by other software staff, perhaps requiring recognition of different styles.

Characteristics that can help identify the use of look-up tables are:

- Recognition of large data areas.

- Recognition of parameters that are used to index the data area, their data type and the data type of the information extracted.
- Identification and tracking of overlaying type commands (that is, programming commands that are used to rename a particular data area and therefore obscure the true source).

7. System integrity

   System integrity is very important in the real-time domain. The system may be operating standalone for considerable periods of time. This may not be hours or days, but weeks and months. Also the equipment may be performing partly, or entirely, life-critical monitoring or control operations. The system on detecting a fault can not wait for an operator to view the operations monitor and decide upon a course of action, there is a need for the system to take positive action.

   Areas of the system code to be identified:

   - Watchdog or non-maskable interrupt operations.
   - Handling of peripheral exceptions, such as divide by 0, buffer overflow, corrupted data.
   - Handling of interface exceptions, for instance data out of range.
   - Coding standards, for instance parameter range checks in SWITCH or CASE statements.
   - Power up testing.

8. Areas for re-engineering

   The process of reverse engineering is examining in varying levels of detail the source code and structure of the system. In that process of examination it should be possible to apply some metrics to identify areas that represent a high risk to the integrity of the system. Such metrics could consider:

   - The use of unstructured techniques within a structured programming language e.g. GOTOs.
   - High usage of 'common' data, this will make the function strongly dependent on changes to the data elsewhere. In such cases changes are usually achieved by creating new variables (to avoid having to consider the effects of the change elsewhere), which may then have very similar data content, reducing the efficiency and comprehensibility of the system. Changing to the use of information hiding modules is a more rigorous solution.
   - Recognition of repetitious pieces of code, where replacement by a procedure could improve maintainability.
   - Procedures, functions or program modules that exceed a certain size. There are limits beyond which the ability of the human brain to conceptualize and summarize the functionality begin to diminish. Breaking up into two or more separate units will improve this process.

There could be many valid reasons as to why one or more of the above techniques has been used within the source code. The identification of such areas though, permits a rational assessment to be made and a plan of action to be proposed.

15

Understanding Programs through Formal Methods

P.T. Breuer, K. Lano, J. Bowen,
Oxford Laboratory Computing Laboratory, Programming Research Group, Oxford, UK

15.1 Introduction

'Finding out what a program does' is often thought of as an informal activity, involving a thorough walkthrough of the code by an experienced programmer, perhaps, but certainly no deep mathematics. At most, the examining engineer may construct tables of variables and attempt to write down the formulae connecting their values at significant points in the code – immediately after initialization and just before program termination, for example. However, the conscientious may go on to *annotate* the program with what they have found to hold true at each point, as in the REMs placed around the following simple loop:

REM $\textit{acct-sum}_i = 0$

```
for (j=1;j<=acct-count[i];j++) do
     acct-sum[i] += transact[i,j]
```

REM $\textit{acct-sum}_i = \sum_{j=1}^{\textit{acct-count}_i} \textit{transact}_{i,j}$

and mathematics will be used by the practising engineer as a means of expressing the knowledge gained. As is the case here, it may be simplest to present the information using a mathematical *notation*. Furthermore, it can often be necessary to enter into mathematical *argument* in order to demonstrate that a claim is true and, indeed, the method of mathematical annotation hinted at above lies at the root of the technique of formal validation through proof [264] which is looked upon today as one of the most useful and convincing ways of showing that a program satisfies a given specification (and which has been adapted also to reverse engineering [190] through the use of *partially instantiated* annotations – these become filled in as examination of the program proceeds, and always represent a consistent, albeit incomplete, state of knowledge about the code).

Mathematical argument is often needed in practice to demonstrate that two different program structures are equivalent for the task at hand. The simple loop code above has the structure:

```
for (a;p;b) do c;
```

(denoting the command statements by a, b, c and the expressional statement in the test by p) but in fact one might equally likely encounter the program structure (diagram at right):

```
a;
L: c; b;
if p then goto L;
```

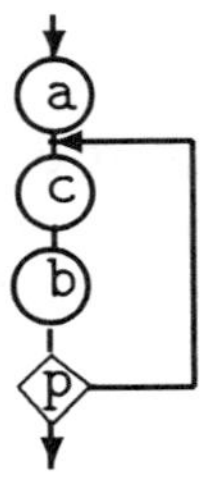

which is altogether less clear, but equivalent whenever the loop can be guaranteed to be traversed at least once, which means only that the loop test p must evaluate to *True* immediately after the loop initialization a, and in this case that condition is:

$$1 \leq \textit{acct-count}_i$$

(every account must have at least one transaction in it per month – perhaps a standing charge?).

This chapter will present an account of the *simple* mathematical representations which must be used to determine equivalences such as the one above. Some mathematical reasoning is required too, of course, but the aim is to achieve an understanding of what the code means, not to demonstrate facility with abstruse formalisms or grand abstractions.

In the following sections

15.2. Describing code mathematically
we describe a convenient mathematical formalism in which to represent programs, then in

15.3. Restructuring through mathematics
we show how to use the formalism to establish structural equivalences between programs, and in

15.4. Presenting mathematics properly
we establish a standard form in which to present program representations aimed at making the semantics clearly readable and easy to compare with other presentations. Finally, in

15.5. Reasoning with the aid of mathematics
we illustrate the use of the techniques by reverse-engineering a scientific programming application code back to its specification.

The example chosen for (15.5.) is a difficult and substantial one, which makes it not the easiest of tutorials, but it demonstrates the power of the techniques on a problem which theory says is as about as hard as it ever could be, and introduces general principles which may be applied to other – easier! – examples as they are encountered in practice.

15.2 Describing Code Mathematically

The simplest way to describe code is as itself. Surprisingly, this representation *can* also lead to increased understanding, but only when the representation is accompanied by various statements of equivalence (mathematically, *axioms*) between different code structures. For example, the following axioms help us to establish the equivalence of the two code structures above:

```
for (a;p;b) do c ≡ a;while p do {c;b}
while p do d     ≡ if p then {d; while p do d}
while p do d     ≡ L: if p then {d; goto L}
```

(assuming only that `a`, `b`, `c`, `d` do not contain any other `goto` statements).

Such axiomatic approaches to programming have been popularized by Hoare [156] and others, and there is a strong appeal in this kind of methodology if one does not wish to have to understand a program with respect to any other frame of reference. The problem is that each set of axiomatic formulations is only appropriate to a particular programming language and a particular implementation of that language. The code above has been written in a C-like language, but different implementations of C [181] may have different semantics, and therefore different axioms are appropriate to each. For example, the following three-line fragment of code has a very surpising semantics – first, it illustrates that assignments of the form $x{=}x$ are not necessarily vacuous when x is compound, particularly when it contains an assignment as a subexpression (in C assignments are commonly used in compound expressions, where they take the value of their RHS as well as effecting the storage operation):

```
int a[2]={2,1};        /* a is an array of length 2, set to (2,1) */
int n=1;               /* n is the array index, initialized to 1  */
a[n=a[n]]=a[n=a[n]];
```

Second, the semantics depends crucially on whether the LHS or the RHS of an assignment is evaluated first. It reduces to `a[2]=a[1]` if the LHS is evaluated first, and to a[1]=a[2] if the *RHS* is evaluated first. The ANSI standard does not specify which is correct.

Faced with such ambiguities, it is necessary to return to basics in the hunt for the meaning of a code segment, and this means discovering the mathematical meaning, which all axiom systems merely reflect. The simplest mathematical representation is that a piece of code c like the following (its strictly linear structure is diagrammed at right):

```
REM declared x1,x2,...,xn

c1; c2; ... ; cm;
```

is a mathematical function c:

$$\begin{aligned}(x'_1,\ldots,x'_n) &= cm(\ldots c2(c1(x_1,\ldots,x_n))\ldots)\\ &= c(x_1,\ldots,x_n)\end{aligned}$$

where the $x'_1, \ldots, x'_n$, are the final values held by the variables x1, ..., xn after execution of the code, and $x_1, \ldots, x_n$ are the initial values. Moreover, the final values are obtained by the composition of the functions $c1, c2, \ldots, cm$ which give the mathematical meaning of individual command statements. For example, the 'ambiguous' C-code above can be rendered as follows under the LHS-first rule (the meaning of each command statement is recorded to the right of the statement):

```
REM declared a[1],a[2], n
REM declare laddr, raddr additionally
```

Code		Meaning		Condition
a[1]=2;	(c1)	$a'_1 = 2$		
a[2]=1;	(c2)	$a'_2 = 1$		
n=1;	(c3)	$n' = 1$		
n=a[n];	(c4)	$n' = a_1,$		if $n = 1$
		$= a_2,$		if $n = 2$
laddr=n;	(c5)	$l' = n$		
n=a[n];	(c6)	$n' = a_1,$		if $n = 1$
		$= a_2,$		if $n = 2$
raddr=n;	(c7)	$r' = n$		
a[laddr]=a[raddr];	(c8)	$a'_1 = a_1,$	$a'_2 = a_2,$	if $l = 1, r = 1$
		$= a_2,$	$= a_2,$	if $l = 1, r = 2$
		$= a_1,$	$= a_1,$	if $l = 2, r = 1$
		$= a_1,$	$= a_2,$	if $l = 2, r = 2$

and the meaning of the whole is as the composition of the functions $c1, \ldots, c8$ on the RHS, giving finally

$$\begin{aligned}(a'_1, a'_2, n', l', r') &= c(a_1, a_2, n, l, r)\\ &= c8(c7(\ldots c2(c1(a_1, a_2, n, l, r))\ldots))\\ &= (2, 2, 1, 2, 1)\end{aligned}$$

for the whole code segment.

Of course this calculation is best represented through a table of values, but the point here is that the mathematical representation also takes care of the difficult case when the initializations ('a(2) = (2, 1); n = 1;') are absent. In that case, the mathematics comes out as

$$
\begin{array}{llllll}
(a_1', a_2', n', l', r') = c8(c7(c6(c5(c4(a_1, a_2, n, l, r))))) & & & & & \\
a_1' = 2, & a_2' = 2, & n' = a_2, & l' = 2, & r' = a_2, & \texttt{if } n = 1, a_1 = 2 \\
\quad = 1, & \quad = a_2, & \quad = 1, & \quad = 1, & \quad = 1, & \texttt{if } n = 1, a_1 = 1 \\
\quad = a_1, & \quad = 2, & \quad = 2, & \quad = 2, & \quad = 2, & \texttt{if } n = 2, a_2 = 2 \\
\quad = a_1, & \quad = 1, & \quad = a_1, & \quad = 1, & \quad = a_1, & \texttt{if } n = 2, a_2 = 1
\end{array}
$$

and this is harder to recognize when filling in tables of trial values. The astute may realize that the effect on the array a is equivalent to the single C instruction

```
n = a[a[n]] = a[a[a[n]]]
```

with n finishing with the value initially in a[a[n]]. One can check this by writing out the mathematical functionality, but one ends up with precisely the same set of equations as those above, and so they are omitted here!

15.3 Restructuring Through Mathematics

More striking yet is the ability of mathematics to represent convoluted control structures, and show which simple structures they are equivalent to. Consider the following code structure (diagram at right):

```
L0:a;
   if b then goto L2;
L1:c;
L2:d;
   if e then goto L1;
   f;
```

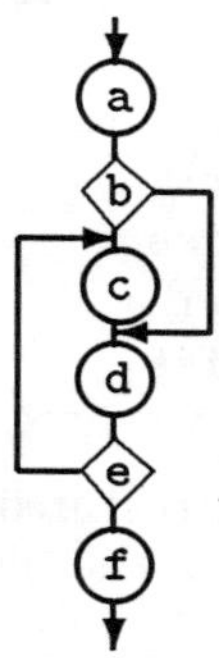

Representing the vector of values of global variables as $\underline{x}$, we write down the functionality of the whole program as

$$\underline{x}' = l_0(\underline{x})$$

where l_0 is expressed in terms of the functionalities of the three significant sections of code labeled. The functionalities l_0, l_1, l_2 each belong to the sections shown below:

```
L0: a;
    if b then goto L2;
    L1: c;
        L2: d;
            if e then goto L1;
            f;
```

and the defining equations are as follows (with the *call graph* – the relationship '*a* is defined using *b*' between functions *a*, *b* – diagrammed at right):

$$
\begin{aligned}
l_0(\underline{x}) &= l_2(a(\underline{x})), && \texttt{if } b(a(\underline{x})) \\
&= l_1(a(\underline{x})), && \texttt{otherwise} \\[1ex]
l_1(\underline{x}) &= l_2(c(\underline{x})) \\[1ex]
l_2(\underline{x}) &= l_1(d(\underline{x})), && \texttt{if } e(d(\underline{x})) \\
&= f(d(\underline{x})), && \texttt{otherwise}
\end{aligned}
$$

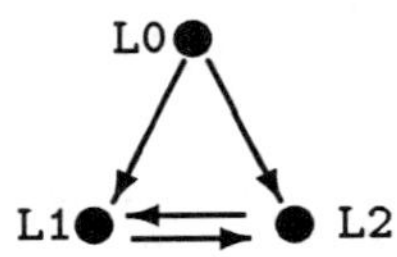

This information is crucial in effecting restructuring because the call graph is closely related to the control flow graph of the source code. The nodes correspond to the labeled lines in the source (including subroutine and function declarations also in the general case). It is clear that to obtain a well-structured program, we should remove the co-routining (mutual call) of `L1` and `L2`. We could in fact express the whole `L1`-`L2` loop as a single self-contained recursion, and express `L0` in terms of that alone. We can choose to express `L1` in terms of `L2` (eliminating `L1` from the equations) or `L2` in terms of `L1` (eliminating `L2` from the equations). Here, quite arbitrarily, we choose the former:

$$
\begin{aligned}
l_0(\underline{x}) &= l_2(a(\underline{x})), && \texttt{if } b(a(\underline{x})) \\
&= l_2(c(a(\underline{x}))), && \texttt{otherwise} \\
l_2(\underline{x}) &= l_2(c(d(\underline{x}))), && \texttt{if } e(d(\underline{x})) \\
&= f(d(\underline{x})), && \texttt{otherwise}
\end{aligned}
$$

from which we can read off the following structured equivalents, with the reduced call graph shown at right below:

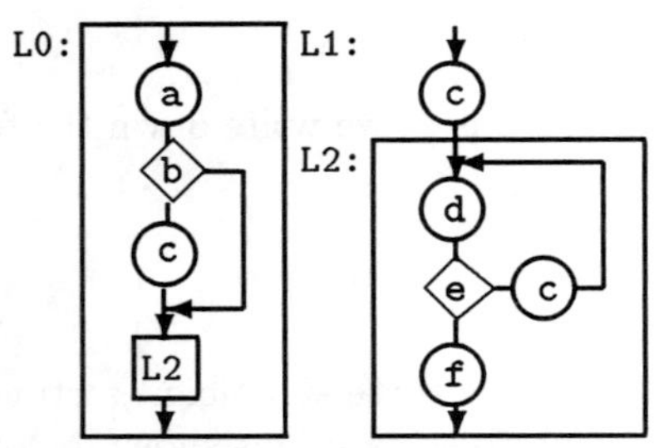

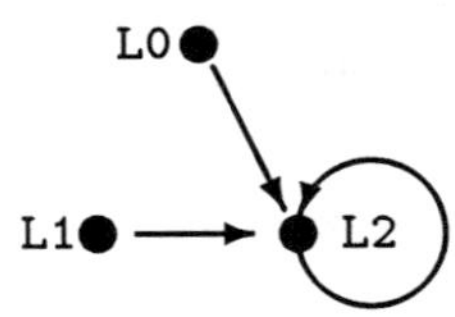

In general, one can decide which equations to substitute out just from looking at the call graph. An equation like '$l_1(\underline{x}) = l_2(c(\underline{x}))$' is responsible for a small part of the call graph, the part which shows the edges leading *from* the node L1 – in this case the single edge 'L1 • → • L2'. The rule is:

> *Substituting the equation for l_1 in the other equations has the effect of replacing all the edges in the call graph which run to* L1 *with edges which run to its immediate successors.*

In this case the successors of L1 in the graph are only L2. So the edge 'L0 • → • L1' becomes (a repetition of) the edge 'L0 • → • L2'. The intention is to choose an equation to substitute out so that the reduced graph contains no new non-trivial cycles, and to be eventually left with a tree-shaped call graph, with possibly a few trivial loops. One can work with trivial loops like 'L1 • → • L1', but not with larger loops like the pair 'L1 • → • L2 • → • L1' in the original call graph above.

Indeed, one is free to substitute using any equation which does not already contain a self-reference but which is referred to in at least one other equation. The point is that the substitution will then definitely remove from the call graph all the edges which point to the node and thus effect a simplification. This is the first step in restructuring the equations (and hence the call graph):

R.I *choose equations without immediate self-references and substitute them into the other equations until the set of remaining equations corresponds to a call graph in which the only cycles are length-*1 *cycles.*

If the substituted node were its own immediate successor in the call graph, then edges which used to point to it would still point to it in the reduced graph. For example, attempting to substitute out the equation for l_2 from the reduced equations above would not alter the reduced call graph at all. The 'L2 • → • L2' edge makes L2 its own successor in the graph (indeed, its only successor) so the two edges running to L2 remain in the reduced graph.

When one gets to the stage that the call graph is protected by trivial (length-1) loops, then one can introduce an explicit *iteration construct* into the graph and the equations which eliminates the loop. The basic iteration construct is the '`L':while p do d`' construct, which transforms an '`L : if p then{d; goto L}`' program (and control-flow graph) as follows:

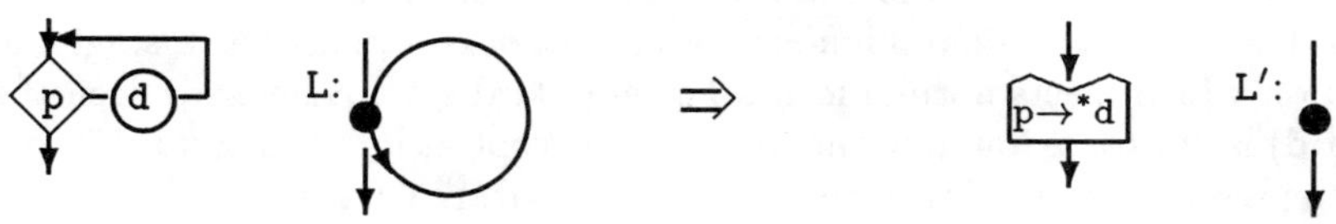

All recursion constructs can be expressed in terms of **while** loops, in particular those which correspond to length-1 loops in the call graph, but it is not necessary to reduce things to this single construct. One can just invent a name (**until**, **for**, etc.) for *whatever* new recursion construct one encounters. In the example overleaf, the recursion construct for L2 could eventually be rendered as a **while** construct thus:

```
L2:d;                                  L2:d;
   if e then {c; goto L2};                while e do {c;d};
   f;                                     f;
```

but it would be perfectly satisfactory to invent the name '`whoops`' for the recursive construct and use that instead:

```
L2:whoops(d;e;c);
   f;
```

(of course, '`whoops(d; e; c)`' is actually the C-language construct '`for(d; e; c) do;`' – a '`for`' loop with an initialization '`d`', a test '`e`', and an iterator '`c`', but nothing in the body of the loop). This is the second step in restructuring the equations and call graph:

R.II *replace length-*1 *loops in the call graph (self-referential equations) with explicit recursion constructs –* `while`*,* `for`*, etc.*

Structuring code by this method always works, in the sense that the call diagrams are eventually broken down into cycle-free ones. The manipulation is performed at the level of the equations which describe the mathematical meaning of the code, however, and so restructuring in this way requires of the engineer some appreciation of the formal mathematical meaning of code. It is to be hoped that the foregoing has demonstrated that the mathematics is not hard.

There is another view which we can take of the restructuring process described above: we can see it as a process for simplifying the equations which describe the mathematical meaning of code before presenting them for inspection, and it is this view which we want to expand upon next. In the next section the simplification of mathematical descriptions is dealt with in detail.

15.4 Presenting Mathematics Properly

In this section we will set out a *normal form* for the equations which one derives to represent the mathematical meaning of code. It is important to use a standard form, because then equations can be compared with one another with greater confidence and previous sections have shown just how useful it can be to use mathematical representations for code, but the word *normal* here carries the special connotation that the standard is completely unambiguous – every set of equations has a single, unique representation which meets normal form. The standard set out here (or even the idea of a standard) is not to be found in the literature, except as informal guides for authors [138], and represents the results of research conducted under the REDO project [42].

All the mathematical equations presented so far have been set out so as to meet the standard. They have been *normalized.* The first thing to do in order to normalize a set of equations is:

N.I *eliminate all equations which are not at the top level by substituting them in higher-level equations.*

This is a set of transformations which are independent of those described in the last section, where top-level equations were substituted in each other in order to eliminate mutual recursions, but this too corresponds to replacing subroutine calls by inline code. The aim is to make hidden effects explicit at the top level. For example, it may be good programming practice to write:

```
total = subtract(transaction,total)
  . .
float subtract(float x,float y){
      return(y-x);
}
```

because this kind of code can be more flexible – one may wish to make all such subtractions incur a charge if the *total* is negative, for example – but, with appropriate module structure, it may give rise to the equation on the left below, which would be much more appropriately written like that at right:

$$total' = subtract(transaction, total) \quad \texttt{where } subtract(x,y) = y - x \qquad \text{or} \qquad total' = total - transaction$$

eliminating the equation for *subtraction*.

In general, subsidiary equations arise when sequences of commands are translated into mathematics. These are represented as the composition of functions, and the intermediate values taken by variables are of no interest to the final result and the equations for them have to be eliminated. A naive translation in particular usually introduces lots of unnecessary intermediates. The second normalization rule seeks to eliminate such redundancies:

N.II *write the final value of a variable* **x** *as x' and its initial value as x. x' may be defined in an equation (so it appears on the LHS there), but it may not appear on the RHS of any equation.*

For example:

```
x=a;        REM x' = a
a+=b;       REM a' = a + b
y=a;        REM y' = a
```

can be transformed by writing the values of **x** taken after successive statements as x', x'', x''', and writing the initial value as x, giving:

$$(a''', b''', x''', y''') = (a'', b'', x'', a'')$$
$$\texttt{where}$$
$$(a'', b'', x'', y'') = (a' + b', b', x', y')$$
$$\texttt{where}$$
$$(a', b', x', y') = (a, b, a, y)$$

which one should write as:

$$
\begin{aligned}
a' &= a + b \\
b' &= b \\
x' &= a \\
y' &= a + b
\end{aligned}
$$

Note that

N.III *Given an n-dimensional vector equation, we write it as n separate scalar equations.*

Another important normalization is connected with '`if`' or '`case`' constructs in code. These can give rise to mathematical expressions with 'cases' buried deep within them. For example, the following code (at left) gives rise in a literal translation to the equation at right:

```
int x;
..
if (x<0) then x= -x;
x=log10(x);
```

x

$$x' = log_{10}\left(\begin{array}{ll} -x, & \texttt{if } x < 0 \\ x, & \texttt{otherwise} \end{array}\right)$$

The normalization rule is:

N.IV *embedded 'cases' must be brought to the top level by writing the guard conditions* outside *all enclosing constructs.*

and the normalized form of the equation for x' above is

x

$$
\begin{aligned}
x' &= log_{10}(-x), & \texttt{if } x < 0 \\
&= log_{10}(\ x), & \texttt{otherwise}
\end{aligned}
$$

and the equations are much more readable in this form, even though they no longer correspond exactly to the underlying code (they give the impression that a separate calculation of $log_{10}(x)$ is carried out in either branch after a ($\mathbf{x} < \mathbf{0}$) test).

One other normalization which must always be performed is the elimination of unnecessary *projections*. A 'projection' means the combination of an array-valued term and an array-index, as in '$a[n]$'. In the previous section we represented the 1×2 array **a** as the vector '(a_1, a_2)', and the expression '$(a_1, a_2)[n]$' is *not* in normal form. It should be written

$$
\begin{array}{ll}
a_1, & \texttt{if } n = 1 \\
a_2, & \texttt{if } n = 2 \\
\perp, & \texttt{otherwise}
\end{array}
$$

(here '$\perp$' signifies an undefined value – this is just for illustrative purposes and, for technical reasons, is only a proper representation if the program is guaranteed to crash when an out-of-range index is attempted. If the program returns an error but continues, we might prefer the representation 'ϵ' – error – instead of '$\perp$').

The example derives from using the following rule:

N.V *always treat an index expression 'n' as though it were a constant guarded by one of several '`if`' cases '1, `if` $n = 1$', '2, `if` $n = 2$', etc., for each possible value 1, 2, ... that the index can take.*

This rule makes indexed expressions much easier to calculate, because it splits the calculation into distinct cases and specific numbers can be used in each component case. Then vectors simply vanish, because the rule for normalizing projections is:

N.VI *always eliminate projections applied to vectors when the vector is written out explicitly.*

And

N.VII *always write out a vector explicitly!*

'Writing out the vector explicitly' means writing (a_1, a_2) in place of the vector a, for example, so that $a[2]$ will reduce to a_2 via $(a_1, a_2)[2]$. This can be a little tedious, but it is very difficult to compare vector calculations unless it is done.

Of course, care will have to be exercized over the level of abstraction appropriate to the program when it comes to writing 'vector' expressions in terms of their components. An integer may be represented in the machine as a vector of 1/0 bits, but it would be foolish to present a program semantics which viewed integer variables like that *unless* that representation were really fundamental to an understanding of the program, and even then one should be very selective over which variables and expressions to treat in that way. So it can sometimes be better *not* to write a vector out explicitly! Other examples of when it is inappropriate to expand vectors occur when matrix or other higher-dimensional operations are being used. Then vectors are best left as single values.

Strictly, 'writing out a vector explicitly' also applies to vector valued functions. If $f(x)$ is an n-dimensional vector, then we should write f as n functions $f(x) = (f_1(x), \ldots, f_n(x))$. But this can lead to many more equational definitions than it might be convenient to deal with by hand, so the rule should be applied sparingly.

Another important normalization determines the presentation of 'guard conditions' in many-case expressions. The 'cases' will have been brought to the top level, and this may have entailed the combining of several test conditions from different '`if then`' commands into single guard conditions. For example, the code below has the effect on the value of variable `r` which is expressed in normalized form at right.

```
    sign=1;
    if (x>0) then goto L1;
         sign=-sign; x=-x;
L1:if (y>0) then goto L2;
         sign=-sign; y=-y;
L2:r=sign*div(y,x);
```

r

$$
\begin{aligned}
r' &= div(\ y,\ x), && \texttt{if } (x > 0)\&(y > 0) \\
&= -div(-y,\ x), && \texttt{if } (x > 0) \\
&= -div(\ y, -x), && \texttt{if } (y > 0) \\
&= div(-y, -x), && \texttt{otherwise}
\end{aligned}
$$

Note that 'cases' in equations have a *fall-through* semantics – the first guard condition in the list which happens to be satisfied determines the active equation. If a guard condition is not satisfied, one 'falls through' to try the next.

The set of guarded equations for r' above is actually a linear pretty print of a two-dimensional tree of tests, which one can draw as follows:

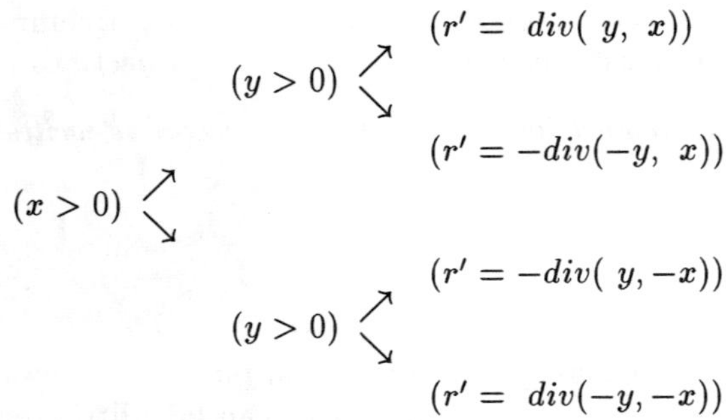

and it is this tree which must be in normal form. The pretty-print is obtained by writing down the leaves of the tree in order (these are each equations), and using as guard conditions for each the '&' of all the *True* conditions encountered in getting from the root to the leaf. One can drop the *False* conditions because of the fall-through semantics.

N.VIII *A 'test tree' may be normalized by the following procedure:*

1. *Remove unreachable branches. These occur when the test is definitely True or False, and one may remove both the test and the untraversible subtree corresponding to the other value of the test condition.*
2. *Remove repetitions of tests along any path through the tree. If the second appearance occurs in the True branch of the first test, then replace it by True. If it is in the False branch, replace it by False. Then renormalize.*
3. *Replace compound tests with multiple simple tests.*
   - *replace a conjunctive test* $(a\&b) \begin{smallmatrix}\nearrow t \\ \searrow f\end{smallmatrix}$ *with the double test*

     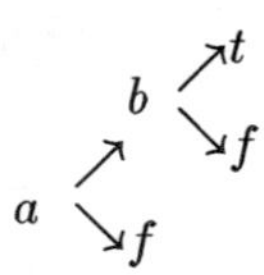

   - *replace a disjunctive test* $(a \vee b) \begin{smallmatrix}\nearrow t \\ \searrow f\end{smallmatrix}$ *with the double test*

     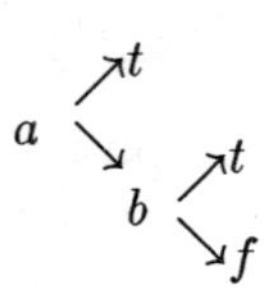

- *if the test is a negative one,* $\neg a \begin{array}{l} \nearrow t \\ \searrow f \end{array}$ *then unnegate it and swap the branches:*

$$a \begin{array}{l} \nearrow f \\ \searrow t \end{array}$$

Then renormalize.

4. *It can happen that a test itself is a guarded 'case' expression. This is a bit of a slow job to unwind, but basically one makes a big test tree which commences with the tree in the condition as root, but its leaves are replaced with copies of the True, False branches,thus:*

$$\left(a \begin{array}{l} \nearrow t \\ \searrow f \end{array} \right) \begin{array}{l} \nearrow T \\ \searrow F \end{array} \qquad \text{maps to} \qquad a \begin{array}{l} \nearrow t \begin{array}{l} \nearrow T \\ \searrow F \end{array} \\ \searrow f \begin{array}{l} \nearrow T \\ \searrow F \end{array} \end{array}$$

Then renormalize.

A normalized test tree is a tree *without logical redundancies.* It can be shown that each normalized tree uniquely specifies a single semantics in the *True*-, *False*-, ϵ-, $\perp$-valued logic which is appropriate to programs (*True*, *False*, *Error*, *Infinite loop*).

For the purposes of reverse engineering, it can often be useful to effect the following additional transformation:

N.IX *After any test of the form '$x = e$' in a test tree, replace x throughout the rest of the True branch by the expression e.*

There is only one occasion in which normalization does not split up existing cases. That is when a test gives the same result in either branch:

N.X *If a test tree has the form*

$$a \begin{array}{l} \nearrow x \\ \searrow x \end{array}$$

in which both branches after the test are the same, then one can remove the test, thus reducing the tree to x. More generally, if the same result x arises in each of a series of tests which disjointly exhaust all possibilities, then one may drop the tests and just write x.

For example, the specification below should appear as just '$y' = x$':

$$\begin{array}{|l}
\hline y: \\
\\
\begin{array}{lcll}
y' & = & x, & \textbf{if } (y = Foo)\&(z = Foo) \\
 & = & x, & \textbf{if } (y = Foo) \\
 & = & x, & \textbf{if } (z = Foo) \\
 & = & x, & \textbf{otherwise}
\end{array} \\
\hline
\end{array}$$

This is an example of the application of logical reasoning to *ordering* information, which will be explained in more detail in the next section, but the example arises also in connection with equalities alone. If we have a data type with just two members, *Foo* and *Bar*, then the schema below must also reduce to '$y' = x$':

$$
\begin{array}{l}
y \\
\hline
\begin{array}{rcll}
y' & = & x, & \texttt{if } (y = Foo) \\
 & = & x, & \texttt{if } (y = Bar)
\end{array}
\end{array}
$$

The converse rule is the following:

N.XI *If the tests in a path of a test tree are impossible to satisfy simultaneously, then that path may be dropped.*

but this rule *follows* from **N.IX** above in the case when all the tests are simple equalities of the form '$x = e$' for some expression e not involving x. One of the tests in the path will reduce to something like '$1 = 2$' after replacement of x by e throughout, if the tests are not simultaneously infeasible, and the rest of the path will drop away. In the more general case when the tests may not be of this simple form, the methods of the next section must be applied.

15.4.1 Dealing with Order Constraints and Arithmetic

The normalization operations given in the sections above essentially deal with *discrete* domains. There, the technique is to enumerate all the separate cases disjointly, but in a *continuous* domain, like the real numbers, it is not at all obvious how one may divide up the domain into different areas for separate treatment. Fortunately, there is a general algorithm for reducing guard conditions of the form:

$$\bigwedge\!\!\!\bigwedge\ (\textit{arithmetic expression}_1\ [<=>]\ \textit{arithmetic expression}_2)$$

to a simplest form (the '$\bigwedge\!\!\!\bigwedge$' is an abbreviation for 'the conjunction of terms like ...'), when the arithmetic expressions are just weighted sums of variables. For example, the condition:

$$(x - y > 0)\ \&\ (x < 2)\ \&\ (y > 3)$$

is unsatisfiable. Shading the excluded areas, the graph looks like:

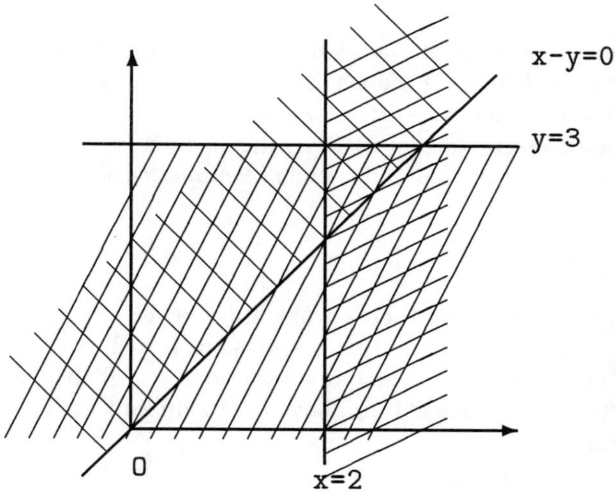

In general, deciding whether such a conjunction of inequalities is *empty* (infeasible) requires the following procedure: write the inequalities as:

$$A\underline{x} = \underline{b} + \underline{z}$$

where $\underline{z}$ is a new set of 'padding' variables, variously constrained to be less than greater than, strictly less than, or strictly greater than zero, as appropriate (or *equal* to zero, if the corresponding condition is an equation, not an inequality). Now one adds another set of 'loosening' variables $\underline{w}$ and writes

$$A\underline{x} = \underline{b} + \underline{z} - \underline{w}$$

so that there will definitely be a solution (it is $\underline{x} = \underline{0}$ and $\underline{w} - \underline{z} = \underline{b}$). Then one uses a standard linear optimization package to find:

$$\min\ |\underline{w}|$$

under the constraints of sign on the components z_i. If the minimum is zero, then there is a simultaneous solution for the $\underline{x}$ and the system of inequalities is not infeasible. Otherwise the system has no solution and the conjunction of the constraints is always *False*.

This procedure also determines when a *disjunction* of conjunctive tests is empty. Each disjunct must be empty if the whole is to be empty. If any disjunct has a feasible solution, then so does the whole.

Now, one can also decide when a disjunction of simple tests is the *whole space* by this method. Consider the disjunction:

$$(x - y \leq 0) \vee (x \geq 2) \vee (y \leq 3)$$

this is plainly the complement of the conjunction '$(x - y > 0)$ & $(x < 2)$ & $(y > 3)$' which the graph above shows to be empty. So it is the full space. This is how to test if any disjunction of tests always comes out *True*: its complement will be an empty conjunction.

This procedure also determines when a *conjunction* of disjunctive tests is the full space. Each conjunct must be the full space if the whole is to be the full space. If any conjunct fails to cover the full space, then so does the whole.

But one can write any propositional statement as *either* the disjunction of conjuncts (*disjunctive* normal form) or as the conjunction of disjuncts (*conjunctive* normal form). One may either write:

$$a\&b \vee c \qquad or \qquad (a \vee c)\&(b \vee c)$$

for example. Therefore one can tell by the method set out above whether *any* propositional combination of tests between linear arithmetic expressions is definitely always *False* or definitely always *True*. Of course, in most situations it will be neither one nor the other, but, interestingly, the algorithm above then suffices to reduce the proposition to its simplest form.

To test whether a new inequality is implied by those already in force:

$$p_1 \ \& \ \ldots \ \& \ p_n \ \Rightarrow \ p$$

one has to test if the space defined by the proposition:

$$\neg p_1 \vee \ldots \vee \neg p_n \vee p$$

covers the whole space or not (here $\neg(x > y)$, for example, means the complementary proposition, $x \leq y$). And this can be checked by the procedure outlined above. This test enables one to reduce any conjunction of inequalities to a *minimal form*, in which no inequality in the set is forced by the conjunction of the others.

This minimal form is not necessarily unique, however. For example, the closed interval [0,1] on the x-axis in 2-D space is (over-) specified by the following conjunction:

$$(x \geq 0)\&(y \geq 0)\&(y \leq 0)\&(x \leq 1)\&(x - y \leq 1)$$

since one may drop *either* $(x \leq 1)$ or $(x - y \leq 1)$ from the list. Once the line $y = 0$ has been determined by the other equations, both $(x \leq 1)$ and $(x - y \leq 1)$ mean the same thing, but the line is nowhere declared explicitly. Nor, in higher dimensions, is there a unique way to specify the line determined by the x-axis. It could be the intersection of the surfaces $y + z = y - z = 0$, for example, or of $y = z = 0$, or of any two planes which intersect on this axis. So in general, there is not going to be a unique way to represent areas defined in a multi-dimensional real continuum.

If the area is not 'flat', however, then there is a unique way. Lines are'flat' in 2-D space, and surfaces are 'flat' in 3-D space (as are lines and points). 'Flat' means 'of less than maximal dimensionality'. Conjunctions of inequalities define *convex* (i.e. 'ball-like') shapes. If the shape is not 'flat', then it is *uniquely* expressible as the intersection of the planes which touch its sides, not at points or edges, but at *surfaces*. In other words, if one extends the 'faces' of the convex shape into planes, then the shape is the intersect of inequalities based on these planes.

The result can be extended to a more complex shape, defined as the union and intersection of inequalities. Such a shape is *always* expressible as the union of convex shapes, and it is expressible as the union of *maximal* convex shapes (i.e. there is no larger convex shape which will fit within the area available). Provided each of the summands in the union is of maximal dimensionality, then it is *uniquely* expressible as the conjunction of the inequalities based on the plane surfaces which extend its faces.

N.XII *Organize each specification so that guard conditions guarding a given result are all grouped together as a disjunction of conjuncts of inequalities and equalities,*

$$foo,\ p_1 \ \vee \ p_2 \ \ldots \ \vee \ p_n$$

and then express the condition $p_1 \ \vee \ \ldots \ \vee \ p_n$ *in normal form, as the union* $q_1 \ \vee \ \ldots \ \vee \ q_k$ *of the conjunctions of inequalities based on the surfaces of its (maximal) convex components. Writing the final specification as the normalization of:*

$$foo,\ q_1 \ \vee \ q_2 \ \ldots \ \vee \ q_k$$

For example, the specification fragment below dictates the result '$y' = x$' in three cases, each specifying a region of the (x, y)-plane, respectively the unit square, a triangular region above it, and the unit square shifted two units to the right, as shown:

$$\begin{array}{ll} y' = x, & (x \geq 0)\&(y \geq 0)\&(x \leq 1)\&(y \leq 1) \\ y' = x, & (x \geq 0)\&(y \geq 1)\&(x + y \leq 2)\&(y \leq 2) \\ y' = x, & (x \geq 2)\&(y \geq 0)\&(x \leq 3)\&(y \leq 1) \end{array}$$

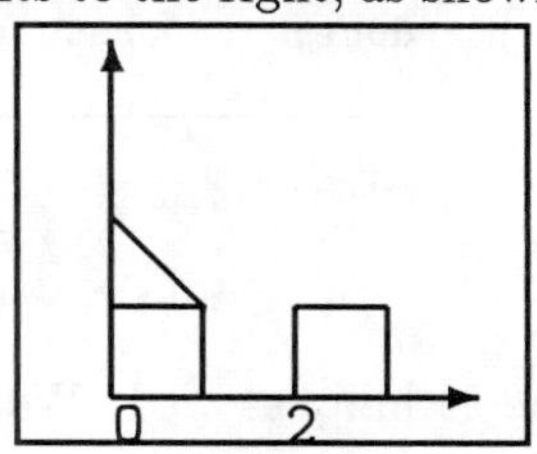

In this situation, the unique decomposition into the union of convex objects produces two components, the four-sided shape at left, and the square at right. These are each defined as the intersection of four half-planes (i.e. by four inequalities), leading to the normalized specification below:

$$\begin{array}{ll} y' = x, & (x \geq 0)\&(y \geq 0)\&(x + y \leq 2)\&(x \leq 1) \\ y' = x, & (x \geq 2)\&(y \geq 0)\&(x \leq 3)\&(y \leq 1) \end{array}$$

That concludes the description of the normalization of sets of equations, such as may result when one expresses the mathematical meaning of segments of code. For information on how to organize, represent and set out larger modules of code, look at section 16 in this manual.

15.5 Reasoning with the Aid of Mathematics

In this section we show how a scientific programming application may be reverse-engineered using the techniques introduced above, plus some reasoning in the transformed domain. The example chosen is a technically difficult one, but it illustrates

```
E:  init();                                     --LABEL Entry
    read m; read n;
    do
          do
A:              if m=0                          --LABEL A
                      then n=n+1; break(1);     --JUMP  out of loop
                elsif n=0
                      then push(1); m=m-1; n=1;
                      else push(0); n=n-1;
                fi;
          done;
          do
R:              if empty()                      --LABEL Reentry
                      then break(2);            --JUMP  two loops
                fi;
                pop(d)
                if d=0 then push(1); m=m-1; break(1);
                      else m=m+1;
                fi;
          done;
    done;       return(n)
```

Figure 15.1: Source code **A**

the techniques well. We start with the code **A** in figure 15.1, introducing the labels shown at left.

The first thing to do with this code is *restructure* it. In general, reverse engineering requires one to cycle continuously between different formalisms, one of which is the original programming language. The cycle [43] is (1) *clean*, (2) *specify*, (3) *simplify*:

1. **Clean**: transform (restructure) the subject matter within the original formalism, the source code, into a form suitable for translation. Here this means:

    - Switch to a smaller and well-understood set of constructs, for example, one might eliminate `break` statements (jumps out of enclosing loops) in favour of `goto`s, and `do if` statements with `while` or `until` loops.
    - Introduce global variables explicitly as arguments and results from subroutine calls which influence them. Here we introduce an explicit variable `s` representing the *stack* of integers which is manipulated by the subroutine `push` (which takes a single integer argument and pushes it onto the front of the stack) and the subroutine `pop` (which takes a *reference* as argument and pops the top value off the stack into the address supplied by the reference). For example, `push` becomes retyped as:

```
int stack       push(int,int stack)
```

so that one writes '`s=push(x,s)`' instead of '`push(x)`'. Similarly, `empty` and `init` become typed as:

```
bool            empty(int stack)
int stack       init()
```

- Replace call-by-reference semantics with the equivalent call-by-value semantics. This means replacing the subroutine `pop` with a 'side-effecting function' which instead of taking the address `d` as parameter, returns a *value* which can be written into `d` later. Then '`pop d`' can be replaced by '`d` = `pop()`', and, incorporating the global variable `s`, this finally becomes written as '`(d,s)=pop(s)`'.

2. **Specify**: translate into the new formalism, mathematical equations, as described in section 15.4.

3. **Simplify**: restructure the representation in the new formalism to make it simpler and to take advantage of whatever insights it affords.

It is not necessary to do all this in one step, or even to do all of it in sequence, provided that one is confident of ones overall ability to transform the code correctly. The sections below take one through the process for the application program **A**:

15.5.1. **Restructuring and Specification**
('Clean') clean the source code and form the initial translation ('specify') into a mathematical formalism.

15.5.2. **Syntactic Simplification**
('Simplify') normalize the set of equations, and

15.5.3. **Mathematical Simplification**
reason about the equations in order to reduce the complexity of the mathematics.

Only during the last section (15.5.3) is any mathematical ability required. A machine could carry out the processes described in (15.5.1) and (15.5.2), and it requires no effort of a human engineer either, but in (15.5.3) a distinctly human intelligence begins to be required. We introduce the concept of *data equivalence* – different ways of encoding the same information – as a means of shifting between one mathematical representation and another with the minimum of effort, and show that the technique succeeds in revealing the semantics hidden in the example application code.

15.5.1 Restructuring and Specification

It is often easier to replace all `while/until` loops with `goto`s for the purposes of specification, but this has not been done below. `Break`s have been removed, however. Restructuring delivers the code shown in figure 15.2, and we can specify the three functions involved as shown in figure 15.3(a).

```
E: init(); read m; read n;
A: until(m=0) do
            if (n=0) then s=push(1,s); m=m-1; n=1;
                     else s=push(0,s); n=n-1;
            fi;
   done;
   n=n+1;
R: until(empty(s)) do
            (d,s)=pop(s);
            if (d=0) then s=push(1,s); m=m-1; goto A;
                     else m=m+1;
            fi;
   done;
   return(n);
```

Figure 15.2: Restructured source code **A**

15.5.2 Syntactic Simplification

We *simplify* in the mathematical formalism by first *normalizing* the equations. Here this means:

- eliminating the low-level intermediate equations for d, s' and n' (**N.I**). It is also convenient to
- use a more concise notation for the *push*, *pop* and *init* functions (equivalent in fact to introducing the underlying structures on which stacks are built). We
  - adopt the notation '$(x : s)$' or just '$x : s$' in place of '$push(x, s)$'. Then
  - one can write '$(d : s') = s$' in place of '$(d, s') = pop(s)$', because the latter is equivalent to testing if '$push(d, s') = s$'. And so we can replace an equation of the form '$foo(s) = bar(d, s')\ldots$ `where` $(d, s') = pop(s)$' with '$foo(d : s') = bar(d, s')$'. We also
  - write '$init()$' as '[ ]', and consequently the test '$empty(s)$' as '$s = [\ ]$', because it is equivalent to asking if '$s = init()$'.

That gives one the specification shown in figure 15.3(b).

- apply the rules **N.II-N.VIII** to normalize each equation, and particularly useful here,
- substitute occurrences of x by foo in equations guarded by $x = foo$ (rule **N.IX**).

This gives one the specification in figure 15.3(c). Notice that the '`otherwise`' in the equation for r must mean '`if` $d = 1$' as the stack is only ever loaded with 1s and 0s. Thus far the work can be carried out completely *automatically*, but from now on human guidance is very definitely required, although heuristics ('rules') will be given as often as possible below.

$$
\begin{aligned}
e(m,n) &= n' \\
&\ \texttt{where } (m',n',s') = a(m,n,init())
\end{aligned}
$$

$$
\begin{aligned}
a(m,n,s) &= r(m,n+1,s) && , \ \texttt{if } m=0 \\
&= a(m-1,1,push(1,s)) && , \ \texttt{if } n=0 \\
&= a(m,n-1,push(0,s)) && , \ \texttt{otherwise}
\end{aligned}
$$

$$
\begin{aligned}
r(m,n,s) &= (m,n,s) && , \ \texttt{if } empty(s) \\
&= a(m-1,n,push(1,s')) && , \ \texttt{if } d=0 \\
&= r(m+1,n,s') && , \ \texttt{otherwise} \\
&\ \texttt{where } (d,s') = pop(s)
\end{aligned}
$$

(a) Initial specification – translate literally.

$$
e(m,n) = a(m,n,[\,])[2]
$$

$$
\begin{aligned}
a(m,n,s) &= r(m,n+1,s) && , \ \texttt{if } m=0 \\
&= a(m-1,1,1:s) && , \ \texttt{if } n=0 \\
&= a(m,n-1,0:s) && , \ \texttt{otherwise}
\end{aligned}
$$

$$
\begin{aligned}
r(m,n,[\,]) &= (m,n,[\,]) \\
r(m,n,d:s') &= a(m-1,n,1:s') && , \ \texttt{if } d=0 \\
&= r(m+1,n,s') && , \ \texttt{otherwise}
\end{aligned}
$$

(b) Simplified specification – use structures instead of calls and eliminate local definitions.

$$
e(m,n) = a(m,n,[\,])[2]
$$

$$
\begin{aligned}
a(0,n,s) &= r(0,n+1,s) \\
a(m,0,s) &= a(m-1,1,1:s) \\
a(m,n,s) &= a(m,n-1,0:s)
\end{aligned}
$$

$$
\begin{aligned}
r(m,n,[\,]) &= (m,n,[\,]) \\
r(m,n,0:s') &= a(m-1,n,1:s') \\
r(m,n,1:s') &= r(m+1,n,s')
\end{aligned}
$$

(c) Final specification – replace guards with pattern-matches.

Figure 15.3: Stages in the production of a *literal* specification for source code A

15.5.3 Mathematical Simplification

Now we can do some reasoning: first of all, it is apparent that function a just calls itself continuously until $m = 0$, when it calls r. So it is sensible to invent a new function a_1 which represents the action of a up to and just *before* it calls r. We write $a(m,n,s) = r(a_1(n,m,s))$ and eliminate r from the three equations for a by cancelling it where it appears on both sides. The result is shown in figure 15.4(a), where the changes are indicated in boldface. The general rule is:

M.I *when the equations for function a are such that substituting 'don't know' ('$\perp$') for a everywhere reduces them to either '$a(\ldots) = \perp$' or '$a(\ldots) = r(\ldots)$' in every case, then r is a* factor *of a, and one writes $a(\ldots) = r(a_1(\ldots))$. The equations for a then become equations for a_1 with the 'r' dropping out.*

The mathematical justification (it needs justifying) for the elimination of r is that at this point we are looking for *some* solution of the equations, not necessarily *all* of them. As the source program is deterministic, if we find a solution by this means, then it will be the uniquely correct one.

It is now apparent that a_1 always delivers the result $m = 0$, so that we can, instead of writing '$a_1(m,n,s)$' always write '$(0, a_2(m,n,s))$', letting a_2 stand for the function which delivers n and s alone. Simplifying, this gives one the specification shown in figure 15.4(b). This is an application of a rule which itself merely specializes the previous one, writing '$(foo, \ldots)$' in place of '$r(\ldots)$':

M.II *when the equations for function a_1 are such that substituting 'don't know' ('$\perp$') for a_1 everywhere reduces them to either '$a_1(\ldots) = \perp$' or '$a(\ldots) = (foo, \ldots)$' in every case, where foo is some explicit, unvarying pattern such as '0' (here), or '$2x + y$', then* `foo` *is a* component *of a_1, and one writes $a_1(\ldots) = (foo, a_2(\ldots))$. The equations for a_1 then become (lower dimension) equations for a_2, and the 'foo' drops out.*

Furthermore, only the second element of the triple delivered by r is ever required, so we can slim things down a little by replacing the equations for $r(\_,\_,\_)$ with equations for $r_2(\_,\_,\_) = r(\_,\_,\_)[2]$ throughout, as shown in figure 15.4(c). The rule is:

M.III *when function r never appears in any other equation except as part of some more complicated expression '$foo(r(\ldots))$', then r is an* intermediate *and should be eliminated. Replace the equations for r with equations for $r_2(\ldots) = foo(r(\ldots))$.*

15.5.4 Data Equivalences

At this point one has gone as far as possible without applying any intelligence. What comes next must rely somewhat on inspiration, because the equivalence of different programs is not something which can be checked or discovered by a machine (an automatic procedure) acting on its own. Notice that whenever a 1 is pushed onto the front of the stack ($1 : s$ appears on the right of an equation), the variable `m` is decremented, and whenever a 1 is popped off the stack ($1 : s'$ appears on the left of an

$$
\begin{aligned}
e(m,n) &= \mathbf{r}(\mathbf{a_1}(m,n,[\,]))[2] \\
\\
\mathbf{a_1}(0,n,s) &= (0,n+1,s) \\
\mathbf{a_1}(m,0,s) &= \mathbf{a_1}(m-1,1,1:s) \\
\mathbf{a_1}(m,n,s) &= \mathbf{a_1}(m,n-1,0:s) \\
\\
r(m,n,[\,]) &= (m,n,[\,]) \\
r(m,n,0:s') &= \mathbf{r}(\mathbf{a_1}(m-1,n,1:s')) \\
r(m,n,1:s') &= r(m+1,n,s')
\end{aligned}
$$

(a) Isolate the calls in a prior to r as function a_1 (rule **M.I**).

$$
\begin{aligned}
e(m,n) &= r(\mathbf{0},\mathbf{a_2}(m,n,[\,]))[2] \\
\\
\mathbf{a_2}(0,n,s) &= (n+1,s) \\
\mathbf{a_2}(m,0,s) &= \mathbf{a_2}(m-1,1,1:s) \\
\mathbf{a_2}(m,n,s) &= \mathbf{a_2}(m,n-1,0:s) \\
\\
r(m,n,[\,]) &= (m,n,[\,]) \\
r(m,n,0:s') &= r(\mathbf{0},\mathbf{a_2}(m-1,n,1:s')) \\
r(m,n,1:s') &= r(m+1,n,s')
\end{aligned}
$$

(b) Notice that $a_1 = (0,\ldots)$ always, and re-express in terms of a_2 (rule **M.II**).

$$
\begin{aligned}
e(m,n) &= \mathbf{r_2}(0,a_2(m,n,[\,])) \\
\\
a_2(m,n,s) &= \ldots \\
\\
\mathbf{r_2}(m,n,[\,]) &= \mathbf{n} \\
\mathbf{r_2}(m,n,0:s') &= \mathbf{r_2}(0,a_2(m-1,n,1:s')) \\
\mathbf{r_2}(m,n,1:s') &= \mathbf{r_2}(m+1,n,s')
\end{aligned}
$$

(c) Notice that only the second component of $r(\ldots)$ is needed (rule **M.III**).

Figure 15.4: Reasoning about the specification to achieve mathematical simplification

equation) the variable m is incremented. We hypothesize that the stack is really just acting as a store for past values of m. Knowing the current value of m and how many 1s are on the stack allows us to reconstruct all the old information.

Imagine a parallel stack t which contains these old values. The diagram 15.5 shows the relationship between t and s. From stack t and the current value of m, one can always reconstruct s (and m). The formal relationship expressed in this *data equivalence* is as follows (skip to the next paragraph for an explanation):

$$\begin{array}{lcll} (m-1, 1:s) & \equiv & (m'-1, t) & \texttt{if } (m,s) \equiv (m',t) \\ (m, 0:s) & \equiv & (m, m':t) & \texttt{if } (m,s) \equiv (m',t) \\ (m, [\,]) & \equiv & (m, [\,]) & \end{array}$$

Each clause of the equivalence states what happens in one representation when a change occurs in the other. The first line says what happens if one pushes a 1 onto stack s and simultaneously decrements variable m. The change is from a stack with shape s to one with shape $1:s$, and from a value m in m to a value $m-1$ in m, and it is represented by the:

$$(m-1, 1:s) \equiv \ldots \ \texttt{if } (m,s) \equiv \ldots$$

part of the statement. The corresponding change in the other representation is that the stack t is unchanged – the decrement in m cancels the external visibilty of the 'push 1' because t only records the *sum* of m and the number of 1's on s – but the value in m is still seen to decrease, from m' to $m'-1$. Using the value m' instead of m helps ensure that we do not prejudge that these values are always the same. The contribution to the equivalence statement is:

$$\ldots \equiv (m'-1, t) \ \texttt{if} \ \ldots \equiv (m', t)$$

and putting the two parts together gives the clause of the data equivalence.

This allows us to rewrite the equations as shown below (the relevant instantiations of the data equivalence which have been used to obtain each equation are shown to the right of that equation). The rule being used is:

M.IV *If one has a* data equivalence *which states that 'data of pattern A_1 carries the same information as data of pattern B_1', and 'data of pattern A_2 carries the same information as data of pattern B_2', and so on, then one may replace patterns A_i with B_i systematically in all equations and thus obtain new functions which behave equivalently to the originals. If the inputs (arguments) and outputs (result values) are unaffected, then they are the* same *as the old.*

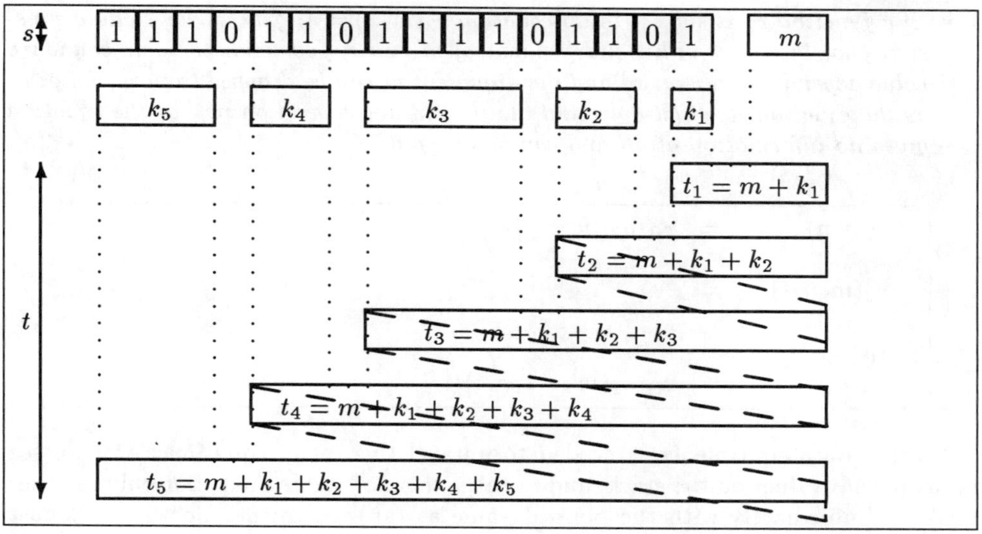

Figure 15.5: The relationship between stacks s and t

$$
\begin{array}{lcll}
e(m,n) & = & r_2(0, a_2(m,n,[\,])) & \\
a_2(0,n,t) & = & (n+1,t) & \\
a_2(m,0,t) & = & a_2(m-1,1,t) & \begin{cases}(m,s) \equiv (m,t)\\ (m-1, 1:s) \equiv (m-1,t)\end{cases}\\
a_2(m,n,t) & = & a_2(m,n-1,m:t) & \begin{cases}(m,s) \equiv (m,t)\\ (0:s) \equiv (m, m:t)\end{cases}\\
r_2(m,n,[\,]) & = & n & \\
r_2(m,n,m':t) & = & r_2(0, a_2(m'-1,n,t)) & \begin{cases}(m,s) \equiv (m',t)\\ (m,0:s) \equiv (m,m':t)\\ (m-1,1:s) \equiv (m'-1,t)\end{cases}\\
r_2(m,n,t) & = & r_2(m+1,n,t) & \begin{cases}(m+1,s) \equiv (m+1,t)\\ (m,1:s) \equiv (m,t)\end{cases}
\end{array}
$$

The last equation shows that r_2 depends only on n and t, not on m. The recursion is towards an (unstated) boundary condition when m is as big as the value at the front of stack t.

The reason for considering this data equivalence in the first place was the observation that all the original equations preserve the sum of m and the number of 1s in the group at the head of stack s across the '=' sign. This value is plainly an important quantifier of the state of the system, and it is the value always held at the back of the stack t. The next value from the back is the sum of m and the number of 1s in the first two groups (separated by a zero) at the head of s, and so on.

Because of r_2's dependence only on n and t, one can consider r_2 to be never called except with $m = 0$, so it is useful to give a name to $r_2(0,n,t)$: we replace it with $r_0(n,t)$ everywhere, and dispense with the last equation above. The rule is:

M.V *If a function r_2 is subject to an equation $r_2(m, x) = r_2(foo, x)$ for some expression foo, then it is either independent of m (when foo tends to some boundary value dependent only on x) and the argument m can be dropped from r_2, followed by the equation itself (it only said that r_2 did not depend on m), or the equation gives no information at all and can be dropped.*

$$
\begin{array}{lcl}
e(m,n) & = & \mathbf{r_0}(a_2(m,n,[\,])) \\[1em]
a_2(m,n,t) & = & \ldots \\[1em]
\mathbf{r_0}(n,[\,]) & = & n \\
\mathbf{r_0}(n,m':t) & = & \mathbf{r_0}(a_2(m'-1,n,t))
\end{array}
$$

Another data equivalence is needed to unravel this set of equations: we can see that a_2 pushes values on the stack, and r_0 takes them off again later, but only in order to call a_2 immediately with the popped value as (an) argument. So the stack just serves as a reservoir of arguments to a_2 for use when it is executed again *later*. What we can do is give $k = r_0(\_, t)$ as an argument to a_2 instead of t, writing '$a_2(m, n, k)$' instead of '$a_2(m, n, t)$', and in the clause where a_2 finally returns the pair $(n+1, t)$ for use by r_0, have it instead execute $r_0(n+1, t)$ directly by writing '$a_2(0, n, k) = k(n+1)$' instead of '$a_2(0, n, t) = (n + 1, t)$'. The function k is called a *continuation function.*

We carry out this procedure below. (Technically, this is an operation of *generalization* on the equations, because we recover the original equations by setting k to be the function $\nu \mapsto (\nu, t)$ for any particular fixed t.)

$$
\begin{array}{lcl}
e(m,n) & = & a_2(m,n,r_0(\_,[\,])) \\[1em]
a_2(0,n,k) & = & k(n+1) \\
a_2(m,0,k) & = & a_2(m-1,1,k) \\
a_2(m,n,k) & = & a_2(m,n-1,k') \\
 & & \texttt{where } k'(\nu,t) \;=\; k(\nu, m:t) \\[1em]
r_0(n,[\,]) & = & n \\
r_0(n,m':t) & = & a_2(m'-1,n,r_0(\_,t))
\end{array}
$$

Moreover, we can abstract away the stack argument t from the equations by writing r_0 as a *curried* function, '$r_0(n)(t)$' instead of '$r_0(n, t)$', and generalizing a_2 slightly by writing '$a_2(m, n, f)(t)$' instead of '$a_2(m, n, f(t))$'.

M.VI *One may generalize a function $a(\_)$ in any of several ways:*

- *Replace a subexpression foo which appears on the RHS of the equations defining a with a new variable x, and declare x to be an extra parameter to a.*
- *If a often appears in equations with a compound expression foo as parameter, as in 'a(foo)', and foo uses a subexpression x repeatedly, then one may*

write it as a function: $a(e, x)$, where '$e(x)$' can be instantiated to foo. This introduces a function as (an extra) parameter 'e', as well as the ordinary parameter 'x'.

- *One may drop one of the equations which governs the function.*
- *One may replace any subexpression foo on the RHS of the defining equations with a generalization (this is a recursive definition!).*
- *One may explicitly replace any expression on the RHS of the governing equation with '$\perp$' ('don't know').*

The second option is the course followed here! We have 'foo' as $f(t)$, and we introduce f and t as separate parameters to a_2. Then we cancel the '(t)' where it appears on both sides, in '$a_2(0, n, k)(t) = k(n+1)(t)$', for example:

$$
\begin{array}{lcl}
e(m, n) & = & a_2(m, n, r_0)[\,] \\
\\
a_2(0, n, k) & = & k(n+1) \\
a_2(m, 0, k) & = & a_2(m-1, 1, k) \\
a_2(m, n, k) & = & a_2(m, n-1, k') \\
 & & \texttt{where } k'\ \nu\ t \ = \ k\ \nu\ (m : t) \\
\\
r_0(n)[\,] & = & n \\
r_0(n)(m' : t) & = & a_2(m'-1, n, r_0)(t)
\end{array}
$$

That is another rule:

M.VII *We can harmlessly replace an equation of the form '$a(t) = b(t)$' where t does not appear in either 'a' or in 'b', with '$a = b$.*

(this is usually called the *eta*-law (η) of the lambda-calculus – the other laws are (α) that one may change the name of any argument variable, and (β) that one may calculate $a(foo)$ by writing out the definition of a with its formal definitional parameter t replaced by 'foo' everywhere). Rule (**M.I**) dealt with equations of the form '$t(a) = t(b)$'. Dropping the 't' gives a generalization there.

The two steps, which we have justified with proper mathematical reasoning above, can be carried through in a single step by using the data equivalence below – 'data is equivalent to function which encodes data':

$$
\begin{array}{l}
(m' : t) \equiv k' \ \texttt{if}\ t \equiv k \\
\texttt{where } k'\ \nu\ \tau \ = \ k\ \nu\ (m' : \tau)
\end{array}
$$

The assertion is that the stack of shape t is equivalent to some function $k(\_, \_)$ (parameterized as $k(\_)(\_)$ in the equivalence) which takes an index ν and a reference stack τ as its parameters. If one changes t to $m' : t$, then this is reflected in a change from $k(\nu)$ to $k'(\nu)$ (for each given ν), where $k'(\nu)$ acts on the reference stack τ as $k(\nu)$ would have acted on a reference stack $m' : \tau$. If one first synchronizes t and τ at the stage when they are both empty, then k has encoded into it precisely the manner in which t is composed at any point. This is tricky to visualize, but it is really just an algebraic device to make the following sequence of mathematical transformations work.

Now we set out the few final steps to the answer. Looking for a solution, we assume that $a_2(m,n,k) = k(A(m,n))$ for some function A, and so we get the equations in figure 15.6(a). The important rule here is:

M.VIII *If a function $a(x,k)$ represents a real working program from a sequential computer, where x corresponds to the input parameters, but k represents an artificially introduced* continuation function, *then we can assume that the value of a is given by $a(x,k) = k(A(x))$ for some function A which does* not *take the continuation function as a parameter. Replacing $a(x,k)$ by $k(A(x))$ everywhere, and setting k to the identity function, gives a set of equations for $A(x)$ alone.*

The idea is that a real computer does not pass functions about – so one should be able to eliminate the function k if a is computable. Here, letting $RA(m,n)$ stand for $r_0(A(m,n))$, and replacing $k(\_)(t)$ with $r_0(\_)(t)$ throughout, we get the equations in figure 15.6(b).

Setting t to [ ] throughout and using the equation $RA(m,n)[\,] = A(m,n)$, finally we get the equations in figure 15.6(c). This allows us to see that $e(m,n)$ is precisely the *Ackerman* function $A(m,n)$, since these are its defining equations.

15.6 Summary

We have set out ways of converting application code written in a procedural programming language into formal statements of what the code does, expressed in mathematical equations. The process is largely automatic, and it produces readable output because of *normalizations* built into the procedure. The contention is that this results in the following:

- (from the automatic part of the process) a statement of what the code does which is clear and comprehensible in itself, and
- (from the human-mediated part) it induces in the engineer who carries the process through successfully a thorough understanding of the meaning of the application code.

The 'further reasoning' part of the process has been presented for the engineer as the invention of suitable *data equivalences* which are to be applied in order to transform one mathematical representation into a simpler one. The 'computerizable' initial part of the process has been presented in detail and it has been seen to be practible to execute it by hand for small chunks of code.

$$
\begin{array}{lll}
e(m,n) & = & r_0(A(m,n))[\,] \\
 & & \\
k(A(0,n)) & = & k(n+1) \\
k(A(m,0)) & = & k(A(m-1,1)) \\
k(A(m,n)) & = & k'(A(m,n-1)) \\
 & & \texttt{where } k'\ \nu\ t\ =\ k\ \nu\ (m':t) \\
r_0(n)[\,] & = & n \\
r_0(n)(m':t) & = & r_0(A(m'-1,n)))(t)
\end{array}
$$

(a) Assume $a_2(m,n,k) = k(A(m,n))$.

$$
\begin{array}{llll}
e(m,n) & = & RA(m,n)[\,] & \\
 & = & A(m,n) & \{\ r_0(n)[\,] \quad = n \quad \} \\
 & & & \\
RA(0,n)(t) & = & r_0(n+1)(t) & \\
RA(m,0)(t) & = & RA(m-1,1)(t) & \\
RA(m,n)(t) & = & r_0(A(m,n-1))(m:t) & \{\ r_0(n)(m:t) = r_0(A(m-1,n))(t)\ \} \\
 & = & r_0(A(m-1,A(m,n-1))(t) & \\
 & = & RA(m-1,A(m,n-1))(t) &
\end{array}
$$

(b) Instantiate $k(\_)(t)$ to $r_0(\_)(t)$ throughout & rename $r_0(A(\_,\_)$ as $RA(\_,\_)$.

A

$$
\begin{array}{lll}
e(m,n) & = & A(m,n) \\
 & & \\
A(0,n) & = & n+1 \\
A(m,0) & = & A(m-1,1) \\
A(m,n) & = & A(m-1,A(m,n-1))
\end{array}
$$

(c) Instantiate t to $[\,]$ throughout and use $RA(m,n)[\,] = A(m,n)$.

Figure 15.6: Mathematical reasoning on the equations describing code **A**

16

Reverse Engineering COBOL via Formal Methods

K.C. Lano and P.T. Breuer,
Oxford University Computer Laboratory, Programming Research Group, Oxford, UK
H. Haughton,
Performance Technology Group, Lloyds Register of Shipping, Lloyds Register House, UK [1]

16.1 Introduction

The COBOL language hinders program comprehension in several ways: by its use of formats instead of types (which means that each assignment between variables usually involves an implicit conversion of data from one format to another), by the mixed use of `PERFORM` statements and the ordinary *fall-through* execution of paragraphs, by the inclusion of unstructured constructs such as `GOTO`s and `ALTER GOTO`s, and by excessive proliferation of specialized verbs and variants of verbs, the exact semantics of which in turn requires very specialized knowledge on the part of the programmer.

All these features make an organized programme for using reverse engineering COBOL applications a *necessity*, and in the following sections we will set out just how to go about it using the tools which we have developed at Oxford (of course it is possible to do what the tools do without using the tools themselves).

[1] An extended version of this chapter will appear in the *Journal of Software Maintenance*, 1992

16.1.1 Picking up Clues from COBOL

On the positive side, COBOL *data declarations* provide significant information abcut the structuring of the data that the program is expected to manipulate: they bind record names and field names to files, and specific index variables to arrays. This means that one can tell which file a record belongs to from its name alone. COBOL therefore already contains some rudimentary *object-oriented* features, and we seek to enhance these as reverse-engineering proceeds.

Moreover, in addition to the expected type and value bindings, one can pick up from the *data division* of a COBOL program some *global invariants*. In general, invariants are useful items of high-level information, being statements of the relationships between runtime values, such as '$sum \geq 0$' or '$0 < n \leq acct\_tot \Rightarrow acct\_rec_n \in acct\_file$' (literally 'if n is in the range $(0, acct\_tot]$, then the n'th *acct_rec* is listed in the *acct_file*'). For example consider a 'level 88' condition name:

```
02 V PIC X.
  88 A1 VALUE IS B1.
  88 A2 VALUE IS B2.
```

where `B1` and `B2` are literal values in the type `X` (which denotes the type of single characters in COBOL). One can read this as asserting that the properties

$$(\texttt{V} = \texttt{B1}) \Leftrightarrow \texttt{A1}$$
$$(\texttt{V} = \texttt{B2}) \Leftrightarrow \texttt{A2}$$

hold invariantly throughout the program, i.e. that `A1` is a Boolean which may be treated as an abbreviation for the condition-test '$\texttt{V} = \texttt{B1}$', and `A2` likewise.

One also gets invariants (although more trivial ones) from 'redefinitions' (or 'casted equivalences', more properly). For example, the declaration

```
LevNum A PIC F1.
LevNum B PIC F2 REDEFINES A.
```

asserts that, throughout the program

$$b = [\texttt{F1} \rightarrow \texttt{F2}](a)$$

holds true, where a, b are the values returned by a use of `A`, `B` respectively, and $[\texttt{F1} \rightarrow \texttt{F2}]$ is the function performing translations of quantities with format `F1` to quantities with format `F2`. These examples illustrate the kind of information that automatic tools can pick up from the raw COBOL source of an application program on their own, but it is not enough. One wants to produce meaningful *abstractions* from the source, and to this end we have developed a method which is summarised in Figure 16.1. Software tools are used to progressively transform the application code into object-oriented abstractions.

The three steps of the process ('clean', 'specify' and 'simplify' in the terminology of Breuer and Lano [43]) are:

Step 1: ('clean') Translation to the intermediate language UNIFORM, eliminating redundant language constructs. For example, '`MOVE X TO Y`' becomes '$\texttt{Y} := [\texttt{FX} \rightarrow$

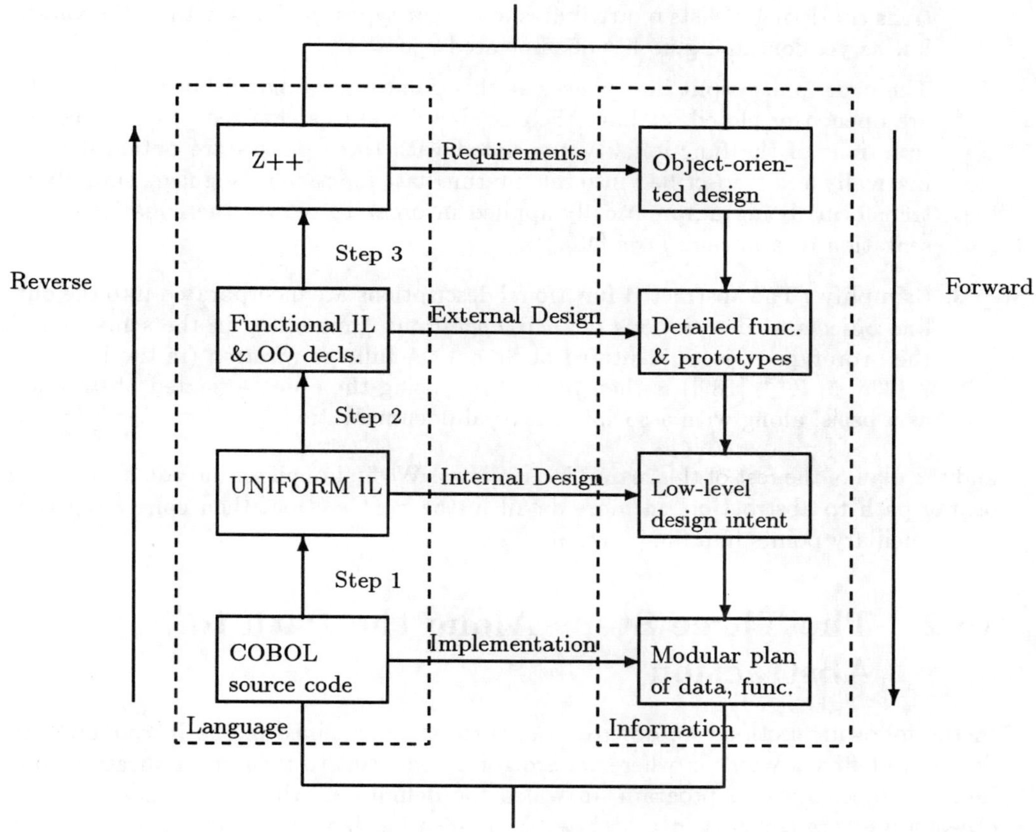

Figure 16.1: The abstraction from COBOL to Z

`FY]`(`X`)', where `FX` and `FY` are the types of `X` and `Y` respectively. Also, asserted relationships between data values (as in the '`REDEFINES`' statement above) are translated into statements about invariants in the programs runtime behavior. This step can be seen as restricting the original language to a small subset of permissible constructs, because UNIFORM is not an inherently different language to COBOL, just more compact.

Step 2: ('specify') Using dataflow diagrams for guidance, associated variables are grouped together to create prototype *objects* – these are object-oriented entity descriptions consisting of lists of attributes and their types, perhaps with initial values, but as yet containing no list of associated *operators*.

The code is also split into *phases* at this point – sections within which no files are opened or closed, or have their read/write status changed. Equational descriptions of the functionality associated with these phases are obtained automatically and transcribed into the intermediate functional language, simplifying transforms being automatically applied in order to reduce the equational presentation to a *normal form* [43].

Step 3: ('simplify') The abstracted functional descriptions are incorporated into the outline objects as descriptions of their *operations*, thus filling in the semantics of the prototype objects identified at Step 1. A full *specification* (in the language Z [296] or Z^{++} [189]) is then printed out using the object-oriented abstraction as a basis, along with associated textual documentation.

and the plan of the rest of this article is as follows. We first of all set out the 'three steps on the path to abstraction' in more detail in the next section, then collect together some ancillary points in a final section.

16.2 The Three Steps Along the Path to Abstraction

In the following sections we describe the three steps outlined in the Introduction in detail. But first a word on where we are going: we want to turn an application code into an object-oriented program, in which the definitions within each class (generic object type) are couched in a high-level specification language (here, Z [296]). The application code will then reduce to a series of calls for an object method to be applied to an object. It will be much shorter, the bulk of the 'program' having shifted to lie within the class definitions. If one chooses to regard the classes as opaque, then one will have achieved an abstraction away from the details of the implementation, and if one does not wish to 'forget' the definitions within the classes, one can go on to provide real abstractions of each operations semantics, simply by replacing the captured functionality with a looser specification.

For a full description of a COBOL application however, we have to construct classes of objects for the *standard* COBOL concepts such as files and sequences. This is a necessary preliminary – one could look up the descriptions in a manual if any such existed, but failing such a source, we give some examples here, as an indication of the kind of description we would expect to obtain from the rest of the application code too. In fact, COBOL provides seven varieties of file:

- *sequential*
- *relative*, with either
  - sequential,
  - random or
  - dynamic access, and
- *indexed*, also with
  - the above three modes of access (access mode cannot be changed within a program).

and each of these types of files is describable as an *object class*. Each class interprets the operations **RECEIVE**, **SEND**, etc., in its own particular way (the advantage of an object-oriented model is that the meaning of a 'command verb' in the code will be dependent on the object to which it is applied, but the semantics will nevertheless be unambiguous and, it is to be hoped, will correspond to the natural meaning of the name chosen for the operation).

The description of dynamic files is shown in figure 16.2 (when **ALTERNATE KEY**s are to be allowed for the file [254], an extra initial operation '**SETKEY**' which sets a given key to be the access key will be included amongst the operations of the class). The description language is Z^{++} [189] – an object-oriented enhancement of the specification language Z [296]. It will be seen that the specification language allows one to use abstractions such as sets – the '$\{\ldots\}$' notation – and functions, and provides names for relations like '$x \in y$' (x is a member of set y) and operators like '$a \lhd f$' (restriction of function f by removing the part a of its domain set) and '$f \oplus g$' (overwrite function f with function g on the points in the domain set where g is defined).

For each class of file described, one has to settle on a suitable carrier type for the internal data structure, and then the operations are described as changes to the contents of the structure. We use *functions* to represent the internal structure of indexed files and sequences to represent sequential and relative files, and these basic representations are to be preferred over some uniquely tailored structure because this reduces the number and complexity of possible operations that need to be considered overall (and whose properties need to be known during *validation*).

The COBOL **REPORT WRITER** can also be described as a class in much the same way. The class takes as parameters list of associated record types, and contains the operations **INITIATE**, **GENERATE** and **TERMINATE**.

16.2.1 Step 1: Translation to UNIFORM

Our reverse-engineering toolset first of all translates COBOL code into UNIFORM [298] intermediate code. In the process (which is automatic on loading a COBOL application) it generates and stores additional information, such as the initial values

```
class reldynfile[Data]
types                                       /* locally defined types*/
  Status ≝ {closed, input, output, i_o}
owns                                        /* local variables      */
  contents : sequence[Data];
  fkey     : ℕ    ;                         /* the natural numbers */
  frec     : Data;
  status   : Status
invariant
   fkey ∈ dom  contents ⇒  frec =  contents( fkey)
returns                                     /* operation types      */
  AT_END   :          → Bool  ;
operations                                  /* operation types      */
  OPEN     : Status → ()    ;
  DELETE   : ()     → ()    ;
  READ     : ()     → Data  ;
  SET      : ℕ      → ()    ;
  WRITE    : Data   → ()    ;
  REWRITE  : Data   → ()    ;
  CLOSE    : ()     → ()
actions                                     /* operation semantics  */
  OPEN x      ≝
              x = i_o     ⇒
                   fkey'     = 1
                   status'   = i_o
              x = input   ⇒
                   fkey'     = 1
                   status'   = input
              x = output  ⇒
                   fkey'     = 1
                   contents' = ∅
                   status'   = output   /* x = closed ⇒ False*/
  AT_END      ≝ fkey > # contents;
  WRITE x     ≝ status = output ⇒
                   contents' = contents ⊕ {fkey ↦ x};
                                        /* status ≠ output ⇒ False */
  READ x      ≝ status ∈ {i_o, input} ⇒
                     x = contents(fkey) ;
                                        /* status ∉ {i_o, input} ⇒ False */
  DELETE      ≝ status = i_o ⇒
                    contents' = squash({fkey} ⩤ contents);
                                        /* status ≠ i_o ⇒ False */
  SET n       ≝ fkey' = n;
  REWRITE x   ≝ status = i_o ⇒   WRITE x;
                                        /* status ≠ i_o ⇒ False */
  CLOSE       ≝ status' = close
end class
```

Figure 16.2: The object class reldynfile corresponding to COBOL 'relative dynamic' files

of variables. The resulting UNIFORM code is semantically equivalent to the original, and forms the basis for all further reasoning.

One can carry out what the tool does quite easily oneself. The intention is simply to eliminate the redundant constructions in COBOL and replace them with a smaller and clearer set.

- Re-express all **PERFORM UNTIL** statements as **DO UNTIL** loops. **PERFORM TIMES** and **PERFORM THRU** statements can also be eliminated, at the cost of introducing a new local variable.

- Eliminate the **DEPENDING ON** clause in **GO TO** statements by using an explicit **IF** ... **THEN** construct.

- Transform all arithmetic verbs (**ADD**, **SUBTRACT**, **COMPUTE**, and so forth) into assignments – or conditional assignments, when it is necessary to take account of **ON SIZE ERROR** clauses.

- A basic complication of COBOL is the significance of data formats in **MOVE** and other statements. We have to re-express a statement

  ```
  MOVE X TO Y
  ```

  where X and Y are variables, with formats FX, FY respectively, as the explicit assignment

  $$\mathtt{Y} := [\mathtt{FX} \rightarrow \mathtt{FY}](\mathtt{X})$$

  and not as just 'Y := X'. Here, for example, $[\mathtt{X}[3] \rightarrow \mathtt{X}[2]](\_)$ ($\mathtt{X}[n]$ is the type of length n character arrays) denotes the function which left-aligns the input characters, possibly losing the rightmost character.

- A function $no\_overflow_F(\_)$ must also be used to express the fact that COBOL looks to see if an overflow error occurs when a specific data item is moved into a variable with format F. It is often necessary to introduce this in order to express arithmetic calculations in COBOL.

- Replace **SORT** statements by calls of a *stream-based* function of the same name, as shown below. The function receives an input $\mathtt{P1}_{out}$ (the stream of records released by the procedure or file P1), sorts it according to the sort specification, and returns it in sorted order as $\mathtt{P2}_{in}$ (the stream of records to be read by the procedure or file $P2$). If the COBOL statement specifies that the work will be done in some specified temporary file space (sequence of records), say **tempfile**, one identifies the initial sequence of records in **tempfile** with the output from P1 before the sort, and its final state with the input to P2 after the sort. Thus a statement

  ```
  SORT tempfile
   ON ⟨sort_spec⟩
   INPUT  PROCEDURE IS P1
   OUTPUT PROCEDURE IS P2.
  ```

will be abstracted to

$$\begin{array}{ll} \mathtt{P2}(\underline{v}', \mathtt{P2}_{\mathtt{in}}) & \\ \textit{where} & \\ \mathtt{P2}_{in} & = \mathtt{SORT}(\mathtt{P1}_{out}, \textit{sort\_spec}) \\ (\underline{v}', \mathtt{P1}_{out}) & = \mathtt{P1}(\underline{v}) \\ \mathbf{tempfile} & = \mathtt{P1}_{out} \\ \mathbf{tempfile}' & = \mathtt{P2}_{in} \end{array}$$

(the $\underline{v}$ are the program global variables, written out explicitly). The information here is that the **SORT** has no side-effect on the program variables, but depends on the *sort_spec* for its precise action. In contrast, **P1** and **P2** can have side-effects on the program globals.

The procedures **P1** and **P2** will contain COBOL '**RELEASE** ⟨*rec*⟩ **TO** *workfile*' statements and
'**RETURN** ⟨*rec*⟩ **FROM** *workfile*' statements respectively. If files **F1** and **F2**, rather than procedures **P1** and **P2**, are used as the inputs or outputs to a **SORT**, we simply replace $\mathtt{P1}_{out}$ with **F1** and $\mathtt{P2}_{in}$ with **F1**.

- A similar replacement takes place for **MERGE**, a command which takes a set of files (not input procedures) and produces a new merged file.
- Replace calls to an operating system, or to a transaction processing system such as CICS, by calls to object-oriented operations. The environment systems can each be represented as (single object) classes, with private variables which can only be changed from the program by means of calls of the operations of the class (an outline description of the CICS API system in this style is given in [TN-PRG-1025], and provides a concise way to define the necessary parts of these environments).

Note that any 'callable subprogram' in the COBOL source also corresponds to an object. The class in this case has two operations: **CALL** and **CANCEL** (the latter to reset the values of the subprogram's variables to their initial values, corresponding to a COBOL command '**CANCEL** ⟨*subprog*⟩'). Different instances correspond to different subprograms, and accordingly, have different codes which are executed when a **CALL** call is made. Of course one cannot set up these objects before examining a particular application code.

Overall, the transformation into UNIFORM can be viewed as a translation into a small subset of COBOL. The aim is simply to facilitate the later steps of abstraction by reducing the number of constructs that those steps need to deal with, and by making more explicit certain details which are only implicit in the COBOL text. This will reduce the need to later correlate information from different sources, for example, the *data division* and the *procedure division*.

16.2.2 Step 2: Finding Higher Abstractions

Examination of the *file section* and *environment division* yields the files of the program and their associated flags and counters, but the precise connection and arrangement has to be established by looking at the UNIFORM intermediate language translation. Dataflow diagrams give information on what might be the outline shapes of objects in the application code: we first of all designate the files, indexed arrays and reports as *main variables* of an application – they will be represented as objects with themselves as the chief attribute – and then try to pick up the flags, counters and so on which are associated with them. The details of the procedure are set out below.

Collecting Together Data and Functions

Looking at the dataflow analysis of the UNIFORM translation of the program allows us to find the variables logically associated with the main data structures of the program, as well as the dataflows between the main variables themselves. For instance, if there is dataflow from a simple variable `X` into a file `F`:

$$\mathtt{X} \longrightarrow \mathtt{F}$$

and `F` is the only variable which receives an immediate dataflow from X, then we must produce an object corresponding to `F` that has:

- `X` as a hidden attribute `F.X`, and
- an operation `foo` that takes an input value of the same type as `X`, and updates the object:

$$\mathtt{F.foo}(x) \stackrel{\mathbf{def}}{=} \mathtt{F.X} := x$$

- similarly, for output, an operation `bar` which reports the value of `X` to the outside world:

$$\mathtt{F.bar} \stackrel{\mathbf{def}}{=} \mathtt{return(F.X)}$$

A global dataflow from `F` to another main variable `G`:

$$\mathtt{F} \longrightarrow \mathtt{G}$$

suggests a high-level function $\mathtt{foo}_{\mathtt{F,G}}$, that is, a method `foo` of `G` which uses some function `bar` of `F` to update `G` internally:

$$\mathtt{G.foo} \stackrel{\mathbf{def}}{=} \ \ldots\ \mathtt{F.bar}\ \ldots$$

where the description of $\mathtt{foo}_{\mathtt{F,G}}$ as dependent on `F` and `G` *both* arises because the action of `foo` depends on the object `G` to which it is applied. In this object one finds a description of the action which refers to the class of `F`.

In this way one gradually adds new attributes to the basic objects that describe the types of the main variables as one goes through an application program. One also has to add in invariants which (it is believed) link these attributes to the existing attributes of the file. For example, with a suitable definition of the predicate *atend*, the statement

$$\texttt{csfatend} = \mathit{atend}(\texttt{accountfile})$$

asserts that the variable **csfatend** serves as the 'end of file flag' for the file **accountfile**. Whenever the file pointer points to the end of the file, the value in **csfatend** will be '*True*'. These 'believed invariants' will eventually need to be checked and validated.

A sensible order of working using the abstraction tools is as follows:

- For each putative object class, identify global functions (represented by dataflows between the main structures of the program) whose destination is the main structure in the class.

- Each such dataflow identifies a candidate operation that updates the present class, and one then undertakes a more detailed analysis in order to find the precise functionality and the meaning of this operation.

and other techniques which aid in breaking up the functionality of the program into manageable chunks are detailed below.

Phases

One should always attempt to split the program into *phases* before beginning a semantic analysis. A phase is a maximal logically-connected piece of code which contains no `OPEN` or `CLOSE` statements.

A phase represents an execution period in which the files are processed in a particular *mode* (append, overwrite, etc.), and hence should represent a single input-output function on these files. The modalities of the files during a phase give a clue to what the overall form of this function could be (see section 16.2.2), and the details can then be extracted from the code of the phase by more detailed functional abstraction.

Slices

If useful phases cannot be identified (if, for instance, all `OPEN` statements are in an initiation paragraph, all `CLOSE` statements in a termination paragraph), one should use program *slicing* on the variables of an object `C` – and those variables already identified as likely to be used in a method of `C` – to distinguish the code which touches these variables from that with irrelevant functionality.

For a set of variables `f` and code `C`, the operation $\mathit{slice}_{\texttt{f}}(\texttt{C})$ returns a piece of code that *on the variables* `G`, has the same functionality as `C`. For instance:

$$\mathit{slice}_{\{\texttt{f}\}}\begin{pmatrix}\texttt{x} := \texttt{y} + \texttt{10}\ ; \\ \texttt{z} := \texttt{x} * \texttt{x}\ ; \\ \texttt{SEND x TO f}\end{pmatrix} = \begin{array}{l}\texttt{x} := \texttt{y} + \texttt{10}\ ; \\ \texttt{SEND x TO f}\end{array}$$

Once this code has been obtained, one uses (the tool for) functional abstraction to simplify the description of the function corresponding to the slice.

Heuristics for Code Purpose Determination

In order to get an idea of the basic intention of a program or subprogram, we categorize according to its modalities, as determined during the analysis into phases. Figure 16.3 summarizes the plausible purposes of a piece of code, working from the number of input and output files and streams.

# Inputs	# Outputs	Purpose
0	0	Arithmetic function, or string manipulation
1 (stdin)	0	Building up data in an internal table or value
0	1 (stdout)	Output routine
1 (file)	1	Data extraction, summarization, or rearrangement
1 (stdin)	1	Building up data in file
1	2	Data validation or data extraction
2	1	Master-transaction updating
2	2	Master-transaction updating with error reports

Figure 16.3: The likely purpose of code according to overall form

These are only the most plausible explanations of the purpose, further details are needed to decide whether these are reasonable descriptions or not. For example, are there flags which select whether records are to be inserted, deleted or updated in the old file, do the files have suggestive names – like `OLD-MASTER`, `NEW-MASTER`, etc.? Clearly there is scope here for the application of knowledge-based techniques and more sophisticated heuristics. At least COBOL does have certain high-level functions built-in, such as `SORT`, `MERGE` and `SEARCH`, so simplifying some of this analysis.

The output from this step of the abstraction process is a set of comments attached to the named slices or phases.

Business Rules and Implementation Operations

There are two different design aspects in most programs: there are

- *embedded business rules*, such as 'derive the maximum allowable loan for account x', which operate at a low level, typically on a per record basis. These are at bottom of the

- *implemented operations*, such as a file-processing procedure, which typically incorporate several different business rules in the operations on each record of the file.

and our approach enables us to isolate both these components of the functionality.

The implementation operations are identified by enumerating the phases and dataflows of the program, and then are broken down into logically coherent sub-operations by inspection of the derived functional descriptions. Some of the sub-operations will correspond to business rules, usually of the form, 'if X then $Y = Z$'. A description of the procedure which abstracts the functionality of a source program follows below.

Functional Abstraction and Transformation

We assume now that we have identified suitable sections of translated code for further analysis. This code is ('dirty') UNIFORM, that is, it still contains the **PARAGRAPH**s and **GOTO**s of COBOL, and it retains a fall-through semantics which complicates reasoning about it. One converts this into a set of equations which give the mathematical meaning of the code, set out in a simple 'functional intermediate language'. The process is described in detail in Breuer *et al.* [41]. Here we note only that there are just two essential constructs: functional application, '$f(a_1, \ldots, a_n)$', and conditional expressions, '$cond(e, a, b)$', also written as '$e \rightarrow a, b$', which return value a if e is true, b otherwise.

The reverse engineer has some choice over how paragraphs and loops and sections in the original program are represented as functions: one may either

- produce a new function L for every loop in the original program (which is defined then by a tail recursion in the abstraction), and a function P for every paragraph `P`, which expresses the 'fall through' semantics of `P`. A **`GOTO P`** will then be represented simply by a call of P, but a **`PERFORM P`** will be more complicated to represent. Or one may choose to

- represent the **PERFORM** semantics of a paragraph or section **P** as the named function P. This differs from the fall-through semantics in that it does not go on to execute the rest of the program following it, but instead **RETURN**s at the end of paragraph. Then a **`PERFORM P`** call is simply represented.

In some cases it will be *necessary* to use the **PERFORM** semantics in order to avoid an infinite series of expansions as the abstraction transformation replaces **PERFORM** statements by the code of the performed paragraph. Such infinite expansions will occur if there is a loop in the paragraph call graph and if all of the calls in the loop are **PERFORM** calls rather than **GO TO** calls.

Having obtained the equations which describe the program, one then simplifies them. A set of normalizing transformations are described in [TN-PRG-1031], and these are applied after every high-level modification to produce a consistent and standard form for the user. Afterwards, one may apply the following higher-level transformations in order to simplify the equations:

1. Substitution of a function body for its calls ('unfolding' in the terminology of Darlington [89]).

2. Eliminating recursion by recognizing a simple iteration.

3. Adding in new equations, either as properties to be proved, or as assumptions to simplify the description.

4. Using invariants or other equations to substitute one expression for another inside a function description ('folding').

5. Renaming a function.

6. Deleting a function.

7. Proving properties of a function (including induction when the function is recursively defined).

See Breuer *et al.* [41] for a fuller description.

These operations have been built into the reverse engineering tool produced at Oxford. In (3) new equations are added to the list of global hypotheses (assertions still to be proved) which pertain, whereas in (7) the property will be removed from the global hypotheses after successful proof.

Validation of the equations describing the meaning of the code against some set of specifications can be carried out mechanically using the reverse engineering tool by adding properties of the form $P(f(v))$ to the set of equations (where f is one of the functions defined by the equations), and using the transformations listed above (this is equivalent to more conventional methods of generating preconditions, although it does not directly provide documentation.)

Examples

As an example, the COBOL program in figure 16.4(a) is not immediately comprehensible for a variety of reasons (below), but after translation to UNIFORM it becomes as shown in figure 16.4(b). It has the functional abstraction in figure 16.4(c), and after substitution, the definition of $p1(X)$ simplifies to:

$$p1(X) = 10$$

and note that the equation '$p1(X) = p2(5)$' in the abstraction *is not a mistake*, even though the code for paragraph **p1** begins with '**MOVE 0 TO X**', which might lead one to suppose that it then executes paragraph **p2** with **X** set to 0, not 5! In fact, the final line in the code for paragraph **p1** specifies a preliminary operation '**PERFORM p2 THRU p4**' prior to executing **p2**, and it is this preliminary which sets **X** to 5. It is merely coincidental that the first action of the preliminary is to '**PERFORM p2**' also.

An example involving files is the program shown in figure 16.5(a). This code is abstracted to the description in figure 16.5(b), from which we prove the invariant:

$$eof = atend(file)$$

where eof', $file'$ are the actual values of these parameters in the nested calls of *loop*.

There is only one phase, with mode:

$$file \longrightarrow file$$

so we derive the outline class in figure 16.6. The program itself becomes, after replacement of the scattered parts of the object-oriented functionality with explicit calls:

```
type1 : ....;
file : file_class
begin
  OPEN I-O file;
  ELIMOW of file;
  CLOSE file
end
```

and all the operational details have moved to the interior of the definition of the object class.

```
DATA DIVISION.
WORKING-STORAGE SECTION.
 02 X PIC 99.

PROCEDURE DIVISION.
pd SECTION.
p1.
MOVE 0 TO X.
PERFORM p2 THRU p4.
p2.
PERFORM p3.
p3.
ADD 1 TO X.
IF X = 5 MOVE 0 TO X.
p4.
ADD 3 TO X.
```

(a)

```
X : N[2]
begin
 pd section
   paragraph p1:
     X := 0;
     perform thru p2, p3, p4
   endpara p1;
   paragraph p2:
     perform p3
   endpara p2;
   paragraph p3:
     X := X + 1;
     if  X = 5 then X := 0
     end if
   endpara p3;
   paragraph p4:
     X := X + 3
   endpara p4
end
```

(b)

$$
\begin{aligned}
pd(X) &= p1(X) \\
p1(X) &= p2(5) \\
p2(X) &= p3(0) && \text{if } (X+1) = 5 \\
&= p3(X+1) && \text{otherwise.} \\
p3(X) &= p4(0) && \text{if } (X+1) = 5 \\
&= p4(X+1) && \text{otherwise.} \\
p4(X) &= X + 3
\end{aligned}
$$

(c)

Figure 16.4: (a) COBOL program, (b) UNIFORM translation, (c) Functional abstraction.

```
ENVIRONMENT DIVISION.
  INPUT-OUTPUT SECTION.
    FILE-CONTROL.
    SELECT extf ASSIGN TO file
      ORGANIZATION IS RELATIVE
      ACCESS MODE IS DYNAMIC
      RELATIVE KEY IS ptr
      FILE STATUS IS status.
DATA DIVISION.
  FILE SECTION.
  FD file LABEL RECORDS OMITTED.
  01 frec.
   02 height PIC 9(3).
   02 weight PIC 9(3).
  WORKING-STORAGE SECTION.
  01 ptr PIC 9(5).
```

```
PROCEDURE DIVISION.
 a SECTION.
  b.
   OPEN I-O file.
   READ file AT END MOVE true TO eof.
   PERFORM filter UNTIL eof.
   CLOSE file.
   STOP RUN.
  filter.
   IF (weight>250) DELETE file.
   ADD 1 TO ptr.
   READ file AT END MOVE true TO eof.
```

(a)

INITIALLY : $eof = false$

INVARIANT : $frec = string(height, weight)$
$file = extf$

EQUATIONS :

$$
\begin{aligned}
b(file, frec, ptr, eof) &= (file, frec, 1, true) && \text{if } atend(file)\\
&= loop(file, file(1), 1, eof) && \text{otherwise.}
\end{aligned}
$$

$$
\begin{aligned}
loop(file, frec, ptr, eof) &= (file, frec, ptr, eof)\\
&\quad \text{if } eof\\
&= loop(\text{DELETE } file(ptr), frec, ptr+1, true)\\
&\quad \text{if } weight > 250 \wedge atend(\text{DELETE } file(ptr))\\
&= loop(\text{DELETE } file(ptr), \text{DELETE } file(ptr)(ptr+1), ptr+1, eof)\\
&\quad \text{if } weight > 250\\
&= loop(file, frec, ptr+1, true)\\
&\quad \text{if } atend(file)\\
&= loop(file, file(ptr+1), ptr+1, eof)\\
&\quad \text{otherwise.}
\end{aligned}
$$

(b)

Figure 16.5: (a) An example COBOL program which involves file handling ...
(b) ... and the initial abstraction of functionality.

```
class file_class
  extends reldynfile[type1][ptr/fkey]
owns
  eof    : X[1];
  weight: N [3]
invariant
  eof   = atend(contents)
  frec = string(height,weight)
operations
  ELIMOW: () → ()
actions
  ELIMOW ≝
  (contents',frec',ptr',eof')  =  loop(contents,contents(ptr),ptr,eof)  if ¬ eof
                               = (contents,frec,ptr, true)               otherwise.
end class
```

Figure 16.6: The Object Class abstracted from the COBOL source.

Modifications to Objects

The example above demonstrated the modification of a program by replacing its scattered variables by single objects and attributes and calls on objects. We can then transform these objects, using the refinement rules derived in Lano and Haughton [191] to simplify their presentation and eliminate redundancies. The class hierarchy structure gives information on the design of a system, and will provide suggestions for improvement and modification of this design, for example, by making two similar methods instantiations of a parameterized and more general method.

16.2.3 Step 3: Final Steps – Z and Structured Documentation

From the set of functions that describe the functionality of a code section, we can derive a Z specification, whose state is the set of declarations used in the code, constrained by the known invariants, and whose operations are the individual functions of the code.

Each of these Z descriptions can then replace the function inside the object class within which it is defined, so that we obtain a Z^{++} description of the overall program. This is a set of classes, whose internal actions are described by means of (a subset of) Z.

A lot of detail from the original program has been lost in this description – for instance, which order certain assignments occurred in, or whether **GOTO**s or **PERFORM**s were used to implement a recursion, and so forth. But knowledge has been accumulated and integrated, so that the functions and operations of the code are now clearer and closer to the level at which a person unfamiliar with the source code could understand and modify. Reuse is also enhanced, as the object operations have been separated from their particular use in the given program (which is now just a series of object method calls).

Further documentation can now be produced: from the objects we can extract whole/part graphs [137], which reveal the class inheritances, and dataflow graphs for each method, corresponding to SSADM dataflow graphs. *Entity life histories* can be produced from the transformed source code program to show the order in which particular operations are performed. Thus we can present the extracted design of the application in a way that requires no mathematical notation, with simply a graphical presentation of object hierarchies and method input/output modalities.

Metrics are available from the dataflow graphs produced in the first phase of abstraction: these give an indication of the complexity of variable interactions in the code: the weight of each variable (the number of vertices in the dataflow graph that are incident with it) gives an indication of how difficult it may be to change that variable or its roles, or to comprehend these roles. Thus both the average weighting of variables throughout the program, and abnormally high weightings should be examined. A weighting of 0 of course means that a variable is redundant (logically at least).

We can also give suggestions for improving the positioning of file `OPEN` and `CLOSE` statements, for instance, moving them so that files are open for the minimum extent of program scope necessary; which is useful for code comprehension in addition to being safer. We would expect that only one input/output function is represented in each phase, that is, the subset of the dataflow graph of the phase determined by the active file variables, is connected.

As an example of the production of Z from code, we take the factorial function:

```
i: integer;
x: integer;
begin
x:=1;
do while (i > 1):
   x := x*i;
   i := i - 1
end do
end
```

which becomes abstracted to:

$$\begin{array}{lll} prog1(x,i) & = loop(i, i-1) & \text{if } i > 1 \\ & = (1, i) & \text{otherwise.} \\ loop(x,i) & = loop(x * i, i-1) & \text{if } i > 1 \\ & = (x, i) & \text{otherwise.} \end{array}$$

which can be pretty-printed as the set of Z declarations:

STATE

$$\begin{array}{lll} x & : & \mathbb{R} \\ i & : & \mathbb{R} \end{array}$$

$$loop : \mathbb{R} \times \mathbb{R} \rightarrow \mathbb{R} \times \mathbb{R}$$

$$\begin{array}{lll} \forall x : \mathbb{R};\ i : \mathbb{R} \bullet & & \\ loop(x,i) & = loop(x * i, i-1) & \text{if } i > 1 \\ & = (x, i) & \text{otherwise.} \end{array}$$

*prog*1

$\Delta STATE$

$$
\begin{aligned}
(x', i') &= loop(i, i-1) \quad && \text{if } i > 1 \\
&= (1, i) && \text{otherwise.}
\end{aligned}
$$

Production of Summaries

Each program will give rise to a summary of the form:

```
The main structures of the program are:
...
The functions on these structures are:
...   details of inputs and outputs for each identified function
...
The business rules or purpose associated with these functions are:
...   details of the rules and identified purpose of each function
...
```

16.3 Further Points

In this section we collect together some points which are valuable in themselves, but which do not form part of the 'how to' guide which we have tried to set out in the previous section.

16.3.1 Other Languages

Although the techniques have been devised with COBOL, and specifically COBOL 74, as the priority, the processes of object recognition and functional abstraction apply to any procedural language. Techniques originally designed for UNIFORM have been adapted to deal with COBOL. However, a generic sublanguage of both COBOL and FORTRAN would be a useful intermediate step in the production of abstractions for these languages, and UNIFORM can serve this purpose in our system. A large subset of Pascal could also be handled by our approach.

16.3.2 Change Requests

We can give guidelines for using the reverse-engineered code to facilitate modifications requested by users or by internal enhancement decisions. Each high-level identified function will possess an attached comment, stating what it does, and what business rules it is associated with. A modification request will lead to a specific functional modification request upon one or more of these rules, and hence to the functions that implement them. An enhancement request for additional functionality will require the identification of a suitable set of input and output structures, and this will provide a list of classes in which the new functionality can be expressed. Environmental modifications are interpreted as modifications to the low-level classes that represent the operating system or specific devices. By representing these interactions at a sufficiently abstract level, we have reduced the dependence of the application on a particular operating environment, and we will require only certain abstract algebraic properties of these environment classes to be preserved under the modification for the correctness of the design to be maintained.

16.3.3 Presentation of Equations as COBOL

It is possible, to an extent, to present the derived abstractions as COBOL or pseudo-COBOL code. For example, a recursive function of the form:

$$\begin{aligned} f(x) &= a(x) && \text{if } e \\ &= f(b(x)) && \text{otherwise.} \end{aligned}$$

can be expressed (with more prolixity than is strictly necessary, in order to show the generic technique) as:

```
f.
PERFORM f0 UNTIL e.
PERFORM f1.

f1.
COMPUTE x = a(x).

f0.
COMPUTE x = b(x).
```

in COBOL, where e is the appropriate COBOL expression.

In general, the technique for producing pseudo-code relies on the normalization procedure [TN-PRG-1031] to produce equations of a very specific shape. Because, after normalization, the equations are not as arbitrary as they might be, the technique for converting them can be made quite simple in design. An equation in normalized form [TN-PRG-1031] will have a RHS which is either:

1. a nontrivial conditional $b \to e1, e2$, for some further (vector) expressions $e1$, $e2$ and a simple (scalar) Boolean expression b, or

2. a simple vector expression e which does not contain any conditionals. These take the form $(v_1, \ldots, v_n)$ (possibly with $n = 1$), where the v_i are each *scalar* expressions without conditionals, which are either

   (i) the application of an atomic scalar function `foo` to its arguments: `foo`$(\mathtt{a_1}, \ldots, \mathtt{a_n})$, where the $\mathtt{a_i}$ are further simple 1-dimensional expressions without conditionals, or

   (ii) an infix operator expression $e1$ *op* $e2$ between two simple scalar expressions without conditionals, or

   (iii) an atomic scalar constant or local parameter, e.g. 'π' or 'x', or a reference to the scalar components of atomic vector values, for instance, $b[2]$.

and we can easily say how to translate an equation of this form into COBOL. Note that the LHS of an equation is either:

(a) a name without parameters, for instance, 'a', defining a (possibly vector-valued) data item, or

(b) a function name followed by one or more variable names standing in for its parameters: $f(x_1, \ldots, x_n)$, defining a 1-dimensional function with arguments. N-dimensional functions can be regarded as n 1-dimensional functions.

and the two cases have to be treated differently. Below we sketch the technique for producing the pseudo-COBOL translation.

We deal with the case (a) of an equation defining a data item (a non-function) first. There is then no possibility of encountering a local parameter name in the case 2(iii) for a RHS.

To translate an equation '`a` = ...', where `a` is a vector quantity, first of all we allocate storage within the data division:

```
01 a.
 02 a1 PIC 9(16).
 ...
 02 an PIC 9(16).
```

for example, assuming that the vector components each require 16 bytes.

Next, we write a paragraph in the procedure division which fills it with the correct value. To save time in explanations here we call the paragraph by the same name, '`a`'. If the defining equation was a conditional $b \rightarrow e1, e2$ (case 1), the paragraph contains code which calls two unique subparagraphs `a1` and `a2` corresponding to $e1$, $e2$, depending on the result b deposited in a fixed global variable ('`EXPRVAL`' say) by a paragraph `a0`. So '`a`' looks like:

```
a.
PERFORM a0.
IF EXPRVAL NOT = 0
PERFORM a1
ELSE PERFORM a2.
```

We define the paragraphs `a0`, `a1`, `a2` according to the structure of the expressions b, $e1$, $e2$ too – but `a0` at least will not have any conditionals in it, although `a1` and `a2` might.

Eventually the naming convention descends to using names for paragraphs like '`a1212112`' and no more conditional tests occur within paragraphs (case 2). The paragraph simply corresponds to an unconditional vector expression $(v_1, \ldots, v_n)$, and contains code which calls subparagraphs which calculate the scalar components of the vector in turn and put them in the correct place in array `a`. Each of these stores its scalar result in '`EXPRVAL`', and the paragraph `a1212112` which fills the vector looks like this:

```
a1212112.
PERFORM a12121121
MOVE EXPRVAL TO a1
...
PERFORM a1212112n
MOVE EXPRVAL TO an.
```

Now all one has to do is translate simple scalar expressions. Function applications (case 2(i)) are translated to paragraphs which first of all fill a vector with the argument values, then apply the function. This requires a certain amount of storage space to be set aside for 'concurrent' calculations for the argument values, which cannot all take place in the single storage variable '**EXPRVAL**'. If the function **foo** takes *n* arguments, then one has to declare:

```
01 fooPARAMS.
 02 fooPARAM1 PIC 9(16).
 ...
 02 fooPARAMn PIC 9(16).
```

in the data division. One then can translate function applications of built-in **foo** of n arguments, such as *sin* (the sine function with n = 1), for example:

```
a12121123.
 PERFORM a121211231
 MOVE EXPRVAL TO fooPARAM1
 ...
 PERFORM a12121123n
 MOVE EXPRVAL TO fooPARAMn
 COMPUTE EXPRVAL = foo(fooPARAM1,...,fooPARAMn).
```

If, on the other hand, the function **foo** is defined locally in an equation, then we replace the '**COMPUTE EXPRVAL =...**' in the above with '**PERFORM foo**', on the understanding that we will have defined a paragraph **foo** which takes values cached in the global parameter array **fooPARAMS** and calculates a result value in **EXPRVAL**. It is perhaps safest to do so always, and write a special paragraph for each built-in function **foo** too, which says, in effect 'calculate **foo(fooPARAMS)** and put the result in **EXPRVAL**'. Obviously, infix operations (case 2(ii)) are a special (2-parameter) case of functions.

The only case (case 2(iii)) left to consider is that of scalar constants as subexpressions. Clearly one just writes a paragraph which returns their value in **EXPRVAL**. If they are a 1-dimensional component of another global, say **b**[3], one just returns **b3** into **EXPRVAL** instead of **b**. For example:

```
a121211231.
MOVE b3 TO EXPRVAL.
```

Now consider the case when the equation defines a function **a** with parameters. This will be translated as a paragraph which looks in the **aPARAMS** array for its arguments, and returns a value in **EXPRVAL**. The only extra translation required is to look up a variable **x** which is encountered as an atomic subexpression in the correct component of the **aPARAMS** array. This case did not have to be considered when the equation defined a data item alone, because there were no local parameters.

Notice that one *has* to construct a *separate* copy of the **PARAMS** array unique to each paragraph representing represents a functional call. This is because an expression **foo**(...**bar**(...)...) needs the values placed in **fooPARAMS** for **foo**s benefit to be undisturbed by those placed in **barPARAMS** afterwards (but before **foo** stops needing them) for **bar**s benefit. So one cannot use the same storage space for both **fooPARAMS** and **barPARAMS**, *unless* there are no nested calls of one from the other.

Once code has been produced according to the above recipe, however, one still has to make a second pass in order to disambiguate some remaining parameter clashes. One has to make a separate copy of the paragraph representing a function call of **foo** for each occurrence of **foo** in an expression. Say these are **foo1**, **foo2**, etc., then one calls paragraph **foo1** instead of **foo** when translating the first occurrence, and **foo2** instead of **foo** when translating the second, and so on. This requires one also to make extra copies **fooPARAMS1**, **fooPARAMS2**, etc., of the **fooPARAMS** array.

There are two reasons behind this:

- expressions like **foo**(...**foo**(...)...) may occur, and therefore different parameter tables are required for the two (intertwined) calls, and second
- a COBOL paragraph does not behave exactly like a subroutine on execution. Nested calls will not cause a return from each call to the place the paragraph was called ('perform'ed) from – instead the first (outer) call will return to the later (inner) calls return address. This is because the return addresses are not stacked but overwritten.

To combat the latter effect, one has to make sure that each paragraph is called from only one place. So one makes a different copy of the paragraph for each call statement, to be safe, and this amounts to a different copy for each occurrence of the basic function call in the generating equation.

The code has to be cleaned up considerably after the initial translation! One can replace **PERFORM** ⟨*para*⟩ calls which only appear once with the body of the paragraph (if the call occurs twice, it is probably shorter to leave the paragraph alone), and make many of the storage arrays used occupy the same physical space: a single physical space can be made to correspond to a single *maximal anti-chain* in the graph. An anti-chain is a maximum set of function names (nodes in the graph) with no direct or indirect call relationship (directed path) between any two. All the functions in an anti-chain on the call-graph can utilize the same physical space to store their parameter values, because they never call each other. Obviously the *minimum* physical storage required is the minimal number of (maximal) anti-chains which will cover the directed graph completely. This is an invariant which can be extracted from the graph alone.

The complete forward engineering program can be seen to follow the same 'clean, specify, then simplify' plan [43] as the reverse engineering program;

- 'Clean': normalize the specifications to the standard form given in the report [TN-PRG-1031].
- 'Specify': translate the normalized set of functional equations into COBOL, as outlined above.

- 'Simplify': increase the readability of the generated COBOL code by replacing calls to paragraphs with their bodies when the paragraphs do not correspond to any high-level concept.

In the regenerated code, each function is represented by a paragraph, and a function call is represented by a `PERFORM` of this paragraph. So no `GOTO` statements are necessary.

Thus a limited form of re-engineering is possible; by reverse engineering, then forward engineering again. We are also investigating the automatic rewriting of equational abstractions to produce `WHILE-IF` forms of code (in which there is no mutual or multiple recursion). Much research on such transformations exists in the functional programming world [89, 57].

16.3.4 Comparison with Other Techniques

As is argued in Zimmer [358], using objects in the reverse-engineered abstractions reduces the effort needed to understand the interactions between data, and the technique set out here achieves this: the number of global variables is reduced, and the data is partitioned into distinct objects, where it cannot be affected by remote operations. Our approach also incorporates that of Linger [205], in producing explicit functional abstractions of the 'business rules' and file-to-file mappings present in the code (for large application codes, prior partitioning of the application into objects at the data level, and into object methods and processes at the procedural level, must be essential, and this is advocated here).

But the strategy laid out here is distinct from that of the REFORM project [320], at least. There assembly code is first translated into a 'wide-spectrum language', which contains both Pascal-like and Z-like sub-languages, and code transformations are performed on the Pascal-like language in order to achieve simplifications (our strategy is to perform transformations on the higher-level language, not the lower). There is a large library of transformations, and some guidance about the applicable transformations is given at each point, but selecting the right sequence of transformations remains difficult and exacting. We have avoided the need for a large library of transformations by working at the more abstract level, where there are fewer constructs, and the effects of transformations are clearer. Fewer transforms are needed, and automation is straightforward. So the REFORM approach relies on the reverse engineer's understanding of conventional procedural code, whereas the assumption here is that simple mathematical equations will be more accessible than the procedural code (COBOL). It may be true, however, that a presentation in a more accessible procedural pseudocode might eventually be preferable, and we have set out here a scheme for converting equations back to COBOL which can be adapted – in fact, eased! – to other procedural languages. Certainly, the REFORM strategy, if applied to COBOL, would result in the reverse engineer being presented with an unmanageable number of choices of transformation at each step!

16.4 Conclusion

We have described techniques by which COBOL code can be abstracted to produce explicit mathematical descriptions of functionality, and object classes representing the design of the application. The resulting representation is suitable for the application of theorem-proving techniques, and for transformations to simplify and clarify the design. It is related to the well-known process view of systems, since the global functions identified as methods of the object classes correspond exactly to such processes: the output routines, for instance, become methods that update the class built around the output stream.

The overall design of the tools that use these techniques is itself object-oriented, allowing components, such as abstracted functions, to be named, and used as attributes or method definitions at any suitable point in the descriptions. Thus the system is very flexible and easy to use, although it does require a familiarity with mathematical notation. About 40% of COBOL has been treated, but the basic concepts will be applicable to the remainder of the language.

17

Quality Management and Reverse Engineering

H.J. van Zuylen,
Delft Hydraulics, The Netherlands

17.1 Introduction

Quality management for the development of new programs has become fashionable in the last few years. Standards laid down in for instance the ISO 9000 series [166] and the *IEEE Guide for Software Quality Assurance* are often used as a basis for the quality strategy for the development of new software systems. In the proposed standards 9001-3 [167] an attempt is made to apply the 9001 and 9004 standard to the development, supply and maintenance of software. The ISO standards are mainly concerned with the development of new products. Maintenance does not get much attention. The same applies to the ISO guidelines ISO 9001-3 [167]. This means that the most important activity in software engineering, maintenance (by some authors estimated as 70% of the effort) still has had little attention from the point of view of quality assurance. The draft IEEE standards for software maintenance consider to the 'normal' maintenance process, analogous to the forward engineering process. A meta-process in which a decision fits to change the maintenance policy and, for instance, to reverse engineer an application, is not discussed in [167]. The reverse engineering process itself is also outside the scope of these proposed standards.

For reverse engineering much of the standards can be taken over from forward engineering or maintenance. Reverse engineering is also a process with some input, which produces some output. The process itself can be quality controlled, as well as the product. The question of the software system which is delivered after reverse engineering satisfies the standards of quality software will be discussed later in this section.

17.2 Quality Management

Quality control can be applied to the:

- process
- product
- tools
- people involved

The first step to control the quality of reverse engineering is to have it organized properly. Responsibilities, authorities and interrelations of all personnel involved should be defined. Also the qualification of people, such as their professional education and experience, should be specified for all functions. Further the standards on organization, verification of the organization etc., can be followed from the ISO standard 9001 [166].

17.3 Products

Understanding is often the most important product of reverse engineering. Since it is difficult to verify the quality of understanding, the verification should be aimed at the secondary products: the documentation, the definition of tests, test reports and other reports and the source code after processing.

DIS 9001-3 [167] requires that "*the quality system should be an integrated process throughout the whole life cycle*". This is not applicable to most systems which are reverse engineered. These systems are in most cases developed in a pre-quality situation or have gone out of the quality control in the maintenance phase. What one can do in reverse engineering is:

- to make *reverse engineering* a part of the quality system,
- to assure that the software system after reverse engineering satisfies most standards which are applicable to systems which have been developed under quality control.

The later point can not be taken too literally, because quality assurance imposes requirements, both to the development process and the products. One may build development documentation afterwards, but one can not have them reviewed before the system is implemented, which is a requirement in the ISO standard [166]. One could argue that the requirements [166] are too strict and sometimes irrelevant for software which is reverse engineered. For instance the requirement that "*specification and design should be such that the product or service is producible, verifiable and controllable under the proposed production, installation or operational conditions*" is not appropriate for software which has been completed already as a whole or in part. Some adjustments to the standards may be necessary.

To make reverse engineering a part of a quality system, ISO 9001 [166] can be followed:

- A quality system documentation should be made [167]. This documents all the elements, requirements and provisions for reverse engineering.
- A part of the planning should include the drawing up of a reverse engineering quality plan.

The REDO method can be worked out to form a work plan. Reviews and verification of the products and corrective actions should be prescribed in the reverse engineering Quality Assurance plan.

17.4 Requirements and Criteria

The formulation of precise requirements and criteria for reverse engineering is in general rather difficult or even impossible. For the source code criteria can be formulated, for instance in terms of complexity and coding standards. The metrication tools described in section 21.8 give the possibility to assess the complexity before or after restructuring of the sofwtare. The static analysis tools of chapter 21 can be applied to verify the conformance of the code to coding standards.

It is more complicated to apply standards to the documentation generated in the reverse engineering process. The simple requirement that *all* development documentation should be generated, is very demanding and in most cases too heavy. Some parts of the system may be very stable, such that they can treated as black boxes or as library routines. Reverse engineering is only necessary for the level of interfaces and a functional description. The decision which part has to be redocumented and to which level, may depend on the function and complexity of that part, which may not be known in advance. Sometimes the paradigm is used of reverse engineering as a kind of laundry: the untidy, badly documented software comes in, is treated by a well-defined standard process and leaves the 'laundry' in a well-structured, well-documented state. The metaphor of a predefined product which is obtained by a predictable process, is often not very appropriate. Reverse engineering is more like a health clinic where a system with problems comes in, is analyzed by experts and possibly supported by assistants and tools. The quality assurance is in the validity of the method used, the quality of the tools and first of all in the experience of the expert. Not every analysis need to be done, but the analysis done should conform to certain standards and also the decision whether or not some analysis is done should be verifiable.

The state-of-the-art is not that far, that we can present such standards in this book. there are possibilities to define quality standards for the source code, for instance with respect to data structure and control flow. The tools described in chapters 20 and 22 give the possibility to restructure existing code, so that it satisfies such standards. A further possibility, which is described in chapter 21, is to use the metrication tools to quantify some aspects of the software quality. Standards could be defined based on them, while re-engineering tools can be used to satisfy such standards.

Apart from possible standards for the software, it is important to have standards for the reverse engineering process. One of the safeguards one should build in, is that all decisions should be documented and can be reviewed and that the methods and tools satisfy the best current standards. The quality plan should prescribe this.

17.5 Progress Control

The Reverse Engineering Quality Plan (REQP) should also describe the management of the process. A part of the management is the progress control. The ISO standards mention that maintenance activities are unpredictable. Therefore, progress in terms of what has been achieved is not the most important. More important is how much still has to be done. In maintenance and also in reverse engineering, new problems may come out when some problem is solved. Progress control should consider the activities done, the new problems to be solved and the activities which have been planned and those which have become redundant.

17.6 Configuration and Version Management

Reverse engineering produces documentation of different views on different levels of detail. The system may be restructured during the reverse engineering process, such that a clear link should be made between versions of the system and the documentation and between the documentation items. A configuration and version management of all these products will be necessary in order to keep an overview over the reverse engineering process and the products. In REDO this information is stored in the SDDB, together with the source code and documentation itself.

Officially approved documents have to be placed under version control. Modifications or replacements should be reviewed before they are included.

17.7 Standards and Verification

In the REQP standards should be defined for the products of reverse engineering. The preferred style of documentation has to be chosen and a minimum list of required views can be given. The verification of the products of reverse engineering should be done with respect to the following requirements:

- Does the documentation satisfy the standards?
- Does it accurately and correctly describe the appropriate aspect of the system in a satisfactory complete way?
- Is it suited as a means to comprehend the system and to support future maintenance?

The last issue is the most important. It should be covered, as far as possible, by the requirements for the reverse engineering process and in the standards.

The verification could be done, just as in forward engineering, by introducing an independent review after a milestone in the project. After a review, the approved documents should be placed under configuration control.

17.8 Tools

The quality of all tools used for reverse engineering should be verified. The problem that tools sometimes are used in a wrong way, should be prevented by a good training of the users and provisions in the user interface to make it unlikely that the tools are used for tasks which are outside their domain.

17.9 Conclusions

To a certain extent reverse engineering can be considered as a production process. Standards can be applied as for any other production process. Such standards should apply to the reverse engineering process as well as the reverse engineering products. Although it remains unlikely that a complete, literal application of standards is very useful, many parts of the standards for forward engineering can be applied to reverse engineering too.

There is certainly a need for standards, as mentioned above. It is not sufficient to build new quality systems. Standards for maintenance have to be defined as well as for bringing an existing system to a satisfactory quality level.

Part IV

TOOLS

18

The REDO Architecture

J. Estdale, P. Katsoulakos, M. Tobin,
Lloyd's Register, Croydon, UK

18.1 Introduction

In this chapter the architecture of the REDO toolkit is described. Section 18.2 identifies a number of ideas which had an important influence on project thinking and contributed to the current design of the REDO architecture. The notion of an IMPSE is introduced. Section 18.3 provides an overview of the REDO IMPSE, describing the repository, user interface and tools. (Other chapters of this book provide a more detailed discussion of particular components.) Finally, section 18.4 identifies the technology selected as the implementation environment of the project and lists its advantages and disadvantages.

18.2 Seminal Influences

The Stoneman report [60] introduced the idea of a specialist software development environment for ADA: the ADA Programming Support Environment or APSE. This recognized the need for an underlying database rather than a traditional hierarchical file system. However, its original purpose was to support configuration management. The idea of a common intermediate representation of ADA source, usable by a wide variety of tools was taken up (producing for instance DIANA), but such representations were not intended to identify individual database entities, although later work has recognized that items such as symbol table entries could be stored as database objects [215].

The APSE concept has since led to the more general idea of the Integrated Project Support Environment (IPSE) and the Software Engineering Environment (SEE), which are intended to support every aspect of the developer's work [31]. The REDO project has its own variant: the Integrated Maintenance Project Support Environment or IMPSE. Efforts in the project have been concentrated on the reverse engineering and re-engineering aspects, producing the 'IRSE' defined in section 13.4.2.

Today's Computer Aided Software Engineering (CASE) tools bring together a number of important ideas: large bit-mapped displays and mice supporting good drawing facilities and multiple independently controllable windows; the use of a database supporting independent access to individual design elements; the need to transfer information between different development methods, leading to a better understanding of how they differ and to efforts to agree standards for interchange. This kind of technology is very useful for documenting one's growing understanding of an application and suggests the idea of using a single toolkit and supporting database for reverse engineering and for subsequent redesign, re-implementation and maintenance. A significant limitation in most CASE tools to date has been the failure to integrate the refinement and derivation of design views with the versioning provided by traditional configuration management, particularly at the level of individual design elements.

'Hypertext' has become popular ever since it was first supplied with the Apple Macintosh in 1987. Over the years, hypertext has attracted many who had the objective of helping humans to solve their problems cooperatively and more effectively such as Ted Nelson with his Xanadu [105] and Conklin and Begeman's Gibis [106]. This fits well with the task of a reverse engineering team, which is to understand and document an application, and to provide a sound base for future maintainers to refine.

Another seminal influence on REDO, is the notion of 'live data' [126]: a display shows some data, can be typed over or otherwise edited to permanently change the record of that data to the new version, to be shown in any future displays. This goes back to the first non-command-driven screen-based text editors and to forms-based transaction processing systems which display existing values for update. Although this may seem trivial to users of spreadsheets and Microsoft Windows, most operating systems still supply their commands without this feature. They treat the terminal as two separate, sequential files, one for input and one for output, which are entirely independent although occupying interleaved lines on a display device.

Many authors have suggested that source code should include its own design documentation, to minimize the danger of inconsistencies appearing during maintenance [109]. Knuth's method of 'literate programming' [186] , discussed in section 8.4, goes further, organizing an underlying file in such a way that compilable code, design documents etc., can all be generated directly from it. Unfortunately, this rather complicated file has to be created using a normal text editor, as there are no tools to support its preparation. This approach of associating code with documentation has much to offer; most of the problems are resolved if the concept is re-interpreted using a database and hypertext links to separate out the various different kinds of material.

18.3 The REDO IMPSE

The project strategy in REDO has been to produce two platforms. The first is aimed at early exploitation of project results relying on SQL as an interface to a relational database of the data required for technical documentation and restructuring using a directed graph-based method. The second with longer term objectives relies on a fine grain object management repository with associated schema descriptions for infrastructure, quality management and application understanding tools.

This section concentrates on this second platform, the REDO IMPSE, which is described in figure 18.1.

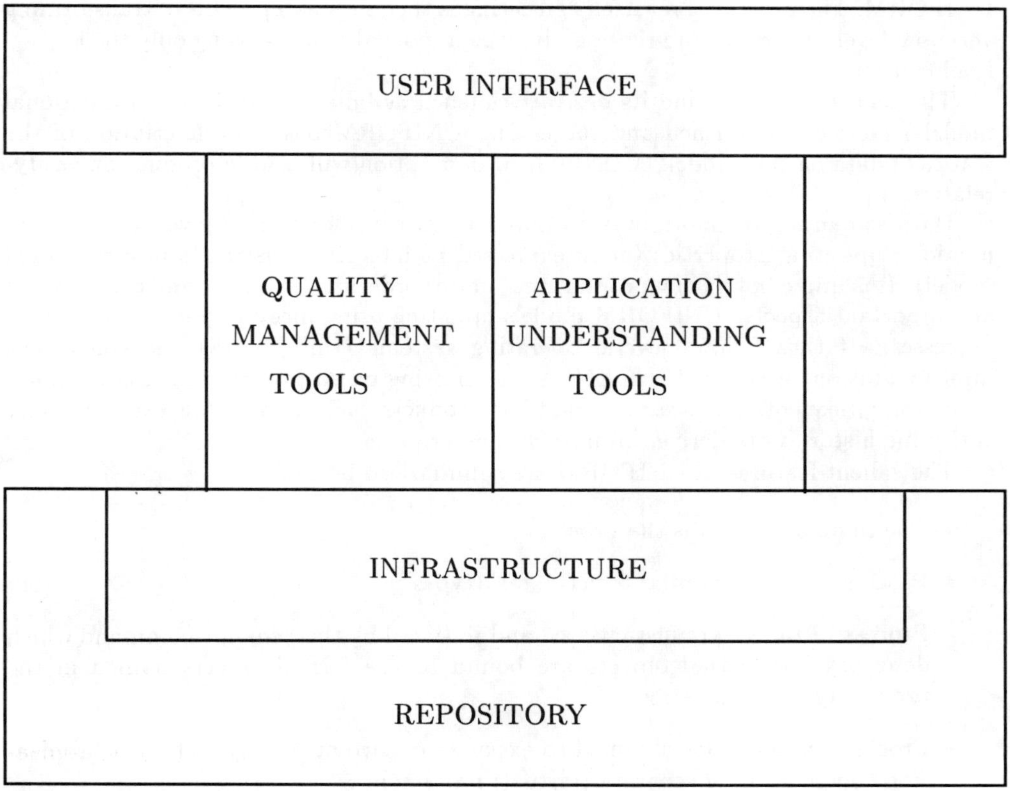

Figure 18.1: The REDO IMPSE

18.3.1 The REDO Repository

The UNIFORM Intermediate Representation

REDO aims to support a wide spectrum of activities which lie between code restructuring and reverse engineering. UNIFORM [298] is an intermediate representation of the application logic, which allows a system to be described at the various levels required and provides a common framework for the representation of environmental dependencies. Chapter 9 describes the role of UNIFORM in the project. UNIFORM supports a reasonably direct translation of the source to be restructured, and therefore contains the equivalent of all the language constructs of the source languages (presently COBOL and FORTRAN). It also contains features which support code 'improvements' at a higher level than restructuring. One example is the provision of user-defined types, supporting the search of the source for types which were intended but have not been directly expressed.

A prerequisite for reverse engineering is the provision of a suitable set of notations to express the system description: these are the 'high-level' language constructs of UNIFORM. The process of reverse engineering is then seen as a process of transforming very low-level constructs and representing them more abstractly using only the higher-level constructs.

The relational model and its derivatives (such as binary-relational and functional models) are well-established and successful. UNIFORM bases its description of the statics of data on this model. A UNIFORM description will readily produce an entity-relationship data model.

Data semantics are more fully captured when consideration is given to their dynamic or updating properties (often expressed as integrity constraints in a relational model). It is immediately obvious that the time or ordering dimension and concurrency are important aspects. UNIFORM models updating using message-passing sequential processes. It thus follows several operating systems (Unix, VMS) and concurrent implementation languages (OCCAM, ADA) in being based (loosely) on Hoare's Communicating Sequential Processes. Familiar products such as dataflow diagrams and entity life histories are derived from such a description.

The salient features of UNIFORM are summarized below.

- The main construct is the process.
- Process types are similar to ADA task types.
- Process instances are instantiated and initiated by the *generate* command which describes how actual objects are bound to the formal objects named in the process type specification.
- Process instances are assumed to execute concurrently, subject to synchronization constraints, on separate (virtual) processors.
- Processes send and receive messages through buffers of appropriate types.
- It is easy to represent vectors, arrays, and direct access files as functions.

The System Description Database

The REDO repository called the System Description DataBase (SDDB), provides:

- a central store, shared by the REDO tools, of all information about the maintained application;

- explicit representation of the application structure and logic;
- common repository services (such as loaders, parsers and browsers);
- communication between tools;
- version control.

It was clear from the outset of the project that REDO would require a repository of all the diverse maintenance data used and produced by its tools. Such data includes original textual source code, parsed abstract syntax trees, life cycle documents, design annotations, data models, formal specifications, metrics etc. Not only should this data be stored centrally; it should also be integrated to capture structurally the inter-relations between its elements and to eliminate as far as possible duplication of information between different elements. Nonetheless, the repository must facilitate appropriately simplified views of subsets of the data, as required by individual tools.

To represent explicitly the structure and logic of the application, it was agreed that the structural representation of the parsed source code should optimize queries relating to semantics rather than to incidental syntax. However, the abstract syntax (but not necessarily the concrete syntax) of the source code should be recoverable. To enable tools to work on the same code representation, the data structures of UNIFORM are used to define a representation into which applications written in a range of third-generation languages can be parsed.

As an interim measure, to provide an early version of the SDDB for tools to use and to enable recovery of source code abstract syntax, it was decided also to design an intermediate representation of COBOL applications which would use generic UNIFORM structures where possible without losing language [7] specificity. This is called 'COBOL-IF', the *COBOL Intermediate Form* and represents structurally ANSI '74 COBOL semantics and abstract syntax, including programs, variables, procedures, statements and expressions, and stores explicitly a program's control structure, its data definitions and its data usage. COBOL applications are parsed into COBOL-IF. Subsequently they can be translated and restructured into UNIFORM as required. The SDDB schema has been extended to meet the needs of several tools which annotate the nodes of COBOL-IF and link them with design information.

The storage of a persistent representation of a program's semantics and abstract syntax has proved to be of considerable benefit to the project. Instead of each tool having to conduct its own parse of the source code at the beginning of its invocation, all tools have been able to share the same parser, and the parser needs to be run only once for each source file. The structured representation of source code can be readily linked at a fine-grain level to other maintenance information. This has been found particularly useful for reverse engineering tools which allow the user to browse the code and annotate it. The results of any tool, once written, are immediately available to other tools, as they use the same data store.

The schema for COBOL-IF is very complex (around 120 entity types and 160 relationship types) and its design requires considerable resources. Although this complexity is partly a result of the size of the COBOL language, any such representation of a third-generation language will not be trivial. The network data model of the Object Management System (OMS) used is well suited to the representation of the recursive structures which pervade programming languages and software engineering. The data model is also suited to the representation of relationships for which there are no natural key fields. The query language of the OMS has been found to be powerful and concise, combining attribute pattern matching, network path specification and functional composition of queries. Importantly for a project of this type, it has been found relatively straightforward to extend the SDDB schema, both through the application of new attributes and links to entities and through the definition of new views and domains.

18.3.2 Repository Infrastructure

Infrastructure tools can be categorized as follows:

- loaders to populate the SDDB with source code and documentation;
- parsers to produce parsed code structures and information about environmental dependencies;
- general purpose tools, which support editing and querying of all data stored in the SDDB;
- incremental documentation tool, which may be used to annotate any element of data in the SDDB;
- link tool, which may be used to associate two or more data elements in the SDDB;
- facilities to browse documentation in the SDDB;
- facilities to access source code in the SDDB in a controlled manner, providing a range of views on that data. Views may be structured using the abstract syntax of the code or as defined by the user. Facilities include pretty printing and structured editing. The code may be viewed at different levels of granularity (e.g. the contents of code blocks may be hidden from view). The user may also traverse the source code, for instance by 'navigating' to the usage of a variable, from its definition, or by stepping through a sequence of statements of a specified type.

For a more detailed account of the SDDB and its infrastructure, the reader is referred to chapter 19.

18.3.3 The REDO User Interface

The basic principles of the REDO user interface are described below. The goal of the REDO project was 'integratability' rather than 'integration', so the level of achievement of these principles varies from tool to tool.

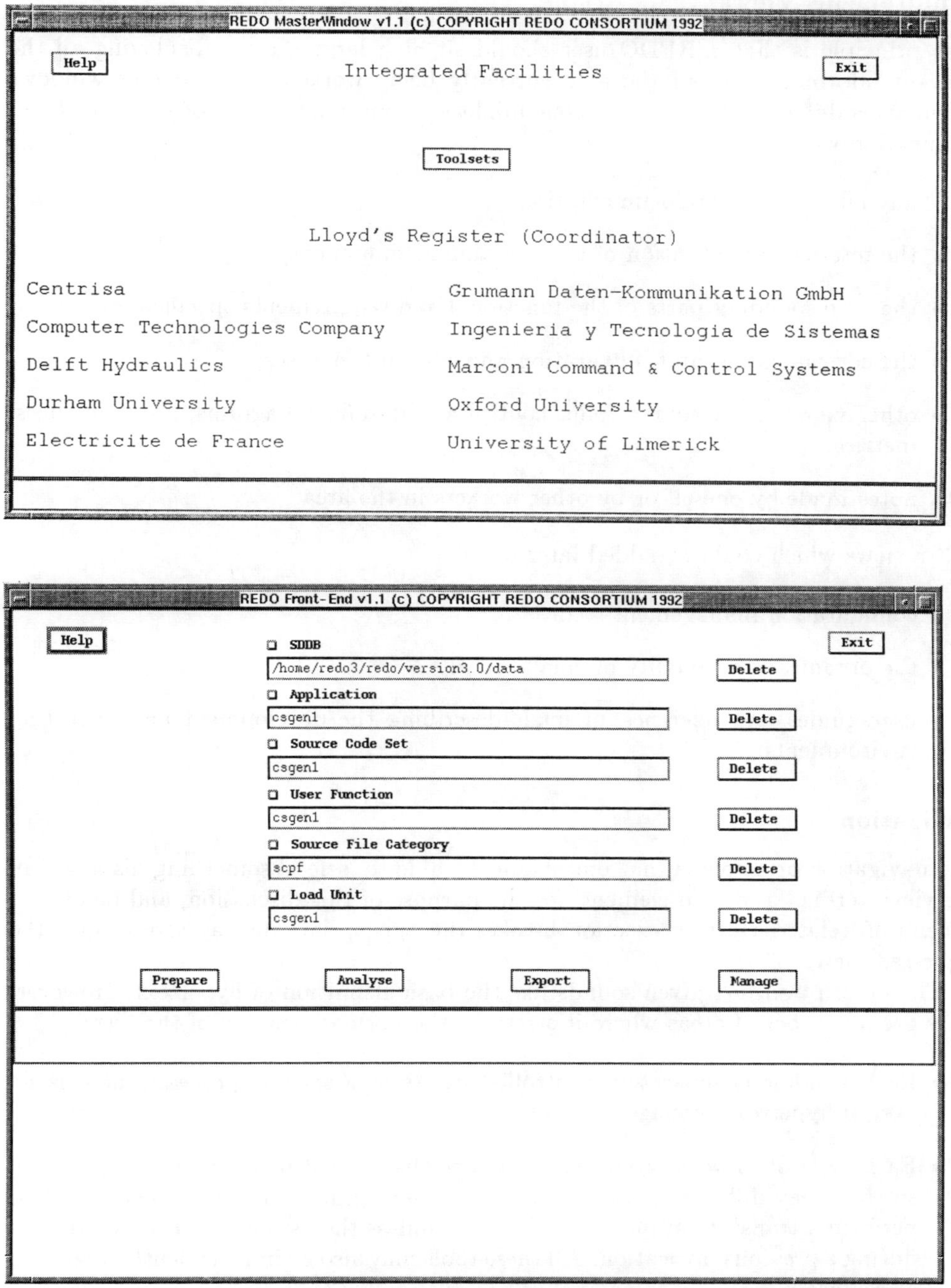

Figure 18.2: The first screen of the REDO user interface

Simultaneous Views

This principle is that a REDO user should sit at a large screen, displaying all the relevant information about the area currently being worked on. Different windows would show different aspects. Thus one might be examining a piece of source code, in conjunction with:

- any relevant design documentation;
- the interface specification of the containing component;
- the corresponding parts of the functional and requirements specifications;
- the corresponding unit, integration and system test cases;
- other views of the source code: control and dataflow diagrams, program slices, metrics;
- notes made by oneself or by other workers in the area.

Other views which could be added later include:

- configuration management records;
- the organization's quality manual;
- user guides and reference manuals describing the development and operating environments.

Navigation

The navigation principle is that one should be able to 'select' something displayed in one view, termed a 'design element' for the purpose of this discussion, and be offered a menu of 'related views'. Selection invokes the appropriate display tool to give the requested view.

The description just given sounds like the basic definition of hypertext. However, there are a number of areas where it stretches the normal meaning of the term.

- Each window is separately controlled by its own specific process; there is no overall hypertext manager present.
- Each type of view is produced by a specialist tool dedicated to that purpose, so they may differ in content, style, scope and implementation. Some need to perform a transformation on the database unless they stored appropriate details during a previous invocation. All these tools may also be independently upgraded or replaced.
- Views may be generated on invocation rather than being stored in a database. Views may be linked so that a change in one causes corresponding changes in others.

It is also important to make clear that although the network of hypertext 'connections' between views is related to the network of database links between entities, there are significant differences:

- a single design element may be represented by many linked database entities;
- a hypertext connection corresponds to invoking a specified display tool on some portion of the database, which need not have a database link to the design element whose related views menu is being considered;
- database links of the same type will normally be part of the same view(s).

Visibility

Each type of view is composed of various fragments of information. Rather than dictate the precise contents of each view, as much potential information as possible is provided, allowing users to control the visibility so that they can limit the display to the most appropriate for the particular circumstances.

The REDO IMPSE needs to be sufficiently easy to use that experienced users find it more natural and more cost-effective than using listings and writing on them. The benefits of using REDO include:

- all existing views are immediately accessible;
- views can be seen and compared side-by-side;
- useful views can be produced by automated analysis tools;
- repeated change does not produce illegible results. The latest version is as legible as the first; earlier versions and changes can be viewed on request.

18.3.4 REDO Quality Management Tools

The main objectives of the REDO project in this area are:

- to identify the quality factors of an application that affect the maintainability of that software product and to define appropriate measures. These measures should help identify applications or parts of applications, that can benefit from restructuring, and should help qualify the usefulness of the restructuring carried out in REDO;
- to investigate the maintenance process and to model this process with a view to providing aid to management in determining the optimal allocation of maintenance resources to maintenance requests;
- to construct a cost estimation model for maintenance, in particular maintenance in the REDO environment. This estimation model should provide estimates for annual maintenance effort based on various product, process and environmental factors;

- to construct a suite of validation and verification tools for use in the maintenance process.

These objectives are addressed in the following sections.

Metrics

A number of metrication schemes were investigated, with particular emphasis on the Fenton and Whitty approach [119], which allows the extraction of control flow metrics from flow graphs. This technique allows decomposition of a flow graph into a hierarchy of primes, and the definition of metrics as recursive functions on these primes. The scheme was extended to enable the definition of metrics dependent on the data declarations in a program. As the application is being represented in terms of an abstract syntax tree in the SDDB, metrics can be implemented quite naturally as recursive functions on this tree structure. Advantages of this approach are:

- data and control flow are defined in a unified way;
- definition of the metrics becomes more formal;
- users can define their own metrics provided that they can be expressed as recursive functions.

It seems likely that system level metrics, such as those dependent on the identification of logical and physical files, can be defined in a similar way.

Process Modeling

Queuing networks have been applied to describe a request driven maintenance process within a software maintenance department. Software maintenance management has been considered as the allocation of departmental resources to the various maintenance tasks. A formal description of the model has been produced in terms of a predicate net, allowing various intelligent server allocation strategies to be evaluated. The predicate net has been interpreted using logical programming techniques and a Prolog research prototype has been built.

Cost Estimation

A survey of existing cost estimation models was carried out. Boehm's COCOMO model [28] was selected as the basis for the REDO cost model RECOMO. The adaptation includes the appropriate modifications for REDO. An examination is carried out on how 'historical data' is used to adjust the program quality characterization so that the cost estimation is as accurate as possible.

Validation Tools

A number of validation tools are being developed to ensure that validation and verification needs during the maintenance process in the REDO environment are met. Some of these tools are described below.

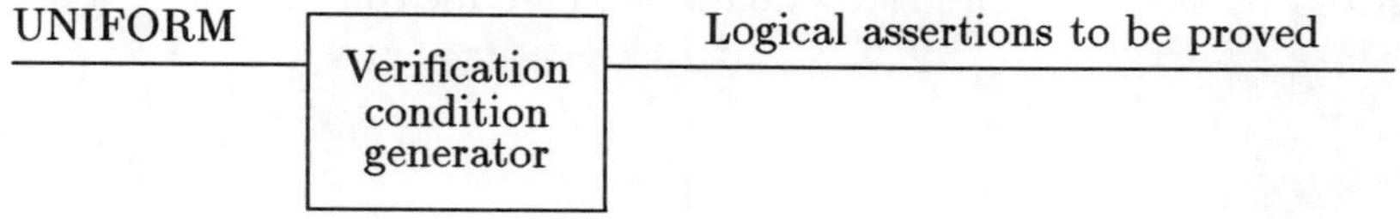

The verification condition generator is a tool which provides facilities for verifying properties of UNIFORM programs. These properties are expressed in terms of predicate calculus and correspond to assertions about the values of variables under various transformations. The verification method employed is a variant of the Gries weakest pre-condition approach.

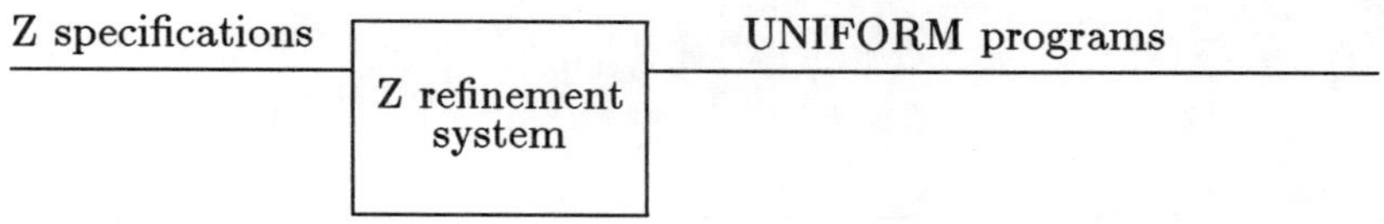

The Z refinement system is a tool that translates Z specifications into procedural UNIFORM code. A number of well-known transformations are used, for instance, set membership is converted to a search for an element in an array. The objective of the refinement system is to allow for the constructive (correct) translation of specifications into UNIFORM programs.

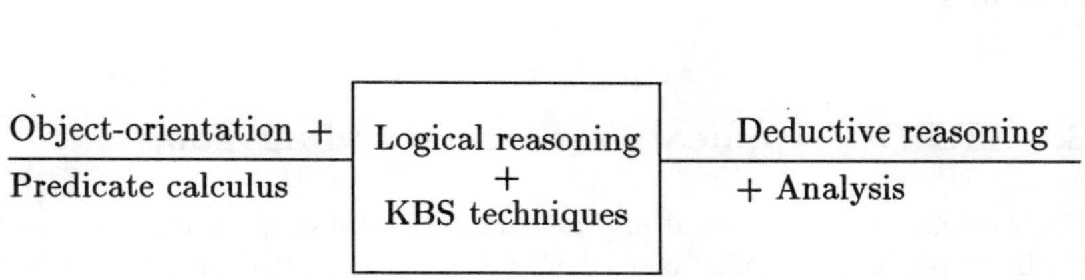

The logical knowledge-based (KBS) reasoning system provides verification of logical properties described by an object. The object-oriented description is derived from analysis of COBOL code, in particular file declarations and read and write access to files. A formal semantics, in terms of category theory has been provided for the object-oriented language Z++ which is a novel extension of the specification language Z and is derived by the function abstraction tools, described in section 18.3.5. The static

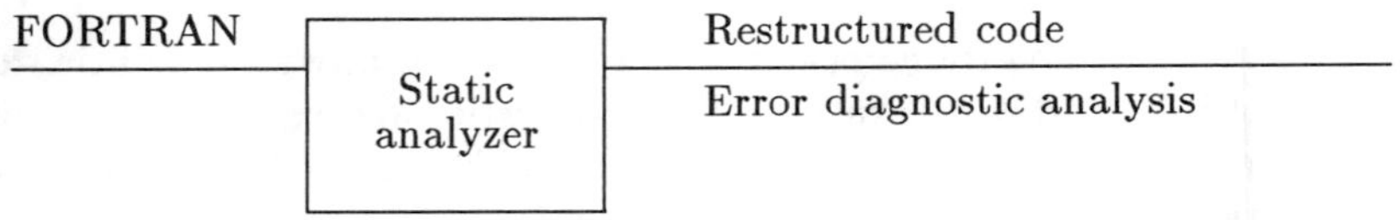

analysis system takes code as input and undertakes limited forms of restructuring and diagnostic analysis. The functionality is typical of many such analyzers.

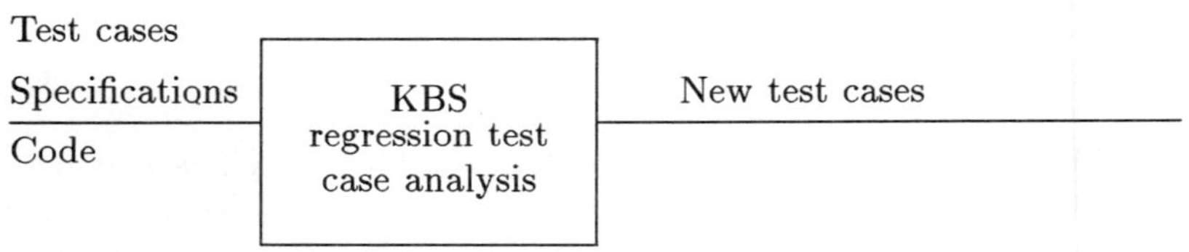

The regression and test case analysis tools provide assistance in identifying which existing set of test cases are to be rerun and which new set of tests are required, when modifications are made to program code. The work attempts to identify new test cases from specifications.

18.3.5 REDO Application Understanding Tools

REDO is adopting a number of application understanding techniques: some are well-established and have already proved useful in commercial projects; others are more novel. They cover issues associated with reverse engineering and restructuring code, environmental and user interactions, and documentation. The main tools and techniques under development are described briefly in the following sections.

Function Abstraction Tools Using Formal Methods

A suite of prototype function abstraction tools have been developed exploring different approaches. In the first approach, appropriately structured code is automatically transformed into a functional specification of itself (i.e. translated into a functional language.) The result is not itself a helpful specification. The next phase is to produce a concise normal form of the application by applying transformations automatically. Once such a specification is produced, more expert methods may be employed to determine what the specification means in a more profound sense, but, often, the initial specification itself will be enough. Text may be added giving the inferred design intention.

In an alternative approach, code is logically tested against theories formulated about it, and, in the process of validation (or refutation), a satisfactory and accurate specification for the code is gradually arrived at by the validation expert. This method assumes the (predicate transformer) semantics of the IL, and is based on the weakest pre-condition method of Gries.

In the final approach, a COBOL program restructured to remove `GOTO`s and other unstructured constructs is transformed into the logical objects present in an application represented by Z++. The approach is based on first collecting together all flags and associated data structures in working storage which act as subordinate functions for the main data structures of the program. The user can then conjecture relationships between these variables and the main data structure. The program is then divided into distinct procedures which perform a single input/output function, possibly on several files or internal data structures. This can be obtained by examining the places at which files are opened or closed. The conditions which need to be satisfied in order for the function to hold true can then be obtained. The derivation of these conditions can be best achieved via an interactive process with a user providing detailed domain knowledge as to the functionality of the code.

Control-flow Restructuring

Control-flow restructuring transforms programs with arbitrary control structure into ones containing only the base constructs of sequence, selection and iteration. In REDO, this is performed as a prerequisite for the function abstraction techniques although control-flow restructuring should also prove useful in its own right.

Analysis and Remodularization Based on Dataflow

Code is remodularized by the application of various transformations to UNIFORM, guided by information derived from dataflow analysis. The resulting code reflects the logical structure of the application as a set of UNIFORM processes and more closely conforms to the object-oriented paradigm than the original.

Data Remodeling

Functional (many-one) dependencies among the data are deduced from access keys to indexed files and sort keys to sequential files. A normal form (probably Third Normal Form) is computed, if possible, within user-supplied constraints (for example, that a given relation must appear in the decomposition). The resulting normalized model is presented as an ERA diagram using a combination of heuristics and further assertions.

The REDO data remodeling tool differs from many existing data modeling tools in being 'bottom-up' as opposed to 'top-down': the starting point is an un-normalized physical data model, which is progressively brought closer to normal form, as opposed to starting with nothing and maintaining a normal form as new entities and dependencies are added.

Design Information Management and Recovery

The generation of design diagrams was discussed in chapter 11. REDO provides a default design editor with a wide range of symbols, so that users who have not configured suitable design editors may nevertheless approximate the required notation. Diagrams can be created 'by-hand' using the interactive facilities of these design editors to document findings as they emerge, or be generated automatically by analysis tools on the SDDB.

REDO is considering the notion of 'correlation' of design diagrams with source code, from the level of entire diagrams (with programs) down to diagram elements (with fragments of source code). This is helpful when studying source code, as one's emerging understanding of the underlying design can be recorded, checked and improved. REDO has developed this concept to create the generic 'design component' which consists of a name, a textual description and database links to its 'contents', whatever they may be, such as fragments of source code or documents. All references to the component are linked to the corresponding design component entity, so that these too can be explored. Design components are useful in enabling the reverse engineer to:

- give a single meaningful identity to any desired collection of material;
- give the design components shown in design diagrams a permanent existence not dependent on the continuation of their presence in such a design diagram. This is necessary in order to allow radical editing of such diagrams, for instance moving a design component from one diagram to another;
- provide a standard means of representing the components found by analysis tools, so that a mixture of approaches can be combined.

REDO supports explicitly a variety of views on the SDDB. However, there will always be a need for further ad hoc views and the generic design recovery facilities are designed to support this. Straightforward examples include:

cross-reference variable usage: list all lines where a specified variable occurs;

module call tree: list all modules, and within each, list all the modules it calls.

It seems that a sophisticated pattern-matching query language could well be sufficient to handle the extraction of this information. This is being explored with the REDO Query Tool, described in chapter 19. The results could be presented in various ways, for instance:

- simple list of instances with associated attribute values;
- structured report of instances and their details;
- instances highlighted in source code;
- diagrams of instances and their relationships.

For example, possible diagrams include:

data dependency graph :
nodes: all variables
links: all use of variable <source> in updating variable <destination>

call tree :
nodes: all paragraphs
links: all calls of paragraph <destination> in paragraph <source>

flowchart :
nodes: all source statements
links: all possible control flows

dataflow diagram :
nodes: all processes in JCL
links: all files written by process <source> and read by process <destination>

Documentation Tools

Documentation is crucially important as an aid to understanding the application. The process of redocumentation generates new documentation for an existing system, either to replace or augment any documentation which already exists.

Conceptually, complex relationships exist between an application and the documentation which describes it. These vary in granularity; at the highest level, a document describes an application. At a lower level, particular parts of a document refer to specific parts of the application. These references may be explicit, for example they may represent the development path from an initial statement of a requirement through to the code which implements the required functionality. Others may be implicit, in the sense that they may be inferred by the user during the comprehension process. Some of these implicit references may be specific to a particular user's mental model; a second user may make different logical connections.

References from documentation to the application are generally represented in conventional linear documentation by explicitly naming part of the application in the text. These references are unidirectional, from the documentation to the application. References back from the application to the documentation may occur in module header commentary, but are otherwise rare. Some systems exist which allow and encourage more extensive documentation to be embedded in the application itself, a good example being Knuth's WEB system [182].

Where the application and documentation are stored in a repository, it is possible to represent references by links. Explicit links can be set up permanently when the database is loaded. Implicit or conceptual links are built up as part of the incremental comprehension and redocumentation process; it may also be appropriate to annotate the links themselves to explain the relationships which they represent.

Work on documentation in REDO has been based directly on European standards in this area such as ISO 8613 and ISO/DIS 9541. A graphics-based logical structure editor is being built on the SDDB. This tool will allow users to specify, design and instantiate (using a graphics-based interface) their own document structure according to their own company documentation standards. The documentation tools will also provide efficient modification and updating facilities.

Technical Documentation Of Data Processing Applications: Control And Data Graph Analysis

Technical documentation is the precursor to a multitude of commercial activities based on technical DP information extracted for verification, auditing, metrication, validation, porting, maintenance, extension, and last but not least restructuring purposes. The graph technical documentation tools capture the entire and complete application as an application graph consisting of a series of connected functional directed graphs which allow the projection of information about the application into various spaces, the most well known of which are the control space and the data space.

While it is not possible to extract the functional specification from the application in a coded form, it is possible to document the function in such a manner that meaningful decisions can be made about whether the application should be overhauled, including possible restructuring. Logical inconsistencies in the program such as unused code, bad control structure, unused data etc., can be marked for attention. Actual structure and flow paths of control and data can be extracted and checked for consistency with either a functional specification, if this is available, or with the users of the application. Only once this information has been extracted in the desired form can meaningful management decisions be made about what maintenance strategy should be adopted for the application. Technical documentation is, in the last instance, a method for extracting and presenting commercial information about technical DP matters.

18.4 Choice Of Technology

Although the REDO project's precise technology requirements were not available at the start of the project, sufficient was known to be able to agree a set of standards.

The following were selected after much debate:

Sun Workstation : This was chosen for its large bit-mapped display and mouse, its fast 32-bit processor and large address space, its multitasking operating system and the availability of research and product software (primarily PCTE, Unix, X Window and MOTIF and Prolog so far).

IPSYS Toolbuilder's Kit : The main reasons for choosing this were that it provided:

- a database capable of handling both fine and coarse-grain data;
- availability on a variety of platforms, including SunOS and PCTE;
- a design editor which could be configured to support a wide range of diagrammatic notations common amongst users and which could be used to display, edit and print those diagrams;
- a structure editor which could be configured to display contents from the database in a range of user-specifiable formats;
- a configurable user interface which would help ensure consistency across tools developed by independent teams at separate sites.

X Window and MOTIF : It was clear that the emerging GUI standards would be helpful in ensuring consistency, although it was unclear whether the technology being used would migrate to these standards within the project timescale.

Prolog : It was decided to use Prolog for reasoning and rule-based programming. This has necessitated the building of an interface between Prolog and the IPSYS database. It has also been useful as a sophisticated pattern-based search capability embedded in REDO tools.

There is no doubt that the best available technology in the circumstances was chosen and those issues to which most weight was given have generally proved to be the most important.

The resulting deficiencies were many and varied:

- The Sun workstation is little used in commercial data processing.
- There is poor inter-operability between Sun and IBM mainframes running the COBOL, CICS and TOTAL to be supported by REDO.
- The database lacked some important features: wide commercial acceptance, multiple writers at the fine-grain level, easy interfacing to third-party tools, SQL interface, resilience.
- There are no explicit hypertext facilities and no support for combining diagrams and structured text within a single window.
- Tool-to-tool communication is poor; there is no standard for passing formatted information.
- No OCR scanner was available for loading existing documentation into the Sun.

Apart from the lack of a scanner, these issues were known in advance. If the choice had to be made again today, the decision would be the same.

19

The System Description Database and its Infrastructure

G. Ostrolenk, M. Tobin, *Lloyd's Register, Croydon, UK*
A. Altes, *Centrisa, Barcelona, Spain*
E. Younger, *Centre for Software Maintenance, University of Durham, UK*

19.1 Introduction

At an early stage of the REDO project it was decided to develop a reverse engineering repository, called the *System Description DataBase* (SDDB). The objectives of the SDDB are:

- to provide a central store, shared by the REDO tools, of all information about the reverse engineered application,
- to represent explicitly the structure and logic of the application,
- to enable the REDO tools to manipulate applications written in a range of source languages, supported by different environments,
- to maximize integrity and consistency of data,

- to save development resources where possible through the sharing of database loaders (including parsers) and access and update functions,
- to act as a means of communication between tools, and
- to enable version control of information during the reverse engineering process.

The ANSI/SPARC architecture for DataBase Management Systems (DBMS) [312] defines three levels of data representation: the *internal*, the *conceptual* and the *external.* The internal level is concerned with physical storage of the data. The external level is concerned with how data is presented to the user and involves a number of views, each based on some part of the total database. The conceptual level is concerned with a logical representation of the entire database; it is an intermediary level between the other two.

Discussions of database analysis and design [268] distinguish three activities: data analysis (yielding a *conceptual schema*), logical design (yielding a *logical schema*) and physical design (yielding an *internal schema*). The conceptual schema is DBMS-independent. The logical schema maps the conceptual schema into the data constructs of a particular DBMS (for instance, the relations of a relational DBMS (RDBMS) or the logical records of a CODASYL system).

A *data model* is a formal system of object types, operators and integrity rules which can be used to specify a conceptual or a logical schema. The data model underlying an RDBMS is the Relational Model. The data model underlying a CODASYL DBMS is the Network Model. Neither the Relational Model nor the Network Model capture sufficient semantic information to serve adequately as the data model underlying the conceptual schema. A number of 'semantic' data models have been developed for this purpose, including the extended relational model, RM/T, and the Entity-Relationship model.

If the data model underlying the DBMS is the same as that used to specify the conceptual schema, there is no distinction between data analysis and logical design. This is the case for the SDDB.

Sections 19.2 and 19.3 discuss the rationale and requirements for the SDDB. Section 19.4 discusses the data model underlying both the conceptual schema and the DBMS chosen to implement the SDDB. Section 19.5 discusses the conceptual schema itself. Section 19.6 looks at the process of loading an SDDB, and section 19.7 discusses several tools which offer access to the data at the conceptual and external levels of the ANSI/SPARC architecture.

The physical level (the internal schema) of the SDDB is not discussed here.

19.2 The Need for a Central, Shared Database

There are many reasons why an integrated reverse engineering toolkit requires a central, shared database (a repository[1]), to store the diverse data used and produced by its constituent tools.

[1] The term 'repository' has been in vogue since it was coined by IBM for the database facility they will provide as part of their AD/Cycle product. The term has been used subsequently in diverse ways. Some people use it to refer to any database within a software engineering environment which describes life cycle information and source code. Other people use it to refer to software engineering

For any realistic application, the quantity and complexity of data involved in reverse engineering demands a persistent data store. An application may be composed of many programs, each containing hundreds of thousands of lines of source code. Each line of source code can represent a complex group of facts with associated documentation. Such complexity and quantity of information precludes the exclusive use of primary memory by tools.

The various tools required to support reverse engineering manipulate interconnected and overlapping data types. They also often manipulate the same data instances. The same program may be viewed by the user through a source code browser, restructured by a tool concerned with its control structure, and measured by a metrics tool concerned with its dataflow patterns. Rather than attempting to maintain many (mutually consistent) copies of the same data, it is preferable to integrate the representations required by each tool within a single database. Tools then derive their own views of the information they require.

Reverse engineering a large application is neither simple nor brief. The process is likely to involve several engineers working over an extended period. As with CAD and CASE tools [53], transactions are likely to last days rather than seconds and may execute in sequence or asynchronously. There is therefore a need to enable and control complex patterns of read and write access by multiple users.

The data types of reverse engineering tend to be highly complex structures like control flow graphs. Unstructured representations of such data are easily corrupted. Data integrity is particularly important when many tools share the same data. Database technology provides techniques for the enforcement of data integrity.

Finally, there are a number of functions common to many different reverse engineering activities. If the tools are implemented to share the same data, they can share a library of common utilities such as source code parsers and browsers.

19.3 Project Requirements on the SDDB

It is worth considering some of the specific requirements that a reverse engineering toolkit is likely to place on an SDDB.

The SDDB is required to store and interrelate all the information about an application which is used or generated by REDO's reverse engineering tools, including source code, historical life cycle documents, diagrams, ad-hoc notes and links created by the reverse engineer, metrics, application data models and formal specifications.

Clearly the most important domain of data is the source code of the application which is to be reverse engineered. This includes not only compilable programming language modules (for instance COBOL programs), but also job control language scripts, DBMS schema definitions and transaction specifications (such as CICS tables).

Six categories of information about source code have been identified:

Original Source Text, including the layout and appearance of the source code (white-space) and optional key words that have no effect on the functionality of the program ('noise');

databases which implement an Entity-Relationship model and which provide facilities to customize and query meta-data. The latter and fuller definition is true of the SDDB.

Abstract Syntax, specifying the particular (compiler or interpreter-significant) source language constructs used to express the functionality of the program;

Module Semantics, including:

- **Statement Semantics,** defined in terms of the requirements that a compiler or interpreter must satisfy when generating machine code for statements of that type, and modeled as an abstraction from the textual and syntactic constructs available in the particular language used to express program functionality[2];
- **Data Usage,** specifying the type and location of all explicit references to variables, constants and files (including evaluations, updates and parameter-passing);
- **Control Flow,** i.e. all information directly affecting the sequence of statement, procedure, program and job execution;
- **Data Definitions** of the types of all variables, constants and files.

Different representations are suited to storing and manipulating different categories of information about source code. The choice of a representation determines the integrity constraints that are enforced by the schema and the kinds of queries which it optimizes. A requirements specification for a repository should identify the categories with which its tools and users are primarily concerned.

The difference between abstract syntax and semantics in representing a program statement is significant when there is not a 1:1 mapping between the two for a particular language. For example, in COBOL the two statements below have precisely the same semantics:

1. `ADD A, B GIVING C.`
2. `COMPUTE C = A + B.`

While a simple abstract syntax representation would not manifest the similarity between the two statements, an exclusively semantic representation would not capture their differences. Those differences might be important to a tool concerned, for instance, with programming style.

REDO's restructuring and reverse engineering tools are primarily concerned with information from the semantics categories. This is also the range of information to which a reverse engineer would most need access. Abstract syntax is, however, important in the early stages of reverse engineering, before descriptions have been generated which are not source language specific.

Other kinds of information required by reverse engineering tools can be derived from the above categories. For instance, dataflow (the map of possible sequences of explicit references to variables, constants and files) can be derived from data usage and control flow. Data dependency (the set of variables, constants and files which can

[2]In fact, the semantics of the target language is never *defined* in REDO. The objective is to *model* the semantics' structure explicitly, to meet the needs of reverse engineering tools. The REDO representation of semantics does not presuppose any particular denotational, operational or axiomatic definition.

affect the value of a data item at runtime) can be derived from data usage, control flow and statement semantics.

A further requirement on the representation of source code is that it enables REDO tools to manipulate applications written in a range of source languages, supported by different environments. In other words, there is a requirement to maximize source language independence.

19.4 The Choice of a Non-Relational Data Model

Having decided to build a central repository for the REDO toolkit, the project had to decide which database technology to use. The advantages of an established DBMS implementing the relational data model are considerable: proven reliability, extensive data and transaction management, automatic query optimization, a standard declarative query language (SQL), and a sound theoretical base in relational algebra and set theory. Nonetheless, many recent developments in database technology, especially in the fields of CAD/CAM and CASE, have moved away from the pure relational data model. Examples include the Portable Common Tool Environment (PCTE) [107] and the Common ADA Programming Support Environment Interface Set (CAIS) [99], the IBM Repository Manager [273, 344] and a range of general-purpose object-oriented and/or deductive DBMSs such as O2, GEMSTONE and POSTGRES. Much of the rationale driving these new technologies is true of the reverse engineering domain. The project chose the IPSYS Tool Builders' Kit (TBK) [31] as its platform, a software engineering environment which extends PCTE with additional database facilities. The reasons for this choice are discussed in sections 19.4.1 and 19.4.2. For general discussion of the relative merits of relational and object database technologies, see Loomish [210], section 3.3 of Brown and Childs [53] and chapters 22 and 25 of Date [90].

19.4.1 The Data Model Underlying the Conceptual Schema

The subset of the SDDB's conceptual schema which is used to represent COBOL defines around 120 entity types and 160 relationship types. The subset used to represent calls to the TOTAL DBMS defines 50 more entity types and 50 more relationship types. Techniques of semantic data modeling are required to minimize such complexity and to enforce data integrity.

In particular, reverse engineering data (such as programs, structure charts and dataflow diagrams) is highly structured and lends itself to representation in networks of nodes and arcs. Moreover, much reverse engineering data is recursive in structure. Recursive data structures can be naturally and concisely expressed using subtypes, as figure 19.1 illustrates. A section of a document can be composed of further (sub)sections, units of text, or a sequenced mixture of both. This fact can be captured using a single relationship if it is possible to declare sections and units of text as subtypes of some supertype, and to define the supertype to be the destination of the relationship.

For these reasons, an Entity-Relationship-Attribute model incorporating subtyping, multiple inheritance and logical sequence was chosen for specification of the SDDB's conceptual schema.

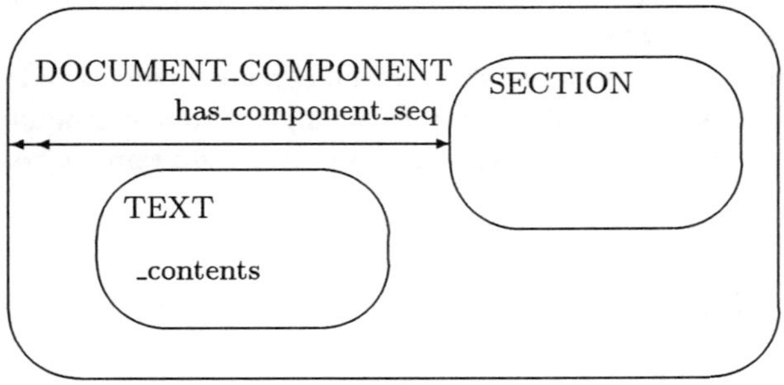

Figure 19.1: Document Sections: An example of recursive data structures

19.4.2 The choice of a database management system

It was decided not to use an RDBMS for several reasons:

1. The mapping from the Entity-Relationship-Attribute model to the relational model is complicated and indirect. Given the complexity of the SDDB's conceptual schema, and the prototyping nature of the REDO project, it is important that the mapping from the conceptual to the logical schema is simple and direct.

2. It is not possible to capture many of the integrity constraints imposed by the structure of the SDDB's conceptual schema using the Data Definition Language (DDL) of an RDBMS, simply because the RDBMS implements the relational model rather than the Entity-Relationship-Attribute model.

3. The following are typical of queries on reverse engineering data:

   (i) `What is the first statement in the COBOL paragraph called by this 'PERFORM' statement?`

   (ii) `What is the next statement in that paragraph?`

   (iii) `Which section contains the paragraph which is the destination of this 'GOTO' statement?`

   (iv) `Which variables were evaluated in the statements in which this variable was previously updated?`

   Such queries are naturally represented as navigations across a network, requiring the evaluation of a succession of links from some given starting point. They are *one-at-a-time* queries. Relational DBMSs optimize *set-at-a-time* queries, because they store and manipulate data as relations rather than as objects. The restrictions and joins required to implement *one-at-a-time* queries in an RDBMS can be both clumsy and inefficient. Although *set-at-a-time* queries also occur in reverse engineering, the predominance of *one-at-a-time* queries makes their evaluation response time critical.

In particular, and importantly in reverse engineering, recursive data queries are not handled well by RDBMSs, precisely because they operate *set-at-a-time*. Rather than navigating the arcs of a graph selectively, an RDBMS has to repeatedly *join* entire relations and store each of the results in temporary relations.

Rather than using an RDBMS, the project decided to use a DBMS implementing the Entity-Relationship-Attribute model of the conceptual schema.

PCTE implements the Entity-Relationship-Attribute model. However, on its own it is inadequate as an SDDB platform. There are two reasons:

1. The SDDB contains data of diverse granularity: source code files, documents, diagrams, variables, procedures, statements and expressions must all be represented and manipulated. Some of these objects contain other objects. Documents contain sections, subsections and diagrams, and diagrams contain nodes and arcs. PCTE is suited to the representation of coarse-grain data. However, because objects are implemented with the overheads of operating system files and directories, they are very inefficient for the representation of large quantities of fine-grain data.

2. Although PCTE supports *one-at-a-time* queries, it has very limited support for *set-at-a-time* queries. It is not possible, for instance, to retrieve all the entities of some type in a PCTE database using a single query. Entities are always retrieved by specifying their position in the database network.

The TBK is an extension of PCTE. It was chosen for the following reasons:

1. The TBK provides a second tier to the PCTE database, efficiently implementing large complex structures. Such structures can be manipulated as simple objects at the first tier.

2. The TBK DataBase Interface uses a functional data model. The model integrates PCTE's facilities to support the composition of links and attributes for succinct navigation with facilities for SQL-style keyed set queries. The functional data model is discussed further in section 19.7.

3. The TBK database supports the Entity-Relationship-Attribute model directly, providing a straightforward mapping from specification to implementation. Hence, structural constraints on data integrity imposed by the specification are automatically enforced in the database.

19.5 The Conceptual Schema

This section discusses the conceptual schema of the SDDB[3]. In particular, this section discusses how the conceptual schema satisfies the requirements for the representation of information in the SDDB (as described in section 19.3) using an Entity-Relationship-Attribute model incorporating subtyping, multiple inheritance and logical sequence (see section 19.4).

[3] As the same data model underlies both the conceptual schema and the DBMS in which it is implemented, there is no distinction between the conceptual schema and the logical schema (see section 19.4).

19.5.1 The representation of source code

Section 19.3 discussed the requirement that priority be given to semantic information over abstract syntax, and of abstract syntax over original text appearance, in the SDDB's representation of source code. Section 19.3 also stated the need to enable manipulation of a range of source languages and environments. The solutions to these requirements were found to be closely related.

A representation in which semantics is separated from abstract syntax enables tools which access the semantic representation to be relatively independent of the source language in which the application was written. Extensions to the scope of the toolkit to include additional application source languages require changes only to the tools which *load* the semantic representation. The semantic representation naturally integrates the different elements of an application (such as jobs, programs and schema definitions) by abstracting from their language-specific features.

UNIFORM [TN-UL-1002], a language developed at the University of Limerick as part of the REDO project, is designed to capture explicitly the semantic structure of third-generation programming languages and the environments in which they operate. The *structures* of UNIFORM are used as the basis of a data model for the semantic representation of source code in the SDDB. Generation of source text from the semantic structure is viewed as an unparsing process from an internal to an external representation, i.e. to one of several alternative source languages such as COBOL (see Section 19.7.3).

There are four conceptual stages in the transition from the original source code of an application to its UNIFORM semantic representation in the SDDB:

1. loading and parsing of the original source code (see section 19.6);

2. construction of relationships between the different components of the application (see section 19.6);

3. low-level restructuring (for instance to remove COBOL `GOTO` and `PERFORM THROUGH` statements) (see chapter 22.3);

4. translation of source language structures not available in pure UNIFORM (e.g. replacement of COBOL paragraphs by UNIFORM procedures, and replacement of any COBOL `STRING` statements by an equivalent series of UNIFORM assignments) (see chapters 9 and 22.3).

Rather than implementing all these stages in a single tool, the SDDB defines an 'Intermediate Form' for each source language and layered product, enabling the task to be decomposed.

The source of an application is parsed into the appropriate Intermediate Forms. The next two stages (construction of the application and low-level restructuring) are carried out on the Intermediate Form representation. The Intermediate Forms are then translated into UNIFORM. Higher-level restructuring is performed on the UNIFORM representation.

Although each Intermediate Form retains the abstract syntax of its associated source language or layered product, its underlying structure is derived from the semantics of that language or product. The semantics of most languages and products have much in common. These shared features are expressed in UNIFORM. Hence, it is often possible for the Intermediate Forms to use UNIFORM's semantic structures and to extend them with abstract syntax information.

This considerable overlap is captured in the conceptual schema through the declaration of generic types, with attributes and relations, and of subtypes which inherit their generic type's definitions and extend them with further attributes and relations. In some cases, the UNIFORM representation is encapsulated in the generic type definition. In other cases, a UNIFORM subtype is required. A single conceptual schema is defined for UNIFORM and the Intermediate Forms: they are alternative specializations of the same generic types.

In translation, say from COBOL to UNIFORM, the relations and attributes defined at the subtype level for COBOL are analyzed and redefined, but those at the generic level are left unaltered. Tools which manipulate only the generic features can be used on any of the subtypes.

The source code of an application may include a wide range of components, utilizing third-generation, compiled programming languages, job control languages, transaction processing monitors, DBMSs, etc. REDO's approach to the representation of source code has been to start with particular application platforms and to generalize from them. The discussion below is divided between the representation of third-generation, compiled programming languages and the representation of interactions with the environment, including layered services. Particular languages and products will be used as examples of the REDO approach.

Third-generation, Compiled Programming Languages

This section uses COBOL-IF [TN-LR-1057], the Intermediate Form for COBOL[4], to illustrate REDO's approach to the representation of third-generation, compiled programming languages in the conceptual schema of the SDDB. In particular, the representation of assignment is used as an example of the separation of semantics from abstract syntax.

Cross-references

COBOL-IF is concerned with the semantics of the (syntactically correct) language constructs used in a program. For example, the occurrence of a variable name in an expression is treated explicitly as a reference to an entity, a variable, which also has a definition and to which there may be references elsewhere in the program. Similarly, the occurrence of a paragraph name in a `PERFORM` statement is represented as a call to a paragraph entity, which contains a sequence of statements, occupies a position within a sequence of sections and paragraphs, and may be called by other statements in the program. Capture of the meaning of cross-references (the relationship between definition and use) necessitates a network representation, rather than the tree structures typically used for abstract syntax representations.

[4] To be more precise, COBOL-IF is the Intermediate Form for ANSI 74 COBOL [295] and its extensions and refinements in IBM VS COBOL for OS/VS [164].

An Example: Assignment

The representation of assignment in COBOL-IF is a good example of how an Intermediate Form can capture semantic information structurally and extend it with abstract syntax. It also illustrates the relationship between the Intermediate Forms and UNIFORM.

There are many COBOL constructs which can be used for assignment, including `ADD`, `DIVIDE`, `MULTIPLY`, `SUBTRACT`, `COMPUTE`, `SET` and `MOVE`. Each of these statement types has various alternative forms. Although their abstract syntax is different, they share much in common semantically. Each can be considered as a set of one or more simple assignments. In each simple assignment, the value of an expression is assigned to a variable. The expression may be an arithmetic expression, a reference to a variable or a literal value. Each arithmetic expression applies an operator to one or two arithmetic expressions, variable values and/or literal values.

The way in which a COBOL statement is constructed from its constituent simple assignments varies depending on its abstract syntax. Consider the following COBOL statements:

1. `ADD VAR1, VAR2 TO VAR3.`

2. `ADD VAR1, VAR2, VAR3 GIVING VAR3.`

3. `COMPUTE VAR3 = VAR1 + VAR2 + VAR3.`

4. `DIVIDE VAR4 INTO VAR3 GIVING VAR1, VAR2.`

5. `DIVIDE VAR3 BY VAR4 GIVING VAR1, VAR2.`

Each of the first three statements assigns to `VAR3` the sum of the values of `VAR1`, `VAR2` and `VAR3`. Similarly, the last two statements both carry out the same two assignments, assigning to `VAR1` the result of dividing `VAR3` by `VAR4` and assigning the same result to `VAR2`.

A (simplified) Entity-Relationship-Attribute model of assignment is shown in figure 19.2. COBOL-IF captures the similarity between statements (1), (2) and (3), and between statements (4) and (5), by representing their constituent simple assignments identically, but by separately attributing information about their abstract syntax using the *multi_assign_type* attribute of MULTIPLE_ASSIGNMENT.

Figure 19.3 shows the actual entities, relationships and attributes that would be created in the SDDB to represent statement (1). The representation of statements (2) and (3) would differ in only one way: their *multi_assign_type* values would be `ADD_GIVING` and `COMPUTE` respectively.

Figure 19.3 also illustrates the representation of cross-references. The entity of type VARIABLE, whose *name* is `VAR3`, is assigned a value by a SINGLE_ASSIGNMENT and evaluated by an ARITHMETIC_EXPRESSION.

Figure 19.4 shows the actual entities, relationships and attributes that would be created in the SDDB to represent statement (4). The representation of statement (5) would differ in only one respect: its *multi_assign_type* value would be `DIVIDE_BY_GIVING`.

Figure 19.4 is also of interest for its representation of a COBOL statement which involves two assignments, both with the same right hand side.

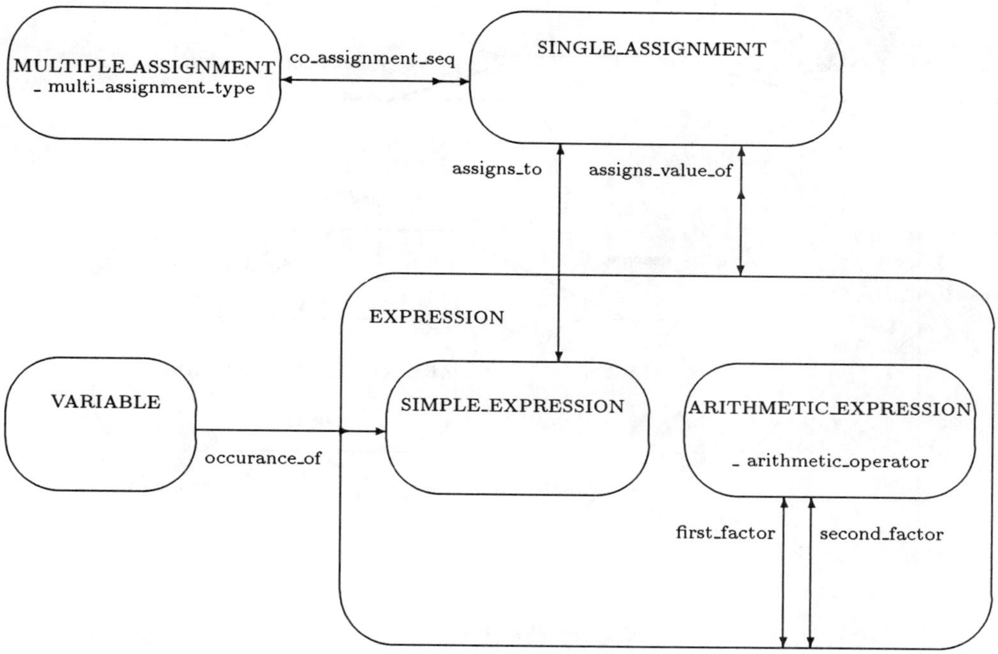

Figure 19.2: The COBOL-IF schema for assignment

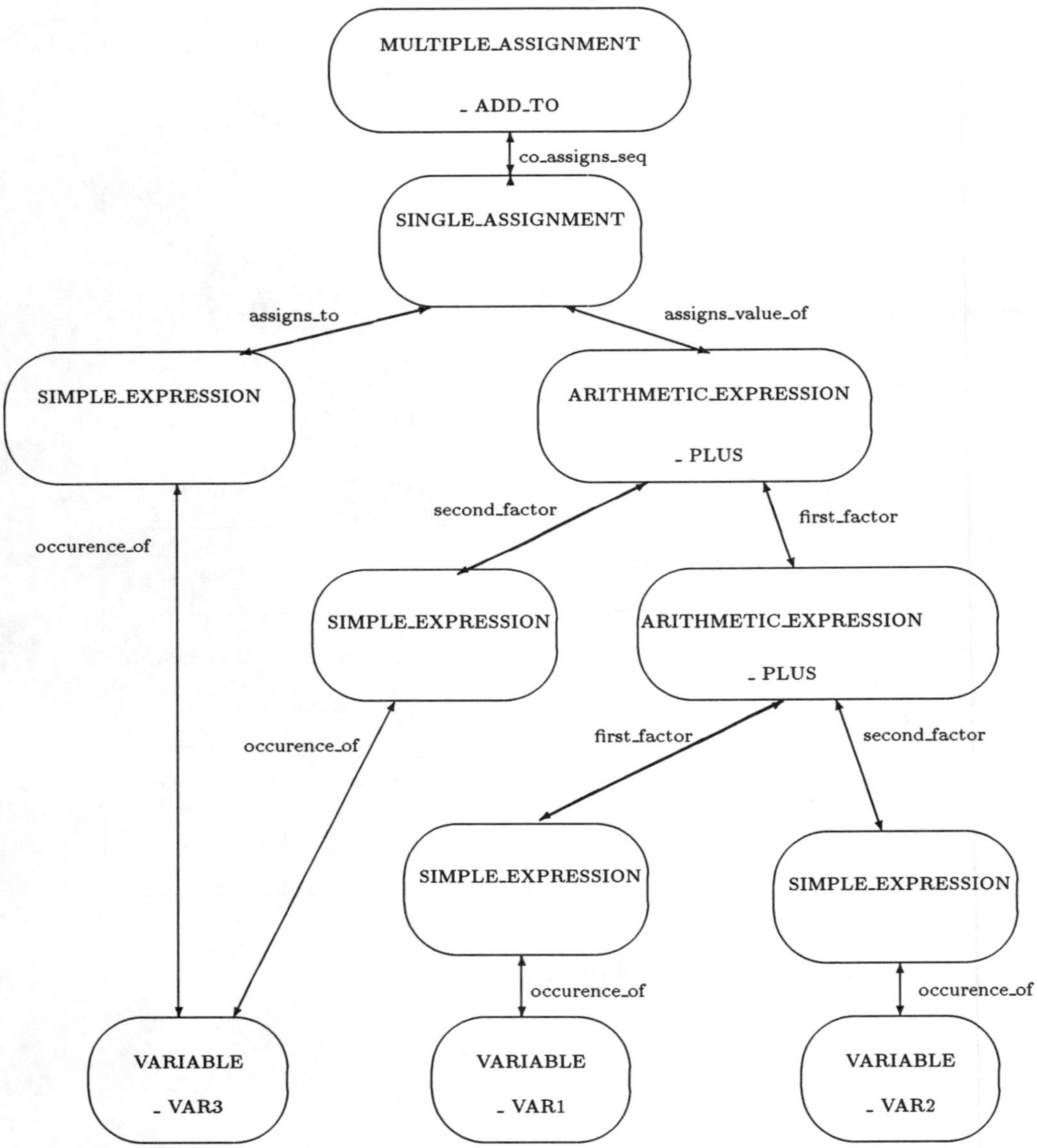

Figure 19.3: The representation of '`ADD VAR1, VAR2 TO VAR3`'

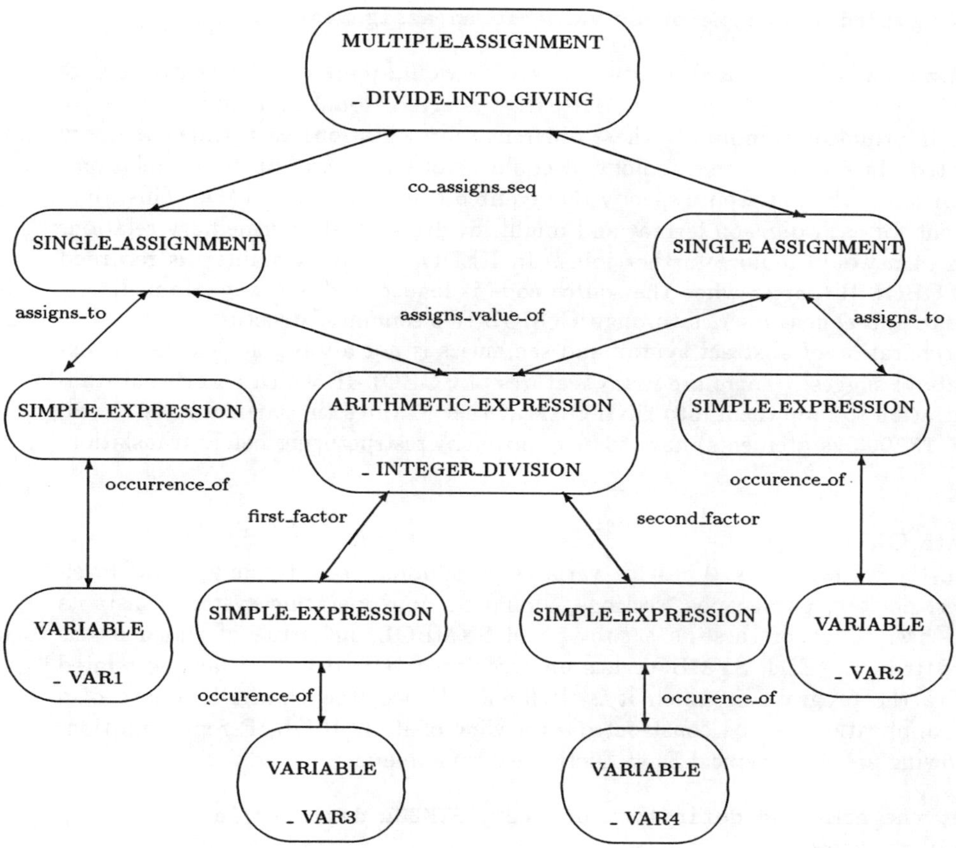

Figure 19.4: The representation of '`DIVIDE VAR4 INTO VAR3 GIVING VAR1, VAR2`'

The UNIFORM model of assignment has no *multi_assign_type* attribute. Otherwise, it is identical to that of COBOL-IF. Hence, translation of assignment statements into UNIFORM is relatively straightforward.

Section 19.3 stipulated that the conceptual schema should optimize queries about semantics. Consider the following query, useful for detecting arithmetic exceptions if `VAR4` is discovered to have a value of zero:

```
Get all the statements in this program in which VAR4
is divided into some other value in an assignment.
```

A conceptual schema based on abstract syntax would represent differently each of the six COBOL formats for division. Extensive analysis would be required to derive semantic information common to these different representations each time the query is evaluated. In relational terminology, it could involve a *join* of up to six relations. The condition of the join would specify the required connection with `VAR4`. This could be different for each division format and might involve several intermediary relations which in turn would require further joins. In REDO, the full semantics is recorded by the COBOL-IF parser when the source code is loaded and is always immediately available to subsequent queries through COBOL-IF's semantic structure.

The separation of abstract syntax and semantics is not always as clear as the examples above suggest. There are many features of COBOL-IF which require substantial translation to map them into UNIFORM. Other features (in particular, `GOTO` and `PERFORM THROUGH` statements) have to be removed by restructuring before translation.

The Data Dictionary

COBOL-IF defines entity types for variables (including records, arrays and level-88s), files, devices, paragraphs, sections, alphabets and operating system constants and switches. Each of these is a subtype of SYMBOL, in virtue of which it has a *name* attribute. Each SYMBOL has an associated type definition and is related directly to the program in which it is declared. Hence, the Data Dictionary of a COBOL application can be constructed as a view of its COBOL-IF representation. The following are some typical Data Dictionary-type queries:

1. `Get the name and definition of every SYMBOL declared in this program.`
2. `Get the name and definition of every VARIABLE declared in all the programs of this application.`
3. `Get the name and definition of every SYMBOL whose name is also the name of some other SYMBOL.`

The Statement Sequence

The notion of a sequence of statements is central to the representation of control structure, particularly to meet the needs of low-level restructuring tools (see chapter 22.3). Clearly, the COBOL paragraph can be modeled as an entity composed of a sequence of statements. There are many other statement sequences in a COBOL program which are less obvious, but which it is useful to treat in the same way as paragraphs. Examples include the contents of the `THEN` and `ELSE` clauses of `IF` statements, and of exception clauses such as `ON SIZE ERROR`. If these statement sequences are represented as entities in their own right, they can be manipulated and interchanged along with paragraphs in a standard way.

Environment Software

REDO is aimed at application software systems running on common operational environments. Generally, these applications utilize software components of the operating environment such as job control languages, file handlers and transaction processing monitors. Interactions between application programs and the environment in which they operate are modeled by the conceptual schema of the SDDB. This enables the SDDB to store information about the application in its entirety, and to support reverse engineers in identifying the parameters of individual programs and in restructuring the boundaries between them.

REDO provides explanations of *what* the environment software does when a request is issued by an application, using language familiar to the maintainer. Most service calls to the software environment found within application programs are formulated by means of `CALL` statements (or some equivalent) to a specific module, passing a parameter list. As there is often no comment attached to such statements, and as the run-time values of their parameters determine their meaning, maintainers often have difficulty in understanding them. REDO aims to support this process of understanding.

The remainder of this section discusses the SDDB's representation of database management systems, transaction processing monitors and job control languages.

Database Management Systems

There is a wide range of different types of database management system now on the market. REDO concentrates on the representation of database management systems with an opaque interface. For this reason, the project does not deal with relational DBMSs, but instead represents the TOTAL DBMS from Cincom Systems. TOTAL has a hybrid nature. It was designed to implement an early network model but it has retained the style of DBMSs which implement the hierarchical model.

The TOTAL DBMS

Although the same COBOL verb, `CALL`, is used for each interaction with the TOTAL DBMS, a wide range of operations can be requested by it. These operations are similar to the COBOL file input and output commands, `OPEN`, `CLOSE`, `READ`, `WRITE`, `REWRITE` and `DELETE`.

Each `CALL` statement is analyzed to identify the operation it requests. The analyzed statements are classified according to their functional similarity to COBOL commands. Once the requested operation of a `CALL` statement has been identified, the purpose of each of its parameters can be made structurally explicit, and shown to the reverse engineer.

Consider the simplified COBOL fragment in figure 19.5. The final `CALL` statement of the fragment instructs the DBMS to retrieve the name and address of the employee

```
MOVE 'READV' TO FUNCTION-PARAMETER.
MOVE 'EMPLOYEE' TO FILE-PARAMETER.
MOVE 'D532' TO EMP-ID.
MOVE 'NAME, ADDRESS' TO ELEMENT-PARAMETER.
MOVE 'NEXT-EMP' TO INTO-PARAMETER.
CALL 'DATBAS' USING FUNCTION-PARAMETER, ..., FILE-PARAMETER,
                    ..., EMP-ID, ELEMENT-PARAMETER,
                     INTO-PARAMETER, ...
```

Figure 19.5: An example request to the TOTAL DBMS from COBOL

whose record occurs after that of employee **D532** in the **EMPLOYEE** file, and to place them in the variable, **NEXT-EMP**. The specific DBMS function is indicated by the value of the first parameter, the name of the file to be read is indicated by the second parameter, and so on. (Of course, there is no guarantee that the original programmer will have used variable names as suggestive as the ones chosen here.)

This use of the **CALL** verb is similar to the COBOL **READ** verb. Both read data from a file into a variable and specify a key. However, the COBOL **READ** statement selects the entire record referenced by the key, whereas the TOTAL **READV** operation selects particular fields of the record which follows the keyed record. A (simplified) Entity-Relationship-Attribute model of these two file reading operations is shown in figure 19.6. It captures the similarities and differences between them by creating a supertype of both operations, called **GENERAL_READ**. Shared attributes and relationships are defined for the supertype and are inherited by the more specific **COBOL_READ** and **TOTAL_DIRECT_READ**. Each of these specific operations has further attributes and relationships defined for it. These are not shared.

As figure 19.6 shows, interaction with the TOTAL DBMS has been modeled by extending COBOL-IF. Many entities, relationships and attributes in the conceptual schema are shared between the representations of COBOL and TOTAL. (Another example is found in the representation of TOTAL's Data Definition Language: the same data types are used to define both TOTAL schema and COBOL data items.) This close integration assists reverse engineers in reasoning about environment interaction and helps software tools to navigate and manipulate the parsed structure of an entire application.

The **CALL** statement in figure 19.5 can be shown to the engineer after analysis in the form of figure 19.7. Practitioners shown this textual presentation have reacted very enthusiastically and foresee significant gains in productivity during the program understanding process.

The analysis of TOTAL DML command described above is not trivial. The variables passed as parameters in a **CALL** statement can have values assigned anywhere in the **PROCEDURE DIVISION** of the program. Unlike the fragment in figure 19.5, the assignments may be in distant and obscurely related paragraphs. Different values may be assigned to the parameters depending on the runtime values of other data items, some of which may be input by the user.

Ddataflow analysis techniques and tools (described in section 22.1) are used to

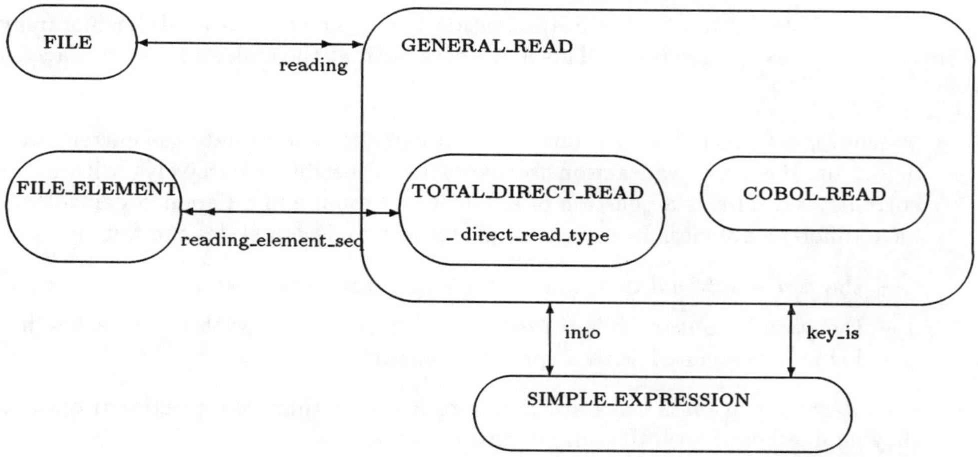

Figure 19.6: An example of the integration of COBOL and TOTAL file operations in the conceptual schema

```
TOTAL_READV
        read from file     : EMPLOYEE;
        key is             : D532;
        file elements are  : NAME, ADDRESS;
        read record into   : NEXT-EMP.
```

Figure 19.7: The users' view of a request to the TOTAL DBMS after analysis

determine dynamic data values wherever this is possible. If it is not possible to identify the operation requested by a `CALL` statement, the reverse engineer is informed.

Transaction Processing Monitors

Transaction processing monitors are used to build applications implementing complex interactive tasks. They offer a wide range of services such as transaction and program execution control, file handling, terminal control, user interface layout management, database interfacing, main storage management and intersystem communication. REDO focuses on a particular transaction processing monitor, namely the Customer Information Control System (CICS) of IBM.

Customer Information Control System

In CICS applications, a task is made of transactions. Each transaction triggers a program. Different tasks can share a common set of transactions. Similarly, transactions can share programs and programs can share modules. Every interactive task has a *header* transaction. The program associated with a header transaction can call other programs.

The control structure of a CICS application is not, however, a modular hierarchy of one-entry, one-exit procedures. This is the case both at the task and the transaction level.

- Whenever a transaction is about to end it can either terminate the current task or set up the next transaction for execution (possibly recursively) within the current task. This is a question of application design and different organizations have different policies. In industrial practice, two design styles are found:

  - the *conversational task*, made of a single transaction, and
  - the *pseudo-conversational task*, in which every step within the task's dialogue is associated with a specific transaction.

  Pseudo-conversational tasks are far more frequent than conversational ones as they enable better overall computer throughput.

- During its execution a CICS program can execute some other module. Control returns to the program on completion of the module. However, the program can also terminate itself and pass control to another program. One program can have several alternative statements, each transferring control to a different transaction. Only one of these statements will be executed, but the selection is determined dynamically. Control does not return to the original transaction. Again, use of this facility is a question of design and programming standards. However, as IBM recommend that CICS programs are kept as small as possible, the facility is used extensively. In particular, most programs directly associated with a CICS transaction are developed in this way.

This complex pattern of control flow across tasks, transactions and programs is modeled in the SDDB using a graph structure tightly integrated with that of the control-flow representation in COBOL-IF. This enables engineers and tools to navigate, manipulate and reason about the whole application.

CICS commands within COBOL programs are similar to TOTAL queries: they are all issued using the `EXEC` verb, and their meaning is determined dynamically by the values of their parameters. `EXEC CICS` statements are analyzed and modeled using the approach developed for TOTAL queries. Wherever parameter values can be determined statically using dataflow analysis, the statement is transformed into a COBOL-like verb attached to a set of arguments whose role is explicit [5]. Analyzed CICS commands can be presented to the user in a similar textual form to those of TOTAL, with equivalent benefits (as in figure 19.7).

Once the CICS commands that handle task execution have been identified and understood in this way, the application's task execution graph can be derived.

The SDDB represents not only the semantics of CICS commands found within programs, but also CICS tables and the start-up job which has to be run in a computer partition or region to start a CICS session. The integration of this information with the representations of COBOL and TOTAL provides a sound industry-based platform for REDO demonstration and exploitation.

[5] This takes the analysis a step further than CICS compiler preprocessors, which translate EXEC CICS commands into CALL statements.

Job Control Languages

The job control language scripts of a batch application define an often complex control structure. This is the context in which individual COBOL programs are executed. In REDO's chosen target job control language, IBM DOS/VSE/AF System Control Statements (SCS), the application is decomposed into *jobs* and each job into *steps.* The job step executes an *image* of machine code, compiled from one or more files of source code. There may be no record of the way in which the image was generated from source code: often this is a matter for empirical investigation by the reverse engineer. The representation of SCS models the control structure of jobs and steps. It also provides a framework within which the maintainer can identify the source code programs executed in each job step's image. Hence it enables an integrated representation of the control structure of an entire application.

In the File Control entries of a COBOL program's Environment Division, the program's logical file names are associated with 'implementor' names. These are in fact logical file names themselves, and must be assigned to physical devices in SCS before they are understood by the operating system. This assignment is made by job steps.

By representing the assignment of 'implementor' names to devices in SCS, and by integrating such assignments with the representation of COBOL's Environment and Data Divisions, the SDDB provides the maintainer with a full understanding of the logical and physical definition of files from the viewpoint either of the job or of the program.

19.5.2 The Representation of Documentation

The REDO SDDB contains a variety of information about the application in addition to the application itself. In so far as this additional information is descriptive of or derived from the application, it can be regarded as documentation in a most general sense. It will include 'conventional' documentation in the form of life cycle documents (specifications, design documents, user documentation etc.), documentation extracted from the application (control and dataflow, etc.) and also some more novel forms of descriptive material made possible by the SDDB itself (see the discussion of notes and links later in this section). A populated SDDB can be regarded as self–documenting, in the sense that an SDDB instantiated to reverse engineer a particular application will also contain information to describe the application. This will include any existing documentation and information generated incrementally during the iterative process of reverse engineering and added to the SDDB.

The REDO approach to reverse engineering (described in chapter 13) is documentation-intensive: it focuses on the creation of a documentary description of the application geared towards improving its maintainability. The aim of the documentation tools is to computerize this process, using the SDDB to store the information, and thus to provide views of the required information which are more useable and more powerful than their paper equivalents.

Life cycle Documents

Life cycle documents are those which are produced to document particular stages in the life cycle of an application. They include development documents, user documentation and any formal documentation produced during the maintenance phase of the life cycle.

The structure of life cycle documents is very much dependent on the methods used by a particular organization in the development and maintenance phases, and on the organization's standards for documentation. In the development phase, the expected documentation can be categorized broadly: requirements definition, functional specification, design description, etc. However the details of each type of document are highly dependent on which if any of the many formalized development methods has been used. Organizations may also have their own internal standards for the format of standard development documents. The situation with regard to any maintenance documentation which may exist is even less well defined. Not only are there no formalized methods for software maintenance, there are not even any accepted broad categories of documentation that ought to be produced during maintenance (a possible exception being a 'change request' or 'fault report' document of some kind).

Using the REDO toolkit, existing documentation for an application can be imported into the SDDB. The end user is also able to store in the SDDB any new documentation generated during reverse engineering. The method used to represent life cycle documents must therefore be sufficiently flexible to cope with the many and varied document types which may be employed by developers and maintainers.

For these reasons it is considered inappropriate to constrain either the logical or the physical structure of documents which may be stored in the SDDB.

Conventional paper-based documents have a naturally hierarchical structure of sections, subsections, paragraphs, etc. The leaves of this tree contain the text and graphics which make up the body of the document. This generic logical structure is readily represented in the SDDB. Specific document types are specializations of this generic structure, in which the structure and contents of each structural element (section, subsection, etc.) are more closely defined. By defining a library of document types we may define the structures of each type of document which we wish to store. Every document stored in the SDDB will be an instance of a type defined in the types library. End users can then configure the system to their own requirements by defining in the types library the structure of the various document types which they require. These type definitions can then be modified, or new types added to the library, as the users' requirements or standards change.

In addition to the types library, there is a document library containing the actual documents associated with a project or application. These documents are all instances of document types defined in the types library.

Version control of documentation is particularly important in a maintenance environment, where modification of an application ought to be reflected by new versions of life cycle documents. Each document in the SDDB is identifiable by version, and the DBMS allows searches to be performed using the version effectively as a key. Links may also be established between a specific version of a document and the application (see the discussion below of notes and links). Versions of a document may be 'frozen', so that further editing is prohibited. This corresponds to the document's entry into the documentation library.

Notes And Links

Notes and links together form a mechanism to support redocumentation in the environment provided by the SDDB. Links are, as the name suggests, a means of connecting two entities stored in the SDDB; notes are a means of annotating entities.

Annotation and linking demonstrate the power of a common information repository. Storage of heterogeneous types of information in the same database allows links to be created between information of completely different types, such as code and documentation, as well as material of the same type, for instance code-to-code links.

Links were originally devised as a means of linking documentation to the application code which it describes. This linking is required at all levels of granularity, from documents or programs at one extreme to paragraphs or source code lexical tokens at the other. The very general mechanism required for such linking may be extended trivially to provide an 'anything-to-anything' linking mechanism. This mechanism may then be used to represent relationships between any types of information in the SDDB. A network of links may be built up incrementally as relationships are discovered during the process of reverse engineering. The structure of this network forms part of, in a general sense, the documentation of the application.

As links provide a mechanism to document incrementally relationships between information already present in the SDDB, so notes provide a means to add information incrementally to the SDDB. Notes consist of unstructured text, and are linked to entities in the SDDB. They are intended to record information about the entity to which they are linked. For this reason, they exist only when linked to some entity in this way.

The semantics of notes and links are entirely defined by the user; thus they provide a completely generic mechanism for representing relationships between entities in the SDDB, and for annotating these entities. The semantics of individual notes are defined by the text which they contain. In the case of links, a similar method for defining their semantics on an individual basis is required. The approach adopted is the most general possible: a text field is provided in each link into which the user enters a free-text description of the relationship which the link represents, at the time at which the link is created. In addition, two special subtypes of link whose semantics *are* defined are used by certain tools. They are used in one case to link notes to the entities which they annotate, and in the other to relate abstract design objects created by the reverse engineering tools to the code which corresponds to the implementation of these objects 18.3.5.

As noted in chapter 8, systems which allow incremental addition of information tend to degenerate unless quality control of their contents is carried out. Quality control of notes and links takes the form of 'manual' inspection of their contents (notes) or the relationships they purport to represent. Notes and links each have a flag which is set once they have passed a quality control inspection. In addition, notes and links are each 'stamped' on creation with the identity of their creator and the date of creation. These three attributes (date, author, and QA status) are made visible by the tools which access notes and links to help the user to judge the quality and reliability of the information which they represent.

19.5.3 The Representation of Other Information

A wide range of other information is represented and integrated in the SDDB. The SDDB records metrics derived from analysis of its representation of source code, and slices and traces of program modules and statements to support data and control-flow analysis and restructuring. It provides an extended Entity-Relationship model to support reverse engineering from COBOL file definitions, and a representation of Z++ formal specifications, with a means of linking them to the programs from which they are reverse engineered. The SDDB also makes *meta-data* available about the schema of the SDDB. This can be queried by tools and can be presented in a graphical form to toolkit users as a 'help' facility.

19.6 Loading Source Code into the SDDB

One of the first activities of the REDO software maintenance method is to load the existing source code of the application into the SDDB. A process model has been defined for this activity and much of the process has been automated.

The objectives of the process are:

- to load into the SDDB the text of all source code components of the application, and to parse them;
- to ensure the consistency of the components and the completeness of the application.

Often the incompleteness or inconsistency of a set of source code components is realized only during the loading and parsing process. Therefore an iterative process model has been defined, covering initial loading, complete reloading and individual component addition, deletion and replacement. Incomplete subsets of an application can be maintained as long as the missing components are explicitly identified. Inconsistencies are drawn to the reverse engineer's attention.

Application Completeness

It is necessary to define the types of component which must be present for an application to be complete.

An application corresponds to a discrete user function. An application is complete if all the interrelated software components which implement the user function and for which source code is available are present. Hence the source code for proprietary environment services would not usually be part of the application, whereas a library of modules developed in-house would be part of it.

Linger, Mills and Witt make a useful distinction between two layers of software components: the *job* and the *procedure* [205]. The job is the immediate physical realization of the user function, "the highest level of program execution invoked on demand by an external agency (user, operator, scheduled clock time, etc.) and executed to completion." It is "a program intended for immediate execution ... whereas a procedure is a program intended to be stored for later invocation by other programs."

The specific types of job and procedure required for an application to be complete depend on two factors:

The application's operational environment, specified for REDO to be IBM's mainframe DOS/VSE operating system (with SAM, ISAM, DAM and VSAM access methods, the POWER/VS spool manager and the job control language), COBOL/VS, CICS and the TOTAL DBMS.

The application's mode of operation: whether the application is batch or conversational. Batch applications are relatively straightforward to define: the job is the top-level job control language script. The procedures include any job control language scripts called by the job, and any COBOL programs called either by the job or by its procedures.

Conversational applications are more difficult to define. The user function of a conversational application is the task. However, the job of a conversational application is defined to be the CICS job control language start-up script. Although this is not specific to any particular user function, it contains information essential to an understanding of each user function and it is at the highest level of each application's control structure.

Neither tasks nor transactions are implemented directly by files of source code. Instead, the mapping between tasks and transactions and between transactions and programs, and the control flow between them, is defined by CICS tables and by `EXEC CICS` statements in programs.

As a result of the high level of integration between interactive applications, it is sometimes difficult to define the boundaries of user functions. Their tasks can overlap by sharing transactions, and the transactions by sharing programs (as described in section 19.5.1). The boundaries are identified by control-flow analysis of parsed tables and programs.

Both batch and conversational applications may also contain Data Definition Language files for the TOTAL DBMS and COBOL `COPY` files.

The Loading Process Model

The process of loading a single user function into the SDDB is organized into four sequential stages. More than one process cycle is usually required to accomplish a successful load and it is often necessary to iterate over some of the stages during a process cycle.

Stage 1: Conduct an initial validation of the consistency of the application's source files and load them into the SDDB. The operational mode of the application is identified and a number of consistency rules are enforced, such as the need to have at most one job file, at least one procedure file, and if the application is conversational, at least two CICS table files (the Task Control Table and the Program Process Table).

Stage 2: Parse the job and validate its completeness. The source files containing the application job, CICS tables and TOTAL DDL are parsed. The call graph of the job is derived. The procedure files are checked to ensure that for every node of the job's call graph there exists a corresponding source file.

Stage 3: Parse the procedures and validate their completeness. Starting with the job's call graph, three steps are applied recursively: the procedure associated with each node of the call graph is parsed, its own call graph is derived, and the procedure files are checked to ensure that for every node in the new call graph there exists a corresponding source file.

Stage 4: Re-validate the consistency and completeness of the application. Any redundant files of source code are identified and removed. These include procedure files that do not occur in the application call graph and DDL files that define unused database schema.

19.7 Accessing the SDDB

The ANSI/SPARC architecture, described at the beginning of this chapter, provides a framework for considering how the reverse engineer accesses the SDDB.

Access At The External Level
The external level of the SDDB is addressed by a range of tools such as the Source Code Browser (section 19.7.3), the Documentation Browser (section 19.7.4), the Note Tool (section 19.7.5) and the Link Tool (section 19.7.6). These tools abstract from the full conceptual schema and are partial in that they concentrate on particular areas of the application. The mapping from the internal representation (in the conceptual schema) to the external representation required for a particular view may involve the definition of details not available in the conceptual schema such as formatting conventions.

Access At The Conceptual Level
The reverse engineer may sometimes need to view all the data 'as it really is' in the SDDB, rather than be constrained by its presentation in external views. During the development of tools on the SDDB, toolbuilders require a similar capability to test their tools.

At the conceptual level, the SDDB can be accessed from a procedural language (such as C) using a binding of the TBK DataBase Interface (DBI). This interface implements a functional model [31]. Data is represented as typed entities and the type of an entity determines what attributes it has. Attributes are typed and may be printable (such as string, integer) or entity-valued, namely links. In either case, they are understood as functions. Database navigation corresponds to functional composition. (Note that a function in this model may return multiple values.) The DBI consists of a small set of basic functions, enabling the user to access all SDDB data. The database schema is represented within a database and can be interrogated using the DBI. However, to achieve this level of visibility of SDDB data and schema, the user must become familiar with how the data is accessed at an implementation level.

There is no high-level, declarative, easy-to-use database query facility in the TBK. However, one of the DBI functions can be used to obtain the values of attributes:

```
value_of_attribute: entity * attribute -> attribute_value
```

The result is implemented as a discriminated union with a number of cases, including printable (string, integer etc.), entity (link) and sequence. Entities can be identified from the values of their attributes by exact matches, pattern matching and the use of comparison and Boolean operators.

The DBI can be used to query the SDDB, but raises a number of issues. For example, the user must know how to handle multi-valued attributes, compose attribute searches in a single DBI call and specify complex queries requiring more than one DBI call. In addition, 'housekeeping' issues, such as how errors are handled, need to be considered. Changes in the SDDB schema would have a considerable impact on access software using the DBI.

To summarize, SDDB access facilities at the conceptual level must fulfill the following requirements:

- they must facilitate access (for edits and queries) to all parts of the SDDB (data and schema);
- they must provide an interactive, easy-to-use interface to the SDDB;
- they must shield the user from DBI implementation details;
- they must be resilient to changes in the SDDB schema.

In REDO, two interactive tools provide a conceptual view of the SDDB in terms of entities and attributes. Although these tools assume familiarity with the underlying data model, they shield the user from having to know how to access this information. Hiding procedural details not only simplifies use of the SDDB, but also improves the maintainability of the access software. These tools are intended to be of general use; although particular examples of usage are identified, these do not constrain their functionality nor define their scope.

The first, an SDDB Editor, facilitates the viewing and editing of all entity details in the database. It is discussed in section 19.7.1. The second, a Query Tool, facilitates queries (in the SQL sense) of SDDB data and schema. It is discussed in section 19.7.2.

19.7.1 The DataBase Editor

This tool enables the REDO toolbuilder to set up test data and examine the SDDB output of tools. It also provides the REDO reverse engineer with a facility for viewing and editing SDDB data.

The data to be edited is considered as a graph of attributed entities. The integrity constraints enforced by the tool are those constraints embodied by the Data Definition Language (DDL) implementation of the schema. Validation of data is performed as it is entered, so that only 'correct' data is ever written to the database. In particular, referential integrity is enforced. Where a link is being instantiated, the user is provided with a choice of possible options for the target entity. References to entities are maintained by the editor, for instance if an entity is deleted, then all links, for which that entity is the destination, are also deleted.

The tool enables the user to load, view and change entity-level data. An individual entity entry may be displayed in one of two formats:

unfolded which means that its contents (namely all attribute details) are visible. This includes links whose destinations have not yet been defined and all printable attributes (which may have default values).

folded in this case its contents are not visible. All that is displayed is the entity type and identifier.

When entities are created, their contents are *folded.* They may be *unfolded* by selecting an appropriate field. An *unfolded* entry may then be *folded* in a similar manner. The state of an entry is stored in the database, so that it may be 'remembered' from one invocation of the tool to the next.

The tool enables the user to edit all the data in the database and create data of any data type supported by the database. An exception is made for those constructs used internally by the tool to store visibility information, described above. In addition to interactive use, it is possible to save the edit display to an ASCII file for further analysis.

Editor Generator
If the editor were tied to a particular SDDB schema, then it would need to be maintained in parallel with revisions to the schema. As the approach to schema development in REDO has been iterative, manual updates to the editor would have presented a severe overhead. Instead, an editor generator is provided. This meta-tool can generate editing functions for any data type, as defined in the underlying DDL of the database. It uses the particular SDDB schema (written in DDL) to identify the data types to be included for the corresponding editor.

19.7.2 The Query Tool

This section begins by discussing the scope of the Query Tool. It then discusses briefly some issues with regard to the design of the tool.

Scope
The Query Tool enables the REDO reverse engineer to interact with the SDDB at a conceptual level on an ad hoc basis. For example, the application code in the SDDB can be interrogated for information about data usage, control flow and program structure. Examples of typical queries are provided in section 19.4.2. The tool also supports checking of static semantics; it can indicate the presence of errors such as:

- uses of undeclared variables;
- calls to undeclared procedures;
- calls to procedures with the wrong number of arguments or with arguments of an incorrect type.

Anomalies can also be detected. An *anomaly* is something that, although correct in terms of syntax and static semantics, indicates a possible logical error. Examples include:

- procedures that are never called;
- declared variables that are never used;
- modifications of an input parameter;
- failure to assign a value to an output parameter.

SDDB interrogation is not confined to the application source code; any information modeled on the SDDB can be queried using this tool. In addition, the SDDB schema itself can be interrogated, providing the reverse engineer with ready access to details of the conceptual schema itself.

The tool can also be run in conjunction with other REDO tools. For example, the Note Tool, described in section 19.7.5, provides local information about notes, at the level of a specified second-tier entity. The Query Tool could be used to obtain global information, by querying structured fields in notes. The tool can also be used to generate input for tools, such as slicers and tracers (see section 22.1).

The tool can be used in conjunction with the DataBase Editor, described in section 19.7.1. The latter provides access to all second-tier entities in the SDDB, but does not facilitate the selection of entities by attribute value. The Query Tool would provide this capability.

Design

The Query Tool is based on the SQL `SELECT` statement [90]. The general form of the statement (concentrating on major features) is given below:

```
SELECT [DISTINCT] item(s)
FROM table(s)
[WHERE condition]
```

When using the Query Tool, the *item(s)* that are selected for output are attribute types. These can be printable attributes or links, single-valued or sequences. Attribute types can be atomic or (functionally) composed from other attribute types. Each database entity is known to the user by a unique, system-assigned attribute. The domain of the query (corresponding to *table(s)*) is a collection of entities, identified by type. The selection *condition* specifies attribute values and can include pattern matching constructs, comparison and Boolean operators.

To maximize ease-of-use, the tool interface is not purely command-driven. Instead, the user chooses items from a menu or fills in items on a form. The database schema is interrogated by the tool to compile choice lists, for instance, of possible attribute and entity types. There is also a facility to store queries for later retrieval. In addition to interactive use, query output can be written to an ASCII file for further analysis or use in subsequent queries.

19.7.3 The Source Code Browser

This section begins by considering the reverse engineer's requirements for tool support in accessing source code in general, and then discusses the design of the REDO Source Code Browser.

The reverse engineer's requirements for a facility to access source code fall within three categories: viewing, editing and browsing.

Viewing

Essential in a reverse engineering toolkit is the capability of viewing the source code in a textual form. It should be possible for this information to be written to the screen, a file or a printer without significant regeneration costs. The use of pretty printing, in particular the adoption of a single display format, provides a uniform appearance which facilitates the comprehension task (see section 6.5).

As discussed in section 19.3, there are many categories of information which the reverse engineer must be able to retrieve from the reverse engineering repository and, although these may be extracted from a purely textual representation, it is not efficient to do so.

The formatting required is influenced by the difference between the internal representation of the source code and its external textual representation.

1. At a basic level, issues of code layout need to be considered, such as indentation of substructures, style of comments, and use of spaces and blank lines. Code layout may be constrained by the application language (for instance in the case of COBOL, there is no notion of a blank line, reflecting the language's punched-card origins).

2. Concrete syntax details may need to be considered, such as the use of optional literals and punctuation. In COBOL, examples include the `TO` which may follow a `GO` and the period which may separate statements.

3. It is possible that the internal representation stores semantic information rather than abstract syntax. For example, it may be deemed sufficient to represent the fact that a single assignment has been used, without identifying it, for instance as a COBOL `ADD` or `COMPUTE`. If abstract syntax details are to be displayed, then this information must be defined.

The separation of formatting details from the internal representation of the source code facilitates the customization of the source code appearance. It also supports the definition of additional or alternative formats.

Editing

In general, the application source code will remain unchanged during the reverse engineering process. However, there are occasions when an editing facility is required, for example to manually restructure code to facilitate its future understanding or to correct coding errors.

It is sensible to use the textual representation of the source code, described above, as the view for this editing. This provides the reverse engineer with a familiar view of the application which can be readily manipulated. Editing functions may be textual, for instance to manipulate comments embedded in the code, or directed towards syntax or semantics. When code changes are made, the reverse engineer is often thinking in terms of the code's syntactic or semantic structure. A syntax/semantic-directed editor facilitates this approach and ensures the integrity or correctness of the edited data. It also removes the need to separately parse the entire application to take account of the changes made and update the repository accordingly.

Edits may range from making minor revisions to existing code to creating new sections of code using predefined templates. For both categories, the editing facilities are based on the constraints of the formatting environment. By controlling changes to the code in this way, the chosen display format is enforced.

Browsing

Some of the facilities described so far can be found in programming development environments, although largely confined to individual application programs or subroutines. Reverse engineering and maintenance environments are concerned with aspects of the entire application and so introduce issues of magnitude (the sheer volume of code to be considered) and diversity (the range of languages and packages used).

A single complete view of the source code is unlikely to be adequate in these circumstances. The reverse engineer may wish to focus on a small specific part of the code, viewing it in the context of an entire program or application. This raises the issue of what control the engineer has over which parts of the code are displayed and how this visibility can be specified. It also identifies the need to ensure that the engineer does not lose track of where the visible part fits into the broader picture.

Some visibility functions may be readily identified. The hierarchical structure of the application may be used to step through the code at different levels of detail. This is best illustrated by providing an example: consider a COBOL application consisting of a JCL file, a number of program files and a number of data files. These components could form an initial high-level view of the application. Information at lower levels of detail is not shown (but indicated in some way). The reverse engineer could selectively 'open up' lower levels, for example to expand a program into its component modules (such as subprograms in COBOL), a module into its component divisions and so on. This hierarchy of views has the advantage of enabling the reverse engineer to focus on those parts of the application which are of interest. As these parts are presented in the context of the entire application, users are not disoriented as they step through the code.

These hierarchical views can be used to document the overall structure of the application. As this structure can be derived directly from up-to-date source code, the reverse engineer does not need to use separately generated documents whose relevance and correctness have to be ascertained.

Non-structural views can also be identified. For example, the reverse engineer may be interested in the usage of a particular variable and wish to view only those statements which change its value. Attention can be focused on the dataflow between particular modules, whether explicit (in argument lists) or implicit (in global variables) and the data dependencies of particular variables or files. The usage of particular statement types, for instance COBOL `GOTO` and `ON SIZE ERROR` exception conditions, can also be detected, in context. This flexible interactive capability complements the use of automatic tools, such as control flow analyzers (as described in section 22.3) and program slicers (as described in section 22.1).

It is impossible to categorically specify all the different views which all reverse engineers require. Requirements may be influenced by their approach to the comprehension task, their domain knowledge and general expertise. Instead, efforts should be focused on providing the reverse engineer with the capability of customizing predefined views and defining new ones.

In addition to the selective viewing facility described above, it is useful for the reverse engineer to be able to traverse the source code. For example, the reverse engineer can select a variable name in an assignment statement and navigate to the definition of that variable elsewhere in the code. A COBOL `GOTO` statement can be selected and the reverse engineer can step to its destination.

Design Issues

In ANSI/SPARC terminology, the code is displayed to the reverse engineer by mapping the conceptual schema to one or more external views. (For a detailed discussion of this *unparsing* process, the reader is referred to Garlan [130].)

The implementation of views is largely determined by the capabilities of the unparser. The mapping from objects in the database to views must be considered as a bi-directional one. On the one hand, it must support the display of objects; on the other, it must allow operations performed on the visible display to be translated into corresponding database operations.

The representation chosen to display the code may be textual, graphical or a combination thereof. If there is an unwieldy volume of code to be displayed, a number of solutions could be provided. One approach is to provide a higher level graphical representation of the application, such as a module hierarchy, from which the user can select the specific area of code of interest. This combination of graphical and textual information may prove confusing, in that the context of the code being viewed may no longer be readily available. In addition, the choice of graphical representation(s) may constrain how the code may be viewed.

Another approach is to use the concept of *source text elision*, a viewing paradigm used in programming development environments. Rather than displaying the source text for an entire application, the user can specify which parts should be visible and which parts elided. Those parts of the code which are not displayed are indicated to the user, who can then select them for expansion. Figure 19.8 provides an example of a COBOL program, showing its constituent divisions.

```
IDENTIFICATION DIVISION.
...
ENVIRONMENT DIVISION.
...
DATA DIVISION.
...
PROCEDURE DIVISION.
...
```

Figure 19.8: A COBOL program showing constituent divisions

The user may 'open up' the procedure division, by selecting the appropriate elision marker. Figure 19.9 shows the resulting display.

```
PROCEDURE DIVISION.
MAIN
     ...
START_PROG
     ...
PROCESS
     ...
END_PROG
     ...
```

Figure 19.9: A COBOL procedure division showing constituent paragraphs

Within the procedure division, the user has a choice of several possible paths to expand. If the **MAIN** paragraph is of interest, it can be expanded to show the first level of its logic, as given in Figure 19.10.

```
MAIN.
     PERFORM ...
     PERFORM ...
     PERFORM ...
```

Figure 19.10: A COBOL paragraph showing constituent statements

Each **PERFORM** statement may be then expanded, as given in figure 19.11.

```
MAIN.
     PERFORM START_PROG.
     PERFORM PROCESS.
     PERFORM END_PROG.
```

Figure 19.11: A COBOL paragraph with statements expanded

The elision paradigm is discussed in Cordy *et al.* [84], in the context of a user interface for software maintenance, called the *TuringTool.* The tool provides structural and non-structural views of program source code in a textual context. It draws on the idea of visibility rules to define views; these rules may be combined using set theoretic operations to form new views. In addition, users may augment the default set of rules with additional rules which meet their particular needs. This enables the tool to be tailored for individual users and also facilitates the development of a library of rules which may prove useful to others.

This viewing paradigm is adopted in the REDO project. The TuringTool's internal representation of a program is a tokenized line-structured version of the source text. In REDO, the SDDB representation of the source code, primarily in terms of semantics and abstract syntax, is used instead. This facilitates the use of semantic and syntactic information about the application captured in the SDDB. For example, instead of being a set of lines, a view can be defined to be a set of statements and variable definitions. The TuringTool's limitation to consideration of the source code of a single program written in a single language, is avoided in REDO by considering the entire application.

19.7.4 The Documentation Browser

The notion of *elision*, discussed previously in the context of source code (section 19.7.3), is also applied to life cycle documents. A range of views of a document may be generated as different representations of the same underlying data. Using the Documentation Browser, the logical components of a document can be 'expanded', to show their substructure or contents, or 'collapsed' to hide their contents. For example, it is possible for the user to start from a view of a document which shows only the titles of its chapters – this corresponds to a contents listing. The user may selectively expand or 'open' chapters to view their substructure in terms of sections and subsections, then selectively open sections which are of interest to view their text. Thus the user can create a customized view of a document showing only the information required at that time. Similarly the various attributes of a document such as its author, date of entry, status etc., may be displayed if relevant or hidden if not. The objectives are to aid the user in locating the required information in a (probably large) document and to display this information in a context chosen by the user.

19.7.5 The Note Tool

Notes are intended to provide an online analogue of the annotation of a paper listing or document. They are used to record the maintainer's emerging knowledge about the application or components thereof. The immediate and obvious advantage of doing this online is that the notes can be preserved in the repository, and so the knowledge gained by previous maintainers is made available to their successors. The Note Tool creates, displays and manages notes, which are attached to other entities in the SDDB such as source code and documentation by links (see section 19.5.2).

The thinking behind the tool has been influenced by previous research projects in redocumentation carried out at Durham University in collaboration with British Telecom Research Laboratories (BTRL). A toolset known as DOCMAN has been developed at BTRL and is used there by maintenance staff [125]. The toolset is based on a sophisticated program cross-referencer which generates documentation from source code. It also provides facilities to attach annotation to identifier names which appear in the cross-reference tables. This means that its capabilities are restricted to annotating named entities in a program. A second project involved the use of a commercial hypertext tool in the redocumentation of programs (see references [53, 123]).

The actual task of the users of the REDO tools is centered on understanding the application, and various tools are to be provided to assist in this task by extracting

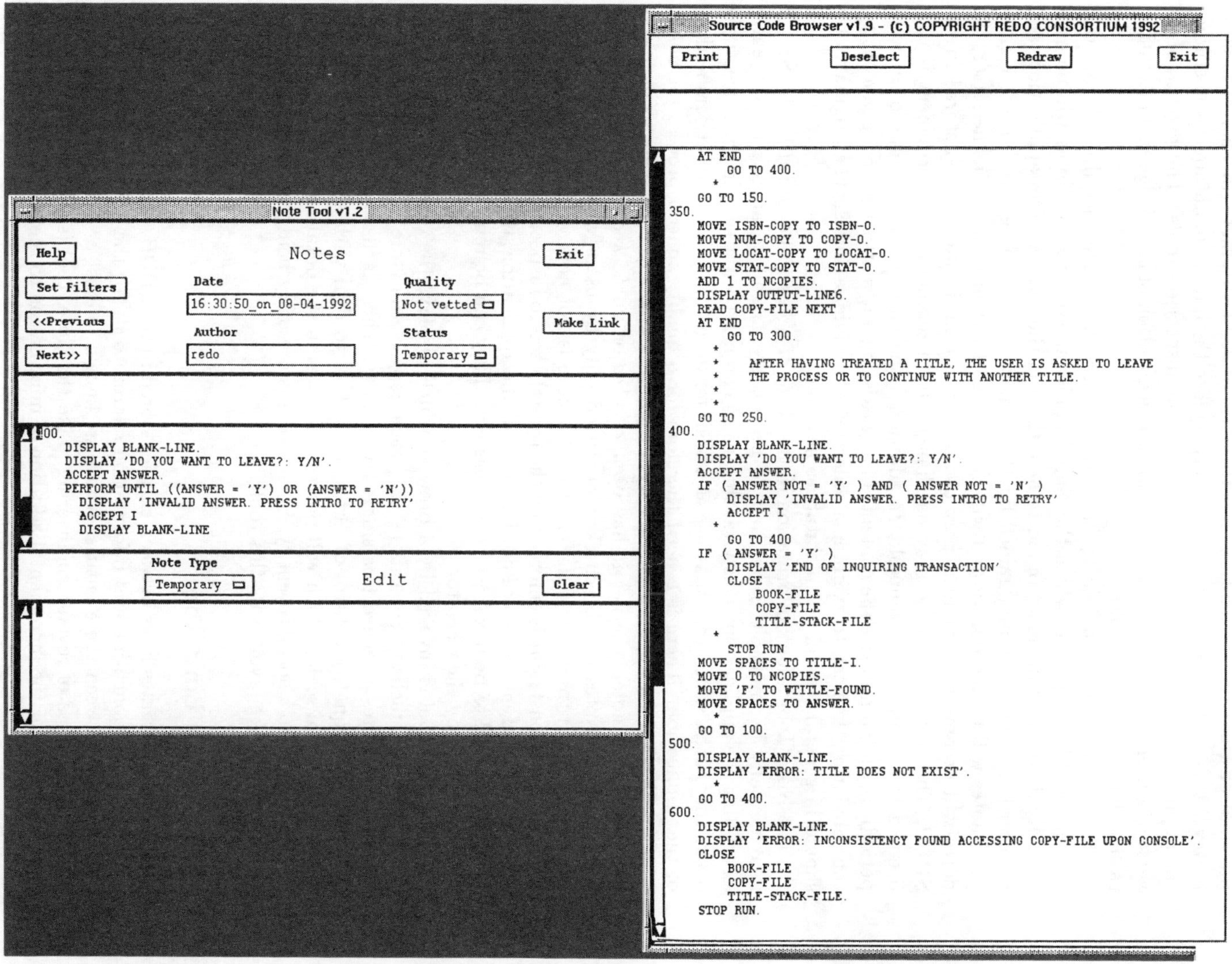

Figure 19.12: The user interface of the Note Tool

information from the application by automatic or semi-automatic means. It is clear however that such tools will not completely replace the human maintainer who studies the application 'manually', aided by the various inspection tools. The process of reverse engineering is seen as one of incremental acquisition of knowledge in an iterative, rather than a linear fashion.

There is a need for a tool to be used to record knowledge acquired during this process, and it is this role which the Note Tool is intended to fill. Notes will be used by individual maintainers as an aid to help them in their study of an application, and to record the understanding gained for the benefit of their successors. In the former case, notes will be temporary and will be removed by their creator. In the latter, the notes will become a permanent part of the application documentation stored in the SDDB. The status of a note may be changed from temporary to permanent if it is deemed to be sufficiently valuable. In addition a special type of note may be created periodically to summarize the contents of any existing notes attached to a given entity, thus obviating the need to examine a collection of individual notes. The original notes should in general remain in the database however.

The Note Tool allows information in the form of notes to be added to the SDDB incrementally by multiple users, and to be made available to anyone subsequently examining the application. It is vital that users can have confidence in the correctness of existing notes, which they may use as a basis for developing their own understanding of the application. There is a need therefore for a quality control process for notes, which will allow for their inspection by a quality controller. The Note Tool makes the status of a note, whether it has been *checked* or *unchecked*, visible to any user who reads it. Notes can be checked or vetted only by users who have appropriate authorization. In particular, the creator of a note is not able to mark it as quality-checked. This constraint is enforced by the tool(s) used to inspect the notes. Similarly, since notes represent valuable knowledge about the application, they should be deleted only when found to be incorrect or inconsistent. They can be removed only by quality controllers and by their creator.

The Note Tool is invoked by a browser which displays the object to which notes are or will be attached. For this reason, each copy of the Note Tool provides access only to those notes attached to a single given entity. There is also a need, particularly with regard to quality control of notes, for a tool to deal with the management of notes on a global scale, which will process all notes in the database rather than only those attached to a specified entity. Such a tool is presently being considered, and the Note Tool may be invoked by this tool.

19.7.6 The Link Tool

The Link Tool creates links between entities stored in the SDDB, which represent components of an application and information related to it, for the purpose of recording relationships between these entities which are known to exist or which are discovered during the process of reverse engineering. Like the Note Tool (section 19.7.5) it provides a facility for the incremental addition of information to the SDDB describing an application.

The original purpose envisaged for this tool was to link documentation with other contents in the SDDB. This was intended to make it possible for the maintainer to

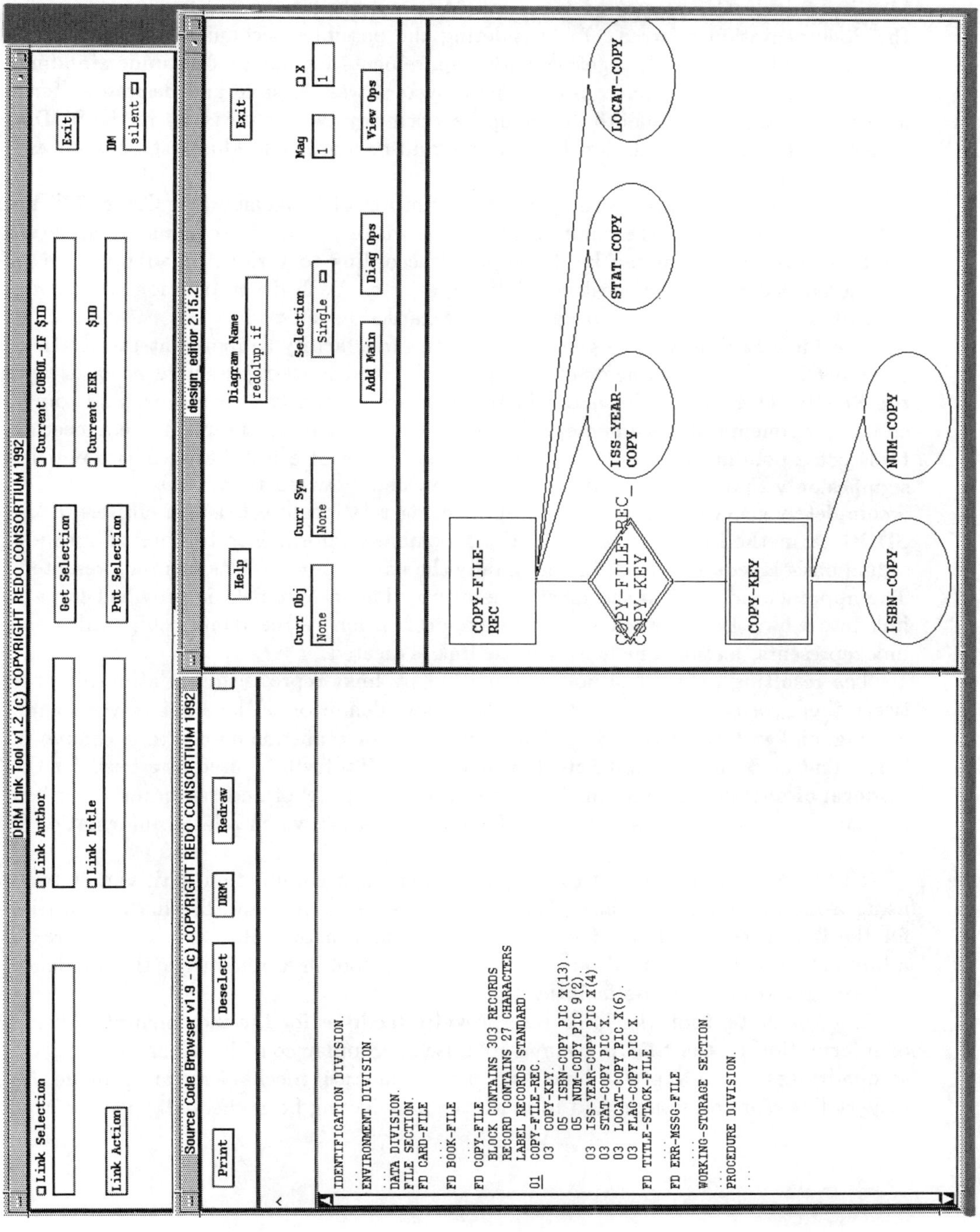

Figure 19.13: The user interface of the Link Tool

identify quickly the part(s) of the application to which a particular component of the documentation referred. In considering the possible mechanisms by which this system could be realized, together with requirements for application understanding, it became clear that a much more general system was possible and desirable. Such a system would allow links to be set up between any two entity types in the SDDB, reflecting the fact that relationships of one kind or another might exist between any types of entity.

Reverse engineering, according to the definition of Chikofsky and Cross [71], involves identification of the components which make up the system and their interrelationships. A system can be decomposed according to various paradigms such as functional decomposition, abstract data types, etc. Each decomposition constitutes an abstract view of the system and can be regarded as a design.

The Link Tool provides a generic, semantics-free facility to represent the relationships between any components of the application which are represented as entities in the SDDB. These might be nodes in the abstract syntax tree of the original source code, components of documents, or abstractions created by the reverse engineering tools corresponding to design objects. The existence of a link between two entities signifies only that a relationship of some kind exists between them: thus they provide a completely generic mechanism for representing relationships between entities in the SDDB. A method for attaching additional semantic information to links on an individual basis is required, to define more fully the nature of the relationship represented. The approach adopted is the most general possible: a text field is provided in each link into which the user enters a free-text description of the relationship which the link represents, at the time at which the link is created.

The resulting network of nodes connected by links representing relationships between them corresponds well both with the above definition of the aim of reverse engineering, and with the model of human knowledge representation described in chapter 6. The intention is that the links created by the Link Tool will be used as a basis for the retrieval of related information. In the terms of the model of understanding described in chapter 6, they will play the role of access paths via which related information is accessed.

The Link Tool is intended to be used primarily in conjunction with viewer tools using a mouse-driven interface. The user selects the source and destination entities for the link in the windows of two viewer tools, and invokes the Link Tool to create a link between them. It is also possible to run the tool in a non–interactive mode, so that other tools can use its facilities to create links.

Like the Note Tool, the Link Tool provides facilities for the incremental addition of information to the SDDB by multiple users. Similar considerations with regard to quality assurance apply to links as to notes; identical mechanisms are provided to inspect links for correctness and to mark them as having been checked.

20

Data Remodeling

A.G. Darlison, N. Sabanis,
Lloyd's Register of Shipping, Croydon, UK

20.1 Rationale

As discussed in chapters 1 and 7, reverse engineering is all about creating models of an existing system, in much the same way as 'normal' system specification is all about making models of an as-yet non-existent system: that is, reverse engineering is more-or-less synonymous with system *understanding*. So in reverse engineering, as in forward engineering, we must be clear about what kinds of model are required, and what they may be used for. Naturally, an assumption of this section is that data models are required for some systems, and we shall describe a tool for making data models from existing code and manipulating them.

An extensive investigation of industry requirements has not been part of REDO, but an assessment of partners' own needs has lead us to the focus of *analysis* and *understanding* existing systems, and, of course, recording in an accessible manner the results of this analysis. We shall not present any reverse engineering case studies or scenaria. The reader is invited to review the many examples in the literature (see for instance, references [203] [145] [65] [274]), and those which will doubtlessly be more and more frequently discussed at the numerous reverse engineering, maintenance and CASE conferences [274]. If we look at these in the light of the REDO focus on analysis, and also its current (but not necessarily permanent) focus on ageing data processing systems written in COBOL, we can draw a number of conclusions (see chapter 7):

- Derived models must be presentable to staff with a particular culture, training and mentality, and must be acceptable to management, who may have recently swallowed the CASE hook and spent considerable sums on tools and training for particular analysis techniques. This indicates that a credible reverse engineering offering must be to some extent tailorable, and will probably have a graphical interface. This is much the same idea as the customizable CASE tool (or CASE meta-tool), and infuses the REDO philosophy. Indeed, REDO itself is built on a platform which can be regarded as a CASE meta-tool. The tool we describe below should be regarded as a particular instance of a more generic REDO analysis tool.

- Many kinds of model or view are required, often simultaneously, in order to gain insight. This is discussed elsewhere in this Compendium. However, in the commercial data processing world great emphasis is placed on data modelling. One of the views available to our would-be reverse engineer must therefore be a data model. We might expect that its means of derivation, presentation and manipulation will be somewhat configurable.

- Models at various 'levels of abstraction' are required, depending upon intended use. For example, change requests are sometimes presented at a functional level, so an up-to-date functional specification, suitably linked to the designs and code which implement it, will be of great benefit for impact analysis and cost estimation. REDO as a whole caters for a range of abstraction levels. The data modelling world generally acknowledges three levels: physical; logical; and conceptual. Data remodeling in REDO aims to reconstruct a conceptual model from information contained in the source code and elsewhere, whilst maintaining links from the model to the source (see below). Lower-level models can be reconstructed from this, much as in normal forward engineering, but with additional cues and clues from the implementation.

- Substantial tool assistance is important [274]. We should not expect maintainers to create models of their system by hand any more than we expect programmers to compile their source by hand. Much useful information can be extracted automatically, and the only barrier to doing this presently is the sheer size of the manual task. This suggests a tool which traverses the SDDB to create a 'first cut' view automatically, rather like a giant query.

- Not all useful information can be derived automatically. It can often be shown by mathematical arguments that some information cannot be extracted automatically – the associated mathematical problem is said to be *undecidable*. In any case, it is common-sense to any seasoned maintenance programmer that, while the source code constitutes a precise description of the implemented system, considerable detective work is required to uncover its meaning. The conclusion is that tools must be interactive. This can happen in two ways:

  1. the tool is interactive to allow users to modify the first cut view on the basis of information which the tool could not possibly have inferred from the source code alone. The tool will, of course, ensure consistency is maintained within certain limits

2. the first cut is created using heuristics, contained in a knowledge base which is maintained by users, and hopefully over time, captures their domain and system knowledge. This is a further sense in which tools must be adaptable, and is one which is emphasized in some existing commercial products (see next section).

- Now that we have a range of powerful reverse engineering tools becoming available we must acknowledge that the 'added information' that a user provides to one particular tool may have been derived using another tool. We thus expect a toolkit to be immensely more valuable if different reverse engineering tools are reasonably tightly integrated. So like all the other REDO tools, a data remodeling tool must provide 'hooks' for invoking other tools. We shall say a little more about these below.

- We would expect to be able to justify the reverse engineered model in terms of the source from which it was derived (in much the same way as we expect to justify implementations with respect to specifications in forward engineering). This leads us to the idea of connecting derived models to the original source via navigable links, with terminators being elements of source code (for example, nodes in the parse tree) and constructs in the derived model (entities, relationships, or whatever). The links may either represent a trace of the automatic tools derivation, or may be subsequently set by users. Different link types will be used for different (user supplied) semantics. This concept is discussed in the wider context of the REDO architecture in chapter 18.

These considerations have strongly influenced the functionality of the REDO data remodeling tool. We ask the reader to bear them in mind while reading the more detailed description in section 22.1. It will be seen that the data remodeling tool may be regarded as just one instance of a more general toolset.

20.2 State-of-the-Art

Before embarking on a discussion of what REDO has to offer, let us pause to examine the current state of the art in this field.

It can generally be said that the state-of-the-art in methods for reverse engineering is currently embodied in the tools available or currently under development. There is no flourishing of 'independent' theoretical work reported in literature. Two early publications [243, 177] on the translation of COBOL file definitions to an Entity-Relationship conceptual model originated from a slightly different viewpoint and, to the best of our knowledge, were not followed by any major thrust of relevant research.

The above phenomenon is probably due to two factors:

1. the strategic and financial importance the field of (Data) Reverse Engineering has for major vendors;

2. the fact that maintenance-related activities have traditionally been perceived as low-status, low-interest.

Judging by the number and content of relevant publications, it appears that in academia the problem of reverse engineering data has been paid less attention than that of reverse engineering process code. The few seminal papers in the field [222, 266, 288, 153, 110] present the case for Data Reverse Engineering. They also provide a first classification of tasks and levels of abstraction, from the implementation (physical design) level, up to and including the 'conceptual level' representation of information.

More particularly, the following three levels of abstraction are identified, which are very much the same as the levels typically recognized in data modeling (forward engineering):

- conceptual design level, where the system and its 'real world' (in ISO terminology, the Universe of Discourse [77]) is described in an implementation-independent manner (independently of the data model used in the logical design)
- logical design level, where data are organized according to a defined implementation model (such as relational, hierarchical or network), but in a DBMS-independent manner
- physical design level, where the actual physical structures (files) of the implementation (for instance DBMS DDL, COBOL files) are created.

By and large, researchers in the field appear to have mostly focused on 'first-degree' reverse engineering: recovering the physical database design from existing schema and subschema code or, accordingly, extracting data dictionary information from COBOL file definitions. Issues addressed also include system-level data re-engineering (e.g. data definition and data value re-engineering [288]), and the introduction of abstract data types to improve existing data structures (see for instance reference [37]).

In the commercial world, most tools concentrate on the lower-levels of the reverse engineering process, capturing physical design information (e.g. DBMS DDL, or COBOL files) and storing it in a repository. This perhaps explains why a large proportion of tool vendors are actually Repository and/or Data Dictionary vendors (e.g. PSL/PSA, PM/SS, etc.).

As found by a recent state-of-the-art study [299], very few tools get above the Logical Design level towards a Conceptual Level representation of the persistent data of a system. Three tools are identified, namely:

- the Bachman Toolset, an IBM market orientated product developed by Bachman Information Systems Ltd., USA, and now also marketed by IBM with its products.
- Synon/2, an IBM mainframe-orientated product developed by Synon Inc., USA.
- Softorg, an IBM mainframe-orientated product developed by Szamalk, Hungary.

Of the above three products, it actually appears that only Bachman provide support for data reverse engineering from COBOL files to an ERA kind of representation.

Finally, we are not aware of explicit plans by any other tool developer to provide a similar level of service in the near future.

20.3 Tool Functions

This section describes the functionality of the data remodeling tool, its source of information and its end product(s). It highlights major areas of research on which this work is to capitalize, as well as areas where the current state-of-the art is advanced for the needs of this task.

The implemented functions are natural ones for the REDO environment and allows the integration of the data remodeling tool with other REDO tools using the SDDB, thereby exploiting one of the main novelties and advantages of the REDO platform.

20.3.1 Create First Cut Model

Outline

This function takes as its input a representation of the subject system in the form of COBOL-IF stored in the SDDB, processes it according to some supplied heuristics, and presents a first cut ERA model. Like other REDO tools, no direct input from COBOL source is catered for, so only information representable in the SDDB [TN-LR-1057] can be processed.

Input

More precisely, the tool takes as input *persistent data information* from COBOL programs. The entire system source will be scanned for information normally residing in the INPUT-OUTPUT SECTION of the ENVIRONMENT DIVISION and the FILE SECTION of the DATA DIVISION of COBOL programs.

Most of the popular file organizations and access methods (e.g. serial, sequential, indexed sequential) are covered, with less emphasis on serial files for which fairly limited information can be derived from COBOL file definitions.

Auxiliary files, such as sort files, are not considered, as they do not embody any information about the system that the main files do not. Internal data (WORKING STORAGE data in COBOL) may contain useful information, and this issue will be addressed during a later research phase of the tool development.

The REDO data remodeling tool does not deal with any other physical file implementations, such as hierarchical, network, or relational data definitions due to the overall emphasis of the project. These have been emphasized in some of the tools discussed in the previous section, and should be in the scope of any mature data reverse engineering product. However, the SDDB does cater for TOTAL DDL and DML, and would be easily extendible to other data definition and manipulation languages. An immediate extension to the REDO data remodeling tool would therefore be to analyze TOTAL DML.

Output

The tool creates, stores and displays a logical/conceptual data model of the persistent data of the system. The target formalism is an *Entity Relationship* (ER) kind of model [288].

The ER is the most widely accepted technique for logical data modeling. It supports the representation of data at a higher level of abstraction by modeling them in terms of entities, their attributes and (inter)relationships. It is generally considered as more conducive to creative thinking and effective communication than data models that are closer to implementation, such as the relational, hierarchical and network models.

The ER appears most often as the meeting point for reverse engineering and forward engineering processes and tools, and for conversion procedures for migration towards new database technology (for example hierarchical to relational). Variations of the ER are also the underlying data model of popular CASE repositories (e.g. AD/Cycle [110], PSL/PSA [32]).

It has been argued that despite ER's general acceptance, it fails to fully capture the data modeler's intent, especially for large and complex applications (e.g. CAD). The most often quoted claim is that, in its original definition, the ER lacks a substructure for entities and relationships: it does not support concepts that are very popular with the object-oriented school of thought, such as generalization/specialization, aggregation, and association [285, 30, 15].

The basis of the formalism used by the data remodeling tool is provided by the enhanced Entity Relationship (EER) model as defined by Navathe *et al.* [22]. The EER supports the following classes of objects:

- **entities** (more accurately, entity sets), which are the principal objects about which information has to be collected. Entities are distinguished by:
  - **strong entities**, which have internal identifiers (see below) that uniquely determine the existence of entity occurrences,
  - **weak entities**, which derive their existence from the identifying attributes of one or more parent entities.
- **attributes**, which are used to provide descriptive information about entities. Two types of attributes are distinguished:
  - **identifiers**, which are used to uniquely distinguish among the occurrences of an entity,
  - **descriptors**, which are used to describe an entity occurrence.
- **relationships** (or relationship sets), which represent real-world associations among one or more entities (degrees greater than two allowed in the EER model). Relationships have semantic meaning which is indicated by the following:
  - the **connectivity** of the relationship: *one-to-one*, *one-to-many*, or *many-to-many*,
  - the **participation** in this connectivity by the member entities: *optional* or *mandatory*.
- **categories**, as defined in Lientz and Swanson [203]. The introduction of the category abstraction results into two additional classes of objects:

  - **subset hierarchies**, where each occurrence of a generic entity may be also be an occurrence of other entities that are potentially overlapping sets,
  - **generalization hierarchies**, where a (generic) entity is partitioned by different values of a common attribute.

- **ternary relationships**.

The extensions to the original ER model defined by Chen are intended to provide adequate expressive power to capture information either derived from COBOL data files or asserted by the user. For example, the concept of generalization is necessary to represent 'exclusive-OR' relationships. Such information is typically reflected on 'DATA-ITEM-1 REDEFINES DATA-ITEM-2' clauses from COBOL file definitions.

The derived, and evolving ERA model of the system will, of course, be stored in the SDDB, and suitable graphical viewers will be provided using TBK's generic Design Editor facility. Sophisticated CASE users will expect an automatic layout facility, and naturally this is provided with the data remodeling tool. A textual (predicate calculus-like) view is also provided for users of the formal reverse engineering tools who may find this style more palatable. Finally, interfaces to other data modeling and case environments must eventually be implemented if REDO's goal of 'openness' is to be achieved.

The initial tool implements a fixed mapping from model to diagram entities, but eventually this will be configurable, to suit users' own house styles of notation. This mapping need not be 'information preserving' if the user is not interested in exploiting the power of the enhanced ERA model we are using.

Processing

Upon invocation the tool commences a traversal of the COBOL-IF stored in the SDDB, applying the rules and heuristics stored in the knowledge base to build up a first cut ER model of the system.

Some of the mappings are rather straightforward. The following are some examples of rules that are applied automatically for mapping COBOL data structures to an ER model:

- COBOL 01 record definitions (01 group items and elementary items) naturally correspond to entities
- a clause of the type 'FIELD-NAME OCCURS N TIMES' can be represented as a separate entity 'FIELD-NAME' related to the parent entity via a 1:N relationship.
- PICTURE clause are used to determine data types and values
- 88 clauses in COBOL data definitions can be ignored in the first-cut ER diagram.

Other correspondences between COBOL structures and ER primitives are less clear-cut than the above. For example, a group item in COBOL can be represented in the ER, either as a separate entity related to the parent entity via a 1:1 relationship (this means an entity plus a 1:1 relationship), or as an attribute of a parent entity, or even be ignored! The tool will provides a choice to the user as to which of the three kinds of representation to adopt. If this choice is made globally by configuring the knowledge base before the tool is invoked then the application of this kind of rule is straightforward. However in many instances we would like the reverse engineer to be able to make a runtime decision, and we must carefully consider what information we will be able to provide him. He will require a view of the source code which is currently being processed together with a minimal (but perhaps expandable) context. He will also be assisted by a view of the partial ERA which has been derived to date, which imposes the constraint that certain kinds of consistency of the evolving ERA model be maintained throughout its derivation.

It is expected that we will require a facility to invoke the first cut tool more than once, each time experimenting with different hypotheses and assumptions. Thus the SDDB will be capable of storing more than one ERA model of a given COBOL-IF instance. It is not expected that facilities for merging these will be required because one or more of the first cut models will be selected for further processing as described in a later section.

Naming of components of the derived data model is naturally be based on the names of corresponding COBOL data items, although naming conventions reflect – to a certain extent – practical limitations imposed by the implementation environment (such as maximum length of entity names).

20.3.2 Maintain Knowledge Base

REDO supplies an initial set of heuristics, probably including those discussed in the previous subsection. However, it is up to the reverse engineer to enlarge and maintain this list, based upon:

- his general knowledge of the domain, and how a particular application relates to it,
- his knowledge of 'house style', that is, how various implementation language constructs are typically used within the organization (both informally, and as formalized in programming standards and so forth),
- his growing experience of using the toolset, and the results it has achieved to date.

Of course, specifying a user-oriented interface for entering and modifying heuristics is not a simple matter. Each rule takes the form of a 'query' or predicate over part of the SDDB. In the prototype implementation these are expressed as code which will access the SDDB via TBK's (low-level) database interface. To make the rule-base accessible to users we require a higher-level query language which will to some extent insulate users from the implementation details of the schema. This is ambitious considering the great flexibility of the TBK conceptual data model. Temporarily we must content ourselves with making the software functions which implement rules highly modular. Users will need to program using the TBK database interface, but they should be left in no doubt about where to insert their user-defined functions, or what values they should return etc.

Eventually users will need to be provided with:

- an interface for entering queries, including those which require data to be supplied by the user at runtime,
- a means of associating the results of the queries with model terms,
- a completeness checker, ensuring that rules exist for all required model constructs.

Statistics functions to monitor rule usage will help rule base development.

Ideally, the meta-model (that is, the specification of SDDB entities used for storing the ERA model terms), and its graphical and textual representations, would also be configurable. Indeed, it would be nice to provide:

- a convenient way for users to specify an arbitrary diagram syntax,
- a generator to convert model syntax to an SDDB subschema,
- an interface to enter and maintain heuristics (effectively giving their diagram a semantics in terms of implementation code), as mentioned above.

Of course, we would not be restricted to data models. Dataflow diagram syntax could be specified, and (assuming the query language were sufficiently powerful) queries with the 'meaning of dataflow' invented. Indeed there would be scope to substitute invocations of other REDO tools (such as the dataflow analyzer) for heuristics.

The long-term view, then, is that the data remodeling tool is just one instance of a more generic design recovery facility.

20.3.3 Maintain Links to IF

We have already seen one instance of an association between a derived model and the original source (when a user is provided with context information to make a choice which is offered by the first cut tool). The idea of setting up a web of links between the original source and various kinds of derived information is pervasive within REDO. For example the Note Tool (see chapter 19) allows link creation between any SDDB entity and user supplied comments.

A data model is just another kind of derived view and so facilities are provided for navigation from the derived model to the original source. Links are created by the first cut tool as it traverses the SDDB and creates the model. These links connect nodes in the parse tree of the source ('pieces of code') to terms in the derived model (entities, relationships, attributes, and so forth) and are navigable in either direction. For example it is possible to point at an ER object and obtain a display of related data definitions within the source, using one of the database editors supplied with REDO. The displayed objects would be elements of source which had somehow contributed to the creation of that ER object, and different link types are provided to express different kinds of relationship. Related source, together with some minimal context will be displayed. Naturally links created by the first cut tool are only to data definitions, and not to procedural code, since only data definitions are used in creating the first-cut model.

Once a model has been created it is possible to create further links between model terms and other database entities. Since we cannot anticipate all of the numerous ways in which such a facility might be used we permit users to create their own link types, with the (non-enforceable) understanding that each type is to be used to express a different kind of relationship.

As an example of the use of such links consider the notion of a *transaction* within the subject system. Some entities in the derived model will have a number of transactions associated with them, implemented as procedural code updating the data items in the implementation which model the real-world entity. Since we have an association between ER entities and data fields we can use an editor, or a more advanced REDO tool (such as a dataflow analyzer) to search for updating code, and once we have found it, link it to the appropriate entity.

20.3.4 Refine and Enhance Model

We recall that the intention behind our effort in data remodeling is not to construct a very sophisticated data modeling environment or a CASE tool based on the ER formalism, but primarily to investigate ways in which to derive as much information as possible from the source code about the persistent data of the system, in order to enhance system understanding and maintainability. However, producing a correct and unambiguous representation will require some further manipulation of the first cut model.

Support for this includes:

- a **interactive graphical environment** that will enable the user to visualize and maintain an ER diagram. This will include:

  - creating and modifying ER diagrams
  - using associated functionality offered by the tool, such as validation and normalization of the diagram (see later)

  This environment is an extension of the graphical display environment discussed above.

- a **knowledge base**, consisting of rules for assisting with aspects of the refinement and enhancement of the ER model. This includes checking for anomalies (such as synonymous entities), and discovering potentially useful properties (for instance hidden relationships, the possibility of ISA hierarchies) in the current model.

  Further aspects of knowledge-based support for ER modeling (for example automatic merging or splitting of an entity in the ER model, or creation of a subtyping hierarchy among a set of entities) would normally be expected to be addressed by a more sophisticated data (re)modeling environment. These functions will certainly be required if the derived models are to be used for any significant re-development, but with the steady move towards open tool interfaces we can foresee that this need may best be addressed by a good connection between REDO and another tool which already offers these features. The REDO tool does not embody a sophisticated data modeling environment, although relevant research has already been identified, for example the work referenced in Chen [70] and Ling [204].

- producing a normalized data model.

The data model we construct should be as correct, accurate and unambiguous as possible. This is where normalization of the data model becomes a necessity.

It is generally considered more natural to reason about the functional interdependencies of data and conceptual similarities between data items at a higher degree of abstraction than that of the implementation code. Therefore the data remodeling tool offers a facility for producing a normal form of the conceptual ER model.

This serves the dual purpose of having a normalized (thus, non-redundant) conceptual representation of the data-independent of the choice of the logical model, and being able to produce a normalized logical data model of our choice (for instance relational) 'at will' in a more straightforward manner.

This latter property is important in linking the outcome of data remodeling task with Forward Engineering (CASE) activities, such as logical database design.

There is no universal agreement on what exactly is meant by a *'normal-form' ER diagram.* It is usually perceived in terms of the following properties:

- all attribute names are distinct and of different semantics,
- the translation of ER structures into relational (network) representation leads directly to relations (records) that are at least in Third Normal Form. This is most often considered a 'good' normal form for relational logical designs (a definition of Normal Forms for the relational data model can be found in Ceri and Gottlob [68]).

The precise approach REDO will adopt to normalization has not yet been determined. We are currently investigating whether current research has managed to produce effective algorithms and methods for the normalization of an ER model. We are aware of research that has developed such algorithms for simplified versions of the ER formalism (see for instance references [92, 145]), but similar procedures for 'richer' ER models present a higher degree of complexity [27].

We are also interested in devising a way of localizing the impact of changes in the 'normality' of an ER diagram, that is reducing as far as possible the overheads involved in re-normalizing the whole ER diagram when a change is requested by the user.

If the alley of normalizing the ER model itself does not bear fruits, an alternative route will be to develop an algorithm for the mapping of ER structures into relations of a relational data model, and then develop an algorithm for the normalization of this relational model.

This capitalizes on vast amounts of research pursued over the years in relational database normalization (see references [68, 21, 111]), and automatic mapping between various data models (see references [22, 307, 176, 270, 316]).

Whichever of the above two approaches is taken, it will be imperative for the tool to offer facilities for asserting further semantics and functional dependencies between data which are not detected automatically in the original data structures, but which have been derived from auxiliary sources such as the procedural code.

Even if the normalization process is aimed at producing a (normalized) relational data model instead of normalizing the ER model itself, it is preferable to store all functional dependency information in the high-level representation (the ER model), rather than hide it somewhere in the accompanying documentation for the produced relational data model.

'Standard' ER formalism does not support a relevant construct, so an appropriate extension to it will be required. Relevant information – which does not need to be visible in the diagrammatic representation of the ER model – will be directly used in the normalization of the data model.

The data remodeling tool will provide facilities for the user to store intermediate as well as final products of both the reverse engineering phase and the normalization process in the SDDB. In this way, the information conveyed by these products will be accessible by any tool connected to the SDDB – for example, conceptual model(s) will be accessible by the diagrammatic facilities (tools) and displayed on request.

First findings indicate that the information provided by the original COBOL file will suffice in deriving information about keys in the new data model. However, as more information is required in order to produce a logical model from the conceptual representation, the whole issue is still under investigation.

The fate of the links described in the previous section as the ER model is refined is not clear at this stage. Maintenance of links will be a subject of future research.

20.3.5 Navigate to/from Other REDO Tools

Typically, in COBOL data processing applications the procedural code is used to formulate transactions and integrity constraints on the data. A significant part of structural information and semantic constraints (e.g. cardinality, inheritance/subtyping information, validation rules), as well as inherent functional dependency information (besides 'primary key' information for files) are typically expressed in the code, rather than asserted declaratively or documented in any form directly accessible to the maintainer/reverse engineer.

For instance, for a given subset of the first-cut conceptual model, such as an entity, the dataflow analyzer [128] can be invoked to provide information on the sequences of code that access and/or update it. A closer inspection of this code can reveal interesting information regarding:

- unspecified internal structures of records. In some occasions, the author(s) of a COBOL program are not interested in assigning structure to their persistent data, as long as they can extract this structure in their programs. This is typically achieved through appropriate 'READ persistent-record INTO working-storage-record statements', as shown in the following example of a COBOL programr:

```
DATA DIVISION.

FILE SECTION.

FD  SALES-PERSON-FILE
    LABEL RECORDS ARE STANDARD
    VALUE OF FILE-ID IS "SLSDO".
01  SALES-PERSON-DATA   PIC X(80).

WORKING-STORAGE SECTION.

01  SALES-PERSON-RECORD.
    05  SP-REGION        PIC XX.
    05  SP-NUMBER        PIC XXXX.
    05  SP-NAME           PIC X(18).
    05  SP-QUOTA-CLASS   PIC X.
    05  SP-COMM-CLASS    PIC X.
    05  SP-YTD-SALES     PIC X(8).
    05  SP-YTD-RETURNS   PIC X(7).
    05  FILLER           PIC XX.
    05  SP-CURRENT       PIC XX.
    05  FILLER           PIC X(35).

PROCEDURE DIVISION.

B020-READ-SALESPERSON-RECORD.
        READ SALES-PERSON-FILE INTO SALES-PERSON-RECORD
                AT END MOVE "Y" TO WS-EOF-FLAG.
```

By isolating the fragments of code that read persistent data into working storage structures (namely READ statements) throughout the entire system, information can be recovered about the inherent structure of data items that was obscured in the implementation code. The reverse engineer may then decide to include this structuring information as part of a consistent record definition.

Particular attention should be paid to records that are accessed by more than one program with different structures extracted in each occasion – view integration is a possibility.

- Any conceptual similarity among data, which will enable the integration/merging of conceptually synonymous concepts. Thus, for instance, two attributes with the same name, or two items which (the reverse engineer thinks) embody similar content/role can be checked, using the dataflow analyzer to slice out relevant code.

- Functional dependencies between data items not covered by the key information of file definitions. This will be very useful not only in reaching a richer conceptual model, but also in deriving information that is necessary for the normalization of the logical data model.

For example, if the value of a data item is always computed by a piece of code based on some other data item, this is a strong indication of an implicit functional dependency between these two data items. The reverse engineer can assess the situation and possibly assert a functional dependency between the two data items.

- The way data structures are updated. This may for instance provide information as to whether a group item in a COBOL file definition is ever accessed on its own, or only as part of a higher-level group item/entity. This can have a bearing as to whether, for example, this group item should be represented as a separate entity related to the parent one, or as an attribute of the parent entity.
- Cardinality constraints not expressed in COBOL OCCURS clauses, as well as optionality information, which are very useful for the semantics of relationships in the ER model.
- 'Mutual exclusion' information not expressed by REDEFINES clauses on a piece of data structure, but defined in the code as a constraint/validation rule.
- Nested loops of updating code may indicate parent-child hierarchy in the data.

This is just one example of the benefits of tight tool integration. However it should be clear from the above discussion that to realize the full power of the data remodeling requires tool navigation. By this we mean that one or more of the following facilities are available:

1. Other REDO tools may be invoked to access the same SDDB as currently being used by a data remodeling tool. (In REDO we have an implementation problem here, because it is not possible to multiply write-lock at a fine-structure level, but this issue is not fundamental.) Invocation of these additional tools should be possible directly from the data remodeling tool interface, or from within a data remodeling function, where appropriate.
2. Currently most REDO tools (including the data remodeling tool) do not take navigation parameters. That is, they take only that name of an FSO, further navigation being done by the tool user. It is planned for some tools (such as the Source Code Browser) to navigate directly to certain regions of the schema upon invocation, provision being made for this in their parameter lists. Indeed one can readily imagine many other modalities for tool invocation.
3. 'Hooks' (that it, an appropriate generic interface) will be provided for the directed invocation of other tools described in the previous bullet. For example, pointing to an ER entity brings down an 'auxiliary tools' menu. A selected tool is provided with a pointer to the entity from where it was selected. Naturally, the data remodeling tool may be regarded as an auxiliary tool by another REDO tool.

The whole issue of tool navigation is under active discussion within REDO. Integration through shared data (the SDDB) has largely been achieved. To harness the full power of the variety of tools in tomorrow's reverse engineering toolkit (REDO), we believe that functional integration as described above will be required.

20.4 A Forward Look

Much fuss is beginning to be made in the trade literature about the new generation of reverse engineering tools which will be used to solve the maintenance crisis. Many pieces of the jigsaw have been developed or are currently being researched. So far they have not been convincingly assembled into an integrated approach although there is almost universal agreement that future developments in reverse engineering will concentrate on four areas:

1. the active use of an open repository for storing both implementation artefacts and higher-level information recovered via reverse engineering;
2. the use of knowledge-based techniques to assist with labor-intensive aspects of the reverse engineering process and increase productivity;
3. a greater degree of synergy between data-reverse-engineering and process/code reverse engineering towards a more coherent, possibly unified, higher-level representation of information concerning both data and processes;
4. the integration of reverse engineering activities with existing and emerging forward engineering tools and methodologies.

The implementation of a basic data reverse engineering tool within the integrated environment of REDO will be a significant step in realizing these four goals. In particular, the Ovum report [270] for example, makes it clear that while a number of commercially available tools are beginning to address the problem of extracting conceptual level data models, there is still a dearth of tools to perform 'process reverse engineering'. Not only does REDO contain both these elements, but also sufficiently tight integration to permit both these complementary approaches to reverse engineering to work in tandem.

21

Static Analysis, Verification and Metrics

H. Haughton, C. Hornsby,
Lloyd's Register, Croydon, UK
P. Jacob,
Department of Computer Science and Information Systems, University of Limerick, Ireland
D. Robson,
Centre for Software Maintenance, University of Durham, UK

In a general sense, validation can be defined as covering all processes, tools and techniques which enable an individual to determine whether a software product is what is expected by the final recipients, namely that it satisfies its requirements.

21.1 Issues Involved in Verification

There is a close connection between reverse engineering of a piece of software, and validation of that software. Both can be seen as a process of obtaining information and understanding about the software. An area of validation known as formal verification, is defined to be a form of validation in which formal mathematical properties of the software are derived or proved. In general reverse engineering efforts have not achieved the extraction of this level of information, being concerned only with overall design. Howeŷer situations arise in practice in which such properties are essential to the understanding of the code domains.
We have identified three processes by which new or old code can be verified:

1. Use of a Verification Condition Generator, to generate weakest pr-conditions for existing program components [85], [155],
2. Generation of code from formal specifications [TN-PRG-1041], in a way that preserves the semantics, so guaranteeing correctness with respect to the specification, although not necessarily with respect to the requirements,
3. Functional abstraction of source code to a simple mathematical language, upon which transformations are employed to facilitate the process of proving properties about the domain implemented by the code.

In the following we will describe only (1) and (3).

21.2 Generation of Verification Conditions

Following the pioneering work of Green [140], Floyd [124], Hoare [155], Dijkstra [98] and others, there has been a strong effort to make software development a more rigorous subject. This has been achieved in the main, by employing mathematics as a means of transforming requirements into a formal (mathematical) notation, then comparing the formal specification with a solution (in the form of some code). The issue of program correctness has formed a central issue of concern for formal software development for more than two decades. The term 'correctness' is defined as a state within which the desired behavior of a program over the whole domain of input data is equivalent to the actual behavior over the same domain. A program may either be proved partially correct or totally correct. Partial correctness assumes that each construct in a program has been proved correct, irrespective of whether this program ever completes its 'function'. Total correctness, in addition to partial correctness, proves that a program will terminate (and thus complete its function). Verification conditions are logical predicates (or propositions) that are derived as a result of finding a solution to a problem of the form $P\ cmd\ Q$ where precondition P is a predicate which must be true to commence execution of the command. A post-condition is a predicate which holds after execution of a program fragment.

An invariant is a logical predicate which expresses the relationship between the variables of some program statement and the values they can take during the statements execution.

The technique of verification condition generation is a well-known and established technique, and is the subject of an ESPRIT project [85]. We have extended these techniques to include a form of concurrency – stream-based message-passing – as implemented in UNIFORM, and to use heuristics for guessing of loop invariants [190]. In a certain sense this approach is equivalent to (3), but encourages the user to interact with the abstraction process, providing meaningful and plausible loop invariants, and making explicit the conditions under which these are correct. An alternative way to represent the verification condition is as follows:

Definition
The notation $\{P\}cmd\{Q\}$ means

$$P \Rightarrow wp(cmd, Q)$$

for predicates P, Q and command cmd. The interpretation is that if the pre-condition P holds, prior to execution of the command, then after execution the predicate Q will be true. The weakest pre-condition is then given by substituting the values of Q in the command cmd.

A simple example of verification involving a communicating program follows, where we interleave the verification conditions between program statements (indeed they can be considered to be *assertion* statements, and can be given rigorous semantics):

21.2.1 Example

The following UNIFORM program fragment is a process declaration, whose instances are processes that remove all duplicates of a particular character **cskip** from the input stream:

```
PROCESS Removeduplicates;
DESTINATION charout:CHAR;
SOURCE charin:CHAR;
USES cskip:CHAR;
OWNS x:CHAR;
     y:CHAR
BEGIN
  RECEIVE x FROM charin;
  SEND x TO charout;
  y := x;
  DO WHILE true :
     RECEIVE x FROM charin;
     IF ((y=x) AND (x=cskip)) THEN SKIP
                                  ELSE SEND x to charout;
                                       y := x
     END IF
  END DO
END
```

This process deterministically maps an input stream to an output stream, and satisfies an assertion of form:

$$charout! = dup\_remove(cskip, charin?)$$

where *charout*! denotes the total sequence of characters output by the process, and *charin*? the total sequence received. We want this function to satisfy:

$$(i) dup\_remove(cskip, \langle x\rangle) = \langle x\rangle$$

$(ii) dup\_remove(cskip, seq\,\hat{}\,\langle cskip, cskip\rangle) =$
$\quad dup\_remove(cskip, seq\,\hat{}\,\langle cskip\rangle)$

$(iii) dup\_remove(cskip, seq\,\hat{}\,\langle x\rangle) =$
$\quad dup\_remove(cskip, seq)\,\hat{}\,\langle x\rangle$

if $x \neq cskip$ in the last.
We can then try to prove the program correct, using the invariant:

$$charout = dup\_remove(cskip, charin) \wedge y = last(charout)$$

for the loop (omitting the *cskip* parameter for brevity). The verification conditions are:

$\{assertion : charout = dup\_remove(charin) \wedge y = last(charout)\}$
DO WHILE true

$$\begin{aligned}\{assertion : \forall v \bullet (y = cskip = v \Rightarrow&\\ &charout = dup\_remove(charin\,\hat{}\,\langle v\rangle)\wedge\\ &y = last(charout))\\ \vee(((y \neq v) \vee (v \neq cskip)) \Rightarrow&\\ &charout\,\hat{}\,\langle v\rangle = dup\_remove(charin\,\hat{}\,\langle v\rangle)))\}\end{aligned}$$

RECEIVE x FROM charin;

$$\begin{aligned}\{assertion : (y = cskip = x \Rightarrow&\\ &charout = dup\_remove(charin)\wedge\\ &y = last(charout))\vee\\ (((y \neq x) \vee (x \neq cskip)) \Rightarrow&\\ &charout\,\hat{}\,\langle x\rangle = dup\_remove(charin))\}\end{aligned}$$

IF $((y = x)$ *AND* $(x = cskip))$ *THEN SKIP*
 ELSE SEND x TO charout;
  $y := x$
 END IF
END DO

This shows the generation of a necessary pre-condition for the body of the loop, assuming that the invariant holds afterwards. y is used to record the last character transmitted. From properties (ii) and (iii) the first assertion implies the second, and the invariant can be taken as the pre-condition of the whole loop, and we trace back the pre-conditions to the beginning of the process:

$\{assertion : \forall w \bullet charout\,\hat{}\,\langle w\rangle = dup\_remove(charin\,\hat{}\,\langle w\rangle)\}$
RECEIVE x FROM charin;
SEND x TO charout;
$y := x$

$\{assertion : charout = dup\_remove(charin) \wedge y = last(charout)\}$

Which, at entry to the process, when $charout! = charin? = \langle\rangle$, is simply property (i) above.

All of this derivation, including some algebraic simplification, was performed automatically, only the formatting into LaTeXwas manual.

21.3 Functional Abstraction and Verification

This approach is the most original of the three mentioned in section 21.1, and is closely linked with reverse engineering work described earlier in the compendium. It is described fully in the section on reverse engineering.

Prototype tools can be developed for all three approaches, and it has been found that (1) proves the most effective for small programs. However the complexity of verification conditions grows beyond the ability of the user to easily manage in larger programs, it is then necessary to use method (3), and attempt to prove properties of the abstraction by building up lemmas and inductive hypotheses, as in Boyer [36].

21.4 Motivations for Validation

There has been an increasing awareness that the traditional validation techniques used within most commercial organizations namely manual code inspection, walkthroughs, human-generated data sets etc., have proved less than adequate in their reliability. This awareness has been created by issues relating to:

- Safety-critical applications, possibly having an effect on human life (such as possible malfunctions of nuclear power plants), require more robust and precise methods of error-detection than before, due to the complexity and importance of such software. Particular emphasis has been placed recently upon the production of reliable software by the new defence standards for software procurement [232] and other requirements from organizations.

- The cost of maintenance for existing programs has become a major issue, leading to the desire to reduce the volume of 'bug-fixes' required.

- The difficulties experienced in controlling and validating modifications to software have been recognized, particularly with respect to retesting.

- The wider use and acceptance of software as a consumer project like any other has lead to the demand of more reliable systems, which conform to the same standards as other products. Thus the UK Consumer Protection Act of 1987 imposed liability for consequence of software failure on the suppliers.

In order to address the above issues, efforts have been focused upon the development of more sophisticated techniques for the production of reliable software, and for the detection of errors and problems within existing programs. In the next section, details are provided of how various analysis techniques (static analysis) can be used to achieve more reliable software.

21.5 Static Analysis

Static analysis is proving to be an important part of validation [162]. This analysis can be defined to be the scanning of source code in order to detect possible anomalies which does not involve direct reference to any item external to that product, and do not require actual execution [162].
There are three basic categories of static analysis:

- Analyses producing general information about a program which is not designed to search for any particular kind of errors. For example, symbolic cross-references, listing of the number of statements, variables, in a program. These are often related to or form the basis of software metrics. They are also linked with checking for standards conformance.
- Techniques designed to detect specific classes of errors or anomalous constructs, such as inconsistencies between actual and formal parameters and the use of un-initialized variables. Such static error analysis techniques can often be automated. The level of sophistication of these techniques varies widely.
- Symbolic execution or evaluation, in which program segments are interpreted to explore input/output relationships and functional dependencies between variables, and subsequently, to prove properties of programs. This procedure is probably the most sophisticated, but for a large program, faces the problem of combinatorial explosion. It is related to the processes used in formal property proving.

Most static analysis tools make use of automatic or semi-automatic translators from programming languages into their own intermediate language. The purpose of this is to enable various types of analysis which a tool can undertake.

In translating an application source code into an intermediate form, it is not the intention of static analysis to maintain the semantics of the code. Instead, certain aspects of the code are extracted, for the purposes of analysis, for instance, the control flow might be represented by a graph. If, on the other hand, a stated objective of using an analysis tool was to restructure an application, it is imperative that the translation maintain the semantic of the original program.

21.5.1 Analysis of Requirements and Design

In addition to code it is possible to validate requirement specifications and designs. These aspects of validation have received much interest over the past few years and have led to significant developments in the areas of formal methods/rapid prototyping [154, 151] and process modeling via executable models [103, 339].

In support of the above endeavors, the area of Computer-Aided Software Engineering (CASE) has been receiving much attention. These software tools support automated techniques for design and specification and facilitate various consistency checks between processes in dataflow analysis.

21.5.2 Types of Analysis

Control-flow analysis is the process of analyzing the sequence of execution of statements in a program. Control-flow analysis can be used for at least four related purposes:

- to provide general information on structure to the programmer, for the identification of possible bugs and the assessment of the complexity and likely bug-status of a program,
- to detect specific types of bugs, such as unreachable code, code having no exists, unconditional branches into DO loops,
- to produce data structures for later use for other analysis purposes,
- to prepare for restructuring of a program.

21.5.3 Interface Analysis and Type Checking

Under this category some checks for the consistency of interfaces between modules and of data definitions are done. Interface analyses include checks for:

- A subprogram called with the wrong number of parameters,
- A subprogram called with the wrong type of parameter,
- A subprogram called with an argument as an input when the corresponding parameter is a constant such as a string,
- A subprogram called with an array or character variable shorter than the dummy parameters.

21.5.4 Dataflow Analysis

Dataflow analysis or data use analysis is the process of analyzing how the data in the program has been used, particularly focusing on the use of variables. This aims to show whether data has been correctly read, written, declared and used in the program.

21.5.5 Cross-references

Perhaps the simplest tools for static analysis are those which provide cross-references between program data items across a program. These provide facilities for determining where data items are set and used.

Most analysis techniques employ the following basic checks:

- use of undefined variables (i.e. variables used and not defined),

- unused variable definitions,
- non-usage of function results,
- misuse of pointers.

21.5.6 Reference Anomaly Detection

The other major technique for dataflow analysis concerns the identification of reference anomalies. this refers to such items as the use of variables written twice without reading, and variables referenced along a program path before they are assigned a value along that path.
Detecting reference anomalies requires an examination of each path in a flow graph. This can be done by a form of depth-first traversal of the flow graph. Such an analysis examines the sequence of definitions, undefinitions and references to variables. There are two basic rules:

- A reference must be preceded by an assignment, without an intervening undefinition. The reasons for this include forgetting to initialize a variable, spelling errors etc.
- A definition must be followed by a reference, before another definition or undefinition.

21.5.7 Expression Analysis

It is possible to detect some common errors found within arithmetic expressions without actual execution. These include:

- Incorrect or incomplete parentheses. These are available if all expressions are parenthesized.
- Out of bounds array index. These can sometimes be detected from source code, without execution, leading to a runtime error. If the array dimensions are constant and the index constant, a simple check can be done. If the dimensions are constant and the reference index constant, a simple check can be done. If the dimensions are constant and the reference index is a variable, it may still be possible to deduce, for instance, within a DO loop, elements are often accessed in order, with the loop index as the array index.
- Division operations can be checked to ensure they can never lead to a divide by zero, by two methods:
  - tracing an expression back to check that values of input variables which could result in zeros are not in program input space,
  - checking for tests to ensure that the value is non-zero.
- Checks for square roots of negative numbers.
- Equality tests on floating point numbers.

21.5.8 Symbolic Execution and Information Flow Analysis

Another major technique for analysis of a program is symbolic execution. The basic idea is to allow variables to take on symbolic as well as numeric value in a simulated execution of the program. Thus, it is possible to maintain a form of record of the relationships between variables within a program, and of the conditions which are required in order to execute a particular path through the program. The technique requires sequentially evaluating the assignments, rewriting the LHS as RHS and evaluating the RHS as far as possible.

One should note here that many of the features of static analysis mentioned above are present in some modern day compilers. However, this does not invalidate the usefulness of analysis tools, as many such tools are developed which are capable of analyzing several dialects of programming languages. In addition, an assumption made in REDO is that the programs are working programs.

21.6 Software Metrication

This section will deal with metrication of software in a maintenance environment. Due to the diverse requirements on metrics in this environment, the approach of REDO was to develop a generic metrication tool, enabling users to define and extract a wide range of metrics using the tool. The generic, and to a certain extent language independent, metrics extraction tool is described, and a description of some of the useful types of metrics that can be defined, is given. The major uses of these metrics, both as an aid to restructuring and as a method of quality assurance for manual maintenance, are outlined.

The software engineering community has long recognized the need to be able to extract meaningful measures from both the software product and the software development and maintenance life cycle, and to be able to relate these measures [257]. Software metrics is the branch of software engineering dealing with this problem. Early work such as that carried out by Halstead [147] and McCabe [223], attempted to obtain a measure of complexity of software that would correlate with many different process metrics. For example, experimental work [280, 114] sought to correlate the metrics proposed by Halstead and McCabe with:

- subsequent reliability of the product,
- ease of understanding of the product,
- ease with which maintainers can locate and fix certain bugs in the software.

A criticism of this early experimental work has been the use of single indicators, rather than introducing a range of metrics to reflect different aspects of the product. Recent software tools with metrics components have used a number of metrics and taken weighted averages of these metrics.

Control flow metrics determine the subsequent testability of the product. In particular relations have been established between control-flow metrics and the number of test cases required to provide test coverage according to certain criteria. Lexical measures determine the level of learning required to become familiar with vocabularies of variables. As such it is expected that both types should have an input to the subsequent maintainability of the product. A benefit of the metrication tool produced for REDO is that both of the above types of measures are defined and extracted in a unified way.

21.7 A Generic Metrication Scheme

Fenton and Whitty have described a control-flow metrication scheme based on a well-defined mathematical theory of program structure [119], which depends on the existence of a unique decomposition of the flow graph of a program into a hierarchy of prime structures. These prime structures are subgraphs and in the case of a well-structured program, represent the control-flow structures that are available in the programming language, used to implement the program. Defining metrics corresponds to defining recursive functions on this hierarchical tree structure.

Noting the recursive nature of arithmetic expressions, data declarations and type definitions, we have extended the above scheme to enable metrication of these other parts or descriptions of programs. [TN-UL-1041] The scheme can also be extended to the Job and Application level. Metricating these descriptions consists of defining recursive functions on appropriate hierarchical or tree structures.

Objects in the structures consist of for example, arrays, records, variant records etc. The objects and structure are general enough to enable the modeling of a wide range of programming languages.

The following is a simple example from COBOL with ordinary and variant record structures

```
01 TRANSACTION
      02 TRANS-CODE PIC X
      02 CREDIT
            03 ....
            03 ....
            03 ....
      02 DEBIT REDEFINES CREDIT
            03 ....
            03 ....
```

The underlying tree structure is:

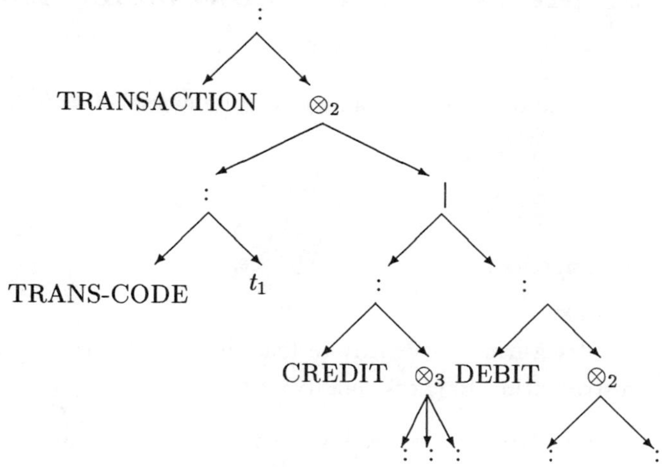

21.8 Implementation of the Metrication Tool

As described elsewhere in this document, a database schema has been defined to enable the storing of a representation of a COBOL application in the database. For metrication purposes, only a small subset of the entities and attributes are relevant for particular metrics. For example, for control-flow metrication, we are concerned only with the control-flow structure of programs. This corresponds to viewing a subset of the database, neglecting certain entities and attributes in the schema. For example, simple statements are considered as terminal constructs and all link and printable attributes of these statements are ignored. This corresponds to ignoring the internal structure of the statements.

This view of a program, and the schema underlying it, will remain unchanged for different programming languages. By restricting the metrication tool to access the appropriate entities and attributes in the schema, and by preserving these attributes when defining a database for different languages, the metrication tool, or at least certain parts of it, is language independent.

In some cases, it is necessary to effect a transformation on the database before metrication. For example, the REDEFINES verb in COBOL is in effect used to define variant records. Variables 'REDEFINE' other variables, and this is captured by having a list of variables that reference the same storage area. If a transformation is carried out, before metrication, that converts this list of variables to a variant record, then the metrication will be directly portable to other programming languages.

Once the general representation is obtained, metrication is carried out by traversing the database, and evaluating functions at the appropriate places. Genericity is built into the tool by having a set of predefined functions to which the metrics functions and elementary metrics values are bound at runtime. The binding of functions is achieved in C with the use of pointers to functions.

21.9 Uses of Metrics in a Maintenance Environment

The uses of metrics in a maintenance environment can be classified as follows.

- cost estimation,
- quality assurance:
  - for ongoing maintenance
  - for restructuring:
    - before restructuring to identify restructurable software
    - after restructuring to check quality.

For manual maintenance, metrics can be used to ensure that certain measures remain within acceptable bounds. Great care must be taken to ensure that other measures are not consequently pushed outside acceptable limits, with a resultant decrease in the maintainability of the product. For the purposes of restructuring, metrics can be used for identifying parts of an application that can usefully benefit by restructuring, as well as for Quality Assurance after restructuring.

21.10 Metrics for Cost Estimation

Lines of code are quite often used as the primary cost driver for estimation purposes. The problem is that some software is necessarily more complex than other software, and this should be taken into account. An approach to this problem is to subjectively rate the complexity of the software [28] but this has the disadvantage that it requires expert analysis of the software. Automatable measures of the complexity of software are a useful aid in the cost estimation process.

Control-flow metrics can and have be interpreted as a measure of the psychological complexity of the program. Complexity has been defined as ".. a characteristic of the software interface which influences the resources another system will expend or commit while interacting with the software."[87]. Therefore psychological complexity is concerned with the characteristics of software which effect programmer performance. Control-flow complexity is a measure of psychological complexity as, in order to understand a program, it is presumably necessary to trace different paths through a program.

As measures of psychological complexity, it is necessarily incomplete. Other factors such as:

- program modularization,
- variable and type vocabulary,
- vocabulary of external calls,
- dataflow.

will of course be relevant. (Indeed, an artificial intelligence approach to program maintenance views comprehension of programs as the production of such descriptions [212].) Measures extracted from these descriptions will contribute to a measure of psychological complexity.

Therefore measures used for cost estimation for maintenance will be dependent on these other factors as well as control flow and the metrication tool provides support for the extraction of these types of metrics.

21.11 Quality Assurance for Ongoing Maintenance

In line with Quality Assurance procedures in other production environments, it is very useful to be able to place limiting values on certain product measures and to insist that values obtained for these measures lie within certain predefined bounds. Values obtained outside these bounds identify errors in the production process.

In the case of software, such Quality Assurance measures would apply both after product development and after any subsequent maintenance activities. Values outside these Quality Assurance limits would point to potential maintenance hotspots.

The most famous example of a recommended Quality Assurance procedure in this vein is the recommendation by McCabe that values for the cyclomatic complexity of a module should be less than or equal to 10 [223]. This, in effect, restricts the number of decision nodes in a module to 9, which in turn would lead to a size restriction on modules. (Experimental work has repeatedly demonstrated the high correlation between cyclomatic complexity and size.)

Bache has similarly proposed such a procedure [14]. REDO suggests that great care should be taken in imposing restrictions of this type. In particular, few studies have been carried out on the resulting effect such restrictions might have on programmer behavior.

If such an approach is to be taken, it is recommended that extensive correlation analysis be carried out in the particular environment, to obtain correlations between proposed quality assurance metrics and relevant process observations. It is also recommended that careful analysis is carried out to identify any side-effects that occur, and to identify any subsequent maintenance behavior caused by these side-effects. The generic metrication tool is an ideal way to obtain the product measures required for the correlation analysis. It is also useful in quantifying any side-effects caused by the Quality Assurance procedure.

21.12 Restructuring

The criteria for restructuring is to transform the software in line with what is currently perceived as good programming practice. This includes the following transformations.

- Removal of GOTOs and PERFORM THRUs,
- Improved modularization of the program,
- Restriction of the scope of data items.

Regarding the first type of transformation, control-flow restructuring, GOTOs can be used to either implement 'structured' or 'unstructured' control-flow constructs. For example, a GOTO has been used to implement an IF statement, if there are no branches out of the code between the forward branching GOTO and the destination. In this case we can restructure the code by removing the GOTO and replacing it with an IF statement. There are no side-effects of this transformation, and the only decision is whether it is worth the effort to remove the GOTO. Most people would of course reply yes. GOTOs can also be used to implement constructs that cannot be implemented using structured programming constructs. In this case, transformation requires either replication of code, or the introduction of new Boolean variables. There is a side-effect and metrics can be defined to reflect the side-effects as well as the primary effect of the transformation.

Software metrics cannot be used to decide if the transformation is advantageous. They can only be defined to reflect, in a useful way, the changes carried out. A decision must then be made as to whether the advantages outweigh the disadvantages, and whether the transformation is to be accepted as a restructuring. In general, there may be a number of transformations and in this case the optimal one should be identified.

The second and third type of restructuring, are naturally treated together. Faced with a size distribution for modules in a system that we judge implies that the size of some of these modules are too large, we divide modules. This requires the identification of which variables are defined and used in the appropriate parts of the program. The scope of these variables should be restricted as far as possible by suitably defining the shared variables as parameters or global variables, and defining non-shared variables as local to modules.

While the size distribution has improved, there are many ways to remodularize and the optimal transformation should be taken.

As described elsewhere in the handbook, it is often possible to slice and trace the program to find a natural separation of the state space. Chunks that reference the same variables should be grouped together. A metric identified as reflecting the success with which this separation is carried out, is a product of statements in modules, and numbers of variables in scope in particular modules. This 'area' measure is low where there is good localization of reference of variables in a program.

A metric of this type, in conjunction with size metrics, is a good candidate for use in the identification of parts of a program that would be amenable to remodularization. Experience of the remodularization process, along with the use of these metrics, will allow the identification of suitable candidates for restructuring.

21.13 Conclusion

Software metrics should be an integral part of the decision-making process during the development and in particular the maintenance and restructuring of software systems. The size and complexity of many systems make it extremely labor intensive to examine these systems. Any support in the way of automatable metrics that capture attributes of the software such as size, complexity and quality, can be a substantial benefit.

The REDO metrics tool makes use of the substantially similar structure of many program languages to obtain measures dependent on the structure of the software.

It allows the user substantial freedom to select from a set of predefined metrics, or to define their own metrics. This is in line with current trends in software metrics, that recognizes the range of uses to which metrics can be put, and the dependence of which metrics are relevant on their intended use and on the software engineering environment.

The approach of REDO to this variability in the requirements on metrics is slightly different than many current approaches. A lot of current work has gone into developing a metrics methodology that can be instantiated to the requirements of an organization. This necessarily implies a process modeling approach. Careful selection of metrics required ensures that the development of instrumentation software is kept to a minimum.

Our approach is to provide instrumentation software that can, due to the genericity of the tool, be of immediate use in an organization.

22

Re-engineering

T. Cahill, C. Stanley-Smith, L. O'Brien, F. McLoughlin,
Department of Computer Science and Information Systems, University of Limerick, Ireland

22.1 Code Transformation

Code transformations are an integral part of any compiler [4]. In compilers, transformations are applied to the source code as it is being translated into object code. In other instances, transformations can be applied to the source code to obtain a *better* version of the code, [211, 216]. Transformations on code have also been used to produce different types of parallel code [252]. Transformations have also been applied to code to improve the readability in the modification process [113].

In the reverse engineering process within REDO, transformations are carried out to help in the maintenance process. The transformations carried out on the code reflect a lot of the processing that would have to be carried out by a maintainer when analyzing the code. The transformations improve the readability of the code as well as highlighting a lot of the hidden information within the code, that the maintainer would have to search for himself, without the aid of such a tool.

The following are a list of the transformations that the tool when complete will carry out :

- redundant variable elimination,
- constant variable recognition,
- initialization of variables,

- redundant code elimination,
- identification of loop invariants,
- parallel execution of statements,
- transformation of WHILE to FOR statement.

The dataflow analyzer provides the information to carry out the above transformations on the code. In the following sections the rationale behind each of the transformations is explored and it is seen that the transformed code is greatly improved as a result.

22.1.1 Identifying Constants and Initialization

The dataflow information that we have provided is used in checking whether or not a data item, used in the code of the program, is really a constant. This is done by analysis of each variable and its uses within the code.

Identifying the program constants is very useful to a maintainer as he can see, at a glance, some of the 'hidden' details of variables. The rationale for identifying the constants has already been elaborated. Showing the initial value of variables also improves the readability of the code.

22.1.2 Identifying Loop Invariants

A loop invariant statement is a statement within a loop that contains variables which are not affected by the execution of the loop. These statements can be optionally moved outside the bounds of the loop.

Discovering loop invariant statements and optionally moving them outside the loop, will reduce the number of statements within the loop. If we reduce the number of statements within the loop we may also reduce the complexity of understanding of the functionality of the loop. At least we will have removed any statements within the loop that are not affected by the execution of the loop.

From a maintainer's point of view, after identifying loop invariants, he will know what statements to consider while working out the functionality of the loop. Statements may have been added to the loop while testing and were not removed. They may not serve any useful purpose. If they are invariant of what the loop is doing they will be identified by this tool and can be moved outside the bounds of the loop.

22.1.3 Identifying Statements for Parallel Execution

The purpose of finding those statements that can be executed in parallel is to highlight the fact that the order of execution of those statements is unimportant. It does not matter which of the statements is executed first or last, as there would be no dependencies between them. Thus parallel execution removes that inherent ordering that seems to apply in a sequential program.

To identify the statements that can be executed in parallel, the tool scans through the program taking several statements at a time and checking if there are any dependencies between the variables. There are 4 types of dependencies that can occur. These are outlined in Padua and Wolfe [252].

If any of the dependencies flow, anti, output or control occur between statements being analyzed we cannot convert them to a parallel assignment statement. Those statements, that can be executed in parallel, can be converted into a single multi-assignment statement and the normal assignments removed.

22.1.4 Other Sections of Code that can be Parallelized

There are other times when we find sections of code that can be executed in parallel. When slices and traces of the code (see later) are found based on a particular set of variables of interest and the slice is equal to the trace, we have an instance where the code, making up the slice, can be executed in parallel with any other segment of code from the original program.

This can be done because there are no data dependencies between the variables in the slice segment and the rest of the code. The effect on any of the variables is localized to the code within the slice segment. Thus, it may be possible to separate a large program into several independent functions, each of which can be executed in parallel.

The rationale for identifying the statements that can be executed in parallel is two-fold. The first is that we can expose the ordering or the lack of ordering that seems to be evident in most programs. Showing the statements that can be executed in parallel, will take away some of the burden from a maintainer in finding the logic of some piece of processing carried out in a program.

The second rationale is that in the future, distributed processing will become more popular. Existing systems can be transformed to fit into this new architecture. In distributed processing there are many processors on which programs or sections of programs can be executed. If we can highlight the code that can be executed in parallel within existing applications, we will be a step along the way to transforming existing systems for this new architecture.

22.1.5 Transformation of WHILE Loops to FOR Loops.

There are certain WHILE loops that exist within a program that iterate over some set of data. These loops can be converted into equivalent FOR loops that have the same effect. The reason for this conversion to a FOR loop is that it is easier to reason about a FOR loop because we know, from the loop, that the statements within it, act on all the members of the set that is being iterated over.

To convert a WHILE loop into a FOR loop there is certain information that must be gathered first. We must know the set that is being iterated over, for instance an array of numbers. The following is an example of a WHILE loop that may occur within a program and that can be converted to a FOR loop.

```
:
control-variable := initial-value
```

```
:
WHILE control-variable < final-value DO
        :
        statements within the loop
        :
        control-value := control-value + increment
END-WHILE
```

Within the program with the WHILE loop we will have to be able to find the loop control variable. The initial value of that variable will have to be found along with the final value. The initial value of the control variable of the loop will be given to it before the loop is encountered. The assignment of the initial value may occur just before the loop is encountered or it may be given to it a number of statements before hand or it may even be given at declaration time. The final value of the control variable will usually be part of the conditional statement that terminates the WHILE loop. The increment value for the control variable will usually be found within the loop itself. The assignment of the increment to the control variable is usually the last statement within the loop body.

Using the dataflow analysis outlined earlier we can find the control variable, its initial, increment, and final values. The WHILE statement above can be converted to a FOR statement as follows:

```
FOR control-var = initial-value TO final-value BY increment
       :
       statements within the loop
       :
END-FOR
```

All of the statements within the loop, except the control variable increment statement can be moved into the FOR loop.

There are conditions that have to be satisfied to be able to convert a WHILE loop to a FOR loop. One of these would be that the loop control variable is not interfered within any other way except, incremented by the one statement within the loop. We would also have to check to make sure that there is only one increment statement and that there are not two different increment statements on different branches of an IF statement within the loop, which increment the control variable by different amounts. If this happens the WHILE loop cannot be changed to a FOR loop because we are not sure whether the loop is iterating over a set or only over part of a set.

Therefore we can only convert a WHILE loop to a FOR loop if we are sure that the loop is iterating over a set and we know the bounds of that set. If we are not sure that this is what the loop is doing, we will not be able to transform it into a FOR loop and we should leave the loop in the format that it is in.

22.2 Modularization

Why should we modularize an existing system? There are a number of reasons for doing this. The main reason for carrying out modularization is that we want to highlight the objects within the system and cluster the code that affects part of these objects into functions. Doing this gives the maintainer a better overall view of the system and the processing that is carried out within.

The functions that affect an object may be in a single program: a program could have several independent functions within it. A program may contain a single very large function that could be broken down into a number of independent sub-functions.

The objective of the modularization process is to analyze each program in the system and to possibly break it into a number of procedures or functions. Thus modularization will separate a large program into a number of smaller programs and separate a single program which contains a large function into a number of smaller functions.

The paradigm that we are using in decomposing a system is the object-oriented paradigm. This paradigm regards a system as being made up of a collection of objects which interact to produce output from the system. The problem that we are facing is that we do not know the objects within such a system. We have an idea as to what objects should be within such a system but we are unable to identify them. We are trying to identify them from the information stored within the system itself. We are not really relying on any domain knowledge.

Research has been done using domain knowledge to reconstruct the design of a system [25]. Within the REDO project, domain information is not being used as part of an overall philosophy for restructuring. None of the restructuring tools have any domain knowledge built into them. The restructuring is based entirely on the information within the system.

An object is a collection of data and operations that can be carried out on the data. Each object has a set of actions that it carries out or is carried out on it. Within a program there may be a number of different objects or actions on objects residing. Each of the actions of an object will manipulate all or some part of the data belonging to that object. An object may either be contained wholly within a single program or there may be a number of different programs where the object is represented. The actions on data may be spread over a number of files.

When we look at an individual program there may be some subset of the overall data in that program that is related to the carrying out of an action on some object. The objective in the modularization process is to try and uncover what this subset of data is and to separate out the code that manipulates each of the subsets. If we can find a number of subsets of the data, the program code can be divided into a number of different subsets, each carrying out a specific operation.

Most actions on objects in the system will be spread over a number of different programs. There are two types of object within a system, persistent and non-persistent. A persistent object is one that is stored after the system has executed. Examples of these would be files within a system. A non-persistent object would not be stored after the execution of the system, it is volatile. An example of a non-persistent object would be a report that is printed while the system is running.

22.2.1 Logical Structure of an Application

The logical structure of a system can be expressed in terms of objects. The objects within the real-world are modeled within the system. Each object has a set of operations that it carries out. These represent operations that are carried out on or by objects in the real world.

The objective of the modularization tool is to convert a system from its existing representation into a more object-oriented representation, highlighting the objects that are in the system. Each object will be represented as a separate UNIFORM process.

The operations that are carried out by an object will be found within the existing system. These will be transformed into procedures and functions in the UNIFORM language. Within the existing system an operation that is carried out on an object may occur in several different places in the code of the system. An objective is to find each occurrence of the operation and to replace the multiple occurrences by a single occurrence.

Operations that are carried out on an object may be spread over a large area of the text of a program. Another objective of the tools will be to bring all the code relating to the carrying out of the operation textually together and to convert it into a procedure. This is done to make the code more understandable and to make it easier for a user to follow the logical structure of the code.

A third objective of the tools will be to separate pieces of the code that are not related to carrying out the same function. Within the code of a program there may be several different functions being carried out. These will be transformed into a number of different procedures or functions that carry out each separate task. This will again make the code more understandable. It will also make it easier to locate places in the code where errors occur or where changes need to be made.

22.2.2 Program Decomposition

Decomposition of a program is based on slicing [329] and tracing [290]. For a given program, a slice based on a subset of behavior is an executable program that reduces the program to a minimal form that still produces the wanted behavior.

The slicing technique has been used for a number of different areas in software engineering. It has been used by Hausler *et al,* [152], for function abstraction. It may also be used in the debugging process as shown in [331], and for integrating non-interfering versions of programs, [161].

In the modularization tool a slice is produced for a set of variables of interest. A set of variables of interest contain output variables from a piece of code. The slice is basically a program that affects these variable the same way as the original program did. Thus a program can be separated into a number of different subprograms that carry out the same functionality as the original program did.

When we have found the slices for the various sets of variables of interest in the system, it is necessary to separate both the data and the code in the program. The code that carries out a particular operation and the data that is used in that code are separated out, forming new procedures and functions. The following section discusses the different aspects associated with the separation of the data and code and the approach that is taken within the **REDO** project.

22.2.3 Data Separation

One of the objectives behind modularization/remodularizsation of an existing system is to separate the variables in the system into independent sets. The way we can go about this is to use different set of the data and to slice the code based on each of the sets. Analysis of the slices tells us what other variables should be included in each of the sets of variables to make them as independent as possible.

Sometimes the separation into independent sets may not be possible, because there may be a lot of overlapping of use of the variables. The idea of obtaining the slice is that a set of output variables are chosen and the slice is found. The variables that are used in the slice will be those that affect the values of the set of output variables. Sometimes variables may be used to derive the value of a number of different output variables. This leads to the sets of variables obtained not being independent. This is shown up by the overlap between the different slices when the slices are analyzed.

The variables that are common to a number of different slices can be used in some interface between the various procedures making up the slices. These variables can be used at a higher level, whereas the variables that are not common can be moved to a lower level (into the procedure created from the statements in the slice). Figure 22.1 shows a program before modularization is attempted.

Original program

No data separation

Figure 22.1: A program before modularization

When the slices are found, the variables are separated into those that are independent (used only within a single slice) and those that are common (used in several slices). Any common variables will show up common statements that are within a number of slices. The common statements within the code are left where they are. The statements that are in only a single slice can be separated out into a procedure.

The slice produced is usually not a contiguous sequence of statements. The slice brings together all the statements that affect a set of variables of interest. Thus the tool clusters the statements in a program around the variables which those statements affect. If we can relate the variables to an object within the program, we can cluster the statements into a function for a particular object. Each independent slice is separated out into a procedure and any slice which has statements that overlap with other slices is checked for possible combination with other slices.

The next step in this process is to move the data which is independent for each of the different slices into the procedure representing the slice. In this way none of the data that is used independently in any of the procedures is accessible to any other procedure. Each procedure is isolated as much as possible from other procedures. The common data that is used in several different procedures can be left in the program at the higher level and the data, that is required in any of the procedures, can be passed as parameters.

The common data can be found by analyzing each of the slices produced and finding the overlapping sets of data. Any data item that is not common must be local to that slice in which it appears. Thus the definitions of those data items can be grouped together and transferred into the definition of the new procedure representing the slice. All the common data will be left in the program at the higher level. Having done this we will have separate groups of data items that can be moved into the newly formed procedures. We will have clustered together data items that affect each other. This will add to the understanding of the code, because at a glance, a maintainer can see what groups of data interfere with one another.

When the above transformations have been carried out on the original program, the understandability of the code will have been increased. The original code will have been separated into independent and common segments. The variables used in each of the different segments will have been identified and the variables grouped on the basis of there affect on each other. This will give the maintainer a greater idea of the processing that is been carried out in the system.

Figure 22.2 shows what the modularization tool achieves.

It has been argued in Zimmer [358] that the use of objects in the reverse engineering abstractions serves to reduce the effort needed by the reader in comprehending the possible interactions between data in the code; the number of global variables will be reduced, and there are no possible interactions between the local attributes of distinct object instances.

22.2.4 System Structure after Modularization

After the system has been modularized what will be the structure of the resultant system? Each program within the original system may have been broken down into several different modules. Parts of the original program will still exist and new statements for controlling the execution of the new modules will have been added. Thus functionality will have been separated and the interface between the different modules in the system should be at a minimum. There may be some pieces of code that are replicated in a number of different modules but these should be few.

The modules produced will be separated into processes, procedures and functions. The original program will now contain GENERATE statements (for the processes) or CALL statements (for the procedure or functions) instead of having the code contained within itself. Each process or procedure should be as self-contained as possible. Each will contain its local variables and only pass information to other procedures and functions as required by them.

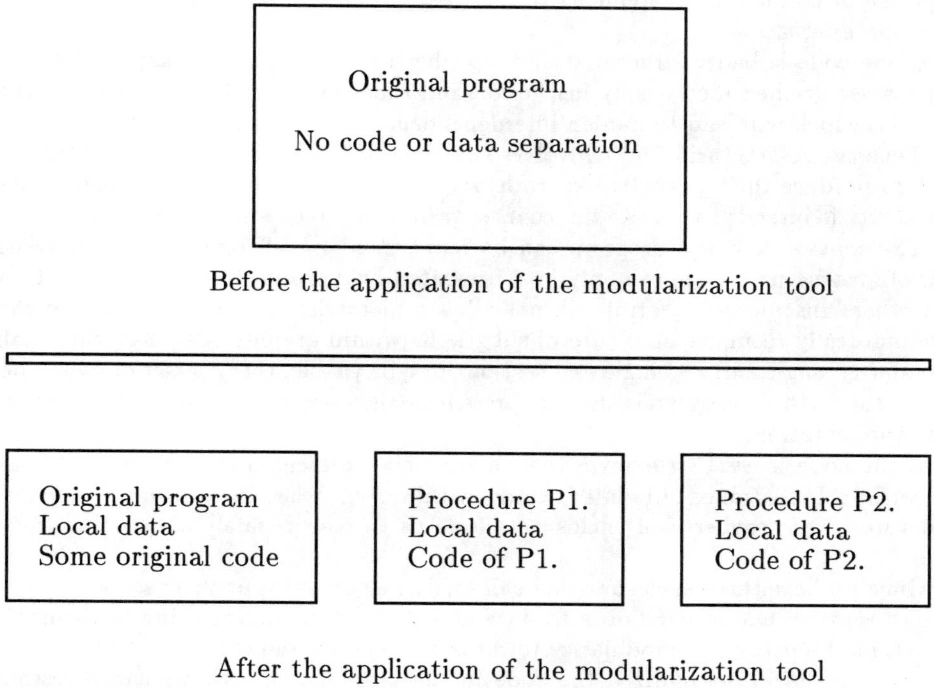

Figure 22.2: The modularization tool

22.3 Control-Flow Analysis and Restructuring

Introduction

A large proportion of the existing software that is subject to maintenance was written in an unstructured style, at a time before the benefits of structured programming had become apparent.

In this section we will discuss methods that perform analysis of the control flow of both structured and unstructured programs and generate control flow restructured code from an *unstructured* program. There are two reasons for this, first these analysis tools will be useful in their own right, for instance COBOL has certain language constructs such as the PERFORM THROUGH, that make the tracing of control flow, by inspection, extremely difficult. Second and more importantly, a great many of the tools and methods that are discussed in this handbook and are being developed in REDO have the pre-condition that the code be *well structured.*

Reasons for Restructuring

In any program, no matter how badly structured, there are identifiable single entry – single exit sections of code. These vary in granularity from blocks representing a sequence of non-control statements to complete 'modules', represented by procedures or subprograms.

If the code is badly structured and 'spaghetti-like' then it not easy to determine the coarser grained modules by inspection and there may also be an overlap of these modules which will lead to hidden interdependencies.

Thus the restructuring that involves the removal constructs such as GOTOs that tend to produce the 'spaghetti-like' code and their replacement with 'well-structured' constructs is intended to make the coarser grain components more apparent.

The control flow of a program can be represented in different ways. The control flow of unstructured code can only be represented by a graph, the presence of GOTOs and other 'unstructured' forms will not allow a hierarchical representation and there is no naturally recursive structure of subgraphs within graphs. Although the smaller granularity single entry – single exit sections maybe visible, the 'coarser grained' modules or the possible subgraphs that are present are not very visible within the spaghetti like representation.

If the code is *well structured*, then it may be represented in a hierarchical fashion with 'self-contained' modules nested within each other in a naturally recursive structure. This property of enclosure allows us to reason safely about a section of code.

Once we have these enclosures, we can safely merge and split them so as to achieve an enclosure around specific objects/data and the actions appertaining to them, thus we can modularize or re-modularize towards an object-orientation.

Once we have modularized the code in the fashion required, we can investigate the data declaration and usage in each enclosure. These enclosures are now becoming 'proto-' procedures and functions. So we now begin to bring the enclosure of the 'scope' of data in line with the enclosure of the use of data by declaring the data in the deepest level of enclosure that is practicable, this means, we make it as non-global as possible. We finish our transformation by separating the parameters to the enclosure from the local data and can now form the enclosures into the fully fledged processes, procedures or functions that they have become.

An Example of a Hierarchical Representation versus a Graph Representation

Figure 22.3 shows a GOTO representation of two nested IF statements marked (B) and (C) within a loop marked (A). The rectangles represent single entry – single exit blocks of code, some of which might be COBOL paragraphs. The diamonds represent predicate nodes, and the circles represent junction points at which two (or more) paths of control through the program rejoin.

The restructuring will recognize that the predicate no. 10 is in fact the control of the loop (A), this is represented by an octagon. The body of the loop is the two nested IF statements governed by predicates 6 (B) and 16 (C). This is described in figure 22.4. The fully hierarchical representation is in figure 22.5 where the enclosure of each subgraph is shown.

In an interactive diagramming system, each subgraph could be expanded or contracted depending on the view that was required and figure 22.5 is a two-dimensional representation of this.

22.3.1 A Method of Automatic Restructuring

A Directed Graph Representation of Control Flow

A directed graph is one desired representation of an application for the analysis and restructuring of control-flow. Its nodes are either sequential (or procedure) nodes or predicate nodes and it will contain only one start node and one stop node.

- Sequential Nodes have only one successor. They represent either some (possibly empty) sequence of statements that have no influence on the control flow or a completely self-contained subgraph. They are represented in the diagrams by rectangles.
- Predicate Nodes have two (or more) possible successors. If they have 2 successors, they represent conditional statements and if more they represent case statements or GOTO DEPENDING etc. Conditional statements are represented in the diagrams by diamonds.
- The WHILE iterative statement will be represented by a predicate node that contains the loop control information, represented in the diagrams by an octagon, and a subgraph that is iterated.
- The Stop Node has no successors. There should only be one Stop Node in the graph.
- The existence of 'Junction Points' that appear as circles on some visual representation of the graph, can be deduced and therefore need not be represented in the machine representation of the graph.

Iterative structures can be formed using conditionals and GOTOs that lead to cycles in the graph. This has been reported in Böhm and Jacopini [13], Ascroft and Manna [11] and others. Figure 22.6 gives the representation of the following:

(i) a WHILE constructed with a GOTO,

(ii) representation of a WHILE,

(iii) a REPEAT UNTIL constructed with a GOTO,

(iv) a REPEAT UNTIL constructed with a WHILE.

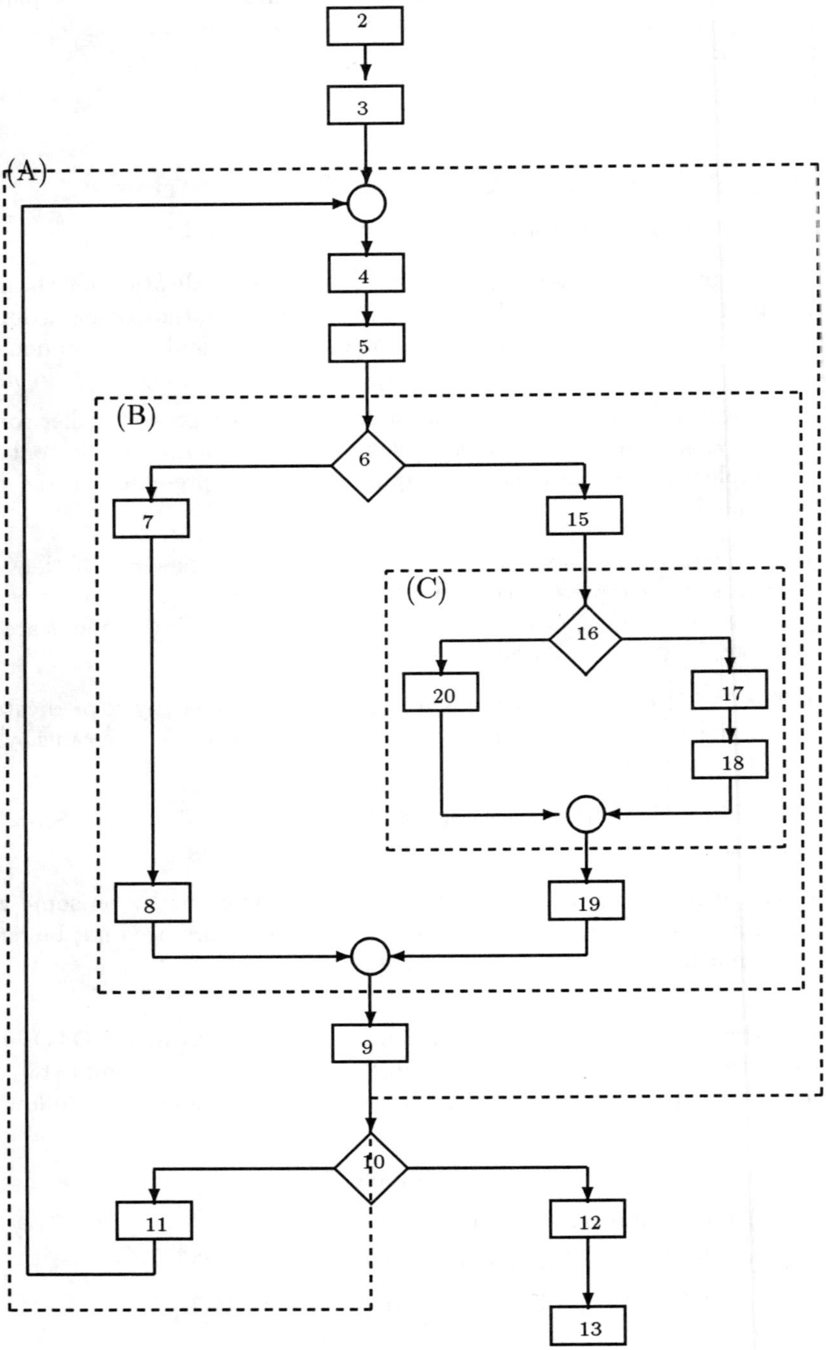

Figure 22.3: Unstructured representation

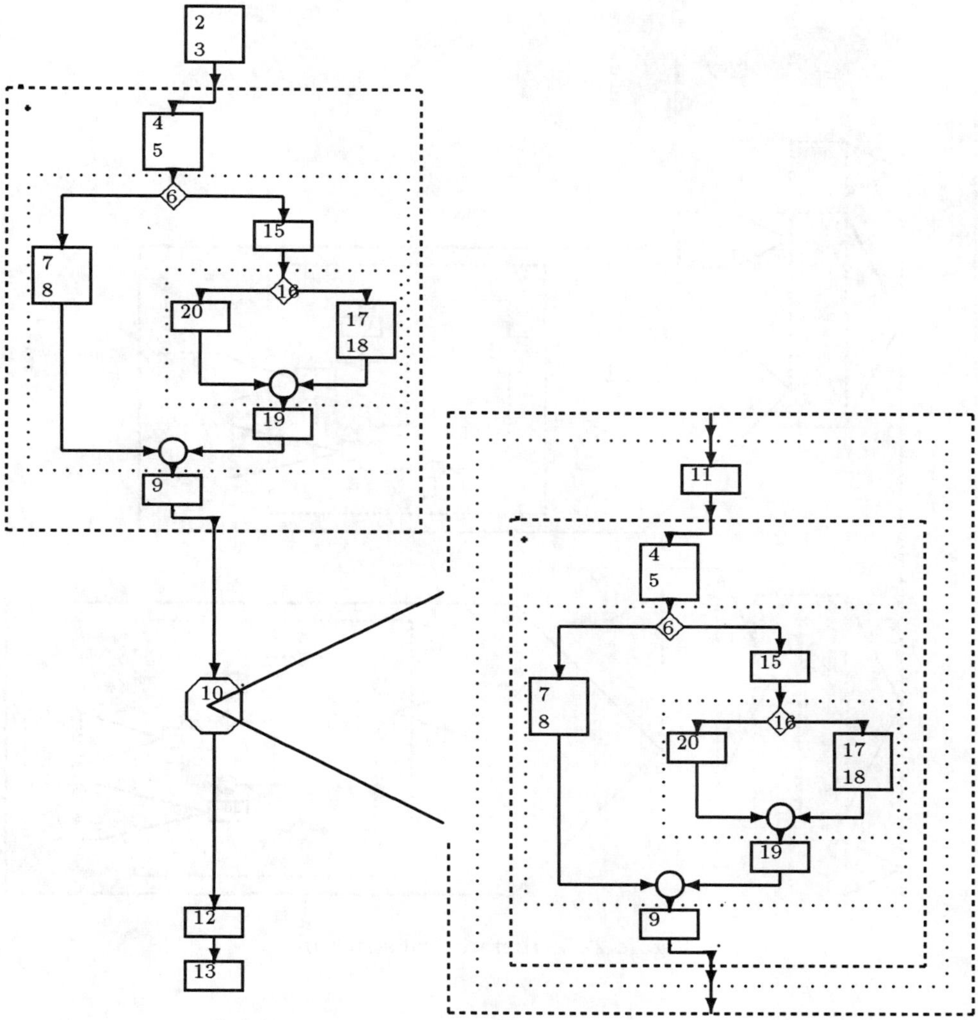

Figure 22.4: More hierarchical representation

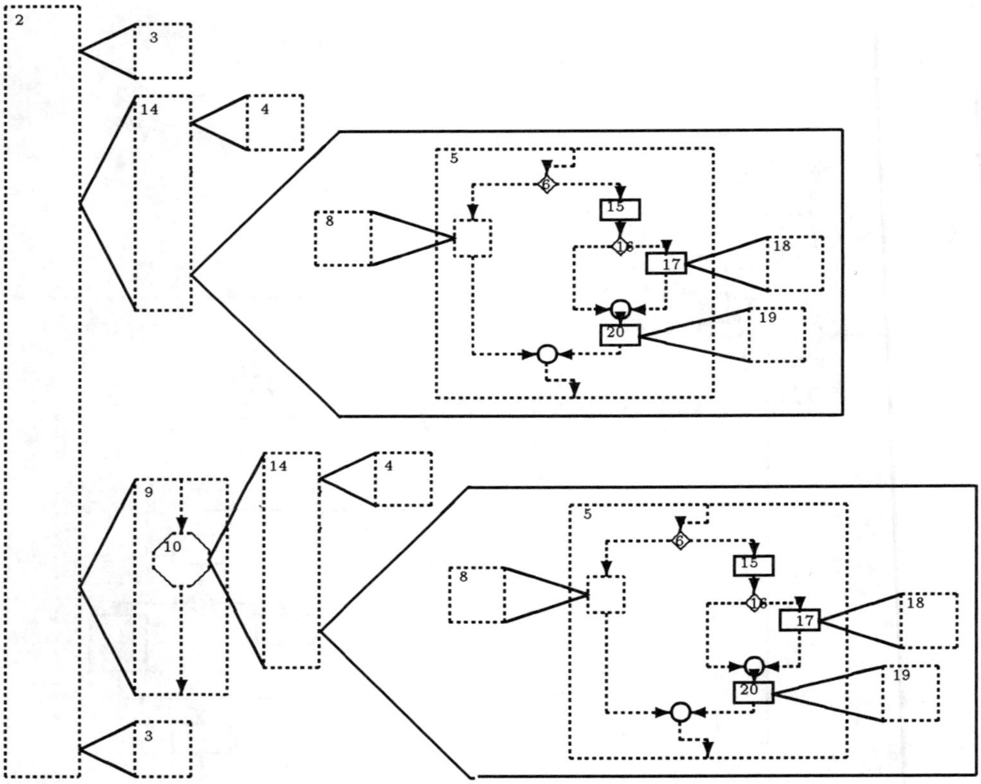

Figure 22.5: Hierarchical structure

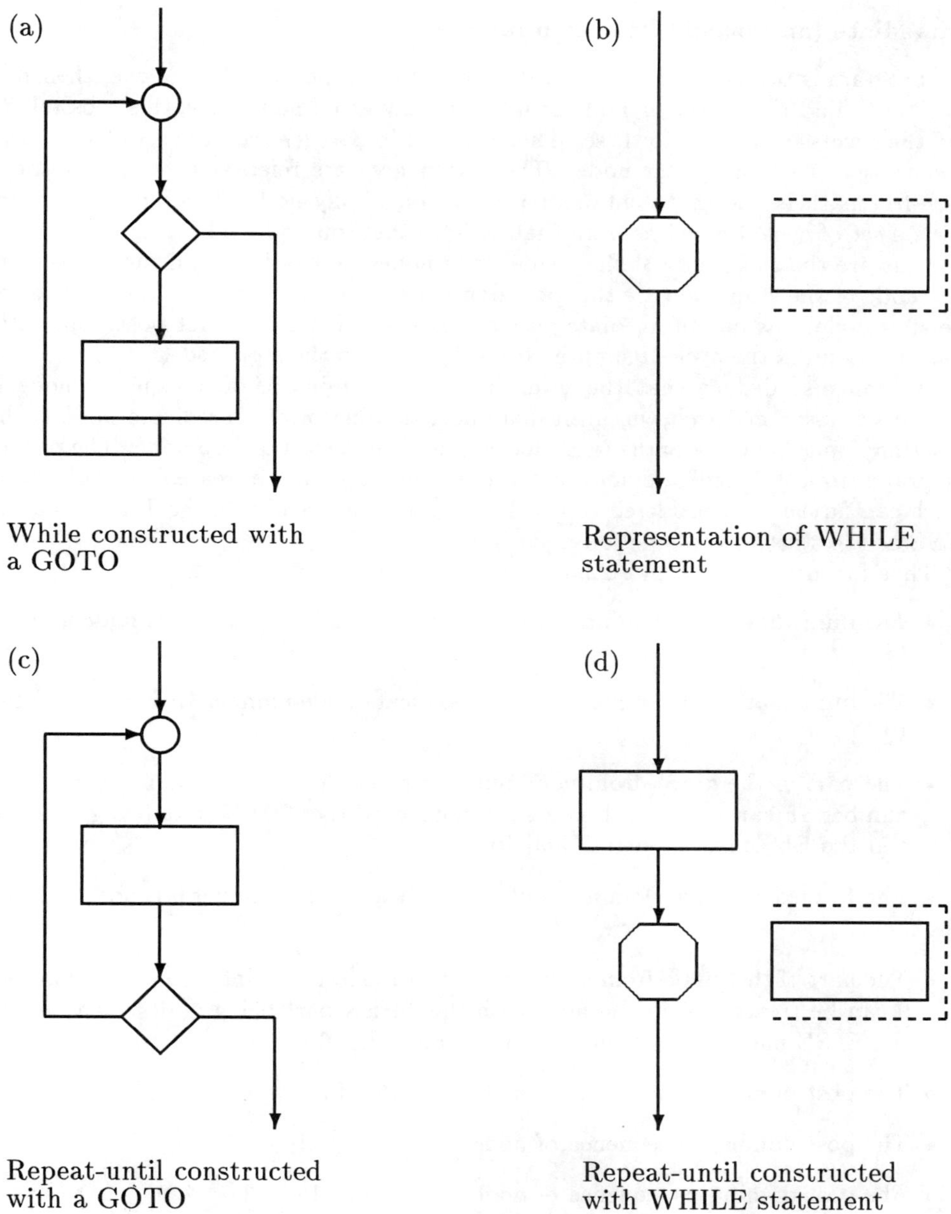

(a) While constructed with a GOTO

(b) Representation of WHILE statement

(c) Repeat-until constructed with a GOTO

(d) Repeat-until constructed with WHILE statement

Figure 22.6: Unstructured and structured constructs

The various graph layout techniques that can be applied to these directed graphs to give many different views of the control-flow are described in chapter 11

Immediate (and other) Post Dominators

If a program is described by a directed graph of the type described above, then it is possible to find the successor node or nodes to any given node. It is then possible to find the successor node(s) to these. Thus it is possible to generate the set of sequences of successors to a particular node. These sequences are referred to as paths and a cycle-free path is one that contains no repetition of any node. For each node there exists a set of cycle-free paths from that node to the stop node. The nodes in that set of paths are the successors of that node. The nodes that occur in all the paths from that node to the stop node are the 'post dominators' of that node. Each node (except the stop node) has one 'immediate post dominator', that is the first post dominator that occurs in all the cycle-free paths from the node to the stop node.

We can also deduce that the immediate post dominator of a sequence node is its sole successor and that the immediate post dominator of a predicate node is the 'junction point' of all the paths from that predicate node to the stop node. The part of the graph from the predicate node to the junction node can be treated as a subgraph, which can further be considered as two subgraphs – one each from the THEN and the ELSE as the start to the junction node.

Thus for instance, in figure 22.3:

- The immediate post dominator of the sequence node number 12 is node number 13.
- The immediate post dominator of the predicate node number 16 is node number 19.
- The part of the graph from node number 16 to the junction point before node number 19 can be treated as a subgraph, with the THEN part being node 20 and the ELSE part nodes 17 and 18.
- The Immediate Post Dominator of the predicate node number 6 is node number 9.
- The part of the graph from node number 6 to junction point before node number 9 can be treated as a subgraph, with the THEN part being nodes 7 and 8 and the ELSE part nodes 16 and the subgraph from 16 to 19.
- The post dominator sequence of node 10 is 12 - 13.
- The post dominator sequence of node 16 is 19 - 9 - 10 - 12 - 13.
- The post dominator sequence of node 6 is 9 - 10 - 12 - 13.
- The post dominator sequence of node 2 is 3 - 4 - 5 - 6 - 9 - 10 - 12 - 13.

Thus as node 2 is the start node and node 13 the stop node, the post dominator sequence of node 2 is actually a special kind of representation of the program and the breakdown of the graph into subgraphs is the same as shown in figures 22.3 and 22.4

A depth-first search of the control-flow graph can yield the immediate post dominator of each node. Depth-first searches and algorithms pertaining to them are given in Tarjan [305]. In fact a modification of a recursive depth-first search will yield not only the immediate post dominator but also the sequence of further post dominators.

Use of Post Dominators in Restructuring

The list of post dominators of the start node forms the program. Each predicate node is replaced by the nodes representing its subgraph. Each of the THEN and ELSE is expanded in turn and if this expansion leads to a cycle in the graph then the predicate is being used to form a loop and the predicate node can be replaced by a WHILE construct.

There are 5 structures that this system will not handle immediately. They are representative of some of the prime structures of [TN-UL-1041] [119, 340]. These 5 cases can be recognized and replaced by their restructured forms which are known.

Williams and Ossher [340] give these 5 unstructured forms as in figure 22.7.

(i) Abnormal selection path,
(ii) Loop with multiple exit points,
(iii) Loop with multiple entry points,
(iv) Overlapping loops,
(v) Parallel loops.

Particular Problems of COBOL

Programs written in COBOL present certain problems :

- The use of paragraph/sections as both the destination of a GOTO (a label) and as parameterless procedures. In the section of code below `PARA-1` is PERFORMED as a parameterless procedure and the target of a GOTO.

```
MAIN.
    PERFORM PARA-1.
    GOTO PARA-1.

PARA-1.
    DISPLAY "PARA-1".

PARA-2.
    DISPLAY "PARA-2".
    STOP RUN.
```

  will display

```
PARA-1
PARA-1
PARA-2
```

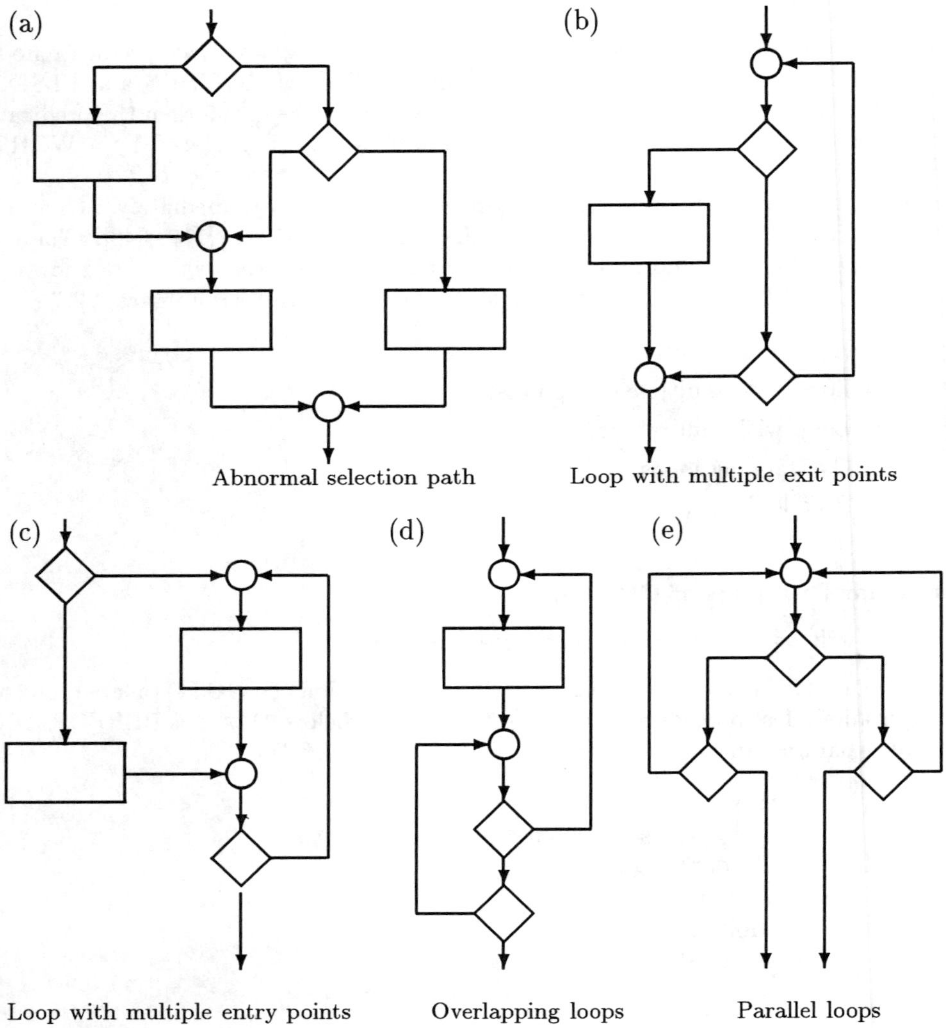

Figure 22.7: Unstructured forms

- The possible fall through from one paragraph to the next. In the section of code above, there is a Fall Through from `PARA-1` to `PARA-2` when `PARA-1` is 'GONE TO' but not when it is 'PERFORMED'.
- If a paragraph is PERFORMED then a marker is placed at the end of the paragraph, which is in effect a RETURN to the next statement after the PERFORM.
- A PERFORM (or PERFORM THROUGH) of a paragraph may never return or return to some unexpected position if a GOTO intervenes.

```
MAIN.
    PERFORM PARA-1.
    GOTO PARA-3.

PARA-1.
    DISPLAY "PARA-1".
    IF ( A = B) GOTO PARA-3.

PARA-3.
    DISPLAY "PARA-3".

PARA-2.
    DISPLAY "PARA-2".
    STOP RUN.
```

The `PARA-1` is PERFORMED and if A = B then `PARA-3` is 'GONE TO' which then falls into `PARA-2` or if A NOT = B then there is a RETURN to `MAIN` and a GOTO `PARA-3` which then falls into `PARA-2` so in both cases the output is:

```
PARA-1
PARA-3
PARA-2
```

- Mixtures of GOTO and PERFORM THROUGH give very unexpected control flow.

These will require a certain amount of preprocessing before they can be described in terms of the graph structure above.

- The PERFORM of a paragraph that contains a GOTO is not actually a PERFORM as it may not be able to RETURN. It may never get to the marker at the end of the paragraph. In this case the marker remains and may later be encountered in some unexpected fashion. Thus :
  - If the end of a paragraph that is PERFORMED is unreachable, then the PERFORM should temporarily be replaced by a GOTO.
  - If the end of a paragraph that is PERFORMED is only conditionally reachable more detailed changes are required.

The example above should be replaced by :

```
MAIN.
    GOTO PARA-1.
MAIN-new1.
    GOTO PARA-3.

PARA-1.
    DISPLAY "PARA-1".
    IF ( A = B) GOTO PARA-3.
    GOTO MAIN-new1

PARA-3.
    DISPLAY "PARA-3".

PARA-2.
    DISPLAY "PARA-2".
    STOP RUN.
```

- If a paragraph is GONE TO (or Fallen into), then if the end of the paragraph is reached then the NEXT paragraph is executed. It is possible to detect the paragraphs that can fall out/fall in. This transfer should be temporarily replaced by a GOTO on the premise that it simplifies the problem to one of GOTO removal and the textual order of the paragraphs is no longer significant.

The example now becomes:

```
MAIN.
    GOTO PARA-1.

MAIN-new1.
    GOTO PARA-3.

PARA-1.
    DISPLAY "PARA-1".
    IF ( A = B) GOTO PARA-3.
    GOTO MAIN-new1

PARA-3.
    DISPLAY "PARA-3".
    GOTO PARA-2.

PARA-2.
    DISPLAY "PARA-2".
    STOP RUN.
```

and the following is equivalent:

```
MAIN.
    GOTO PARA-1.

PARA-1.
    DISPLAY "PARA-1".
    IF ( A = B) GOTO PARA-3.
    GOTO MAIN-new1

PARA-2.
    DISPLAY "PARA-2".
    STOP RUN.

PARA-3.
    DISPLAY "PARA-3".
    GOTO PARA-2.

MAIN-new1.
    GOTO PARA-3.
```

- A PERFORM THROUGH should be replaced by the sequence of PERFORMs which reproduces the logic of the PERFORM THRU. If any intervening paragraphs themselves contain GOTOs or PERFORM THROUGHs then the logic can be quite unexpected and extremely difficult to determine by inspection.

```
MAIN.
    PERFORM PARA-1 THRU PARA-3
    STOP RUN.

PARA-1.
    DISPLAY "PARA-1".

PARA-2.
    DISPLAY "PARA-2".

PARA-3.
    DISPLAY "PARA-3".
```

Should be replaced by :

```
MAIN.
    PERFORM PARA-1
    PERFORM PARA-2
    PERFORM PARA-3
    STOP RUN.

PARA-1.
    DISPLAY "PARA-1".

PARA-2.
    DISPLAY "PARA-2".

PARA-3.
    DISPLAY "PARA-3".
```

- If there are more than 1 STOPs/EXITs then a new paragraph should be provided with just a STOP/EXIT statement and all the STOPs/EXITs replaced by GOTOs of this PARAGRAPH.

Control-flow Analysis and Restructuring undertaken in REDO

As stated in other sections, the programs of the application are held in the REDO SDDB in the form of several 'parse trees'. The REDO control-flow analysis tool recursively descends the 'parse tree' and simultaneously forms the required graph structure in the REDO SDDB as a 'level' above the parse tree and associates each node in the graph with its immediate post dominator and its list of 'post dominators'.

The graph layout tool can be applied to this graph which allows the user to inspect the control-flow structure of the program.

The control-flow restructuring tool is then applied to a copy of the control-flow graph which results in a restructured graph.

Example COBOL Program

```
 PROCEDURE DIVISION.

MAIN.
    DISPLAY "THIS IS THE MAIN PARAGRAPH".
PARA-1.
    DISPLAY "PARA-1"
    ADD AUNT2 TO AUNT4
    GO TO PARA-5.
PARA-2.
    IF AUNT1 EQUAL AUNT2
        GO TO PARA-4
    ELSE
        ADD AUNT3 TO AUNT4 ON SIZE ERROR GO TO PARA-7.
PARA-3.
    DISPLAY "FROM FALL OUT OF PARA-2"
    GO TO PARA-6.
PARA-4.
    DISPLAY "FROM THEN OF PARA-2"
    GO TO PARA-6.
PARA-5.
    GO TO PARA-2.
PARA-6.
    IF AUNT1 EQUAL AUNT3
        GO TO PARA-5
    ELSE
        DISPLAY "ENDS HERE".
    STOP RUN.
PARA-7.
    SUBTRACT AUNT4 FROM AUNT2
    GO TO PARA-3.
```

Example COBOL Program in Required Form, with Nodes Identified

```
PARAGRAPH <2 - MAIN>
           <2 - MAIN>:DISPLAY  "THIS IS THE MAIN PARAGRAPH"
           <2 - MAIN>:GOTO PARA-1 - <3> (Replaces Fall Through)
END-PARAGRAPH <2 - MAIN>
PARAGRAPH <3 - PARA-1>
           <3 - PARA-1>:DISPLAY  "PARA-1" ,
           <3 - PARA-1>: AUNT4  :=  AUNT4  +  AUNT2
           <3 - PARA-1>:GOTO PARA-5 - <4>
END-PARAGRAPH <3 - PARA-1>
PARAGRAPH <5 - PARA-2>
           <5 - PARA-2>:IF <6>   AUNT1  =  AUNT2
             <7 - THEN>:GOTO PARA-4 - <8>
           <5 - PARA-2>:ELSE
             <15 - ELSE>: AUNT4  :=  AUNT4  +  AUNT3  ON SIZE ERROR <16>
                     <17 - OSE>:GOTO PARA-7 - <18>
             <20 - AFTER>:GOTO PARA-3 - <19> (Replaces Fall Through)
END-PARAGRAPH <5 - PARA-2>
PARAGRAPH <19 - PARA-3>
           <19 - PARA-3>:DISPLAY  "FROM FALL OUT OF PARA-2"
           <19 - PARA-3>:GOTO PARA-6 - <9>
END-PARAGRAPH <19 - PARA-3>
PARAGRAPH <8 - PARA-4>
           <8 - PARA-4>:DISPLAY  "FROM THEN OF PARA-2"
           <8 - PARA-4>:GOTO PARA-6 - <9>
END-PARAGRAPH <8 - PARA-4>
PARAGRAPH <4 - PARA-5>
           <4 - PARA-5>:GOTO PARA-2 - <5>
END-PARAGRAPH <4 - PARA-5>
PARAGRAPH <9 - PARA-6>
           <9 - PARA-6>:IF <10>   AUNT1  =  AUNT3
             <11 - THEN>:GOTO PARA-5 - <4>
           <9 - PARA-6>:ELSE
             <12 - ELSE>:DISPLAY  "ENDS HERE"
             <12 - ELSE>:GOTO Redo-Stopper - <13> (Ensure one END)
END-PARAGRAPH <9 - PARA-6>
PARAGRAPH <18 - PARA-7>
           <18 - PARA-7>: AUNT2  :=  AUNT2  -  AUNT4
           <18 - PARA-7>:GOTO PARA-3 - <19>
END-PARAGRAPH <18 - PARA-7>
PARAGRAPH <13 - Redo-Stopper>
           <13 - Redo-Stopper>:STOP
END-PARAGRAPH <13 - Redo-Stopper>
```

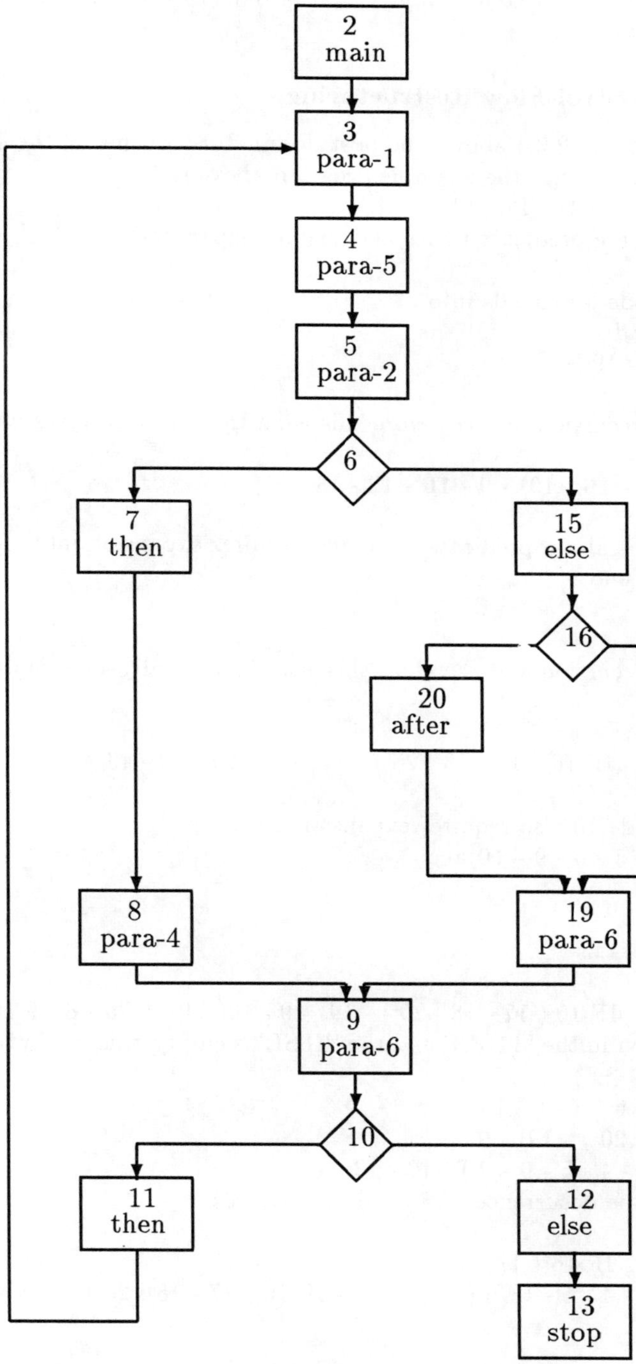

Figure 22.8: Control-flow graph of COBOL example

Figure 22.8 gives the control-flow graph of our example program with the nodes numbered as above.

Example of Control-Flow Restructuring

As stated in section 22.3.1 above, the post dominator sequence of the start node is in effect the program. Thus the example program above is:
2 - 3 - 4 - 5 - **6** - 9 - **10**- 12 - 13
where **6** and **10** are predicate nodes and require expanding.

Predicate node 6 expands into
THEN : 7 - 8 and
ELSE : 15 - **16** - 19

There is no recursion and therefore this is an IF. This now gives us :
2 - 3 - 4 - 5 -
IF 6 (7 - 8 | 15 - **16** - 19) - 9 - **10** - 12 - 13.

However **16** is also a predicate node and requires expansion into
THEN : 17 - 18 and
ELSE : 20

There is no recursion and therefore this is an IF (actually an exception). This now gives us :
2 - 3 - 4 - 5 -
IF 6 (7 - 8 | 15 - IF 16 (17 - 18 | 20) - 19) - 9 - **10** - 12 - 13.

Predicate node 10 also requires expansion into
THEN : 11 - 4 - 5 - 6 - 9 - **10** and
ELSE : 'empty'.

This now gives us :
2 - 3 - 4 - 5 -
IF 6 (7 - 8 | 15 - IF 16 (17 - 18 | 20) - 19) - 9 - 10(11 - 4 - 5 - **6** - 9 **10** |) - 12 - 13.
There is recursion in the 'THEN' and the 'ELSE' is empty, this is a WHILE. This now gives us :
2 - 3 - 4 - 5 - IF 6 (7 - 8 | 15 -
IF 16 (17 - 18 | 20) - 19) - 9 -
WHILE 10 (11 - 4 - 5 - **6** - 9) - 12 - 13.
and expanding the occurrence of **6** as above gives us :
2 - 3 - 4 - 5 -
IF 6 (7 - 8 | 15 - IF 16 (17 - 18 | 20) - 19) - 9 -
WHILE 10 (11 - 4 - 5 - IF 6 (7 - 8 | 15 - IF 16 (17 - 18 | 20) - 19) - 9) - 12 - 13.

Thus the example program can be represented as :

```
2 - 3
4 - 5
IF <predicate 6>
        7 - 8
ELSE
        15
        EXCEPTION <predicate 16>
                17 - 18
        ELSE
                20
        END-EXCEPTION
        19
END-IF
9
WHILE <predicate 10> DO
        11      4 - 5
                IF <predicate 6>
                        7 - 8
                ELSE
                        15
                        EXCEPTION <predicate 16>
                                17 - 18
                        ELSE
                                20
                        END-EXCEPTION
                        19
                END-IF
        9
END-WHILE
12
END
```

Our restructured example is given below, and this program is represented in figure 22.5

```
PROCEDURAL-SECTION
PARAGRAPH <2 - MAIN>
              <2 - MAIN>:DISPLAY  "THIS IS THE MAIN PARAGRAPH" ,
              <2 - MAIN>:PERFORM PARA-1 <3>
              <2 - MAIN>:PERFORM PARA-LOOP <14>
              <2 - MAIN>:PERFORM PARA-6 <9>
              <2 - MAIN>:PERFORM PARA-NEW <12>
              <2 - MAIN>:STOP RUN
END-PARAGRAPH 2 - MAIN
PARAGRAPH <3 - PARA-1>
              <3 - PARA-1>:DISPLAY  "PARA-1" ,
              <3 - PARA-1>: AUNT4  :=  AUNT4  +  AUNT2
END-PARAGRAPH <3 - PARA-1>
PARAGRAPH <14 PARA-LOOP>
              <14 - PARA-LOOP>:PERFORM PARA-5 <4>
              <14 - PARA-LOOP>:PERFORM PARA-2 <5>
END-PARAGRAPH <14 PARA-LOOP>
PARAGRAPH <4 - PARA-5>
END-PARAGRAPH <4 - PARA-5>
PARAGRAPH <5 - PARA-2>
              <5 - PARA-2>:IF <6>   AUNT1  =  AUNT2
                <7 - THEN>:PERFORM PARA-4 <8>
              <5 - PARA-2>:ELSE
                <15 - ELSE>: AUNT4  :=  AUNT4  +  AUNT3  ON SIZE ERROR <16>
                        <17 - OSE>:PERFORM PARA-7 <18>
                <20 - AFTER>:PERFORM PARA-3 <19>
END-PARAGRAPH <5 - PARA-2>
PARAGRAPH 8 - PARA-4
              <8 - PARA-4>:DISPLAY  "FROM THEN OF PARA-2" ,
END-PARAGRAPH 8 - PARA-4
PARAGRAPH <18 - PARA-7>
              <18 - PARA-7>: AUNT2  :=  AUNT2  -  AUNT4
END-PARAGRAPH <18 - PARA-7>
PARAGRAPH <19 - PARA-3>
              <19 - PARA-3>:DISPLAY  "FROM FALL OUT OF PARA-2" ,
END-PARAGRAPH <19 - PARA-3>
PARAGRAPH <9 - PARA-6>
              <9 - PARA-6>:WHILE  <10>   AUNT1  =  AUNT3
                  <11 - LOOP>:PERFORM PARA-LOOP <14>
END-PARAGRAPH <9 - PARA-6>
PARAGRAPH <12 - NEW>
                <12 - NEW>:DISPLAY  "ENDS HERE" ,
END-PARAGRAPH <12 - NEW>
```

This work has been influenced by the work on metrics that is being undertaken as part of the REDO project, specifically by Paul Jacob of the University of Limerick reported in [TN-UL-1041] and consequently this work is also influenced by the theory of prime structures described in the papers [118, 119, 120]. Other relevant papers are [11, 13, 86, 64, 229, 250, 315, 340, 347].

REDO Glossary

- *Documentation*

  Any written or pictorial information describing, defining, specifying, reporting or certifying activities, requirements, procedures, or results.

- *Inverse Engineering*

  The process of discovering the requirements specification for a software system or component, and then re-implementing using modern software engineering methods.

- *Reconstruction*

  The process of augmenting and/or changing the code and/or documentation of a software system without changing its intended functionality.

- *Re-engineering*

  The modification of source code items (code, data structures, documentation etc.) based on modern software engineering principles to improve the maintainability of the software.

- *Reverse Engineering*

  The process of redesigning parts or all of a software system to improve its quality, then re-implementing the design.

- *Validation*

  The process of evaluating software at the end of the software development process to ensure compliance with software requirements.

- *Software Maintenance*

  Software maintenance is the modification of a software product after delivery to correct faults, to improve performance or other attributes, or to adapt the product to a changed environment.

Related REDO documents

[TN-PRG-1008] Abowd, G., Bowen, J., Dix, A., Harrison, M. and Took, R., 1989, **User Interface Languages: a Survey of Existing Methods**, *REDO report 2487-TN-PRG-1008* Also Programming Research Group Technical Report PRG-TR-5-89

[TN-ITS-1003] Alarcon, I., Moreno, J.C., 1989, **Proposal for New Documentation**, *Redo report 2487–TN–ITS–1003*

[TR-CE-1041] Altes, A. and Pegueroles, J., 1991, **The Method for Loading Source Components into the SDDB**, *REDO report 2487-TR-CE-1041*

[TN-LR-1027] Bennett K.H., Martil, R. and van Zuylen H.J., January 1990, **Reconstruction as a Focus of the REDO Project**, *REDO report 2487-TN-LR-1027* version 1.0

[TN-WL-1004] Bosch, P. van den, 1989, **High Performance Computing**, *REDO report 2487-TN-WL-1004* Delft Hydraulics

[TN-WL-1051] Bosch, P. van den, 1991, **Reverse Engineering for Optimization on Vector Computers**, *REDO report 2487-TN-WL-1051* Delft Hydraulics

[TN-PRG-1044] Bowen, J.P., 1991, **From Programs to Object Code and Back Again Using Logic Programming**, *REDO report 2487-TN-PRG-1044* Submitted to the Journal of Software Maintenance

[TN-PRG-1031] Breuer, P.T., 1990, **Inverse Engineering: The First Step Backwards**, *REDO report 2487-TN-PRG-1031* Oxford University Computing Laboratory

[TN-PRG-1037] Breuer, P.T. and Lano, K.C., 1990, **Tackling Reverse Engineering**, *REDO report 2487-TN-PRG-1037*

[TR-PRG-1047] Breuer, P.T., 1990, **Enumerating Types**, *REDO report 2487-TR-PRG-1047* Oxford University Computing Laboratory

[TN-PRG-1031] Breuer P., 1990, **Inverse Engineering: The First Step Backwards**, *REDO report 2487-TN-PRG-1031* Oxford University Computing Laboratory

[TN-UL-1002] Cahill, A., Stanley-Smith, C., 1989, **UNIFORM: A Language Geared To System Description And Transformation**, *REDO report 2487-TN-UL-1002*

[TR-CE-1039] Enrich A., 1990, **CINCOM's TOTAL DBMS: IF Representation, DDL and DML Translation Process**, *REDO report 2487-TR-CE-1039*

[TN-UL-1041] Jacob, P., 1991, **Metrication of Maintainability. Final Report for Task 403**, *REDO report 2487-TN-UL-1041*

[TN-LR-1057] Khabaza, I., Ostrolenk, G. and Tobin, M., 1991, **The ERA Model of COBOL-IF**, *REDO report 2487-TN-LR-1057*

[TN-PRG-1041] Lano, K., 1990, **Validation through Refinement and Execution of Specifications**, *REDO report 2487-TN-PRG-1041*

[TN-PRG-1025] Lano K., 1989, **An Outline Specification of the CICS Application Programmers Interface**, *REDO report 2487-TN-PRG-1025* Oxford University Computing Laboratory

[TN-LR-1039] Martil, R., 1990, **Task Analysis Results**, *REDO report 2487-TN-LR-1039* Lloyd's Register

[TN-UL-1036] O'Brien, L., 1990, **Static Analysis and Program Transformation Techniques**, *REDO report 2487-TN-UL-1036*

[TN-LR-1047] Ostrolenk, G., 1990, **A Step Towards The Definition Of Requirements For Representation Of Source Code In The SDDB**, *REDO report 2487-TN-LR-1047*

[TN-LR-1076] Ostrolenk, G., 1991, **Standard Conventions For The Specification And Implementation Of The SDDB Conceptual Schema**, *REDO report 2487-TN-LR-1076*

[TN-WL-1071] Smit, E.Y.M., 1991, **Method for User Interface Analysis and Redesign**, *REDO report 2487-TN-WL-1071* Delft Hydraulics

[TN-UL-1025] Stanley-Smith, C., O'Brien, L., 1990, **DIRTY UNIFORM And Paragraphs, Sections And Other 'DIRTY' Constructs**, *REDO report 2487-TN-UL-1025*

[TN-UL-1056] Stanley-Smith, C.P., 1991, **A Preliminary E-R-A Model for the Extra Requirements of Control and Data Flow**, *REDO report 2487-TN-UL-1056*

References

[1] Abelson, H., Sussman, G.J. and Sussman, J., with foreword by Perlis, A.J., 1985, **Structure and Interpretation of Computer Programs**, *MIT Press and McGraw-Hill* London

[2] Adelson, B., 1984, **When novices surpass experts: the difficulty of a task may increase with expertise**, *Journal of Exp. Psychology: Learning, Memory and Cognition, Vol. 10, No. 3* pp 483–495

[3] Aho, A.V. and Johnson, S.C., 1974, **Programming utilities and libraries: LR parsing**, *Computing Surveys* June 1974

[4] Aho, A.V., Sethi, R. and Ullman, J.D., 1986, **Compilers: Principles, Techniques, and Tools**, *Addison-Wesley* Reading MA

[5] Allen, F.E. and Cocke, J., 1976, **A program data flow analysis procedure**, *Comm. ACM, Vol. 14, No. 2*

[6] Almasi, G.S. and Gottlieb, A., 1989, **Highly Parallel Computing**, *Benjamin Cummings*

[7] ANSI, 1978, **Programming Language COBOL**, *American National Standard ANSI X3.23-1974 and ISO 1989-1978,* corrected edition July 1978

[8] Antonini, P., Benedusi, P., Cantone, G. and Cimitile, A., September 1987, **Maintenance and reverse engineering: low-level design documents production and improvement**, *Proc. IEEE Conference on Software Maintenance, pp 91-100* Austin, Texas

[9] **Ariadne**,11 May 1991, *New Scientist, Vol. 30, No. 1768*

[10] Arnold, R. (ed.), 1985, **Tutorial on Software Restructuring**, *IEEE Computer Society*

[11] Ashcroft, E. and Manna, Z., 1971, **The translation of 'GOTO' programs into 'WHILE' programs**, *Proc. IFIP Congress 1971, Vol. 1, pp 250–255* North Holland

[12] Atkinson, A., 4–8 June 1989, **Questioning persistent types**, *Proc. 2nd International Workshop on Database Programming Languages* Oregon, Morgan Kaufmann

[13] Böhm, C. and Jacopini, G., 1966, **Flow diagrams, Turing machines and languages with only two formation rules**, *Comm. ACM, Vol. 9, No. 5* pp 366–371

[14] Bache, R. and Neill, M., 1990, **Validating technologies for software certification**, *Proc. Conference on Approving Software Products, Garmisch, Germany, 1990*

[15] Bachman, C., 1988, **A CASE for Reverse Engineering**, *Datamation*

[16] Barron, D.W. and Bishop, J.M., 1984, **Advanced Programming**, *Wiley*

[17] Basili, V. R., January 1990, **Viewing maintenance as reuse oriented software development**, *IEEE Software, Vol. 7, No. 1* pp 19–25

[18] Basili, V.R. and Mills, H.D., 1982, **Understanding and documenting programs**, *Computer* October, 18-37

[19] Bassett, P., 1990, **Software manufacturing techniques and maintenance**, *in [208]*

[20] Batini, C., Talamo, M. and Tamassia, R., 1984, **Computer-aided layout of entity relationship diagrams**, *The Journal of Systems and Software, Vol. 4* pp 163–173

[21] Beeri, C., Bernstein, P.A. and Goodman, N., 1978, **A sophisticate's introduction to database normalisation theory**, *Proc. 4th International Conference on Very Large Data Bases, West Berlin*

[22] Benedusi, P., Benvenuto, V. and Caporaso, M.G., 1990, **Maintenance and prototyping at the entity relationship level**, *Proc. IEEE Conference on Software Maintenance*

[23] Bennett, K.H. (ed.), 1989, **Software Engineering Environments: Research and Practice**, *Ellis Horwood*

[24] Biggerstaff, T.J. and Perlis, A.J., 1989, **Software Reusability**, *Addison-Wesley* ACM Press

[25] Biggerstaff, T., July 1989, **Design recovery for maintenance and reuse**, *IEEE Computer*

[26] Bird, R. and Wadler, P., 1988, **Introduction to Functional Programming**, *Prentice Hall,* International Series in Computer Science

[27] Blaha, M. *et al.*, 1988, **Relational database design using an object-oriented methodology**, *Comm. ACM*

[28] Boehm, B.W., 1981, **Software Engineering Economics**, *Prentice Hall*

[29] Bohm, C. and Jacopini, A., May 1966, **Flow diagrams, Turing machines, and languages with only two formation rules**, *Comm. ACM, Vol. 9, No. 5* pp 366–371

[30] Borgida, A., Mylopoulos, J., and Wong, H.K.T., 1982, **Generalisation and specialisation as a basis for software specification; on conceptual modelling**, *Springer-Verlag*

[31] Bott, F. (ed.), 1989, **Eclipse: An Integrated Project Support Environment**, *IEE Computer Series*

[32] Bouzeghoub, M. *et al.*, 1985, **Database design tools: an expert system approach**, *Proc. International Conference on Very Large Data Bases, Stockholm*

[33] Bowden, B.V. (ed.), 1953, **Faster Than Thought**, *Pitman*

[34] Bowen, J.P., He Jifeng and Pandya, P.K., 1990, **An approach to verifiable compiling specification and prototyping**, *Deransart, P. and Małuszyński, J. (eds.), Programming Language Implementation and Logic Programming, International Workshop PLILP 90* pp 45–59, Springer-Verlag, LNCS 456

[35] Bowen, J.P., 1991, **From programs to object code using logic and logic programming**, *Proc. International Workshop on Code Generation, Schloß Dagstuhl, Germany (20–24 May 1991)* Springer Verlag Workshops in Computing

[36] Boyer, R.S., 1979, **A Computational Logic**, *Academic Press,* New York

[37] Boyle, J.M. and Muralidharan, M.N., 1984, **Program reusability through program transformation**, *IEEE Transactions on Software Engineering*

[38] Brachman, R.J., 1983, **What IS-A is and isn't: an analysis of taxonomic links in semantic networks**, *IEEE Computer*

[39] Brandon, D.H., 1977, **Commercial Software**, *in [54]*

[40] Brereton, P. (ed.), 1988, **Software Engineering Environments**, *Ellis Horwood*

[41] Breuer, P.T. *et al.*, 1991, **Understanding Programs Through Formal Methods**, *Oxford University Computing Laboratory* PRG-TR-1591

[42] Breuer, P.T. and Lano, K.C., 1991, **REDO at Oxford: reverse engineering techniques within REDO**, *In: Hall, P.A.V. (ed.), Workshop in Software Reuse, Utrecht, November 1989* Springer-Verlag Workshops in Computing, pp 39-49

[43] Breuer, P.T. and Lano, K.C., 1991, **Creating specifications from code**, *Journal of Software Maintenance,* September 1991

[44] Breuer, P.T. and Bowen, J., 1992, **Decompilation: the enumeration of types and grammars**, *submitted to Journal of Functional Programming*

[45] Brewer, O., Dongarra, J., Levine, D., Sorensen, D., 1988, **Graphics tools for developing high-performance algorithms**, *Int. Meeting on Parallel Computing, Verona Italy*

[46] Briand, H. *et al.*, 1986, **Expert system for translating an ER diagram into databases**, *In: P.P. Chen (ed.), Entity Relationship Approach: the Use of ER Concepts in Knowledge Representation* IEEE CS Press, North Holland

[47] Brooke, J.B. and Duncan, K.D., 1980, **Experimental studies of flow charts use at different stages of program debugging**, *Ergonomics, Vol. 23, No. 11* pp 1057–1091

[48] Brooks, F.P., 1975, **The Mythical Man-Month**, *Addison-Wesley, Mass*

[49] Brooks, R., 1983, **Towards a theory of the comprehension of computer programs**, *International Journal of Man-Machine Studies, Vol. 18* pp 543–554

[50] Brown, A.R. and Sampson, W.A., 1973, **Program Debugging**, *Macdonald*

[51] Brown, A.W., 1989, **Database Support for Software Engineering**, *New Technology Modular Series, Kogan Page*

[52] Brown, G.D., 1981, **Beyond COBOL – Survival in Business Applications Programming**, *Wiley*

[53] Brown, M. and Childs, B., April 1989, **An interactive tool for literate programming**, *3rd Workshop on Empirical Studies of Programmers,* Austin, Texas (unpublished)

[54] Brown, P.J. (ed.), 1977, **Software Portability**, *Cambridge University Press*

[55] Brown, P.J., 1980, **Writing Interactive Compilers and Interpreters**, *Wiley*

[56] Broy M. and Pepper P., 1986, **Program development as a formal activity**, *Readings in A.I. and Software Engineering, Rich, C. and Waters, R.C. (eds.), Morgan Kaufmann* pp 123–132

[57] Burton C.T.P., 1991, **Verification and transformation of simple recursive programs – an algebraic approach**, *in [241]*

[58] Bush, E., 1990, **Software re-engineering – state of the art**, *Proc. 8th. Software Maintenance and Management Conf., Washington, D.C.* USPDI, 1734, Elton Road, Suite 221, Silver Spring, MD 20903, USA

[59] Butler, J., 1990, **Salvaging existing systems**, *System Development June 1990* pp 6–8

[60] Buxton, J.N., 1980, **STONEMAN: Requirements for Ada Programming Support Environments**, *US DoD,* Washington, D.C.

[61] Caldiera, G. and Basili, V.R., 1991, **Identifying and qualifying reusable software components**, *IEEE Computer February 1991* pp 61 – 70

[62] Callis, F.W., March 1988, **Problems with automatic restructurers**, *ACM SIGPLAN Notices, Vol. 23, No. 3* pp 13–21

[63] Calliss, F.W., Khalil, M., Munro, M., Ward, M., 1988, **A knowledge-based system for software maintenance**, *IEEE Conference on Software Maintenance*

[64] Calliss, F.W., 1988, **Problems with automatic restructures**, *ACM SIGPLAN Notices, Vol. 23, No. 3.* pp 13–21

[65] Callow, H., 1990, **Practise case study**, *Journal of Software Maintenance, Vol. 2, No. 1*

[66] Carlyle, R.E., 1989, **Fighting corporate amnesia**, *Datamation 35(3)* pp 41–44

[67] Carroll, J.M., Kellogg, W.A., Beth Rosson, M., 1991, **The task–artifact cycle**, *In: Carroll, J.M. (ed.), Designing Interaction: Psychology at the Human–Computer Interface,* Cambridge University Press

[68] Ceri, C. and Gottlob, G., 1986, **Normalisation of relations and Prolog**, *Comm. ACM, Vol. 29, No. 6*

[69] Chapin, E., 1985, **Software maintenance: a different view**, *AFIPS Conference Proceedings 54, National Computer Conference*

[70] Chen, P.P., 1976, **The Entity-relationship model: towards a unified view of data**, *ACM TODS, Vol. 1, No. 1*

[71] Chikofsky, E. J. and Cross, J. H., January 1990, **Reverse engineering and design recovery: a taxonomy**, *IEEE Software, Vol. 7, No. 1* pp 13–18

[72] Choobineh, J., Mannino, M. *et al.*, 1988, **An expert database design system based on analysis of forms**, *IEEE Transactions on Software Engineering, Vol. 14, No. 2*

[73] Chung, I., Nakamura, F. and Chen, P.P., 1981, **A decomposition of relations using the entity relationship approach**, *In: Entity Relationship Approach to Information Modelling and Analysis, P.P. Chen (ed.),* ER Institute

[74] Clarke L.A. and Richardson D.J., 1981, **Symbolic evaluation methods – implementations and applications**, *Computer Program Testing, Chandrasekaran, B. and Radicchi S. (eds.), pp 65–101* North-Holland

[75] Clocksin, W.F. and Mellish, C.S., 1987, **Programming in Prolog**, *Springer-Verlag,* 3rd edition

[76] Cohen, J., 1990, **Constraint logic programming languages**, *Comm. ACM, Vol. 33, No. 7* pp 52–68

[77] Colbrook, A. and Smythe, C., 1989, **The retrospective introduction of abstraction into software**, *IEEE International Conference on Software Maintenance*

[78] Collberg, C.S. and Krampell, M.G., 1987, **A property–based method for selecting among multiple implementations of modules**, *1st European Software Engineering Conference ESEC'87, pp 207–215,* Strasbourg

[79] Collins, B.P., Nicholls, J.E. and Sørensen, I.H., 1991, **Introducing formal methods: the CICS experience with Z**, *In: Neumann, B.* et al. *(eds.), Mathematical Structures for Software Engineering,* Oxford University Press

[80] Colmerauer, A., 1990, **An introduction to Prolog III**, *Comm. ACM, Vol. 33, No. 7* pp 69–90

[81] Computer Weekly, 23 April 1981, **Overhaul service prolongs the active life of products**

[82] Coomer Jr, T.N., Comer, J.R., Rodjak, D.J., 1990, **Developing reusable software for military systems – why it is needed and why it isn't working**, *ACM SIGSOFT Software Engineering Notes, Vol. 15 No. 3* pp 33–38

[83] Corbi, T.A., 1989, **Program Understanding for the 1990s**, *IBM Systems Journal 28(2)* pp 294–306

[84] Cordy, J.R., Eliot, N.L., Robertson, M.G., March 1990, **Turing Tool: a user interface to aid in the software maintenance task**, *IEEE Transactions on Software Engineering, Vol. 16, No. 3*

[85] Couturier P. and Puccetti, A., 1990, **ATES: an integrated system for software development and validation**, *ESPRIT '90 Conference Proceedings, Brussels,* Kluwer Academic Publishers

[86] Cowell, D.F., Gillies, D.F. and Kaposi, A.A., 1980, **Synthesis and structural analysis of abstract programs**, *The Computer Journal, Vol. 23, No. 3* pp 243–247

[87] Curtis, B., 1980, **In search of software complexity**, *Proc. Workshop on Quantitative Models for Reliability, Complexity and Cost* pp 95–106

[88] Dahl, O.J., Dijkstra, E.W. and Hoare, C.A.R., 1972, **Structured Programming**, *Academic Press*

[89] Darlington, J., 1981, **An experimental program transformation and synthesis system**, *In: Rich, C. and Waters, R. (eds.) Readings in Artificial Intelligence and Software Engineering,* Morgan Kaufmann

[90] Date, C.J., 1990, **An introduction to database systems**, *The Systems Programming Series, Vol. 1, 5th ed,* Addison-Wesley

[91] Davis R.E. and Kendrick D.A., 1971, **A branch-and-bound algorithm for zero-one mixed integer programming problems**, *Operations Research, Vol. 19* pp 1036–1044

[92] Davis, K.H. and Arora, A.K., 1986, **A methodology for translating a conventional file system into an entity relationship model**, *In: P.P. Chen (ed.) Entity Relationship Approach: the Use of ER Concepts in Knowledge Representation* IEEE CS Press, North Holland

[93] Davis, M., 1985, **A layout algorithm for a graph browser**, *Master's Thesis,* Dept. of Electrical Engineering and Computer Sciences, University of California, Berkeley

[94] De Groot, A.D., 1965, **Thought and choice in chess**, *Mouton,* The Hague

[95] DeMarco, T., 1978, **Structured Analysis and System Specification**, *Yourdon Press*

[96] Diaper, D., Gilmore, D., Cockton, G., Shackel, B. (eds.), 1990, **Human Computer Interaction, Interact '90**, *North Holland* Cambridge

[97] Dijkstra, E.W., March 1968, **GOTO statement considered harmful**, *Comm. ACM, Vol. 11, No. 3* pp 147–148

[98] Dijkstra, E.W., 1976, **A Discipline of Programming**, *Prentice Hall,* Englewood Cliffs

[99] DoD, 1986, **Common APSE Interface Set (CAIS)**, *DoD-STD-1838* DoD, US

[100] Dongarra, J.J. and Sorensen, D.C., 1988, **Algorithm Design for High–Performance Computers, Parallel Systems and Computations**, *North Holland*

[101] Dongerra, J.J., Du Croz, J., Hammarling, S. and Hanson, J., 1986, **An updated notice on the extended BLAS**, *ACM SIGNUM, Vol. 21, No. 4* pp 2–4

[102] Downs, E., Clare, P. and Coe, I., 1988, **Structured Systems Analysis and Design Method**, *Prentice Hall*

[103] Dowson, M., 1987, **Iteration in the software process: review of the 3rd international software process workshop**, *Proc. of the 9th International Conference on Software Engineering*

[104] Duntemann, J. and Marinacci, C., April 1990, **New objects for old structures**, *Byte,* pp 261–266

[105] Durham, T., 1989, **An angel in devil's clothing**, *Computing* 12 January 1989

[106] Durham, T., 1988, **Tracing the seed from which the flower grows**, *Computing* 10 November 1988

[107] ECMA, 1990, **Portable Common Tool Environment (PCTE): abstract specification**, *ECMA* Standard ECMA-149

[108] Edward, A., 1991, Presentation **Weavers Business Solutions** to BCS, West Herts Branch, 8 May 1991.

[109] Einbu, J., 1989, **A Program Architecture for Improved Maintainability in Software Engineering**, *Ellis Horwood*

[110] Elmasri, R., Hevner, A. and Weeldreyer, J., 1985, **The category concept: an extension to the entity-relationship model**, *Data and Knowledge Engineering, Vol. 1, No. 1*

[111] Elmasri, R. and Navathe, S.B., 1989, **Fundamentals of Database Systems**, *Benjamin Cummings*

[112] Elmendorf, W.R., 1974, **Functional analysis using cause-effect graphs**, *Procs. of SHARE XLIII (SHARE, New York)* pp 567–577

[113] Elshoff, J.L. and Marcotty, M., December 1982, **Improving computer program readability to aid modification**, *Comm. ACM, Vol. 25, No. 8* pp 512–521

[114] Elshoff, J.L., 1976, **An analysis of some commercial PL/1 programs**, *IEEE Transactions on Software Engineering* pp 113–120

[115] Essink, L.J.B., 1986, **A modelling approach to information system development**, *In: Olle, T.W., Sol, H.G. and Verrijn-Stuart, A.A. (eds.), Information Systems Design Methodologies: Improving the Practice,* Elsevier North–Holland

[116] European Directive, 1992, *Financial Times*, 16 May 1992

[117] Fedra, K., 19–21 September 1990, **Interactive environmental software: integration, simulation and visualisation**, *in: Pillmann, W. and Jaeschke, A. (eds.), Informatik für den Umweltschutz* 5. Symposium, Wien Österreich

[118] Fenton, N.E. and Kaposi, A., 1987, **Metrics and software structure**, *Journal of Information and Software Technology, Vol. 29, No. 6*

[119] Fenton, N.E. and Whitty, R.W., 1986, **Axiomatic approach to software metrication through program decomposition**, *The Computer Journal, Vol. 24, No. 4* pp 329–339

[120] Fenton, N.E., 1990, **Software metrics: theory tools and validation**, *Software Engineering Journal, pp 65–78* January 1990

[121] Fischer K.F., Raji F. and Chruscicki A., November 1981, **A methodology for re-testing modified software**, *National Telecomms. Conf. Procs.* pp B6.3.1–6

[122] Fischer K.F., November 1977, **A test case selection method for the validation of software maintenance modifications**, *IEEE COMPSAC 77 Int. Conf. Procs.* pp 421–426

[123] Fletton, N.T. and Munro, M., 1988, **Redocumenting software systems using hypertext technology**, *Computer Science Technical Report No. 88/5* University of Durham

[124] Floyd, R., 1967, **Assigning meaning to programs**, *in: Schwartz, J. (ed.), Mathematical Aspects of Computer Science, Vol. 19, pp 19–32,* American Mathematical Society

[125] Foster, J.R. and Munro, M., 1987, **A documentation method based on cross referencing**, *Proc. IEEE Conf. Software Maintenance* Austin, Texas

[126] Fraser, C.W., Krishnamurthy, B., 1990, **Live text**, *Software-practice and experience, Vol 20 No 8,* pp 851-858

[127] Gansner, E.R., North, S.C. and Vo, K. P., 1988, **Dag – a program that draws directed graphs**, *Software – Practice and Experience, Vol. 18* pp 1048–1062

[128] Gardarin, G. and Valduriez, P., 1989, **Relational Databases and Knowledge Bases**, *Addison-Wesley*

[129] Garey M.R. and Johnson D.S., 1979, **Computers and Intractability: A Guide to the Theory of NP-Completeness**, *Klee, V. (ed.), W.H. Freeman,* New York, pp 222–225

[130] Garlan, D., April 1985, **Flexible unparsing in a structure editing environment**, *Department of Computer Science, Carnegie-Mellon University Report CMU-CS-85-129*

[131] Georges, M., Sept 1989, **The MACS project**, *Proc. 3rd. Durham Workshop on Software Maintenance* Computer Science, University of Durham, Durham, UK

[132] Gifford, B., Harrison, W., 1990, **A reverse-Engineering tool set for the adaptation of sequential programs**, *Conference on Software Maintenance 1990* pp 344–346

[133] Gilb, T., July 1979, **A comment on the definition of reliability**, *ACM Software Engineering Notes, Vol. 4, No. 3*

[134] Gilb, T., 1988, **Principles of Software Engineering Management**, *Addison-Wesley*

[135] Gilmore, D., 1990, **Models of debugging**, *Proc. 5th European Conference on Cognitive Ergonomics, ECCE-5,* Urbino, Italy

[136] Gilmore, D., 1990, **Expert programming knowledge: a strategic approach**, *in [158]* chapter 3.2

[137] Goguen J. and Meseguer J., 1987, **Unifying Functional, Object-Oriented and Relational Programming with Logical Semantics**, *SRI International*

[138] Gravell, A., 1990, **What is a good formal specification?**, *In: Nicholls, J.E. (ed.), Z User Workshop,* Oxford 1989, Springer-Verlag

[139] Greef, P. de, Breuker, J. and Jong, T. de, 1987, **Modality, an analysis of functions, user control and communication in knowledge based systems**, *UvA-A4-PR-004,* University of Amsterdam

[140] Green, C., 1969, **The Application of theorem proving to question answering systems**, *Doctoral Dissertation, Comp. Sci. Dept. Stanford University, STAN-CS-69-138*

[141] Green, M., 1985, **The Design of Graphical User Interfaces.**, *Technical Report CSRI-170* Computer Science Research Institute, University of Toronto

[142] Green, T.R.G., 1990, **The nature of programming**, *in [158]* chapter 1.2

[143] Gries, D., 1981, **The Science of Computer Programming**, *Springer-Verlag*

[144] Guide, 1991, **The strategic development of reverse engineering tools**, *Guide Reverse Engineering Project AE-3100*

[145] Hale, H., Haworth, D.A. and Sharpe, S., 1990, **Empirical software studies during the 1980s**, *Proc. IEEE Conference on Software Maintenance,* San Diego, California

[146] Hall, P.A.V., 1991, **Relationship between specification and testing**, *Journal of Information Science and Technology, Vol. 33 No 1*

[147] Halstead, M.H., 1977, **Elements of Software Science**, *Elsevier North Holland*

[148] Harrold M.J. , Gupta R. and Souffa M.L., 1990, **T A methodology for controlling the size of a test suite**, *Proc. of IEEE Conference on Software Maintenance,* pp 302–310

[149] Hartmann J. and Robson D.J., October 1988, **Approaches to regression testing**, *Proc. IEEE Conf. on Software Maintenance (CSM-88)* pp 368–372

[150] Hatley, D.J. and Pribhai, I., 1987, **Strategies for Real Time System Specification**, *Dorset House*

[151] Haughton, H.P., 1989, **Developing communication protocols – a prototypical approach**, *Proc. Seminar Series on New Directions in Software Development, Rapid Prototyping for the Software Developer,* pp 64–78, Wolverhampton Polytechnic

[152] Hausler, P.A., Pleszkoch, R.C., Linger, R.C. and Hevner, A.R., January 1990, **Using function abstraction to Understand program behaviour**, *IEEE Software*

[153] Hawryszkiewycz, I.T., 1986, **A computer aid for E-R modelling**, *In: P.P. Chen (ed.) Entity Relationship Approach: The Use of ER Concepts in Knowledge Representation* IEEE CS Press, North Holland

[154] Henderson P., 1986, **Functional programming, formal specification and rapid prototyping**, *IEEE Transactions on Software Engineering Vol. SE-12, No. 2*

[155] Hoare C.A.R., 1969, **An axiomatic approach to computer programming**, *Comm. ACM*

[156] Hoare, C.A.R., He Jifeng, Bowen, J.P. and Pandya, P.K., 1990, **An algebraic approach to verifiable compiling specification and prototyping of the ProCoS level 0 programming language**, *Directorate-General of the CEC (eds.), ESPRIT '90 Conference Proceedings,* Brussels, pp 804–818, Kluwer Academic Publishers B.V.

[157] Hoare, C.A.R., 1991, **Refinement algebra proves correctness of compiling specifications**, *In: Morgan, C.C. and Woodrock, J.C.P. (eds.) Proc. Refinement Workshop* Springer-Verlag Workshops in Computing

[158] Hoc, J.-M., Green, T.R.G., Samurçay, R. and Gilmore, D.J. (eds.), 1990, **Psychology of Programming**, *Academic Press*

[159] Holloway, S., 1989, **Re-engineering business systems to use the next generation of software**, *in [314]*

[160] Hood Working Group, April 1988, **HOOD Manual**, *CISI Ingenierie Issue 2.2*

[161] Horwitz, S., Prins, J. and Reps, T., July 1982, **Integrating noninterfering versions of programs**, *ACM Trans. on Programming Languages and Systems, Vol. 11, No. 3* pp 345–387

[162] Howden, W.E., 1981, **A survey of static analysis methods**, *In: Miller, E. and Howden, W.E. (eds.) Tutorial Software Testing and Validation Techniques,* IEEE

[163] Hsu, C., 1986, **Structured database system analysis and design through entity relationship approach**, *In: P.P. Chen (ed.) Entity Relationship approach: the use of ER concepts in Knowledge Representation,* IEEE CS Press, North Holland

[164] IBM, 1986, **IBM VS COBOL for OS/VS**, *GC26-3857-4*, Fifth edition, IBM Corporation, San Jose, California

[165] ICL, 2 April 1981, **Keep it simple**, *Computing*

[166] ISO, 1987, **ISO 9001, Quality Systems – Model for Quality Assurance in Design Development, Production, Installation and Servicing**, *International Organisation for Standardization*

[167] ISO, February 1990, **DIS 9001-3, Quality Management and Quality Assurance Standards – Guidelines for the Application of ISO 9001 to the Development, Supply and Maintenance of Software**, *International Organisation for Standardization* Draft

[168] IEEE, 1983, **IEEE Standard Glossary of Software Engineering Terminology**, *ANSI/IEEE Standard 729*

[169] IEEE, 1991, **Standard for Software Maintenance**, *P1219* rev. 8

[170] Illingworth, V. (ed.), 1990, **Dictionary of Computing**, *Oxford University Press* 3rd ed

[171] Ince, D. and Andrews, D., 1990, **The Software Life Cycle**, *Butterworths*

[172] Inglis, J. and King, P.J.H., 1977, **Data portability**, *in [54]*

[173] Jackson, M.A., 1975, **Principles of Program Design**, *Academic Press*

[174] Jackson, M.A., 1983, **System Development**, *Prentice Hall Internation Series in Computer Science, UK*

[175] Jackson, P., 1986, **Going for broke in the clone game**, *Computing* 4 September 1986

[176] Jajodia, S. and Ng, P.A., 1983, **On representation of relational structures by entity relationship diagrams**, *In: Davis, C.C.* et al. *(eds.), Entity Relationship Approach to Software Engineering,* ER Institute

[177] Janssen, R., 1990, **Mapping of TEMPORA's E-R diagram to Prolog-Sybase level**, *E2469/BIM/T4.1/6/1*

[178] Johnson, W.L. and Soloway, E., March 1985, **PROUST – Knowledge-Based Program Understanding**, *IEEE Transactions on Software Engineering, Vol. SE-11* pp 267–275

[179] Kahn, G., 1974, **The semantics of a simple language for parallel programming**, *Information Processing 74, North Holland* pp 471–475

[180] Kenning R., October 1990, **Understanding the configurations of operational systems**, *Proc. IEEE Conference on Software Maintenance,* San Diego, California

[181] Kernighan, B.W. and Ritchie, D.M., 1978, **The C programming language**, *Prentice-Hall Software Series,* Prentice-Hall, London

[182] Knuth, D.E., **The WEB System of Structured Documentation**, *Stanford*

[183] Knuth, D.E., 1963, **Computer-drawn flowcharts**, *Comm. ACM, Vol. 6, No. 9* pp 777–563

[184] Knuth, D.E., 1968, **The Art of Computer Programming Vol. 2 – Fundamental Algorithms**, *Addison-Wesley Publishing Company,* 2nd ed

[185] Knuth, D.E., 1971, **Optimum binary search trees**, *Acta Informatica, Vol. 1* pp 14–25

[186] Knuth, D.E., **Literate Programming**, *The Computer Journal, Vol. 27 No. 2*, pp 97–111

[187] Kowalski, R., 1990, **Problems and promises of computational logic**, *In: Lloyd, J.W. (ed.), Computational Logic Symposium Proceedings, Brussels, November 1990* pp 1–36, Springer-Verlag

[188] Laffey, T.J., Cox, P.A., Schmidt, J.L., Kao, S.M. and Read, J.Y., September 1988, **Real time knowledge based machines**, *Artificial Intelligence* pp 27–45

[189] Lano, K.C., 1991, **Z^{++}, an object-oriented extension to Z**, *In: Nicholls, J. (ed.), Z User Workshop, Oxford 1990* pp 151–172, Springer-Verlag, Workshops in Computing

[190] Lano, K.C. and Breuer, P.T., 1990, **From programs to Z specifications**, *In: Nicholls, J. (ed.), Z User Workshop, Oxford 1989* pp 46–70, Springer-Verlag, Workshops in Computing

[191] Lano, K.C. and Haughton, H., 1991, **A semantics for an object-oriented specification language**, *In: Algebraic Methodology and Software Technology Conf. Proc.* Iowa

[192] Lawson, H.W., Bertran, M., Sanagustin, J., 1978, **The formal definition of human/machine communications**, *Software – Practice and Experience, Vol. 8* pp 51–58

[193] LBMS plc, 1991, **REVENG – Reduce your software maintenance burden**, *Product brochure*

[194] LBMS plc, **LSDM: LBMS Structured Development Method**, *A proprietary method available from Learmonth and Burchett Management Systems Plc,* London

[195] LeBlanc, R.J., Fischer, C.N., 1979, **On implementing separate compilation in block-structured languages**, *Sigplan Notices Vol. 14 No 8 August 1979* Proceedings of the Sigplan Symposium on Compiler Construction, Denver Colorado

[196] Ledin, G. and Ledin, V., 1981, **The Programmer's Book of Rules**, *Lifetime Learning Publications,* USA

[197] Lehman, M.M. and Belady, L.A., 1976, **A model of large program development**, *IBM Syst. J., Vol. 15, No. 3* pp 225–252

[198] Lehman, M.M., 1980, **Programs, life cycles, and laws of software evolution**, *Proc. IEEE, 19 Vol. 68, No. 9* pp 1060–1076

[199] Lehman, M.M., 1984, **Program evolution**, *Information Processing Management, Vol. 20, Nos. 1-2* pp 19–36

[200] Lenzerini, M., 1986, **SERM: a semantic entity relationship model**, *Entity Relationship Approach: the Use of ER Concepts in Knowledge Representation, P.P. Chen (ed.),* IEEE CS Press, North Holland

[201] Leung H.K.N. and White L., September 1988, **A study of regression testing**, *University of Alberta Technical Report TR 88-15*

[202] Lientz, B.P., Swanson, E.B. and Tompkins, G.E., 1978, **Characteristics of application software maintenance**, *Comm. ACM, Vol. 21, No. 6*

[203] Lientz, B.P. and Swanson, E.B., 1980, **Software Maintenance Management**, *Addison-Wesley*

[204] Ling, T.W., 1986, **A normal form for entity-relationship diagrams**, *In: P.P. Chen (ed.) Entity Relationship Approach: the Use of ER Concepts in Knowledge Representation* IEEE CS Press, North Holland

[205] Linger, R.C., Mills, H.D. and Witt, B.I., 1979, **Structured Programming, Theory and Practice**, *Addison-Wesley* pp 79–85

[206] Littman, D.C., Pinto, J., Letovsky, S. and Soloway, E., 1986, **Mental models and software maintenance**, *in: Soloway, E. and Iyengar, S. (eds.), Empirical Studies of Programmers* pp 80–98, Ablex, Norwood, NJ

[207] Lloyd, J.W., 1987, **Foundations of Logic Programming**, *Springer-Verlag* 2nd edition

[208] Longstreet, D.H. (ed.), 1990, **Software Maintenance and Computers**, *IEEE*

[209] Longworth, G. and Nicholls, D., 1986, **SSADM Manual, Version 3**, *NCC*

[210] Loomis, M.E.S., 1990, **ODBMS vs. Relational**, *The Journal of Object-Oriented Programming, July/August 1990* pp 79–82

[211] Loveman, D., January 1977, **Program improvement by source-to-source transformation**, *Journal of the ACM, Vol. 24, No. 1* pp 121–145

[212] Lukey, F.J., 1981, **Comprehending and debugging computer programs**, *In: M.J. and Alty, J.L. Coombs (eds.) Computing Skills and the User Interface* pp 201–209

[213] Lundeberg, M., Goldkuhl, G., Nilsson, A., 1978, **Systemering**

[214] Lyle, J.R., Gallagher, K.B., 1991, **Using Program Slicing in Software Maintenance**, *IEEE Transactions on Software Engineering,* August 1991, pp 751–761

[215] Lyons, T.G.L. and Nissen, J.C.D. (eds.), 1986, **Selecting an Ada Environment**, *Cambridge University Press*

[216] Maher, B., 1982, **A Program Transformation System**, *PhD Thesis*

[217] Martin, C.F., 1988, **Second-generation case tools: A challenge to vendors**, *IEEE Transactions on Software Engineering, Vol. 5, No. 2* pp 46–49

[218] Martin, J. and McClure, C., 1985, **Diagram Techniques for Analysts and Programmers**, *Prentice Hall*

[219] Martin, J., 1986, **Information Engineering**, *Savant*

[220] Martin, J., 1967, **Design of real time computer systems**, *Prentice Hall,* Englewood Cliffs, N.J.

[221] Mascot Suppliers Association, 3 December 1980, **The Official Handbook of MASCOT**,

[222] McWilliams, G., 1988, **Users see a CASE advance in reverse engineering tools**, *Datamation*

[223] McCabe, T.J., 1976, **A complexity measure**, *IEEE Transactions Software Engineering,* December 1976, pp 308–320

[224] McKeithen, K.B., Reitman, J.S.,Rueter, H.H. and Hirtle, S.C., 1981, **Knowledge organisation and skill differences in computer programmers**, *Cognitive Psychology, Vol. 1981 No. 13* pp 307–325

[225] McLaughlin, R., November 1990, **A plea for a readable Prolog programming style**, *ACM SIGPLAN Notices, Vol. 25, No. 11* pp 75–79

[226] Meek, B.L. and Heath, P.M. (eds.), 1980, **Guide to Good Programming Practice**, *Ellis Horwood*

[227] Meyer, B., 1988, **Object-oriented Software Construction**, *Prentice Hall*

[228] Meyer, C., 1983, **A browser for directed graphs**, *Master's thesis,* Dept. of Electrical Engineering and Computer Sciences, University of California, Berkeley

[229] Miller, J.C. and Straus III, B.M., June 1987, **Implications of automatic restructuring of COBOL**, *ACM SIGPLAN Notices, Vol. 22, No. 6* pp 76–82

[230] Mintzberg, H., 1983, **Structure in Fives: Designing Effective Organisations**, *Prentice Hall*

[231] Moad, J., 1990, **Maintaining the competitive edge**, *Datamation 36(4)* pp 61–66

[232] MoD, 5 April 1991, **Interim Defence Standards 00-55 and 00-56**, *Ministry of Defence,* Directorate of Standardization, Glasgow, Issue 1

[233] Morgan, H.L., February 1970, **Spelling correction in systems programs**, *Comm. ACM, Vol. 13, No. 2* pp 90–4

[234] Mosteller, W., 1981, **System Programmer's Problem Solver**, *Winthrop Mass*

[235] Muggleton, S. and Feng, C., October 1990, **Efficient induction of logic programs**, *Proc. 1st Conference on Algorithmic Learning, Tokyo, Japan,* Ohmsha Publications, Japan

[236] Myers, G.J., 1976, **Software Reliability: Principles and Practices**, *John Wiley & Sons, New York*

[237] Myers, B.A., 1989, **Visual programming and program visualisation**, *In Graphics Tools for Software Engineers,* Cambridge University Press. Chapter 1, pp 3–26

[238] Myers, G.J., 1975, **Reliable Software Through Composite Design**, *Van Nostrand Reinhold. New York*

[239] Mynatt, B.T., 1990, **Why program comprehension is (or is not) affected by surface features.**, *In: Diaper, D.* et al. *(eds.), INTERACT'90,* pp 959–963, Elsevier

[240] Naur, P., 1963, **GOTO Statements and good Algol style**, *BIT, Vol. 3* pp 204–5

[241] Neumann B., Simpson D., Slater G. (eds.), 1991, **Mathematical Structures for Software Engineering**, *The Institute of Mathematics and its Applications Conference Series No. 27* Clarendon Press, Oxford

[242] Nijssen, G.M. and Halpin, T.A., 1989, **Conceptual Schema and Relational Database Design: A Fact-Oriented Approach**, *Prentice Hall*

[243] Nillson, E.G., 1986, **The translation of a Cobol data structure to an entity-relationship type conceptual schema**, *In Entity Relationship Approach: The Use of ER Concepts in Knowledge Representation, P.P. Chen (ed.),* IEEE CS Press, North Holland

[244] Nissen, J.C.D. and Wallis, P.J.L. (eds), **Portability and Style in Ada**, *Cambridge University Press*

[245] Oddy, G. C. and Tully, C. J., 1988, **Information Systems Factory Study**, *UK Department of Trade and Industry,* London

[246] Olle, T.W., Hagelstein, J., McDonald, I.G., Rolland, C., Sol, H.G., van Assche, F.J.M. and Verrijn Stuart, A.A., 1988, **Information systems methodology: a framework for understanding**, *IFIP* Working Group 8.1

[247] Olsen, G.M., Sheppard, S. and Soloway, E. (eds.), 1987, **Empirical Studies of Programmers: Second Workshop**, *Ablex, Norwood, NJ*

[248] Orebi-Gann, S., 28th January 1980 et seq., **Ada**, *Datalink*

[249] Osterweil, L.J. and Fosdick, L.D., September 1976, **DAVE – validation, error detection and documentation system for FORTRAN programs**, *Software – Practice and Experience, Vol. 6, No. 4* pp 473–486

[250] Oulsnam, G., 1982, **Unravelling unstructured programs**, *The Computer Journal, Vol. 25, No. 3* pp 379–387

[251] Paakki, J., 1991, **Prolog in practical compiler writing**, *The Computer Journal, Vol. 34, No. 1* pp 64–72

[252] Padua D.A. and Wolfe M.J., December 1986, **Advanced compiler optimizations for supercomputers**, *Comm. ACM, Vol. 29, No. 12*

[253] Parker, J. and Hendley, B., 1988, **The re-use of low-level programming knowledge in the UNIVERSE programming environment**, *in [40]*

[254] Parkin, A., 1984, **COBOL for Students**, *Edward Arnold* London

[255] Pennington, N. and Grabowski, B., 1990, **The Task of Programming**, *in [158]* chapter 1.3

[256] Pennington, N., 1987, **Comprehension strategies in programming**, *in [247]* pp 100–113

[257] Perlis, Sayward and Shaw (eds.), 1981, **Software Metrics**, *MIT Press*

[258] Perry, W.E., 1987, **Effective methods of EDP Quality Assurance**, *In: Schulmeyer, G.G. and McManus, J.I. (eds.), Handbook of Software Quality Assurance,* Van Nostrand Reinbold

[259] Peyton Jones, S.L., 20 March 1984, **Notes on Occam**, *UCL Lecture Notes* v2.0

[260] Quintus, 1990, **Quintus Prolog – Sun 4 User Manual**, *Quintus Computer Systems, Inc., Mountain View, California, USA* Release 2.5

[261] Rekoff, M.G., 1985, **On reverse engineering**, *IEEE Transactions on Systems No. 3/4* pp 244–252

[262] Rönsch, W. and Strauss, H., 1987, **Timing results of some internal sorting algorithms on vector computers**, *Parallel Computing, Vol. 4, No. 1* pp 49–62

[263] Reingold, E.M. and Tilford, J.S., 1981, **Tidier drawing of trees**, *IEEE Transactions on Software Engineering, Vol. 7, No. 1* pp 223–228

[264] Rich C. and Walters, C., (eds.), 1984, **Mechanical proofs about computer programs**, *In: Artificial Intelligence and Software Engineering* Morgan Kaufmann

[265] Richardson D.J. and Clarke L.A., December 1985, **Partition Analysis: A method combining testing and verification**, *IEEE Trans. on Software Engineering, Vol. SE-11, No. 12* pp 1477–1490

[266] Ricketts, J.A., Del Monaco, J.C. and Weeks, M.W., 1989, **Data re-engineering for application systems**, *Proc. IEEE Conference on Software Maintenance, Miami, Florida*

[267] Robertson, S.P., Davis, E.F., Okabe, K., Fitz-Randolf, D., 1990, **Program comprehension beyond the line**, *In: Diaper, D.* et al. *(eds.), INTERACT'90* pp 959-963, Elsevier Publisher B.V.

[268] Robinson, H., 1989, **Database Analysis and Design, 2nd Edition**, *Chartwell-Bratt, Hatfield Polytechnic Computing Series*

[269] Rochfeld, A. and Tardieu, H., 1983, **MERISE, An Information System Design and Development Methodology in Information and Management**,

[270] Rock-Evans, R. and Hales, K., 1990, **Reverse Engineering: Markets, Methods and Tools**, *Ovum*

[271] Rotenstreich, S., 1990, **Enhancement through design transformations: a retroactive case study**, *Journal of Software Maintenance, Vol. 2, No. 4* pp 193–208

[272] Rowe, L.A., Davis, M., Messinger, E., Meyer, C., Spirakis, C. and Tuan, A., 1987, **A browser for directed graphs**, *Software – Practice and Experience, Vol. 17, No. 1* pp 61–76

[273] Sagawa, J.M., 1990, **Repository manager technology**, *IBM Systems Journal, Vol. 32, No. 5*

[274] Salford University Business Services, 1991, **Reverse Engineering, Reality or Hype?**, *The Belfry, Sutton Coldfield*

[275] Scandura, J.M., 1990, **Cognitive approach to systems engineering and re-engineering: integrating new designs with old systems**, *Software Maintenance: Research and Practice Vol. 2* pp 145–156

[276] Schneidewind, N.F., March 1987, **The state of software maintenance**, *IEEE Transactions on Software Engineering, Vol. SE-13, No. 3*

[277] Schuurman, J.J. and Loeve, W., 1989, **Method based system and executive, tools for management and execution of software systems for CAE**, *Cape '89,* Tokyo

[278] Schwanke, R.W., Altucher, R.Z. and Platoff, M.A., 1989, **Discovering, visualizing, and controlling software structure**, *Proc. 5th International Workshop on Software Specification and Design, ACM SIGSOFT Engineering Notes, Vol. 14, No. 3* pp 147–150

[279] Scott, T.L., 1990, **Automated reverse engineering and integrating with forward engineering CASE tools**, *CASE'90,* p. 32

[280] Shepard, S.B., Curtiss, B. and Milliman, P., 1979, **Third time charm: Stronger prediction of programmer performance by software complexity analysis**, pp 356–360

[281] Shlaer, S. and Mellor, S.J., January 1989, **Understanding object-oriented analysis**, *Design Center (Hewlett-Packard)* pp 8–13

[282] Shlaer, S. and Mellor, S.J., 1988, **Object-Oriented Systems Analysis Modelling: The World In Data**, *Yourdon Press*

[283] Shneiderman B., 1980, **Software Psychology**, *Winthrop Publishers* Cambridge, MA

[284] Shneiderman, B. and Mayer, R., 1979, **Syntactic/semantic interactions in programmer behavior: a model and experimental results**, *Int. Journal of Computer and Information Sciences, Vol. 8, No. 3* pp 219–238

[285] Smith, M. and Smith, D.C.P., 1977, **Database abstractions: aggregation and generalisation**, *ACM TODS*

[286] Smythe C., Colbrook, A. and Darlisson, A., April 1990, **Software re-engineering: the next step?**, *Proc. USPDI Software Maintenance Conference* Washington D.C.

[287] Sneed H.M., July 1984, **Software renewal – a case study**, *IEEE Software* pp 56–63

[288] Sneed, H.M. and Jandrasics, G., 1987, **Software recycling**, *Proc. IEEE Conference on Software Maintenance,* Austin, Texas

[289] Sneed, H.M. and Jandrasics, G., 1987, **Inverse transformation of software from code to specification**, *Proc. IEEE Conference on Software Maintenance* Phoenix, Arizona

[290] Sobrinho, F.G., 1984, **Structural Complexity: A Basis for Systematic Software Evolution**, *PhD Thesis,* University of Maryland

[291] Soloway, E. and Iyengar, S. (eds.), 1986, **Empirical Studies of Programmers**, *Ablex, Norwood NJ*

[292] Soloway, E., Bonar, J., Ehrlich, K., 1983, **Cognitive strategies and looping constructs – an empirical survey**, *Comm. ACM, Vol. 26, No. 11* pp 853–860

[293] Soloway, E. and Ehrlich, K., 1984, **Empirical studies of programming knowledge.**, *IEEE Transactions on Software Engineering, Vol. SE-10, No. 5* pp 595–609

[294] Somogyi, E., 1981, **System Development Methods**, *The Butler Cox Foundation*

[295] Sordillo, D.A., 1989, **The Programmer's ANSI COBOL Reference Manual, 2nd Edition**, *Prentice Hall*

[296] Spivey, J.M., 1992, **The Z Notation: A Reference Manual**, *Prentice Hall International Series in Computer Science* 2nd edition

[297] Standish, T.A., 1984, **An essay on software reuse**, *IEEE Transactions on Software Engineering, Vol. SE-10* pp 494–497

[298] Stanley-Smith C. and Cahill A., 1989, **UNIFORM: A Language Geared To System Description and Transformation**, *Management Systems Dept., University of Limerick*

[299] Stehle, G.J., 1989, **The CASE Repository: More than Another Application**, *Meta Systems Ltd.*

[300] Stovers-Korst, J.M.L., 1990, **An Instrument for the Analysis and Diagnosis of User Task Complexity in Existing Application Programs**, *Delft Hydraulics*

[301] Sugiyama, K., Tagawa S. and Toda, M., 1979, **Effective representations of hierarchical structures**, *Technical Report,* Int. Inst. for Advanced Study of Social Info. Science, Fujitsu, pp 1-29

[302] Sugiyama, K. *et al.*, 1979, **Effective representation of hierarchies** *Proc. IEEE Int. Conf. on Cybern. Soc.* October 1979

[303] Svanks, M.I., December 1988, **Integrity analysis**, *Information and Software Technology, Vol. 30, No. 10* pp 595–605

[304] Tamassia, R., di Battista, G. and Batini, C., 1988, **Automatic graph drawing and readability of diagrams**, *IEEE Transactions on Systems, Man and Cybernetics, Vol. 18, No. 1* pp 61–79

[305] Tarjan, R.E., 1972, **Depth-first search and linear graph algorithms**, *SIAM Journal of Computing, Vol. 1* p 146

[306] TeleSoft, 1990, **TeleUSE**, *TeleUSE Reference Manual* TeleSoft AB, Linköping

[307] Teorey, T.J. *et al.*, 1986, **A logical design methodology for relational databases using the extended entity-relationship model**, *ACM Computing Surveys*

[308] Thebaut, S.M., Wilde, N., 1989, **The maintenance assistant: work in progress**, *The Journal of Systems and Software 9* pp 3–17

[309] Tierney, R.A., May 1988, **Modelling complex systems, a graphic approach to CASE using state diagrams**, *VLSI Systems Design* pp 20–23

[310] Tilford, J.S., 1981, **Tree drawing algorithms**, *Master's Thesis,* Dept. of Computer Science, University of Illinois at Urbana-Champaign

[311] Todd, B. and Stamper, R., 1991, **The Formal Specification of Some Diagnostic Systems**, *Oxford University Computing Laboratory, UK*

[312] Tsichritzis, D.C. and Klug, A. (eds.), 1978, **The ANSI/X3/SPARC DBMS Framework: Report of the Study Group on Data Base Management Systems**, *Information Systems 3*

[313] Tully, C. (ed.), June 1989, **Proc. 4th international software process workshop**, *ACM Software Engineering Notes, Vol. 14, No. 4*

[314] Unicom Seminar, 1989, **Reuse, Maintenance and Reverse Engineering of Software: Current Practice and New Directions**, 29 November - 1 December 1989, London

[315] Urschler, G., 1975, **Automatic restructuring of programs**, *IBM Journal of Research and Development, Vol. 19* pp 181–194

[316] Van Griethuysen, J.J. (ed.), 1982, **Concepts and terminology for the conceptual schema and the information base**, *ISO Report ISO/TC9/SC5-N695*

[317] Vaucher, J.G., 1980, **Pretty-printing of trees**, *Software – Practice and Experience, Vol. 10* pp 553–561

[318] Visser, W. and Hoc, J.-M., 1990, **Expert software design strategies**, *in [158]* chapter 3.3

[319] Walden, J., 1987, **More File Formats**, *Wiley*

[320] Ward M., Calliss F.W., Munro M., 1989, **The maintainer's assistant**, *Proc. Conference on Software Maintenance 1989, IEEE Computer Society Press, Miami, Florida* pp 307–315

[321] Ward, M., 1988, **Transforming a program into a specification**, *Centre for Software Maintenance Report 88/1*

[322] Ward, P.T. and Mellor, S.J., 1985, **Structured Development for Real Time Systems**, *Yourdon*

[323] Warden R., May 1990, **The business of software maintenance**, *Proc. Wolverhampton Conference on Software Maintenance,* Wolverhampton Polytechnic, UK

[324] Warden, R., , **Re-engineering – a practical methodology with commercial applications**, *in [314]*

[325] Warfield, J.N., 1977, **Crossing theory and hierarchy mapping**, *IEEE Transactions on Systems, Man and Cybernetics, Vol. 7, No. 7* pp 505–523

[326] Warren, D.H.D., 1980, **Logic programming and compiler writing**, *Software – Practice and Experience, Vol. 10* pp 97–125

[327] Warshall S., 1962, **A theorem on Boolean matrices**, *Journal of the ACM, Vol. 9, No. 1* pp 11–12

[328] Waters, R.C., 1988, **Program translation via abstraction and reimplementation**, *IEEE Transactions on Engineering Software vol. 14 No. 8* pp 1207–1228

[329] Weiser M., July 1984, **Program slicing**, *IEEE Transactions on Software Engineering, Vol. SE-10, No. 4* pp 352–357

[330] Weiser, M. and Shneiderman, B., 1986, **Human Factors of Software Design and Development**, *In Handbook of Human Factors and Ergonomics, Salvendy, G. (ed.)* John Wiley and Sons

[331] Weiser, M., July 1989, **Programmers use slices when debugging**, *Comm. ACM, Vol. 25, No. 7*

[332] Wetherell, C. and Shannon, A., 1979, **Tidy drawing of trees**, *IEEE Transactions on Software Engineering, Vol. 5, No. 5* pp 514–520

[333] Weyuker E. and Ostrand T., May 1980, **Theories of program testing and the application of revealing subdomains**, *IEEE Transactions on Software Engineering, Vol. SE-6, No. 3* pp 236–246

[334] Wickens, R.F., May 1979, **A Guide to the Management of Software-Based Systems for Defence**, *Technical Note 3017* Central Computer Agency

[335] Wiederhold G., 1987, **File Organisation for Database Design**, *McGraw Hill*

[336] Wikstrom, A., 1987, **Functional Programming using Standard ML**, *Prentice Hall*

[337] Wilde, N., 1990, **Understanding Program Dependencies**, *Curriculum Module SEI-CM-26* Carnegie Mellon University

[338] Wilkes, M.V., 1956, **Automatic Digital Computers**, *Methuen*

[339] Williams, L.G., 1988, **Software process modelling: a behavioral approach**, *Proc. of the 10th International Conference on Software Engineering*

[340] Williams, M.H. and Ossher, H.L., 1978, **Conversion of unstructured flow diagrams to structured form**, *The Computer Journal, Vol. 21, No. 2* pp 161–167

[341] Williams, M.H., 1976, **Generating structured flow diagrams: the nature of unstructuredness**, *The Computer Journal, Vol. 20, No. 1* pp 45–50

[342] Wills, L.M. and Rich, C., 1990, **Understanding a program's design: a graph-parsing approach**, *IEEE Software vol. 7 No. 1* pp 82-90

[343] Winograd, T. and Flores, F., 1986, **Understanding Computers and Cognition: A New Foundation for Design**, *Ablex Publishing Corporation* Norwood

[344] Winsberg, P., 1989–90, **IBM AD/Cycle: overview and analysis**, *InfoDB, Vol. 4, No. 4, Winter 1989/90*

[345] Wirth, N., April 1971, **Program development by stepwise refinement**, *Comm. ACM, Vol. 14, No. 4* pp 221–7

[346] Wood, M. and Sommerville, I., 1988, **A knowledge-based software components catalogue**, *in [40]*

[347] Wulf, W.A., 1971, **Programming without the GOTO**, *Proc. IFIP Congress 1971, Vol. 1,* North Holland, pp 408–413

[348] Yates, F.A., 1966, **The Art of Memory**

[349] Yau, S.S. and Collofello, J.S., November 1978, **Ripple effect analysis of software maintenance**, *Proc. IEEE COMPSAC 78 Int. Conf.,* pp 60–65

[350] Yau S.S. and Kishimoto Z., 1987, **A method for revalidating modified programs in the maintenance phase**, *Proc. IEEE COMPSAC 87 Int. Conf.*, pp 272–277

[351] Yau, S.S., Nicholl, R.A., Tsai, J.J.-P., Liu S.S., August 1988, **An integrated life-cycle model for software maintenance**, *IEEE Transactions on Software Engineering, Vol. 14, No. 8* pp 1128–1144

[352] Yip, S.W.L. and Robson, D.J., 1991, **Window user interfaces and software maintenance**, *Journal of Software Maintenance, Vol. 3, No. 2* pp 107–123

[353] Yourdon, E. and Constantine, L.L., 1979, **Structured Design**, *Prentice Hall*

[354] Yourdon, E., 1979, **Managing the Structured Techniques**, *Yourdon*

[355] Yourdon, E., 1989, **Modern Structured Analysis**, *Prentice Hall*

[356] Yu, D., 1991, **A view on three R's: reuse, re-engineering and reverse engineering**, *Software Engineering Notes vol. 16 No. 3* p. 69

[357] Ziegler, J. and Ilg, R., 1989, **Dialog Manager**, *Informationssysteme für Computer Integrierte Automatisierung,* Stuttgart

[358] Zimmer, J.A., 1990, **Restructuring for style**, *Software – Practice and experience, Vol. 20, No. 4* pp 365–389

[359] Zuylen, H.J. van and Gerritsen, H., 1990, **Knowledge based user interfaces for scientific programs**, *in [96]* pp 827–834

[360] Zuylen, H.J. van, 1993, **From scientific computation to decision support**, *Knowledge-Based Systems* March 1993

[361] Zvegintzov, N., August 1990, **Software configuration management**, *Software Maintenance News, Vol. 8, No. 8* pp 13–14

[362] Zvegintzov, N., August 1990, **Glue: software that sticks software together**, *Software Maintenance News, Vol. 8, No. 8* pp 9–12

[363] van 't Veld, S.F.N. *et al.*, 1990, **16 Methoden voor Systeemontwikkeling (16 methods for systems development)**, *Tutein Nolthenius* 90-72194-17-9

[364] IBM, 1990, *IBM Systems Journal, Vol. 29, No. 2*

Index